"This superb volume brings together diverse views of leading scholars on a broad range of China topics. The overview chapter itself is a must-read for anyone interested in key debates on the Chinese economy; the individual papers are written with clarity and sometimes fearless candor. Very informative."

Professor Kenneth Rogoff, Maurits C. Boas Chair of International Economics, Harvard University, and Chief Economist and Director of Research, International Monetary Fund (2001–2003)

"China's economic landscape has changed dramatically over the past decade, and informed analysis of these changes is scarce. This new volume contains insightful, empirically grounded chapters by expert authors on key challenges for China: population aging, downsizing the property sector, enhancing productivity growth, RMB internationalization, and reforming trade and the state sector. It belongs on the shelf of every serious scholar of the Chinese economy."

Dr. Mary Lovely, Anthony M. Solomon Senior Fellow, Peterson Institute for International Economics

"*The Arc of the Chinese Economy* arrives at a critical moment. After four decades of rapid growth, China faces urgent challenges in shifting toward a model emphasizing consumption, productivity, and sustainability – amid an unprecedented trade war initiated by the Trump administration and global economic restructuring. Understanding China's economic trajectory over the next decade is essential yet complex. Hanming Fang and Marshall Meyer have expertly assembled world-leading scholars who provide clear, insightful analyses on various aspects of China's recent economic developments. Their combined expertise makes this volume invaluable and accessible, a must-read for anyone seeking to understand the future direction of the Chinese economy."

Professor Hongbin Cai, Dean of the Faculty of Business and Economics, University of Hong Kong

"*The Arc of the Chinese Economy* brings together top scholars in related fields to provide an in-depth, multidisciplinary analysis – from the perspectives of economics, sociology, demography, and more – of the driving forces behind China's economic rise. It systematically diagnoses the challenges and solutions in China's recent structural transformation. With its broad vision, innovative insights, and thought-provoking perspectives, this is a must-read for anyone interested in the past and future of the Chinese economy."

Professor Li-An Zhou, Boya Professor of Economics, Guanghua School of Management, Peking University

"The chapters in *The Arc of the Chinese Economy* are written by leading experts on the Chinese economy, many drawing unexpected conclusions. It is an important book for anyone thinking about China's long-term economic prospects."

Dr. Weijian Shan, Executive Chairman of private equity firm Pacific Alliance Group and author of *Out of the Gobi, Money Games,* and *Money Machine*

"At a time when there has never been greater uncertainty about China's global economic role and the ability of China's economy to withstand internal pressures such as population aging, a declining property market, and slowing productivity growth, *The Arc of the Chinese Economy* provides illuminating insights into China's current and future economic prospects. With chapters authored by leading global experts on the Chinese economy, this book is full of new ideas, compelling empirical facts, and multiple perspectives on the key challenges facing China's economic future, addressing key debates on China's changing role in the world, past and future drivers of growth, and the role of the state in China's economy."

Dr. Albert Park, Chief Economist and Director General, Economic Research and Development Impact Department, Asian Development Bank

The Arc of the Chinese Economy

This authoritative volume offers a comprehensive exploration of China's rapidly evolving economy from a team of leading specialists. Readers will gain crucial insights into productivity dynamics, innovation, shifting demographics, and the country's ever-changing industrial landscape – encompassing firms, real estate, and trade flows. With a keen focus on the RMB, regulatory frameworks, and the pursuit of common prosperity, this book seamlessly blends cutting-edge research, real-world case studies, and forward-thinking analysis. It delivers a balanced examination of challenges and opportunities, fostering an informed discussion on China's critical role in the global marketplace. Ideal for academics, policymakers, business professionals, and curious readers alike, this timely and accessible resource unveils the many facets of the Chinese economy, guiding you through its complexities and highlighting strategic implications for the future.

HANMING FANG is the Norman C. Grosman Professor of Economics at the University of Pennsylvania. He is a cofounder of VoxChina, a fellow of the Econometric Society, and a research associate at the National Bureau of Economic Research, where he served as the acting director of its Chinese economy working group (2014–2016).

MARSHALL W. MEYER is the Tsai Wan-Tsai Emeritus Professor of Management and Professor of Sociology at the University of Pennsylvania. He is a founding editor of *Management and Organization Review* focusing on management and organizations in China and their global context and is a member of the Macro Organizational Behavior Society.

The Arc of the Chinese Economy

Edited by

HANMING FANG
University of Pennsylvania

MARSHALL W. MEYER
Wharton School, University of Pennsylvania

CAMBRIDGE
UNIVERSITY PRESS

CAMBRIDGE
UNIVERSITY PRESS

Shaftesbury Road, Cambridge CB2 8EA, United Kingdom

One Liberty Plaza, 20th Floor, New York, NY 10006, USA

477 Williamstown Road, Port Melbourne, VIC 3207, Australia

314–321, 3rd Floor, Plot 3, Splendor Forum, Jasola District Centre, New Delhi – 110025, India

103 Penang Road, #05–06/07, Visioncrest Commercial, Singapore 238467

Cambridge University Press is part of Cambridge University Press & Assessment, a department of the University of Cambridge.

We share the University's mission to contribute to society through the pursuit of education, learning and research at the highest international levels of excellence.

www.cambridge.org
Information on this title: www.cambridge.org/9781009649315

DOI: 10.1017/9781009649339

When citing this work, please include a reference to the DOI 10.1017/9781009649339

First published 2025

Cover image: Vanke Centre buildings (万科中心) in Chengdu. Philippe LEJEANVRE / Getty Images

A catalogue record for this publication is available from the British Library

Library of Congress Cataloging-in-Publication Data
Names: Fang, Hanming editor | Meyer, Marshall W. editor
Title: The arc of the Chinese economy / edited by Hanming Fang, University of Pennsylvania, Marshall W. Meyer, Wharton School, University of Pennsylvania.
Description: Cambridge, United Kingdom ; New York, NY : Cambridge University Press, 2025. | Includes bibliographical references and index.
Identifiers: LCCN 2025025045 (print) | LCCN 2025025046 (ebook) | ISBN 9781009649315 hardback | ISBN 9781009649339 ebook
Subjects: LCSH: Economic development – China | China – Economic conditions – 1949– | China – Economic policy – 1949–
Classification: LCC HC427 .A725 2025 (print) | LCC HC427 (ebook) | DDC 330.951–dc23/eng/20250725
LC record available at https://lccn.loc.gov/2025025045
LC ebook record available at https://lccn.loc.gov/2025025046

ISBN 978-1-009-64931-5 Hardback
ISBN 978-1-009-64936-0 Paperback

To David Dollar (November 21, 1954, to October 8, 2023) and William H. Overholt (March 7, 1945, to September 27, 2024), both exemplary scholars of China.

Contents

List of Figures — *page* xi
List of Tables — xiv
List of Contributors — xv
Foreword — xvii
Acknowledgments — xix
List of Abbreviations — xxi

1 The Arc of the Chinese Economy: An Overview — 1
HANMING FANG AND MARSHALL W. MEYER

2 China's Productivity Challenge — 47
XIAODONG ZHU

3 Innovation in China: Drivers, Challenges, and Future Directions — 67
KEVIN ZHENG ZHOU AND MEITONG DONG

4 When the Abundance Ends: Economic Transformation, Population Aging, and Shrinking Lifecycle Surplus in China, 2000–2020 — 99
FENG WANG, KE SHEN, AND YONG CAI

5 Derisking Real Estate in China's Hybrid Economy — 123
WEI XIONG

6 State Ownership in China: An Equity Network Perspective — 156
JUNHUI JEFF CAI, XIAN GU, LINDA ZHAO, AND WU ZHU

7 China's Journey in Embracing Economic Openness: Four Perspectives — 192
SHANG-JIN WEI AND XINDING YU

8 RMB Internalization and Digitization — 214
BIN WEI AND VIVIAN ZHANWEI YUE

9 The Political Economy of Common Prosperity 239
YASHENG HUANG

10 The "Summer of 2021" and the Trajectory of China's Economic System 256
BARRY NAUGHTON

11 China's Coming Era of Slow Growth 288
WILLIAM H. OVERHOLT

Index 317

Figures

1.1 GDP growth of China, Japan, and Korea, 1990–2023 *page* 5
1.2 Evolution of TFP growth rates for selected economies as a function of their per capita GDP relative to the U.S. 8
1.3 Chinese export partner shares, 2012 and 2022 12
2.1 Fixed-capital investment rates 49
2.2 GDP growth and TFP growth in China: 1978–2022 51
2.3 GDP growth rates: 2007–2022 52
2.4 Projected GDP growth rates of China 62
3.1 SIPO granted patents by category, 1986–2021 70
3.2 SIPO granted patents by domestic or foreign patentee, 1986–2021 72
3.3 SIPO granted foreign patents by patentee country, 1986–2021 72
3.4 SIPO granted domestic patents by patentee sector, 1986–2021 74
3.5 Listed firm's granted patents by ownership type, 1990–2021 74
3.6 SIPO granted patents by IPC, 1986–2021 76
3.7 Cumulative number of granted patents by province, various years 77
3.8 The relationship between regional inward FDI and granted patents (cumulative value by 2021) 79
3.9 International granted patents originated from China, 1986–2021 80
3.10 Technology field distribution of granted patents by Chinese enterprises in B&R countries in 2021 (top ten) 83
4.1 Changing population age structure and support ratio, China, 1950–2050 103
4.2 Per capita annual labor income by age, China, 2002, 2010, and 2018 109
4.3 Per capita annual consumption by age, China, 2010, 2014, and 2018 111

4.4 Per capita annual consumption by type and age, China, 2018 112
4.5 Per capita lifecycle surplus by age, China, 2002–2018 114
4.6 Aggregate lifecycle surplus by age, China, 2002–2018 115
4.7 Projected support ratio and relative lifecycle surplus per capita by year 118
5.1 China's real estate sector 125
5.2 Land sales in 2015–2022 138
5.3 Residential land sales in three tiers of cities in 2015–2022 141
5.4 Residential property transactions across three tiers of cities in 2015–2022 142
5.5 Ratio of inventory to annual sales in 2015–2022 144
5.6 Housing price index growth rate 145
6.1 Network visualization of Central Huijin Investment, a significant SOE, in China 170
6.2 Illustration of our searching algorithm to build the ownership tree 172
6.3 Total capital of SOEs and total state capital in Chinese economy 185
6.4 State assets in aggregation: Matched with AIS sample 187
6.5 State capital in firms directly invested by governments 188
7.1 China's trade openness, 1952–2021 196
7.2 International comparison of the degree of economic openness 197
7.3 The actual and expected levels of economic openness 198
7.4 China's trade imbalance 199
7.5 Chinese tariff rates and current account during 1998–2010 200
7.6 Export sophistication of China and other large developing countries 202
7.7 Changes in China's export sophistication 203
7.8 China's FDI to GDP ratio 204
7.9 The actual and expected levels of inward FDI to GDP ratio 205
7.10 Traditional and broad definition of economic openness 207
7.11 China's "above-the-norm" level of economic openness 209
7.12 Different types of FDI-related value-added activities 210
8.1 RMB settlement under the current account 218
8.2 RMB settlement of cross-border direct investment 219

8.3 Average daily turnover of major currencies 220
8.4 RMB currency swaps 222
8.5 Map of RMB currency swap arrangements 222
8.6 SDR basket 225
8.7 Total foreign reserves in major currencies 226

Tables

2.1 Projected GDP growth rates for China 2023–2035 *page* 62

6.1 Misreporting: Comparison between wholly SOE and state capital 166

6.2 Re-identify state-owned enterprises (SOEs): Layer by layer using ownership trees by 2017 174

6.3 Summary statistics of SOEs identified by our proposed measure 180

6.4 Comparison of the proposed and existing definitions of SOEs: 2017 184

7.1 Forward-linkage decomposition framework for identifying the "open economy" portion in GDP 206

8.1 Shares of daily foreign exchange turnover of major currencies (%) 221

8.2 Shares of foreign reserves in major currencies (%) 226

10.1 The regulatory storm: Major milestones 261

Contributors

JUNHUI JEFF CAI is the Patricia and George Schrapf Family Assistant Professor in Real Estate in the IT, Analytics, and Operations Department at the Mendoza College of Business of the University of Notre Dame.

YONG CAI is an associate professor of sociology at the University of North Carolina at Chapel Hill and Faculty Fellow at the Carolina Population Center.

MEITONG DONG is an associate professor in the Faculty of Business for Science and Technology, School of Management, University of Science and Technology of China.

HANMING FANG is the Norman C. Grosman Professor of Economics at the University of Pennsylvania. He is also a professor at the Department of Health Care Management and the Department of Business Economics and Public Policy at the Wharton School of the University of Pennsylvania.

XIAN GU is a professor of finance at Durham University, UK.

YASHENG HUANG is the Epoch Foundation Professor of International Management at the MIT Sloan School of Management.

MARSHALL W. MEYER is the Tsai Wan-Tsai Emeritus Professor of Management and Professor of Sociology in the Wharton School of the University of Pennsylvania.

BARRY NAUGHTON is the So Kwan Lok Chair of Chinese International Affairs at the School of Global Policy and Strategy in the University of California, San Diego.

WILLIAM H. OVERHOLT (March 7, 1945–September 27, 2024) was a senior research fellow at John F. Kennedy School of Government's Mossavar-Rahmani Center for Business and Government at Harvard University and principal of AsiaStrat LLC, a consulting firm.

KE SHEN is a professor of demography at Fudan University in Shanghai, China.

FENG WANG is a professor of sociology at the University of California, Irvine.

BIN WEI is a research economist and adviser in the research department at the Federal Reserve Bank of Atlanta.

SHANG-JIN WEI is the N.T. Wang Professor of Chinese Business and Economy in the Graduate School of Business at Columbia University. He is also the Director of the Chinese Economy Working Group of the National Bureau of Economic Research at Cambridge, Massachusetts.

WEI XIONG is the John H. Scully '66 Professor in Finance and Professor of Economics at Princeton University.

XINDING YU is an associate professor of economics at the University of International Business and Economics, Beijing, China.

VIVIAN ZHANWEI YUE is Samuel Candler Dobbs Professor of Economics at Emory University.

LINDA ZHAO is Professor of Statistics and Data Science in Wharton School of Business at the University of Pennsylvania.

KEVIN ZHENG ZHOU is the Chung Hon-Dak Professor in Strategy and International Business, and the Director of the Centre for Innovation and Entrepreneurship at the University of Hong Kong.

WU ZHU is an assistant professor of finance in the School of Economics and Management at Tsinghua University, Beijing, China.

XIAODONG ZHU is a Chair Professor of Economics at the University of Hong Kong and a professor of economics emeritus in the Department of Economics at the University of Toronto.

Foreword

The Arc of the Chinese Economy is the seventh in a series of edited volumes that originated with a conference organized by the University of Pennsylvania's Center for the Study of Contemporary China (CSCC). An eighth is in progress, and we hope and expect that others will follow. The present book – along with its predecessors – exemplifies the work that CSCC helps to produce. The editors – and the animating forces – behind this book are two valued colleagues at the Center, Hanming Fang from Economics and Marshall W. Meyer from the Wharton School. Other CSCC-supported volumes have been edited by CSCC affiliates from political science, sociology, law, and communications. Contributing authors have been drawn from a still-wider range of disciplines.

Professor Fang and Professor Meyer, like earlier editors in our series, have brought together leading scholars, ranging from the eminent and well-established to emerging new voices, to address important and timely topics comprehensively. The work that CSCC supports, in these publications and in other work, is highly interdisciplinary. It also brings academically rigorous perspectives to bear on questions of contemporary policy significance. The same spirit and goals guide CSCC's other work, including academic talks, policy roundtables, distinguished lectures, and conferences that we provide to the university community and beyond, the postdoctoral fellows program that has helped launch nearly two dozen rising scholars in the field, the colleagues from China that we host, and the nodal point we provide for faculty and students at Penn and in the region whose work focuses on contemporary China, its economy, politics, law, and role in the world.

We at CSCC are proud to have helped make *The Arc of the Chinese Economy* possible.

Jacques deLisle
Director, Center for the Study of Contemporary China
Stephen A. Cozen Professor of Law
Professor of Political Science
University of Pennsylvania

Acknowledgments

We wish to acknowledge the many people contributing to the March 31–April 1, 2023 conference on "The Arc of the Chinese Economy" at the University of Pennsylvania and directly or indirectly to this volume. First and foremost are the authors of the chapters in this book whose names will shortly become even more familiar than they already are. Next are the expert panelists who opened the conference with their midterm forecasts for the Chinese economy. These experts were Justin Lin Yifu (Peking University), Lant Pritchett (Oxford University), Thomas Rawski (University of Pittsburgh), Michael Zheng Song (Chinese University of Hong Kong), and Chenggang Xu (Stanford University). The comments of a dozen discussants also shaped the conversation and, ultimately, the chapters that follow. The discussants were the late David Dollar (The Brookings Institution), Joe Gyourko (University of Pennsylvania), Emily Hannum (University of Pennsylvania), Yue Hou (Hong Kong University of Science and Technology), Nan Jia (University of Southern California), Shi Li (Zhejiang University), Margaret Pearson (University of Maryland), Daniel Rosen (The Rhodium Group), Hui Tong (International Monetary Fund), Susan Wachter (University of Pennsylvania), Hongxin Zhao (St. Louis University), and Minyuan Zhao (Washington University in St. Louis). We would also like to thank Chris Harrison, Publishing Director of Humanities and Social Sciences, and Joe Ng, Acquisitions Editor, of Cambridge University Press and Assessment for shepherding the manuscript of "The Arc ..." through the publication process.

We owe a large debt of gratitude to Yuanyuan Zeng, Associate Director of Penn's Center for the Study of Contemporary China, for making "The Arc ..." conference happen and keeping track of the many moving parts including multiple manuscript revisions and the minutiae of publishing a book. We are also indebted to Jacques de Lisle, director of the Center, who gave us the go-ahead for "The Arc ..." conference and then turned us over to Yuanyuan.

Finally, "The Arc..." conference and this book would not have been possible but for the generous financial support of the China Research and Engagement Fund of the University of Pennsylvania, which is gratefully acknowledged.

Abbreviations

AI	Artificial Intelligence
AIGC	Artificial Intelligence-Generated Content
AIS	Annual Industrial Survey
ASEAN	Association of Southeast Asian Nations
AUD	Australian Dollar
B&R	Belt and Road
BIS	Bank for International Settlements
BRI	One Belt One Road Initiative
CAC	Cybersecurity Administration of China
CAD	Canadian Dollar
CAS	Cybersecurity Administration of China
CBDC	Central Bank Digital Currency
CBRC	China Banking Regulatory Commission
CCP	Chinese Communist Party
CEO	Chief Executive Officer
CFPS	China Family Panel Studies
CHF	Swiss France
CIPS	China International Payment System
CNY	Chinese Yuan
COFER	Currency Composition of Foreign Exchange Reserves
COVID	Coronavirus
CPI	Consumer Price Index
CSMAR	Chinese Securities Market and Accounting Research
DCEP	Digital Currency Electronic Payment/Digital Renminbi/e-CNY
DLT	Distributed Ledger Technology
EPO	European Patent Office
EU	European Union
EUR	Euro
FDI	Foreign Direct Investment
FIE	Foreign Invested Enterprise

FSU	Former Soviet Union
GBP	British Pound
GDP	Gross Domestic Product
GFC	Global Financial Crisis
HRS	Household Responsibility System
IMF	International Monetary Fund
IP	Intellectual Property
IPC	International Patent Classification
IPO	Initial Public Offering
JPO	Japan Patent Office
JPY	Japanese Yen
KIPO	Korean Intellectual Property Office
LDC	Less Developed Country
LGFV	Local Government Financing Vehicle
LLC	Limited Liability Company
MLP	National Medium- and Long-Term Plan 2006
MNE	Multinational Enterprise
NBS	National Bureau of Statistics
NES	Not Elsewhere Specified
NTA	National Transfer Accounts
ODI	Outward Direct Investment
OECD	Organisation for Economic Co-operation and Development
OEM	Original Equipment Manufacturer
PBOC	People's Bank of China
PDK	Process Design Kit
PNC	Private Branch Exchange
POE	Privately Owned Enterprise
PPP	Purchasing Power Parity
PRC	People's Republic of China
QFII	Qualified Foreign Institutional Investor
R&D	Research and Development
RADT	Regionally Administered Totalitarianism
RDA	Regional Decentralized Authoritarinism
RMB	Renminbi
RRR	Reserve Requirement Ratio
SAIC	State Administration for Industry and Commerce
SAMR	State Administration of Market Regulation

SASAC	State-Owned Assets Supervision and Administration Commission of the State Council
S&T	Science and Technology
SDR	Special Drawing Right
SIPO	State Intellectual Property Office
SNA	System of National Account
SOE	State-Owned Enterprise
STEM	Science, Technology, Engineering, and Mathematics
SWIFT	Society for Worldwide Interbank Financial Telecommunication
TFP	Total Factor Productivity
TVE	Township and Village Enterprise
US	United States
USD	United States Dollar
USPTO	United States Patent and Trademark Office
WTO	World Trade Organization
YTT	China's Young Thousand Talents
ZPMC	Zhenhua Port Machinery Corporation

1 *The Arc of the Chinese Economy*

An Overview

HANMING FANG AND MARSHALL W. MEYER

This book is the product of a conference by the same title, "*The Arc of the Chinese Economy*," held under the auspices of the Center for the Study of Contemporary China at the University of Pennsylvania on March 31–April 1, 2023. It is one of a series of edited volumes published by the Center.

The growth of the Chinese economy in the last four decades is one of the most transformative events of global economic history. It is especially dramatic considering China's population of 1.4 billion and its vast territory and heterogeneity. China's gross domestic product (GDP) grew from US$360.86 billion in 1990 to US$17.79 trillion in 2023, a fiftyfold increase in nominal dollars. In comparison with the U.S., Chinese economic growth was tenfold, from 6.1 percent of U.S. GDP in 1990 to 64.2 percent of the U.S. in 2023. In purchasing power parity (PPP) terms, China's GDP grew from 18.6 percent of the U.S. in 1990 to 125.0 percent of the U.S. in 2023, a nearly sevenfold increase. In terms of per capita purchasing power, China grew from 4.1 percent of the U.S. in 1990 to 29.7 percent of the U.S. in 2023, more than a sevenfold increase (World Bank, n.d. (a); n.d. (b); and n.d.(c)).[1] The increase in per capita purchasing power relative to the U.S. was somewhat higher than the increase of GDP in PPP terms in part because China's population grew more slowly than U.S., 23.3 percent (from 1.143 to 1.410 billion) for China versus 34.6 percent (from 248.709 to 334.91 million) for the U.S., from 1990 to 2023.

By World Bank criteria, China became a lower-middle-income country in 2001 and an upper-middle-income country in 2010. And like many middle-income countries, China faces headwinds and, to borrow language from the World Bank website, a "structural slowdown" of the Chinese economy is anticipated in the medium term. The juxtaposition of spectacular past growth with more modest

[1] The same data are reproduced at *Statistics Times* (2024).

growth expectations renders forecasting the arc of the Chinese economy challenging. Forecasts have evolved over time and toward a more cautious outlook. Pre-COVID, continued rapid growth was anticipated. In 2018, the IMF projected that Chinese GDP in nominal dollars (not PPP) would overtake the U.S. by 2030 due to "accelerating rebalancing efforts, increasing the role of market forces, fostering openness, and modernizing policy frameworks" (Saber, 2018). Post-COVID, forecasts have been revised downward and double-digit annual growth statistics accepted as things of the past. Still, the range of predictions regarding the future growth rates of the Chinese economy was substantial through 2023 when the headlines ran the gamut. A sample of October 2023 headlines includes the following: "World Bank Sees China's Growth Sputtering to Slowest Rate Since 1960s;" "IMF sees signs China stabilizing, reforms can boost medium-term growth;" and "JP Morgan, Nomura Raises China 2023 Economic Growth Forecast" (Chaung, 2023; Economic Times, 2023; Reuters, 2023). Concerns about China's long-term growth prospects intensified in early 2024 when it became evident that end of zero-COVID restrictions did not produce the expected economic rebound. This triggered a lively debate about "peak China," the notion that China's GDP in proportion to global GDP was in inexorable decline. The Rhodium Group (2024), in particular, questioned whether the Chinese economy would ever regain its earlier momentum: " ... it is extremely unlikely that China will regain its previous peak as a proportion of the global economy." China's announcement of 5.0 percent GDP 2024 growth – on target – did little to allay these concerns because growth remained unbalanced: Despite a fourth-quarter $1.4 trillion stimulus package, domestic consumption lagged industrial production and nearly a third of 2024 GDP growth was due to China's $1 trillion trade surplus.[2]

The topic of our conference and the title of this book, "*The Arc of the Chinese Economy*," has become exceedingly relevant, more so than nearly two years ago when the conference convened. Where China's economy is going is no longer a technical issue but is rather

[2] Further, in a report on the fourth-quarter sprint that put China exactly at the finish line, *The Guardian* noted, "Some commentators have raised concerns about the accuracy of China's economic data ..." (Stewart, 2025). We are not taking a position on the quality of Chinese economic data and refer readers to excellent articles on the topic, among the more recent Kennedy and Mei (2023).

of consequence for Chinese households whose wealth is at risk, for the global economy reliant on Chinese economic growth despite "de-risking" and "decoupling" from China, and even for the global balance of power. These issues and many others are addressed in the chapters ahead. While the chapters are written mainly by economists (though in one instance by statisticians, another by demographers, and yet another by a political scientist), they are intended for lay readers as well as academicians. The chapters are full of surprises. To mention one: State penetration of the Chinese economy via partial and indirect ownership of enterprises accelerated rapidly following the Global Financial Crisis (GFC) and is far more extensive than most scholars had imagined. Not surprising, perhaps, is that several of the chapters, though not all, envision a slow-growth scenario for China. This raises further questions: Why have expectations for the Chinese economy shifted from robust to little or no growth? What steps might China take, what policy levers it can pull, to inch away from slow growth? And what are China's long-term growth prospects? We hope this book provides suggestive answers – plural as there are no single or simple answers – to these questions and many more.

We begin with a pair of observations. The first concerns GDP, the total output of goods and services within a country's borders. There are settled ways of *measuring* GDP by expenditure or income.[3] However, as in other domains there are no reliable methods for *forecasting* GDP growth, which is why forecasts differ and the forecasting industry flourishes. The IMF, perhaps the most authoritative source of country-level GDP forecasts, acknowledges that it has no standard methodology for forecasting growth. Rather, IMF growth forecasts originate locally and are based on country-specific assumptions and models (International Monetary Fund, 2024). In this regard, a recent

[3] The expenditure approach calculates GDP by summing the amount spent on final goods and services within an economy during a particular period, usually a year; the formula is $GDP = C + I + G + NEX$, where C is consumer spending, I is business investments, G is government spending, and NEX is net exports. The income approach calculates GDP by summing the income earned from the production of goods and services, specifically the total national income, sales tax, depreciation, and net foreign factor income. The expenditure approach is generally preferred because the data on consumption, investment, government spending, and net exports can be collected more accurately and in real time.

research result is startling: From 2010 to 2020, same-year World Bank country GDP forecasts were off by 1.3 percentage points and IMF forecasts by 1.5 percentage points with the IMF consistently more optimistic than the World Bank (Gatti et al., 2024).

Of special relevance to forecasting is the growth accounting model that estimates GDP growth as the sum of growth in capital, labor, and productivity. The term *accounting* is critical: The model accounts for the contributions of capital, labor, and productivity to growth after the fact. But it cannot forecast growth because productivity is a residual derived from observed capital, labor, and GDP growth – in other words, productivity growth is not knowable until GDP growth has been ascertained.[4] Complicating matters, the error or stochastic component of GDP forecasts is magnified several times in developing compared to developed economies (Hong and Tan, 2014).

The second observation concerns China's actual GDP growth that may (or, less likely, may not) have taken a sharp turn. Until recently, the Chinese economy has performed superbly and weathered economic storms better than most countries. Some relevant data are captured in a comparison of the real growth of China, Japan, and Korea from 1990 to 2023. Figure 1.1, from the World Bank, displays the differences in the three countries' growth trajectories. From 1992 to 2021, except for Korea in 1999, China's growth rate remained consistently above Japan's and Korea's. China's GDP performance during the GFC was stellar: China recorded 9.7 percent growth in 2008 and 9.4 percent 2009, while Japan recorded –1.2 percent growth in 2008 and –5.7 percent in 2009, and Korea 3.0 percent growth in 2008 and 0.8 percent in 2009. Since 2021, however, the gap between China, Japan, and Korea has narrowed. China's real GDP growth in 2022 was 3.0 percent compared to 1.0 percent in Japan and 2.6 percent in Korea. And China's 5.2 percent real growth rate in 2023, though higher than Japan's 1.7 percent and Korea's 1.4 percent, hardly compares to its performance in earlier years. Nor is China's growth expected to be exceptional in comparison with the larger region. The World Bank estimates 2024 GDP growth in

[4] Total factor productivity (TFP), also known as Solow's residual, is a measure of the share of production growth that cannot be explained by increases in inputs like capital and labor. It captures the impact of technical development, including more productive allocations of labor and capital, and other unmeasured elements.

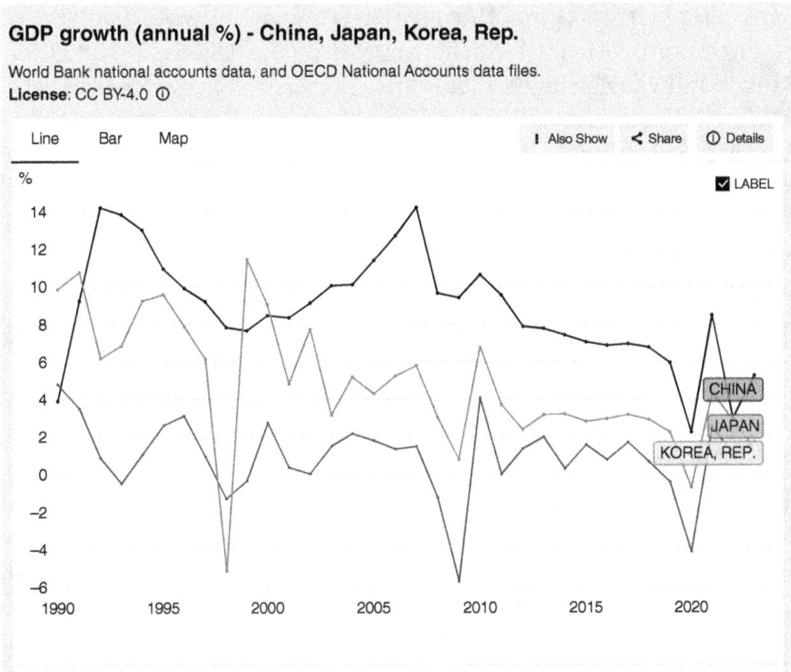

Figure 1.1 GDP growth of China, Japan, and Korea, 1990–2023
Source: World Bank (n.d. (g)).

East Asia ex China and in South Asia at 4.8 percent and 6.4 percent, respectively, compared with China's reported 5.0 percent. Whether China will return to exceptional growth is far from certain but highly consequential.

Expert Forecasts

We began the "*The Arc of the Chinese Economy*" conference with a panel of experts tasked with forecasting the trajectory of the Chinese economy.[5] The panel included Justin Lin Yifu (Peking University),

[5] We should also note that the forecasts in this book are for the mid-run growth prospects of the Chinese economy. The World Bank releases *same-year* forecasts twice a year, usually in January and June, in its global economic prospects (GEP) report; and the International Monetary Fund (IMF) releases its short-term growth forecasts in its World Economic Outlook (WEO), also twice a year and typically in April and October.

Lant Pritchett (Oxford University), Thomas Rawski (University of Pittsburgh), Michael Zheng Song (Chinese University of Hong Kong), and Chenggang Xu (Stanford University). Daniel Rosen (The Rhodium Group) served as discussant. These presentations were brief, not intended as book chapters and, by design, disparate. The panel, like the entire conference, was recorded. Our account of the expert presentations is taken from these recordings and has been approved by the presenters.

Justin Lin began by focusing on the *potential* of the Chinese economy for growth through 2035, which he pegged at around 8 percent. Lin's logic was as follows: According to Penn World Table, China's per capita GDP was 22.6 percent of that of the U.S. in 2019. This ratio was similar to that of Germany's per capita GDP relative to the U.S. in 1946, Japan's relative to the U.S. in 1956, and Korea's relative to the U.S. in 1985. Germany enjoyed annual per capita GDP growth rate of 8.6 percent from 1946 to 1962; Japan also achieved annual per capita GDP growth rate of 8.6 percent from 1956 to 1972; and Korea's annual per capita GDP growth rate was 8.1 percent from 1985 to 2001. Lin thus suggests that China's growth potential from 2019 when it reached 22.6 percent of the U.S., then, should also be in the range 8 percent. Actual growth through 2035, according to Lin, will likely be somewhat lower, averaging 5–6 percent provided there are no "black swan" events such as wars, global recessions, or Covid-like pandemics. Lin cited several factors contributing to the robustness of the Chinese economy including abundant human capital, a large domestic market, short innovation cycles and a comprehensive industrial sector. Interestingly, Lin projected that, going forward, investment will be mainly in productivity-enhancing innovations and account for about 40 percent of Chinese GDP growth, while consumption will drive the remaining 60 percent.

Lant Pritchett, in sharp contrast to Lin, called for a "factual characterization" of growth processes. For Pritchett, the principal fact is this: The reliability of forecasts of GDP growth has historically not been very good, especially for developing economies experiencing high rates of growth. Whereas ten-year growth projections for Organisation for Economic Co-operation and Development (OECD) economies have been relatively accurate with roughly +/– 20 percent error, developing economies often experience sharp turning points or phase transitions where forecasting errors can approach 100 percent.[6] Hence, according to Pritchett, " ... extrapolation [is] a very bad forecast of the future" for these economies. Economic phase transitions have several characteristics: unexpected and massive accelerations or decelerations of growth, regression to the mean where economies of high-growth countries decelerate while low-growth countries accelerate, and underestimation of both the magnitude of change and the duration of the post-transition state. An example cited by Pritchett is Mexico's 1982 bankruptcy and the subsequent LDC (less developed country) debt crisis that lasted seven years. Pritchett then estimates a worst-case scenario for China. Based on the forecast errors for countries with similar growth spurts, China's 2029 real per capita GDP could fall as much as 55 percent below current forecasts and actually contract from 2019 to 2029. He ends with a stark reminder: "...there are often major decelerations in growth and we often miss them...We shouldn't rule out that it can happen because it frequently does happen."

Tom Rawski shares Justin Lin's confidence in the long-run *potential* of the Chinese economy. His confidence is based partly on the historic legacy of entrepreneurship that fueled the post-1978 market explosion and is evident today in the commercial success of overseas Chinese and the abundance of entrepreneurs at home. Rawski also takes reassurance from institutional changes, especially gains in education, health, and infrastructure, as well as "R&D investment on a grand scale." Still, according to Rawski, the whole remains less than the sum of its parts, and China is performing substantially below its production possibility frontier. The proximate explanation lies in the declining growth rate of productivity. For most countries, productivity gains are greatest in the early stages of development. Citing a figure from Rajan and Leng (2022)'s Lowy Institute report reproduced here as Figure 1.2, Rawski argued that the total factor productivity (TFP) slowed at a much earlier stage of China's development, as measured by the output per worker relative to the U.S. level, than that of other East Asian economies. Rawski attributes China's early productivity slowdown to a partial revival of pre-1978 constraints including priority given to the "security sector" in preference to the

[6] Phase transition is synonymous to "regime change" in this context; that is, is the old growth model being replaced by a new growth model or a so-called "new normal."

Figure 1.2 Evolution of TFP growth rates for selected economies as a function of their per capita GDP relative to the U.S.
Source: Rajah and Leng (2022).

commercial sector, criticism of and constraints placed on entrepreneurs, and China's international behavior that has eroded confidence of overseas investors and customers. Absent reforms, Rawski concluded, Chinese productivity and GDP will continue to lag. Rawski also cautioned that consumer prices in China may have risen faster than the reported CPI and hence China's GDP price deflators may be understated and its productivity and GDP growth overstated.

Michael Song is more sanguine than Rawski about the quality of Chinese economic data. His analysis indicates that distortions in local-generated data have been largely corrected by the National Bureau of Statistics such that, nationwide, "misreporting is quite limited." This said, Song's prognosis for the Chinese economy is far less sanguine than Rawski's. The proximate cause of the poor prognosis is declining productivity growth. Not only did China's GDP growth decelerate sharply following the GFC, but also that productivity growth fell in tandem with the GDP growth. Two statistics are illustrative. While productivity growth accounted for 30–40 percent of GDP growth prior to the GFC, Song estimates that the post-GFC contribution of productivity growth to China's GDP growth declined to 10–20 percent. And while the returns to capital were in the range of 20 percent prior to the GFC, these returns plummeted to 10 percent by 2020. Underlying the post-2008 slide in the productivity growth and the returns to capital was a sharp change in government policy. According to Song, prior to the GFC, local governments in China were effectively forbidden from borrowing; however, China's RMB 4 trillion (approximately US$ 586 billion) economic stimulus package announced in late 2008 relied heavily (approximately 70 percent) on local government contributions for which there was no ready cash and could be funded only through indebtedness. Shortly after, the People's Bank of China (PBOC) and the China Banking Regulatory Commission called on local governments "to attract and inspirit banking financial institutions to provide more credit support for centrally-funded projects by increasing the discount interests from the local finance, improving the credit rewarding and compensation mechanism and setting up legal platforms for the governments to make investments and raise funds" (PBOC and China Banking Regulatory Commission, 2009), effectively legalizing local government investment corporations, today known as local government financing vehicles (LGFVs). What followed, according to Song, was a sea change. Aggregate social financing in China ballooned from slightly over 100 percent to nearly 300 percent of GDP from 2008 to 2020. From 2017 to 2022, local government bonds and LGFV debts in proportion to GDP increased from 34 to 50 percent. Song also shows that returns to infrastructure investment in China have fallen below both the U.S. and E.U. since 2008. Song's larger thesis, which deserves attention, is that the role of local government shifted dramatically and decisively during the GFC. Prior to the GFC, local government was entrepreneurial, striking deals benefitting both private enterprises and government. Post-GFC, local governments shifted to financial engineering to rollover their maturing debts and borrow new debt in order to maintain local GDP growth. Ultimately, if Song's thesis is correct, local governments will have to revert to the entrepreneurial model to reignite sustainable growth.

Chenggang Xu is even less sanguine. Fundamentally, Xu believes that today's economy of the People's Republic of China shares certain similarities with the later decades of the former Soviet Union (FSU). According to Xu, prior to 1957 and under the influence of the FSU, China established a Soviet-type totalitarian regime (central planning is an essential part of it). However, since the Great Leap Forward (1958–1962) and the Cultural Revolution (1966–1976), China deviated from a Soviet-type regime and evolved into a regionally administered totalitarian (RADT) regime. The post-Mao reforms inherited this regime, facilitating regional competition across counties, municipalities, and provinces for GDP growth, where such competition was deemed acceptable. The incentives created by this competition were essential for the unintended development of the private sector. This development was key to China's decades-long rapid growth and also evolved Chinese institutions toward a more relaxed regional decentralized authoritarian regime. According to Xu, however, regional competition lost its effectiveness since the mid-2000s, as competition for growth alone became unacceptable due to rising social stability and environmental issues.[7]

The driving force behind China's rise has been the private sector and globalization. However, the Chinese Communist Party (CCP) has regarded key elements of the ever-growing private sector and globalization as threats to its rule. The reversion to totalitarian regime occurred when the Xi government came to office, extending state control over the private sector while international trade and technology transfer became restricted as China's relations with the West deteriorated. In Xu's terms, China has now reverted to RADT, which will persistently enlarge state sector (with soft-budget constraints), depress private sector, and further deteriorate relationships with advanced economies. Putting these together, Xu's forecast for the Chinese economy is as stark as his analysis: persistent weaknesses on both the supply side (cancellation of the Ant Financial IPO, jailing of entrepreneurs, and the collapse of real estate) and the demand side (low levels of secondary education, depressed household consumption, and population decline) indicating a persistent "Brezhnev-era stagnation."[8]

Daniel Rosen, who discussed these expert forecasts, noted that they ranged from 2 to 8 percent medium-term growth of the Chinese economy; and he added that the International Monetary Fund (IMF) forecasts, generally considered the most reliable, anticipate post-2024 growth rates in the range of 3 percent. Rosen then focused on the expected directionality for the key drivers of China's GDP growth. Household and government expenditures, according to Rosen, will remain constrained. Fixed-asset investment will remain severely constrained: Diminished marginal returns will limit infrastructure investment while the real estate sector still needs to shrink by half to balance supply with demand – Rosen commented that there is "no way" for capital expenditures to grow without a leveling-off of real estate. Further, net exports have little room to grow given trade constraints imposed by the West. Underlying these forecasts is Rosen's view of how reversals at the policy level have coursed through

[7] These arguments on regional competition are laid out in detail in Xu (2011).
[8] For detailed arguments and evidence of China's institutional changes, particularly the RADT and RDT, and their impacts on China's economy, see Xu (2025).

the economy. According to Rosen, China continued to pursue neoliberal marketization through Xi Jinping's first term ending in 2018. However commonsensical and nonideological these reforms were, they raised the specter of political instability for the Communist Party. "Compromises were going to need to be made ... each and every one of those next steps in terms of basic policy reform had to be canceled, put on the sidelines," leaving the West profoundly uncomfortable because "China is diverting back to a more intervened-upon approach" with likely negative consequences for innovation and productivity.

Not represented on the expert panel, or elsewhere in "*The Arc of the Chinese Economy*" conference, are the views of investment firms that, perhaps unsurprisingly, tend to support Justin Lin's forecast of robust economic growth, at least of late. There are two key observations. The first is connected with industrial policy. While the academic research about industrial policy is vast and often reaches divergent conclusions,[9] China's manufacturing base is pivoting from heavy industry to digital industries exemplified by online retailing, virtual services (healthcare especially), and digital integration of supply chains. It is also shifting rapidly toward green industries, notably electrification of vehicles (Bu et al. 2021). Growth in China's digital and green economies in 2022 more than offset the contraction in real estate: The digital economy contributed 3.1 percent and the green economy contributed 1.6 percent to China's 2022 GDP growth, more than offsetting the 3.7 percent loss in real estate according to KKR (McVey and Lim, 2023). These new industries are investment-intensive and are anticipated to be productivity-enhancing, with the former contributing to short-term GDP growth and the latter to medium- to long-term growth. Second, just as China's manufacturing base is pivoting, so is its foreign trade. The trade war notwithstanding, U.S.–China trade grew through 2022 (though it declined by 17 percent in 2023 relative to 2022). Still, China's trading partners, especially its export partners, have shifted away from Europe and toward its neighbors in East Asia. As shown in Figure 1.3, the largest shares of 2012 Chinese exports went to the U.S., Hong Kong, Japan, Korea, Germany, the Netherlands, India,

[9] See Juhász et al. (2024) for a recent review of the economics of industrial policy. Naughton (2021) also provides an excellent historical perspective of China's industrial policy. Fang, Li and Lu (2025) provides a comprehensive decoding of China's industrial policies at the central, provincial and city levels for the period of 2000 to 2022.

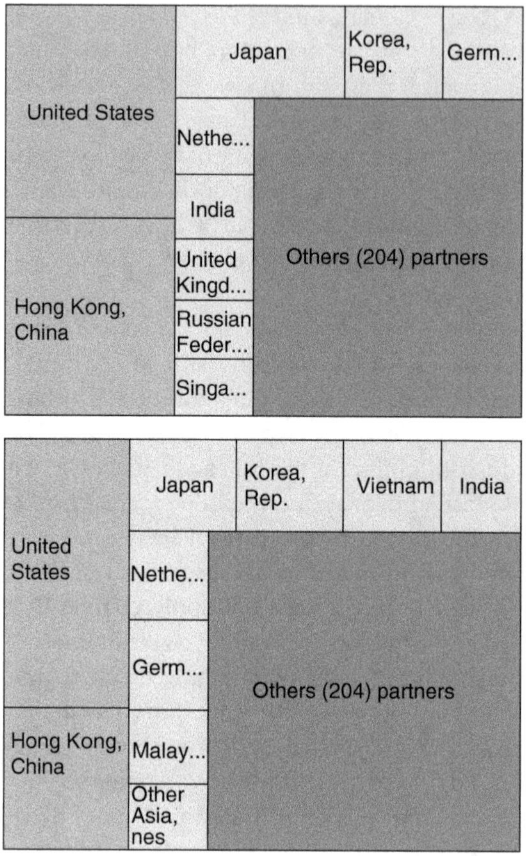

Figure 1.3 Chinese export partner shares, 2012 and 2022. (a) China 2012 export partner share, (b) China 2022 export partner share
Sources: World Integrated Trade Solution (n.d. (a) and (b)).

U.K., Russia, and Singapore in that order. China's largest 2022 export partners were the U.S., Hong Kong, Japan, Korea, Vietnam, India, the Netherlands, Germany, Malaysia, and Taiwan (the euphemism for Taiwan is "Other Asia, NES").[10] The dark spot is that investors are not necessarily impressed by these arguments or, better, that they believe the negative consequences of China's "more intervened-upon approach" to the economy will more than outweigh the gains due to

[10] "Other Asia, NES" stands for Other Asia, not elsewhere specified.

industrial policy and shifting trade partners. In the third quarter of 2023 and for the first time ever since 1998, China posted a net outflow of foreign direct investment (FDI). The outflow was small, $11.8 billion, but signals a waning of confidence in the direction of the Chinese economy. Indeed, the waning confidence, not just of foreign investors as shown by the net outflow of FDI but also of the domestic consumers and investors, in the Chinese economy may be the biggest headwind facing the Chinese economy in the short term.

The question of China's *potential* growth also needs to be revisited. In a recent IMF working paper (Muir et al., 2024), potential growth estimates differ from actual growth or conventional growth projections by assuming efficient allocation of factor inputs across economic sectors. This differs from Justin Lin's approach of estimating China's potential growth by comparison with growth rates of other countries at roughly the same stage of development. Several findings are notable. Looking backward, Muir et al. (2024) find that "China's potential growth peaked in 2005–2006 [at around 10 percent] and has fallen since in line with weaker productivity growth, less productive capital, and a shrinking workforce ..." (p. 12). Looking forward, there are two projections, one a baseline and one a reform model. The baseline model assumes no structural changes while the reform model assumes decelerated capital investment, enhancement of human capital and retirement at age 65, and productivity improvements in the secondary and tertiary sectors of the economy, the last mainly by shifting production into the private sector (see Table 1.1, page 16, for a comparison of the baseline and reform scenarios). Under the baseline projection, 2025, 2030, and 2040 potential growth rates are estimated at 4.2, 3.4, and 2.2 percent, respectively. The 2030 and 2040 estimates correspond almost exactly to the Lowy Institute's forecast that the "Chinese economic growth can be expected to decelerate to roughly 3% by 2030 and 2% by 2040, compared to the pre-Covid trend of a little above 6%" (Rajah and Leng, 2022).[11] The reform scenario increases potential growth rates to 4.6 percent in 2030 and 3.6 percent in 2040. One small step in the direction of reform has been taken. In September 2024, the government announced that the retirement age would inch upward to sixty-three

[11] Rajah and Leng (2022) also summarize twenty other forecasts of Chinese economic growth for 2020–2030 or 2020–2050, ranging from 9 percent to 3 percent annual growth.

for men, fifty-nine for women in white-collar jobs, and fifty-five for other women in the workforce by 2040.

There is danger of losing sight of the forest for the trees. Growth potential in the 2–4 percent range sounds minuscule in comparison with China's heady growth rates of the early 2000s. However, in comparison with other countries, including the U.S., it is still substantial. The Congressional Budget Office (2024) estimates potential U.S. GDP growth at 2.1 percent through 2034 and 1.6 percent for the following two decades. Long-term growth rates on China's periphery, in Vietnam and the Philippines in particular, may exceed 4 percent and India's could be even higher. In comparison with the U.S. and Canada, the E.U., and Japan and Korea, however, China's potential long-term GDP growth is robust.

Has Productivity or Investment Driven GDP?

Xiaodong Zhu's chapter, "*China's Productivity Challenge*," challenges the conventional wisdom about China's rapid economic growth from reform and opening (roughly 1978) to the 2007–2009 GFC and the slowing of growth since. The conventional wisdom, simplified, is this: China's growth throughout has been driven more by investment than consumption, especially investment in heavy industry, infrastructure, and real estate. By most accounts, fixed-asset investment has accounted for about 40 percent of Chinese GDP growth since 2000 despite the emergence of an urban middle class whose size exceeds the entire U.S. population. In the early stages of China's post-1978 development, investment improved living standards and yielded solid economic gains. Later, high levels of investment continued to fuel GDP growth, but excess capacity became legion in industry (China's overcapacity in steel exceeds the total steel output of the EU), infrastructure ("zombie" rail lines and stations abound as China's railway debt approaches US$1 trillion), and real estate (where by some accounts there are enough empty flats to house China's entire population). Ultimately, excess capacity has driven returns downward and today throttles economic growth. The investment story could easily be recast as a productivity story: Excess investment has sapped productivity (because the value of outputs hasn't increased as fast as inputs) and hence economic growth, but the conventional wisdom is that investment per se has been the culprit.

Based on years of research, Zhu challenges the thesis. The key assumption – possibly controversial – is that *real* investment should be compared to *real* GDP, here in 1978 prices, rather than comparing nominal investment to nominal GDP. The difference is quite dramatic: The real investment rate, that is, real investment as a percentage of real GDP, fell from 30 percent in 1978 to 15 percent in 1990 and returned to 25 percent (rather than 40 percent) in the early 2000s. Two key findings follow. One is that real investment contributed only slightly if at all to GDP growth. A simulation using the Solow growth model where the real investment rate was constrained to 15 percent yielded 8.5 percentage point GDP growth per year from 1990 to 2007 in comparison to actual GDP growth of 9.5 percentage points per year. A similar simulation from 2007 to 2022 where the real investment rate was assumed to increase 0.65 percentage points per year from 2014 yielded annual GDP growth rates about 0.5 percent higher than actual GDP growth during this period. The second finding is that TFP growth has tracked Chinese GDP growth closely. Visually, the correspondence of TFP growth with GDP growth is striking as are two key data points: TFP growth averaged 4 percent during China's period of rapid GDP growth through 2007 and has remained 1 percent since when GDP growth has been anemic.

Zhu next asks what lies behind China's initial TFP growth and its subsequent deceleration. While some "potential sources" of productivity growth are well understood, others are surprising, even counterintuitive. Among the early sources of productivity growth was agricultural reform, resulting in increased output and, simultaneously, a shift of agricultural labor to industry, largely to private and township-and-village enterprises rather than state-owned enterprises (SOEs). The most dramatic gains in agricultural productivity occurred well before 2007. Collective production in agriculture (called the team production system) was fully displaced by the household responsibility system by 1983. Zhu notes that gains in agricultural productivity and labor reallocation from farm to industry contributed 1.5 percent to overall Chinese TFP growth from 1978 to 2007 with much of this contribution" occurring in the 1980s when agriculture remained a large portion of the Chinese economy. TFP growth within Chinese agriculture peaked a decade later, from 1995 to 2000, before decelerating sharply and somewhat inexplicably from 2000 to 2007 (Wang et al. 2013).

The account of trade liberalization is more counterintuitive. The conventional wisdom is that China's 2001 accession to the World Trade Organization (WTO) exposed its economy to global competition, forcing productivity improvements. Actually, according to Zhu, international trade liberalization from 2000 to 2005 contributed only 1 percent per year to TFP growth, while during the same period domestic trade liberalization, the diminution of interprovincial trade barriers, contributed 2 percent per year. From 2005 to 2010, however, both international and internal trade costs appear to have *decreased* China's GDP growth (and, by implication, productivity growth), internal trade costs far more than international costs, despite China's massive investment in high-speed rail, railways, and airports (Hao et al. 2020). A better understanding of whether and why domestic trade barriers resurfaced post-2005 (or post-Global Financial Crisis) is essential to understanding the arc of the Chinese economy.

Zhu also cites a series of institutional factors contributing to Chinese productivity growth. *Hukou* (household registration) reform appears to have facilitated internal migration and accelerated productivity growth by 1–1.2 percent per year at least through 2015. What Zhu calls "bottom-up institutional change" encompassing the household responsibility system, the emergence of township-and-village enterprises, and even the mantra of "grasp the large, let go of the small" SOEs in all likelihood contributed substantially to productivity gains prior to 2007. Trade-driven technological innovation may also have contributed to pre-2007 productivity gains.

The details notwithstanding, Zhu's message is clear: Productivity, not investment, drove China's pre-2007 growth; the quantifiable drivers of productivity growth were agricultural productivity, internal migration, and the diminution of internal trade barriers; nonquantifiable institutional changes also contributed significantly to productivity growth. Post-2007, most of the drivers of growth, save for internal migration, were attenuated due largely to an expanded state presence, in response to the GFC, in the Chinese economy.

Has the "Demographic Dividend" Been Spent?

Feng Wang, Ke Shen, and Yong Cai have an entirely different perspective on the Chinese economy. Their chapter, "*When the Abundance Ends*," reserves mention of productivity and GDP until the closing paragraphs. The focus, instead, is principally on the gap between household earnings and consumption: When earnings exceed consumption, there is a surplus and hence abundance, but when consumption exceeds earnings, abundance ends. Moreover, abundance or its reversal in their view is driven principally by the intersection of demography with changing patterns of household consumption, and to a lesser extent, with shifts in ages of peak earnings. The revolution in Chinese agriculture, migration, domestic trade barriers, and institutional changes other than family planning policies are barely mentioned. A key result is a revised understanding of China's "*demographic dividend.*" The demographic dividend is generally understood in population terms as a sharp increase in the working-age population relative to total population caused by a dramatic decline in fertility (from 7.5 births per woman in 1963 to 1.2 births in 2021 per the World Bank (n.d. (d)).[12] The increase in the working-age population in proportion to total population was temporary, however. As smaller cohorts work their way up the population pyramid, the working-age population in proportion to total population begins to shrink so that the demographic dividend turns into a demographic deficit. If working age is defined as 15–64, then the share of working-age adults in China rose from 70 percent in 2000 to 75 percent in 2010 and then fell to 68 percent in 2021 per Feng et al. A narrower definition of working age more consistent with the official retirement age of sixty for men and fifty-five for women yields an even smaller proportion of people currently of working age. According to a recently released National Bureau of Statistics report, China's age 16–59 population was only 62 percent of the total population at the end of 2022 (Cheng, 2023).

Feng et al. think of the "demographic dividend" differently. Rather than a population number, either a low ratio of the under 15 and over 64 population to 15–64 population (the dependency ratio) or, its reciprocal, a high ratio of 15–64 to under 15 and over 64 (the effective support ratio), the demographic dividend is an economic number, surpluses or deficits accruing at the intersection of demography and age-specific income and consumption (or lifecycle surpluses or deficits). To illustrate the difference: China's support ratio peaked in

[12] Note that the one-child policy in effect from 1980 to 2016 reduced births from 2.7 to 1.8 per woman.

2013, about the same time economic growth decelerated sharply, and the support ratio appears to account for 15 percent of China's 1980–2010 increase in per capita income. Income, however, is only half the story. The other half is expenditures since the balance of income and expenditures determines the level of abundance or scarcity people experience. Using National Transfer Accounts (NTA) methodology that has been applied worldwide, Feng et al. calculate per capita lifecycle surpluses and deficits as well as aggregate surpluses and deficits in China for the early 2000s.

The results are striking. Per capita lifecycle surpluses (deficits) have shifted dramatically over time. In 2002, dependent populations had modest lifecycle deficits while surpluses for people of working age were also modest. By 2018, per capita deficits and surpluses were three to four times larger for dependent and working populations, the deficits caused largely by education (for the young) and health care (for the elderly). China's aggregate lifecycle surplus quintupled from 2002 to 2014 but then dropped by 60 percent from 2014 to 2018 due to the combined effects of aging and a sharp increase in lifecycle deficits for the elderly. Looking forward, it appears likely that China's lifecycle surplus will turn to a deficit, and abundance to scarcity. An easing of housing costs could mitigate the scarcity but have untoward effects as well. Raising the official retirement age could reduce lifecycle deficits of the elderly, if wages were maintained with age. A sharp increase in productivity could also shift the balance of incomes and expenditures, but this would depend on a reduced state presence in the Chinese economy, currently uncertain at best.

How Should China Pursue Innovation?

The message of Kevin Zheng Zhou and Meitong Dong's "*Innovation in China: Drivers, Challenges, and Future Directions*" parallels in some respects Xiaodong Xu and Feng et al. It is that the policy-driven, that is, top-down, Chinese innovation system has yielded mixed results. The 1985 PRC patent law was followed closely by the "Decision on the Reforms of the Science & Technology (S&T) System" that reformed the central science and technology apparatus while introducing technology markets into China, the latter "an abrupt departure from previous thinking, which treated the product of mental labor as a public good that could not be privatized," intended to speed the application of research results to production (Simon, 1989: 608–609). China's S&T objectives were subsequently shaped by the 1995 Decision on Accelerating the Progress of S&T and the 2006 National Medium and Long-Term Plan (MLP) for the Development of Science and Technology. The MLP called for increased R&D expenditures, indigenous innovation, and reduced dependence on technology from overseas, the last reversing language in the 1985 Decision aimed at expanding technology imports. The 2006 MLP also set aggressive targets for patents and scientific citations that would place China among the top five nations globally (Sun and Cao, 2021).

The MLP immediately impacted the volume of new patents. Data from the State Intellectual Property Office (SIPO) assembled by Zhou and Dong show that patenting was quiescent before 2006 after which it took off exponentially: Barely 300,000 patents were granted in 2006 compared to 4.6 million in 2021. Recently, however, nearly two-thirds of Chinese patents have been utility patents on minor inventions for which there is no U.S. provision, as distinct from patents on major inventions and designs.[13] Foreign patents as a percentage of SIPO-granted patents peaked in 2005 at about 20 percent and have since fallen below 5 percent. The largest number of foreign patents are granted to Japanese entities. Of firms listed on the Shanghai and Shenzhen stock exchanges, private enterprises have been granted nearly five times as many patents as SOEs. However, patenting by listed private firms has declined since 2018 while patenting by SOEs has increased. Patents are most heavily concentrated in China's coastal regions from Beijing to Guangdong as well as Chongqing but sparse in China's northeastern rust belt of Liaoning, Jilin, and Heilongjiang as well as most interior provinces. Zhou and Dong also show a close correspondence of FDI inflows with patenting. Overseas patenting by Chinese firms, however, appears to be driven mainly by subsidies offered by the Chinese central government. And they question whether collaborative innovation with Belt and Road partners will contribute to China's technological capabilities. They do raise the possibility of breakthrough innovations in electric vehicle technology,

[13] Invention patents in China correspond to what the U.S. Patent and Trademark Office calls utility patents. Utility patents covering minor inventions in China have no USPTO counterpart. Design patents are similar in the U.S. and China.

semiconductors, and digital innovation, the latter exemplified by companies such as ByteDance and Shein. These instances notwithstanding, Zhou and Dong question the long-term efficacy of China's reliance on policy-driven and domestic sources of innovation. Open innovation and openness to innovation from advanced countries, according to Zhou and Dong, will best accelerate China's technological progress and hence China's productivity and growth.

Can the Surfeit of Real Estate Be Unwound?

Wei Xiong's chapter, "*Derisking Real Estate in China's Hybrid Economy*," asks how the risks inherent in an outsized real estate sector can be managed. As to the size of the Chinese real estate sector, though estimates vary, real estate accounts for around 30 percent of Chinese GDP when inputs like supporting infrastructure are included (Rogoff and Yang, 2021). Sixty to seventy percent of household wealth is real estate and the share of local government revenues from land sales peaked at 30 percent in 2021. Xiong argues that a hybrid model of real estate combining ultimate government land ownership with private markets for development and sales could, in principle, manage these risks. Optimally, urban planning would guide government land sales that, in turn, would fund infrastructure development. At the same time, development and sales of residential units by private real estate firms would promote efficient markets and provide market signals that would, in turn, guide government land sales. Under the hybrid model, " … state intervention and the market complement each other, balancing market externalities and promoting economic efficiency."

What has gone awry – why hasn't the hybrid model curbed the excesses of the real estate market? The real estate story parallels Michael Song's account of excessive investment in infrastructure: Local governments lost control of their finances due to Zhu Rongji's 1994 tax reforms, the central government mandated local governments to fund 70 percent of an RMB 4 trillion stimulus package in the wake of the GFC, and the PBOC and CBRC relaxed limitations on local government borrowing and issued guidance for the use of LGFVs to borrow in support of stimulus-mandated projects, real estate especially. Mandated expenditures under the stimulus package in conjunction with career incentives rewarding government officials for local

GDP growth – recall that the calculation of GDP depends on what is spent and is insensitive to debt – fueled a frenzy of LGFV borrowing that has resulted in a vast oversupply of housing where, by some calculations, the entire Mainland population could be accommodated in apartments that currently stand vacant.

Loss of local fiscal autonomy and the excesses of LGFVs, however, are only part of the story. The other part is – or was – the seemingly unlimited appetite for risk of Chinese real estate firms and households. Confirmation bias operated: So many units were built and prices escalated so rapidly that a downturn was unimaginable. And implicit guarantees including government-mandated price floors encouraged widespread discounting of risk. Rather than curbing the excesses of the public sector, then, real estate markets exacerbated these excesses until they were rudely awakened by the August 2020 "three red lines" capping the indebtedness of real estate companies that had been borrowing from LGFVs and their customers. Chinese real estate has since been troubled. Prices are down, especially in second- and third-tier cities, and real estate giants like Country Garden and Evergrande remain perilously close to bankruptcy.

What is the exit path – how can Chinese real estate be restored to health? Xiong suggests that while government policies can be adjusted to avert a hard landing in real estate, only a return to rapid economic growth offers a permanent solution. The question, then, is where China will find a growth engine to replace real estate. And absent a new growth engine, Xiong asks, will the government be tempted to try to restart real estate and infrastructure development and with what consequences for these already overextended sectors?

How Far Does Chinese State Control Extend?

Jeff Cai, Xian Gu, Linda Zhao, and Wu Zhu's chapter, "*State Ownership in China: An Equity Network Perspective*," states that understanding SOEs is the key to studying the Chinese economy if only because of SOEs' inferior performance and reliance on cheap credit and outright subsidies (Harrison et al. 2019). It further argues that widely used data from the Chinese Ministry of Finance, State-Owned Assets Supervision and Administration Commission of the State Council (SASAC), and the National Bureau of Statistics greatly understate the extensiveness of state ownership whether gauged by the number of enterprises or their assets. To gauge actual state ownership, Cai et al. utilize firm registration and ownership data from China's State Administration of Industry and Commerce (SAIC) covering upwards of 90 million firms as of 2017. These data, which include the names of shareholders and their shareholdings, allow the construction of ownership trees whose roots are 127 central government SOEs, 850 provincially owned firms, and nearly a quarter million SOEs directly owned by municipal and county governments. How far the branches of these trees extend and how many firms they encompass then depends on the ownership threshold chosen: 100 percent (wholly state-owned), 50 percent (majority state-owned), 30 percent (here called relative state control), and 10 percent or nonzero (partial state control). At the 100 percent ownership threshold, Cai et al. find a total of 37,991 central, 36,056 provincial, and 299,665 municipal or county SOEs in the SAIC dataset. At the 30 percent ownership threshold, the numbers of central, provincial, and local SOEs are 116,972, 113,336, and 489,872, respectively. Whatever the threshold, the total number of SOEs found in the SAIC data far exceeds other estimates of the reach of Chinese state ownership, though in some instances state ownership is restricted to centrally owned SOEs. Carsten Holz (2018), for example, found the Chinese Finance Ministry claimed full, majority, or relative control of 167,399 firms in 2015, while SASAC claimed a subset of 124,966 of these. Note, however, that the definition of relative control used by Holz is broader than Cai et al., since it encompasses firms less than 30 percent state-owned where the state retains control rights.[14]

The reach of the state into business enterprises, whether measured by the number of enterprises controlled by the state or the aggregate capital of enterprises under state control, may be less significant than how this reach has shifted over time. This shift, consistent with the doctrine of "mixed ownership reform" promulgated by Xi Jinping in 2013, points toward more extensive state ownership at lower thresholds of control and at lower levels of the economy. To

[14] "Relative state control (*guoyou xiangdui konggu*) implies that although the state holds less than 50% of total capital, (i) the state share is relatively large compared to the shares of other ownership categories, i.e., 'relative state control' in its narrow meaning (*xiangdui konggu*) or (ii) even though one or more other ownership categories have a larger capital share than the state, the state in effect holds the control rights by agreement (*xieyi kongzhi*)."

illustrate: From 1999 to 2017, the total capital of SOEs in proportion to the entire Chinese economy decreased if SOEs were defined using 30–100 percent state-ownership control but increased when the SOEs were defined using a threshold of state ownership below 30 percent. Further, from 1999 to 2017, the total capital of SOEs in proportion to the Chinese economy increased sharply for local SOEs, somewhat for provincial SOEs, and actually decreased for central SOEs. The SAIC data, moreover, do not capture increased influence of the Communist Party even in wholly private enterprises, more than half of which today have party branches.

Why ultimate government ownership, especially local government ownership, of business enterprises has spread rapidly in China still requires explanation given the inefficiencies associated with state control. There are two simple – and opposing – explanations. One is that Xi Jinping's calculus places ideological objectives, specifically extending the power of the state, ahead of efficiency, as Kevin Rudd (2023) and many others have argued. The other is the rise of an intermediate form of organization, state shareholding companies relying on private investment managers to deploy state assets. These assets totaled 17 trillion RMB by 2017, nearly half of which were managed by shareholding companies owned by provincial and municipal governments (Chen and Rithmire, 2020). A further explanation is the growth of LGFVs. Daokui Li (2023) has suggested that extended ownership chains may be partly due to nesting or pyramiding of LGFVs. According to Li, many LGFVs are organized vertically such that each is fractionally owned by a parent and, in turn, holds fractional ownership of several layers of subsidiaries: "Typically, local governments register a parent company, such as a local government financing vehicle (LGFV). This parent entity secures financing with, say, 30–40 percent comprising borrowed capital and 60–70 percent being its own funds. This parent company then invests in a subsidiary, which in turn borrows more and invests in a sub-subsidiary, and so on."

The nested financial structure, according to Li, is constructed to conceal the true amount of LGFV indebtedness since much of their reported capital is in fact debt. Li estimates the actual 2020 LGFV debt at 90 trillion RMB or 88 percent of Chinese GDP. This is about 150 percent of IMF and World Bank estimates of LGFV indebtedness and far beyond the capacity of local governments to repay.

How Open Is China – and Will China Remain Open?

The path forward for China's overseas trade and especially its export engine is less fraught than for real estate. Shang-Jin Wei and Xinding Yu's chapter, "*China's Journey in Embracing Economic Openness: Four Perspectives*," begins by asking how China's "dual circulation" strategy should be understood. While several answers are suggested, Wei and Yu argue that the fundamental issue is how China's engagement with the global economy and the development of the domestic economy *as well as the relationship of the two* are to be measured since one is not necessarily the obverse of the other. Their results suggest a dynamic of the Chinese economy not captured by GDP and productivity measures. Wei and Yu begin with a conventional measure of openness, the trade ratio calculated as exports plus imports divided by GDP. China's trade ratio rocketed from 10 in 1978 to 64 percent in 2006, two years before the GFC, before settling back to around 38 percent currently. They next construct a cross-national measure of expected or "normal" openness where the trade ratio is estimated as a function of a country's GDP per capita and GDP using cross-country data. Here, China's actual openness greatly exceeds the predicted openness in 2006 but falls close to its predicted value by 2021. The simplest conclusion is that China's trade openness today is unexceptional, "only slightly higher than what one would have predicted based on cross-country experience." Another measure of concern is China's current account surplus, which increased sharply after its WTO accession and tariff reductions. Wei and Yu suggest counterintuitively that tariff reductions and hence openness may be consistent with growing surpluses: a " ... decrease in the price of imported products leads to a decrease in the price of the 'capital' factor used intensively in the production of imported products ..." and hence " ... a capital outflow and a current account surplus for the country."

Beyond openness, Wei and Yu then explore the quality or sophistication of Chinese exports. The measure of quality is itself sophisticated: It is based on an estimate of the technological level of each product in a country's export bundle (intuitively the weighted average GDP per capita of countries exporting a given product) times the share of that product in the bundle. Here the results are stunning: From 2006, China's export sophistication has greatly exceeded other large developing countries (Brazil, India, Indonesia, and Russia) and the expected level of export sophistication predicted from its GDP per capita and GDP based on a cross-country regression. Wei and Yu also develop several broader measures of openness incorporating both the role of foreign-invested firms in domestic production and trade openness; specifically, the broader measures incorporate the role of foreign-invested firms not only in their direct exporting activities but also in their sales in the local market and in supporting domestic firms' production. China's openness by this broader measure is about 50 percent higher than looking at the export activities alone, but interestingly, the broadly defined economic openness measure also peaked around 2006. Yet China remained above the U.S. and Japan for two decades according to this broader measure of openness. Only time will tell whether China can remain as open in the rapidly evolving geopolitical environment and whether it can continue reaping the benefits of openness while averting the risks. Microsoft's decision on maintaining its China-based artificial intelligence (AI) laboratories is emblematic of the choices ahead.

Will the Renminbi Dominate?

Bin Wei and Vivian Zhanwei Yue's chapter, "*RMB Internationalization and Digitization*," explores the gap between the strength of the Chinese economy, the second largest globally, and the somewhat weaker international position of China's currency, the renminbi (RMB), vis-à-vis the U.S. dollar, the euro, the British pound sterling, and the Japanese yen. Internationalization refers to a currency's acceptance and usage outside of the country where it was issued. A currency is internationalized to the extent that it is used to settle overseas transactions, is freely convertible to other currencies, is held in the reserves of foreign banks, and is regarded as a "safe haven" whose value will hold in periods of economic turbulence. The RMB's recent record on these dimensions is mixed. The use of the RMB to settle trade in goods and services under current account has risen dramatically but unevenly since 2010. The settlement of cross-border investments in RMB also rose unevenly in the 2010s. Though it is the fifth most traded currency globally, the RMB's share of turnover in foreign exchange markets remains small, 7 percent – note that foreign exchange percentages total 200 percent because both sides of transactions are counted – and about 3 percent of foreign reserves globally were in RMB as of the third quarter of

2022. Limited convertibility of the RMB on capital accounts remains an obstacle to its international acceptance as do concerns about the soundness of Chinese financial institutions.

Digitalization of the RMB potentially gives impetus to RMB internationalization since the digital payment system as currently designed will interoperate with many foreign currency platforms. Interoperability potentially advantages the RMB vis-à-vis other currencies by speeding cross-border transactions and lowering costs – and shielding targeted individuals and firms from U.S. sanctions by circumventing correspondent banks. However, a digital RMB may not prove as advantageous domestically where few consumers can see the difference between digital platforms making payments in nondigital currency and payments made directly in digital currency. Together, AliPay and WeChat Pay have more than a billion users and a 92 percent share of China's digital payments market, while the e-RMB's domestic market penetration remains minuscule (Orcutt, 2023). There's also the question of what role remains for commercial banks should e-RMBs issued and traceable by the central bank, the PBOC, become widely circulated.

The End of Reform and Opening?

After more than four decades, has Xi Jinping chosen to end China's grand experiment of "reform and opening"? The experiment appears to have been an unqualified success. The plainest of statistics tell the story of economic growth and poverty alleviation. From 1978 to 2021, China's per capita GDP rose from $381 to $12,175 in constant 2010 U.S. dollars (World Bank, n.d. (f)). The number of Chinese living in extreme poverty shrank by nearly 800 million, accounting for close to three-quarters of the people lifted from extreme poverty globally. Whether any economy can sustain this pace of growth for four decades or longer was addressed in our opening session. Here we confront a somewhat different question: whether China's leadership intends to retain economic growth as a top priority or to subordinate growth to other objectives.

Yasheng Huang suggests that China's leaders may have, for now, strayed from economic growth. In his chapter, "*The Political Economy of Common Prosperity*," he characterizes Xi Jinping's common prosperity program as a "policy pivot" that represents an epochal change with the objective of shifting power away from private capital and toward the state, and he argues that it has little or nothing to do with altering the overall distribution of wealth. In Huang's language, common prosperity aimed to "cut the corporate sector to its appropriate role." To be sure, common prosperity was advertised as evening out imbalances, improving public services, and revitalizing rural communities. But the actual policy target was the immense wealth accumulated by entrepreneurs in industries like private education, online video gaming, entertainment, and technology; yet few, if any, steps were taken to increase labor's share of income or the household share of GDP, which remain intractably low for a country at China's level of development. Huang finds the forced charitable contributions of firms such as Pinduoduo and JD.com all but risible. Ultimately, he argues, the common prosperity program will prove self-defeating since it is fundamentally predatory and will "accentuate the secular economic slowdown that is already well in place" and ultimately detract from China's actual common prosperity goals.

Barry Naughton's chapter in this volume, "The *'Summer of 2021' and the Trajectory of China's Economic System*," by contrast, sees a diastrophism, a reconfiguration of China's economic landscape, "the crystallization of qualitatively different economic system." The reason is not simply the "summer storm" of regulatory crackdown on some of China's most prominent and prosperous firms. It is further, according to Naughton, a much-enlarged set of policy objectives tantamount to new rules for economic decision-making – as to both who makes decisions and how decisions are made. The "summer storm" actually began in August 2020 with the "three red lines" limiting the borrowing of real estate firms, which led to significant liquidity problems and, in several cases, default of the Chinese real estate developers. Two months later, Alibaba's Jack Ma made his now (in)famous speech at the Lujiazui economic forum where he chided bankers and bank regulators for archaic practices. Shortly after, the regulators canceled the listing of Alibaba subsidiary Ant Financial, slated to be the largest IPO ever, and Ma then went into exile in Tokyo for nearly two years. And in July 2021, the Cybersecurity Administration of China (CAC) opened an investigation of Didi Global, the ride-hailing app, that culminated in its delisting from the New York Stock Exchange a year later. The shadow of Didi remains: Currently the CAC is reviewing how Shein, among the leading makers of ultra-fast fashion, handles information about its Chinese contractors and suppliers, which may, like Didi, derail Shein's U.S. listing.

The underlying policy objectives, Naughton argues, multiplied as the "summer storm" intensified. These include common prosperity, a reversal of population decline, strengthening the manufacturing base, information security, and what Naughton calls "self-strengthening" or toughening of society, as, per Xi, hard times may lie ahead: " … we are bound to encounter headwinds" (Ministry of Foreign Affairs, 2023). De-emphasized was GDP growth and the shifting of growth drivers from investment to household consumption. Moreover, " … the multidimensionality of the demands … shows that the objective instead is to generate an ongoing responsiveness to a variety of policy objectives, which can be constantly updated or changed … this [is] a change in the decision-maker's objective function and decision criteria, rather than a change in regulatory framework."

Compounding the multiplicity of goals has been the vagueness or inconsistency of policy instruments with which to reach these goals, for example, tax or welfare reforms that might level income inequalities have been conspicuously absent. This has been coupled with a degradation of Chinese economic and other key data. The consequence is not only that the incentives for economic growth have been significantly weakened since 2021, but the signals needed for businesses and government to adjust to circumstances have also faded.

Naughton raises some extraordinarily interesting questions. For example, was China's phase of rapid growth due to the success of a principal-agent model applied at huge scale – pursuing GDP targets single-mindedly and rewarding officials meeting these targets? And was the subsequent decline in growth rates due to the abandonment of this model as objectives multiplied and their inconsistencies became manifest? Or, contra Naughton, was the setting of GDP targets itself inherently flawed? There is reason to believe the latter. Large-scale target setting is characteristic of command economies. An entire genre of Soviet poster art is captioned, "We shall fulfill and overfulfill the plan for …" or "We shall fulfill the five-year plan …" And a large literature on the economy of the FSU argued that while plans were fulfilled, often they were not fulfilled as intended. A plant with a tonnage quota for iron pipe would make thicker and heavier pipe without producing more pipe. The late Martin Weitzman took this argument a step further in his "ratchet model" of command economies where quotas are shown to be self-defeating: Apparatchiks rewarded for fulfilling quotas would also be punished with higher quotas the following year – this is the ratchet. Anticipating the ratchet, many managers would deliberately miss their quotas causing output to lag rather than grow (Weitzman, 1980).

The peculiar nature of GDP growth compounds the target-setting problem. As we discussed previously, the usual measure of GDP is based on expenditures – consumption, investment, and net exports. Thus, incentivizing GDP growth means incentivizing expenditures, mainly investment, as China has done, because investment is much more amenable to the control of the local government officials. Much of the investment is borrowed – to which simple GDP growth measures do not capture – and, of late, of limited economic value, for example, China's ghost cities and the suspension bridges of Guizhou Province, population 38.5 million or 3 percent of China, with 40 of the 100 highest bridges in the world (Yang, 2020). The consequence of overinvestment, however, is the erosion of productivity growth, which, as argued most forcefully in Chapter 2, is the ultimate driver of GDP growth. Hence, setting GDP growth targets, while effective in the short run to motivate local government officials, ultimately proves self-limiting. As several authors point out, while almost any investment works out in the early stages of development, at later stages investment proves not to be the nostrum it once was. And this seems to have been the case with China.

The method of William H. Overholt's chapter, "*China's Coming Era of Slow Growth*," is different. In Overholt's analysis, the minutiae of GDP are incidental; instead, what is central to his analysis is a developmental construct, the East Asian development model, a distillation of the key elements of the high-growth economies on the periphery of Mainland China.[15] These elements include a priority for economic (read: GDP) growth, centralized and technocratic management, rapid infrastructure development, and gradual opening to foreign trade and investment. GDP growth holds at 10 percent for a generation in the model and 7 percent for "a few years" before settling in the vicinity of 3 percent. Somewhere on this path, the "complexity revolution" is encountered. Though Overholt is not

[15] Overholt's analysis is based on South Korea, Taiwan, and Singapore. Others, for example, Paul Kuznets (1988), treat Japan, South Korea, and Taiwan as exemplars of the East Asian development model.

especially clear as to its details, the general notion is that once everyone has adequate food and shelter, economic diversification (of goods and services) and political diversification (of interests) follow. Central planning and autocracy accommodate complexity poorly, and countries tracking the East Asia development model move toward decentralization and democratization.

China has not done this, however. To paraphrase Overholt, China has chosen to fight the complexity revolution rather than leveraging it. The fight is at multiple levels. And it is likely to be lost due to a "collection of depressive trends" including the insertion of party cadres into senior levels of private and state-owned enterprises, investment in manufacturing industries already rife with overcapacity, discouragement of entrepreneurship, quashing of private and English-language education, a state school system more fit to the twentieth century than the twenty-first century, resistance to property taxation to temper speculative bubbles, resistance to policies favoring household consumption over fixed-asset investment, and choking off discourse with foreign scholars and elites.

China faces a myriad of risks, but for Overholt, the greatest risk lies in the deterioration of the U.S.–China relationship where the U.S. appears to have greatly overestimated China's economic and military capacities as it did with the FSU. The concern is that designation of China as a strategic competitor will descend into an adversarial relationship, economic warfare, and then limited war or worse. Overholt tells us that the tide has changed in China – we prefer to say the tectonics have changed. Overholt, the author of *The Rise of China* (1994), tells us that China's rise is no longer inexorable. And Overholt tells us that elites seldom take cognizance of tidal or tectonic changes until they must, until "institutionalized doctrine hits a brick wall." We are hoping for a landing on a softer surface, for reasoned discourse relying on established knowledge and the work of scholars in this volume, and for recognition that, in the long run, command economies simply don't work very well for a complex modern economy, even with all the advancement in digitization of the economy and in computing power.

The Arc of the Chinese Economy

After forty years of rapid economic growth, China will inevitably shift away from a single-minded focus on GDP growth. The Chinese government has gradually adopted other objectives such as common prosperity, "high-quality growth," and, more importantly, security, including economic, national, and social security.[16] The old growth model, which relied heavily on investment and exports and benefited tremendously from "catching up" and the demographic dividend, no matter how the dividend is construed, will inevitably change. China does not have the choice of staying put.

The transition to a new growth model is challenging and carries myriad risks. For example, for Chinese growth to wean off its reliance on investment and export, domestic consumption must grow. However, China's 2021 household consumption in proportion to GDP was 34 percent, among the lowest in the world, compared to 68 percent in the United States, 60 percent in India, 49 percent in South Korea, and the OECD average of 60 percent.[17] Perhaps the first objective of a common prosperity program should be encouragement of household consumption via a strengthened social safety net. Regrettably, it appears that debt-ridden local governments are currently moving in the opposite direction by reducing retiree medical benefits.

Another risk is the downturn of the real estate sector that, together with real estate-related industries, accounts for nearly 25 percent of the Chinese GDP. The cooling of the Chinese real estate carries significant risk for the local governments, nearly 40 percent of whose revenues have been from land sales. Indeed, the bursting of Chinese real estate sector coupled with declining population for the first time since the 1959–1961 Great Chinese Famine raises the specter of Japanification. The similarities to Japan are indeed real. But as pointed out by Goldman Sachs (2023): "... while deteriorating demographics, a debt overhang, and an asset-bubble-burst were all important ingredients to Japan's malaise at the turn of the century, a key contributor to its Japanification was a fundamental change in longer-term growth expectations."

Avoiding a Japanese-style slump will crucially depend on the Chinese government's ability to manage growth expectations. So far, signs of success are scarce. A key measure of expectations is consumer confidence. The OECD's (2025) composite consumer confidence

[16] See parts 15 and 16 of the 14th Five-Year Plan announced in March 2021 (Center for Security and Emerging Technology, 2021).

[17] See Wang (2023), Figure 8.3, p. 149.

index for China plummeted from the mid-120s to the high 80s in April 2022 and has not recovered since.

Still, several factors could help China avert Japanification. First, China's GDP per capita relative to the United States remains significantly lower than Japan's in the 1990s, hence the Chinese economy arguably has a higher potential growth rate. Second, whatever happens in the Chinese stock market is far less likely to spill over into the real economy than in Japan. Mainland stock markets have consistently underperformed both the Chinese economy and the stock markets of other developing economies. And Chinese stock market bubbles have been far less pronounced than the Japanese market bubble of the late 1980s.[18] Third, while China's deteriorating demography will no doubt exert significant fiscal pressure on the pay-as-you-go pension and health care systems, workforce decline need not be a major drag on Chinese economic growth as it has been for Japan. The quality of Chinese human resources is increasing. Current retirees born in the 1950s and 1960s tend to have low levels of human capital and thus are the least productive, while younger cohorts are far better educated. Further, the impact of an aging workforce can be partially offset by labor-replacing technologies, including robotics and AI. China is currently the country with the largest number of industrial robots, though the robot density remains lower than Korea or Japan. Also critical is repopulating China's workforce, which could be accomplished by raising the retirement age more rapidly than currently planned and to the OECD level of sixty-six for men and women. Reform of the pension system together with job redesign and transition to a more service-oriented economy could facilitate retaining near-retirees in the workforce. And given wide rural-urban and regional imbalances, China's urban workforce could grow even as the overall population and workforce decline (Fang, 2023). These notwithstanding, high youth unemployment rates suggest that there

[18] The Nikkei stock market index rose dramatically from 6615.5 on January 6, 1980, to peak at 38915.9 on December 29, 1989, and then 14309.4 on August 18, 1992 (a decline of 65.8 percent from the peak). In contrast, despite several bubble episodes, the Shanghai Composite Index rose from 1516.6 on January 7, 2000, to 2881.98 on January 12, 2024, an anemic growth for an economy that grew from 1.2 trillion USD to close to 19 trillion USD during the span. For an insightful analysis of the disconnection between the Chinese economy and the Chinese stock market, see Allen et al. (2024).

is no labor shortage in China – for now. Whether due to a statistical anomaly, since rectified, created by classifying student job seekers as unemployed or the cultural anomaly of young people withdrawing from the labor force by "laying flat" or a mismatch between available jobs and the skills of recent graduates, a surfeit rather than a shortage of labor seems to be indicated.

Japanification may also depend on whether the Chinese people and the larger global community retain confidence in China's long-term prospects. There is tangential evidence. Multiple surveys confirm that the Chinese public consistently expresses high levels of trust in government and business.[19] While surveys exaggerate the level of political trust in China due to social desirability, people's tendency to give "right" answers when asked their opinions (Nicholson and Huang, 2023), there is no evidence suggesting that trust in business and government is higher in Japan – and the U.S. – than China.[20] Premier Li Qiang has said, "... we have notable institutional strength" (Embassy of the People's Republic of China in the United States of America, 2023). It is possible that he is right. The confidence of the larger global community is more tenuous as evidenced by a simmering U.S.–China trade war and China's push for "dual circulation," sometimes understood as leveraging a strong domestic base to expand but to rely less on overseas markets.

Ultimately, three sets of forces and their intersection will shape the trajectory of the Chinese economy over the next ten to fifteen years: the political economy, the relationship with the West, and fundamental economic and demographic change (Fang, 2023):

1. ***China's internal political economy will determine the relationship between the state and the market.*** The CCP's primary objective is to maintain its political power, which makes economic growth

[19] The Edelman Trust Institute (2024) reports that 85 percent of Mainland Chinese trust the government "to do what is right." This represents a decline from 89 percent in 2023 and 91 percent in 2022. Trust in business has been steadier though slightly lower: 81 percent in 2024 compared to 84 percent in 2023 and 84 percent in 2022. These results are based on nationwide surveys conducted in November of the previous year, for example, the 2024 Trust Barometer is based on data collected in November 2023.

[20] The Edelman Trust Institute (2024) reports 32 percent confidence in government and 50 percent confidence in business in Japan compared to 40 and 53 percent respectively in the U.S.

secondary to preserving regime stability. In response to perceived internal and external threats, the CCP has turned to more centralized economic policies and tightened regulation of firms in order to solidify its political control.

2. ***China's relationship with the U.S.-led West will determine China's access to foreign technology, finances, and markets.*** U.S.–China relations are at a forty-year low for a number of reasons, including U.S. trade sanctions initiated by President Trump and continued by President Biden, tariffs going into place imminently, the threat the U.S. perceives that China poses to the established global order (such as to the dollar's global dominance), and tensions that often accompany a rising power challenging an established power (the so-called "Thucydides Trap"). Trade sanctions imposed on China by the U.S. and other Western countries have limited China's access to foreign technology, finances, and markets. Citing national security concerns, the U.S. Congress and the Trump and Biden administrations have taken actions, and are considering further actions, to decouple the U.S. economy from China's in several ways, including through new restrictions on trade in response to what the U.S. calls China's unfair trade practices and cybersecurity threats, and restrictions on Chinese military entities' access to advanced technologies. Such actions weaken China's access to the global economic system and further inflame tensions between the two countries. In response to perceived external threats, China is likely to turn further inward as the CCP doubles down on preserving its domestic power through a more centralized economy.
3. ***Fundamental economic and demographic challenges will weaken China's economic growth prospects.*** While China faces serious economic challenges such as an aging population and declining workforce, a real estate bubble, and drastic income inequality, these challenges can be addressed by the right reforms. However, the most significant risk is that necessary reform efforts may be blocked by vested interests (such as executives and workers of SOEs, local governments, and the military) spurred by perceived external threats to China's national security and perceived internal threats to social stability.

We also believe that China's obsession with its GDP growth targets may crimp its long-term growth just as production quotas per Weitzman (1980) may have crimped the economy of the FSU:

> ... targets are always two-edged swords, ... what you measure rather than what you want is most often what you get. The measure – not the cause – of GDP is output. Short-term GDP targets get you greater output, not the creativity and innovation that are the ultimate sources of efficiency and hence economic growth and improvement in peoples' well-being (Meyer, 2024: 940).

To be sure, the rhetoric of high-quality growth abounds in China. But so do national, provincial, and even local GDP targets and headlines comparing performance against targets. And these headlines can be confusing. Twenty-one of twenty-nine Chinese provinces reporting their 2024 GDP as of late January 2025, including Sichuan and Henan, fell short of their targets (Caixin Global, 2025). Guangdong failed to meet its GDP target for the third year in a row (Zou, 2025). We need not reconcile these reports with China's 5.0 percent GDP growth in 2024. However, we would suggest that greater attention to structural reform and less attention to GDP targets would be beneficial.

So, the arc of the Chinese economy is hard to pin down, which is not surprising. In a best-case scenario, China would pursue internal market-deepening reforms and policies and policy instruments to revitalize TFP growth. This would require fundamental reform – a withdrawal of the state from large parts of the economy, an understanding of GDP growth as a desirable outcome instead of a tournament whose winners gain political advancement, and a priority for innovation and productivity. Were TFP growth to return to 4 percent, then Chinese GDP could grow steadily by 6 percent annually in the next 10 to 15 years. Critical, however, is where that growth occurs. If 6 percent growth flowed to households and the social safety net, education, and medical care especially, then the Chinese people would be far better off. If, however, China subordinates its market-oriented reform to centralized decision-making, top-down planned resource allocation, and marginalization of private enterprises, then TFP and economic growth could grind to zero. Much will depend on whether the U.S. and China can mend their relationship, which will in turn depend on the direction taken by the CCP. Bluntly, can the Party grasp that innovation and productivity by command are unlikely, that relaxation rather than tightening of political and economic controls is ultimately best for the Party and the people? We worry that the current dynamics may have put China on a path toward diminished economic growth in the name of social and regime stability.

Epilogue

The Arc of the Chinese Economy conference took place in April 2023. The official real GDP growth rate from China's National Bureau of Statistics for 2023 was 5.2 percent, reaching a total of RMB 129.42 trillion (approximately US$17.79 trillion) after an upward adjustment in December 2024 (National Bureau of Statistics of China, 2024). It should be noted that some analysts held that China's 2023 official growth rate may have been exaggerated. Daniel Rosen (2023), for example, argued that "Taken together, depending on how negative property investment is assumed to have been in 2023, China's 2023 GDP probably grew 0 to 2.5%." The Rhodium Group headed by Rosen estimates China's actual 2024 GDP growth at 2.4–2.8 percent, well below the official 5 percent figure (Rosen et al. 2024). The slowdown of the Chinese economy is driven by both the structural issues and more short-term business cycle issues. The structural issues faced by the Chinese economy are well summarized in William H. Overholt's final chapter in this book. Logan Wright's (2023: 2) Congressional testimony about the Chinese economy concurs with Overholt: "Simply put, most of the factors that contributed to China's rapid growth over the past two decades – an expanding labor force, unprecedented credit and investment growth, a booming property sector, a one-time buildup of infrastructure, and a constructive external environment – cannot be repeated in the next decade."

The second Trump administration may further heighten the U.S.–China trade tension. Regardless of whether, and when, Trump will follow through on his campaign rhetoric that he would impose a 60 percent tariff on all Chinese imports, it is clear that China's external environment for trade and investment with western countries is not expected to improve, and in fact more likely to deteriorate. The Chinese government has finally come to embrace the importance of stimulating domestic consumption in a series of economic stimulus measures. The first bout of the economic stimulus was unveiled on September 24, 2024, and spearheaded by the PBOC, which came amid mounting pressures from a slowing property market, weak consumer demand, and global economic uncertainties. This bout of stimulus focuses on monetary stimulus, and it features key reductions in the reserve requirement ratio (RRR) and policy interest rates. It also includes measures to support the real estate sector, including cuts to mortgage rates and down payment ratios, aiming to stimulate home purchases. Somewhat unconventionally, the PBOC introduced a liquidity support program for securities and loans to companies for stock buybacks, which is aimed at restoring investor confidence in a flagging Chinese stock market (Interesse, 2024). A more significant stimulus came on December 9, 2024, ahead of the annual Politburo Central Economic Work Conference to set key targets and policy interventions for 2025. It officially shifts China's monetary policy to "appropriately loose" for 2025, the first easing of its stance in some fourteen years, alongside a more proactive fiscal policy to spur economic growth. Besides the easing of the monetary policy stance, China will step up "unconventional" counter-cyclical adjustments, focusing on expanding domestic demand and boosting consumption (Yao and Zhang, 2024). The Chinese government has been reluctant in stimulating domestic consumption in dealing with business-cycle downturns and has historically chosen stimulating investment. Stimulating investment has led to production overcapacity, particularly in sectors that are targeted by China's industrial policy that cannot be absorbed by domestic demand, which must rely on export expansion. Such a strategy is no longer sustainable amid the worsening external trade environment, with both the United States and the European Union threatening hefty tariffs against Chinese imports, particularly on EVs and solar panels. The December 2024 policy announcement for the first time introduced a large consumption stimulus, estimated to be on the order of 10 trillion RMB, to subsidize purchases of new electric appliances and home improvements, including rural homes.

These counter-cyclical measures should not be confused with structural reforms that are necessary for sustained growth. China's household consumption share of GDP hovered in the 37–39 percent range over the last ten years and stood at 39 percent in 2023, which is significantly lower than the household consumption share of roughly 56 percent of global GDP and 48 percent of GDP in upper-middle-income countries (World Bank, n.d. (e)). Boosting the consumption share requires fundamental reforms in the income distribution and further strengthening of the social insurance programs. One-time consumption stimulus will not solve the structural problems underlying the low consumption share. Large-scale, government-funded infrastructure investments, such as high-speed railways and highways, as an engine for economic growth have run their course as these projects enter into low-returns territory. Private investment must take on increasing importance as local governments are now increasingly saddled with unsustainable debt burdens. But to boost private investment, it is necessary to restart the market-deepening reforms, and the government must reverse the trend of the resurgence of the state (see Chapter 9) and roll back some of the seemingly arbitrary regulations against private business in the past years (see Chapter 8). In addition, the real estate sector, which accounted for close to 20 percent of Chinese economic growth in the last decade, has experienced significant downturns.

What then will be the next engines of growth? It is easy to imagine industries fueling growth: electric vehicles where China today has a commanding lead; electrical generation and distribution where China dominates solar panel production, has perfected ultra-high voltage transmission and may be close to commercializing fusion energy; or generative artificial intelligence where DeepSeek has taken the world by surprise. The question is who China's customers for its most advanced technologies will be. Domestic demand is likely to remain weak given high levels of household indebtedness, the erosion of household assets as real estate stagnates or worse, and probably more importantly, a less than sanguine outlook among both consumers and producers about the prospect of the engine of economic growth roaring back to life. A rapidly aging population compounds these challenges (Chapter 4). And there will be pushback from overseas markets, including developing countries, should an onslaught of Chinese goods and services threaten jobs or the capacity to develop their own nascent industries. Whether China can achieve balance in several dimensions – economically by encouraging consumption at home, politically by reassuring its trading partners that they will not be swamped by Chinese exports, and socially by rebuilding safety nets making it easier for people to raise children and remain secure in old age – remains to be seen. We believe that the analysis presented by the distinguished authors in this book provides a useful guide to think about these questions and hence the arc of the Chinese economy in the next decade and beyond.

The Arc: Reprise

Two months after submitting the final version of "The Arc ..." to the publisher, the second Trump administration imposed tariffs on virtually all imports entering the U.S. and especially steep tariffs, up to 154 percent, on Chinese imports. China responded with tariffs of their own, and at this writing the two countries are at loggerheads. Stephen Miran, now Chairman of the Council of Economic Advisers, has diagnosed the underlying problem as an imbalanced global trading system where " ... persistent dollar overvaluation ... is driven by inelastic demand for reserve assets. As global GDP grows, it becomes increasingly burdensome for the United States to finance the provision of reserve assets and the defense umbrella, as the manufacturing and tradeable sectors bear the brunt of the costs" (2024: 1). China is clearly in the crosshairs as its persistent and growing trade surplus with the U.S. is perceived, rightly or wrongly, to have caused the displacement of U.S. manufacturing. The solution envisaged by the second Trump Administration involves steep "reciprocal" tariffs to crimp demand for imports alongside realignment of currencies with a softening of the U.S. dollar vis-à-vis the Chinese renminbi. Miran acknowledges that tariffs and currency realignment will be difficult to implement without disrupting the U.S. much less the global economy: the path to reconfiguring global trading and finance to America's advantage "... is narrow, and will require careful planning, precise execution, and attention to steps to minimize adverse consequences" (2004: 38). So far, evidence of careful planning and precise execution is scant, leaving the world awash in uncertainty and markets in disarray.

Does this uncertainty alter China's choices going forward? The reflexive answer is yes, since China's access to U.S. and E.U. markets will likely be further constrained by steep tariffs – the ASEAN countries have already displaced the U.S. and E.U. as China's largest export destinations, and China's trade with the Global South is growing rapidly. Still, in our judgment, the fundamental lessons remain intact. Two are critical at this juncture. One is that China's productivity growth slowdown must be addressed as productivity growth remains the principal driver of continued GDP growth. The other is that household consumption must be buoyed if only to offset the deceleration of exports and fixed-asset investment, especially real estate.

Neither will be easily achieved. Total factor productivity is itself a derived construct ("the Solow residual") making it difficult to pinpoint its exact causes. What is clear is that Chinese TFP growth fell by nearly half following the GFC and has not recovered since, despite gains in high-profile industries like electric vehicles and solar panels. The remedies per a new Asia Development Bank (2025) report include greater investment in human capital, correcting resource misallocation across industrial sectors and provinces, including redoubling the support for the private sector and facilitating market-based merger, acquisition, and bankruptcy, and greater investment in basic research and breakthrough innovation rather than applied research. Stimulating household consumption may prove more daunting. Household wealth suffered with the deterioration of the real estate market, and consumer sentiment remains weak. One-time measures, for example, government rebates on purchases of large appliances, are palliatives but no more. Ideally, the Chinese government would bear more of the risks, especially health care and retirement costs, currently left to households and constraining spending. While the logic of shifting risks from households to the government seems impeccable, whether the government can afford to bear these risks remains uncertain given that tax revenues in China are at best stagnant (Wright, 2025). This said, boosting household consumption and service consumption in particular is now the number one economic priority at all levels of Chinese government. China may finally be focusing on its overdue task of rebalancing its economy away from reliance on exports and fixed-asset investment.

A long-run solution to the consumption shortfall, however, must address China's low labor share of income and extreme income inequality leaving many households without discretionary spending capacity. The Rhodium Group's Logan Wright (2025) has argued that the government should actively rebalance incomes adding, "Consumption growth will remain tethered to household income growth and will remain constrained by income inequality." Asked by the South China Morning Post whether a more equitable wealth distribution would spur household consumption, Peking University economist Michael Pettis stated bluntly, "It's the only solution. It is mainly distortions in the distribution of wealth and GDP that lead to weak domestic consumption" (Yang, 2025).

With or without a world awash in new uncertainties, China's economy faces substantial challenges – as well as opportunities. We hope the chapters in this book inform the conversations and solutions that emerge.

References

Allen, Franklin, Jun Qian, Chenyu Shan and Julie Lei Zhu. 2024. "Dissecting the Long-Term Performance of the Chinese Stock Market." *Journal of Finance*, 79 (2): 993–1054.

Asian Development Bank. 2025. "Promoting Total Factor Productivity Growth of the People's Republic of China." April.

Bu, Lambert, Violet Chung, Nick Leung, Kevin Wei Wang, Bruce Xia and Chenan Xia. 2021. "The Future of Digital Innovation in China: Megatrends Shaping One of the World's Fastest Evolving Digital Ecosystems." *McKinsey & Company*. www.mckinsey.com/featured-insights/china/the-future-of-digital-innovation-in-china-megatrends-shaping-one-of-the-worlds-fastest-evolving-digital-ecosystems.

Caixin Global. 2025. "Most Provinces Miss GDP Growth Targets." January 27. www.caixinglobal.com/2025-01-27/most-provinces-miss-gdp-growth-targets-102284134.html.

Center for Security and Emerging Technology, Georgetown University. 2021. "Outline of the People's Republic of China 14th Five-Year Plan for National Economic and Social Development and Long-Range Objectives for 2035." May 13. https://cset.georgetown.edu/publication/china-14th-five-year-plan/.

Chaung, Chih-wei. 2023. "World Bank Sees China's Growth Sputtering to Slowest Rate since 1960s." VOA News, October 2. www.voanews.com/a/world-bank-sees-china-s-growth-sputtering-to-slowest-rate-since-1960s-/7294359.html.

Chen, Hao and Meg Rithmire. 2020. "The Rise of the Investor State: State Capital in the Chinese Economy." *Studies in Comparative International Development*, 55 (3): 257–277.

Cheng, Si. 2023. "Shrinking Working Population Poses Challenges to Job Market." China Daily, December 23. www.chinadaily.com.cn/a/202312/29/WS658e2484a31040ac301aa165.html.

Congressional Budget Office. 2024. "The Long-Term Budget Outlook: 2024 to 2054." www.cbo.gov/publication/60127#_idTextAnchor030.

Economic Times. 2023. "JP Morgan, Nomura Raise China's 2023 Economic Growth Forecast." October 18. https://economictimes.indiatimes.com/news/international/business/jp-morgan-nomura-raise-chinas-2023-economic-growth-forecast/articleshow/104521550.cms.

Edelman Trust Institute. 2024. "2024 Edelman Trust Barometer: Global Report." www.edelman.com/sites/g/files/aatuss191/files/2024-02/2024%20Edelman%20Trust%20Barometer%20Global%20Report_FINAL.pdf.

Embassy of the People's Republic of China in the United States of America. 2023. "Premier Li Qiang Meets the Press: Full Transcript of Questions and Answers." March 13. http://us.china-embassy.gov.cn/eng/zgyw/202303/t20230314_11040394.htm.

Fang, Hanming. 2023. "Where Is China's Economy Headed?" In *Building a More Resilient US Economy*, edited by Melissa S. Kearney, Justin Schardin, and Luke Pardue. Aspen Economic Strategy Group, November 8. https://doi.org/10.5281/zenodo.13886913.

Fang, Hanming, Li Ming and Guangli Lu. 2025. "Decoding China's Industrial Policies." National Bureau of Economic Research Working Paper Series No. 33814. www.nber.org/papers/w33814

Gatti, Roberta, Daniel Lederman, Asif M. Islam, Ha Nguyen, Rana Lotfi and Mennatallah Emam Mousa. 2024. "Data Transparency and GDP Growth Forecast Errors." *Journal of International Money and Finance*, 140. https://doi.org/10.1016/j.jimonfin.2023.102991.

Goldman Sachs. 2023. "Is China's Economy Facing Japanification?" October 5. www.goldmansachs.com/insights/articles/is-chinas-economy-facing-japanification.html.

Hao, Tongtong, Ruiqi Sun, Trevor Tombe and Xiaodong Zhu. 2020. "The Effect of Migration Policy on Growth, Structural Change, and Regional Inequality in China." *Journal of Monetary Economics*, 113: 112–134. https://doi.org/10.1016/j.jmoneco.2020.03.003.

Harrison, Ann, Marshall Meyer, Peichun Wang, Linda Zhao and Minyuan Zhao. 2019. "Can a Tiger Change Its Stripes? Reform of Chinese State-Owned Enterprises in the Penumbra of the State." NBER working paper 25475. www.nber.org/papers/w25475.

Holz, Carsten. 2018. "The Unfinished Business of State-Owned Enterprise Reform in the People's Republic of China." https://papers.ssrn.com/sol3/papers.cfm?abstract_id=3392986.

Hong, Pingfan and Zhibo Tan. 2014. "A Comparative Study of the Forecasting Performance of Three International Organizations." UN Department of Economic and Social Affairs (DESA) Working Papers. https://doi.org/10.18356/820dbd70-en.

Interesse, Gulia. 2024. "Decoding China's Recent Economic Stimulus Package: What Investors Need to Know." China Briefing, October 9. www.china-briefing.com/news/decoding-chinas-recent-economic-stimulus-package-what-investors-need-to-know/.

International Monetary Fund. 2024. "Frequently Asked Questions" [scroll to "Q. What is the methodology used to produce the forecasts?"]. www.imf.org/en/Publications/WEO/frequently-asked-questions.

Juhász, Réka, Nathan Lane and Dani Rodrik. 2024. "The New Economics of Industrial Policy." *Annual Review of Economics*, 16: 213–242. https://doi.org/10.1146/annurev-economics-081023-024638.

Kennedy, Scott and Qin Mei. 2023. "Measurement Muddle: China's GDP Growth Data and Potential Proxies." Big Data China, September 13. https://bigdatachina.csis.org/measurement-muddle-chinas-gdp-growth-data-and-potential-proxies/.

Kuznets, Paul W. 1988. "An East Asian Model of Economic Development: Japan, Taiwan, and South Korea." *Economic Development and Cultural Change*, 36 (3): S11–43. www.jstor.org/stable/1566537.

Li, David. 2023. "Local Government Debt in China: Dimensions, Causes and Impacts." The East Is Read. December 21. www.eastisread.com/p/chinas-local-govt-debt-in-2020-was?utm_source=substack&publication_id=1151841&post_id=139069083&utm_medium=email&utm_content=share&utm_campaign=email-share&triggerShare=true&isFreemail=true&r=101

Lin, Justin Yifu. 1988. "The Household Responsibility System in China's Agricultural Reform: A Theoretical and Empirical Study." *Economic Development and Cultural Change*, 36 (S3): S199-S224. https://doi.org/10.1086/edcc.36.s3.1566543.

McVey, Henry and Francis Lim. 2023. "Thoughts from the Road." KKR, October. www.kkr.com/content/dam/kkr/insights/pdf/thoughts-from-the-road-asia-october.pdf.

Meyer, Marshall. 2024. "State Management and Malign Growth." *Management and Organization Review*, 20 (6): 936–941. https://doi.org/10.1017/mor.2024.41.

Ministry of Foreign Affairs of the People's Republic of China. 2023. "Full Text of President Xi Jinping's 2024 New Year Message." December 31. www.fmprc.gov.cn/eng./xw/zyxw/202405/t20240530_11332610.html.

Miran, Stephen. 2024. "A User's Guide to Restructuring the Global Trading System. Hudson Bay Capital." November 2024. www.hudsonbaycapital.com/documents/FG/hudsonbay/research/638199_A_Users_Guide_to_Restructuring_the_Global_Trading_System.pdf

Muir, Dirk V., Natalija Novta, and Anne Oeking. 2024. "China's Path to Sustainable and Balanced Growth." IMF Working Papers 2024, 238, accessed May 27, 2025, https://doi.org/10.5089/9798400293467.001.

National Bureau of Statistics of China. 2024. "Bulletin by the National Bureau of China on the Revision of Annual GDP Data for 2023." December 28. www.stats.gov.cn/english/PressRelease/202412/t20241231_1958128.html.

Naughton, Barry. 2021. *The Rise of China's Industrial Policy: 1978–2020*. Lynne Rienner Publishers.

Nicholson, Stephen and Haifeng Huang. 2023. "Making the List: Reevaluating Political Trust and Social Desirability in China." *American Political Science Review*, 117 (3): 1158–1165.

Orcutt, Mike. 2023. "What's Next for China's Digital Currency?" MIT Technology Review, August 3. www.technologyreview.com/2023/08/03/1077181/whats-next-for-chinas-digital-currency/.

Organization for Economic Co-operation and Development. 2025. Consumer Opinion Surveys: Composite Consumer Confidence for China [CSCICP02CNM460S], retrieved from FRED, Federal Reserve Bank of St. Louis, February 9. https://fred.stlouisfed.org/series/CSCICP02CNM460S.

Overholt, William. 1994. *The Rise of China: How Economic Reform Is Creating a New Superpower*. Norton & Company.

People's Bank of China and China Banking Regulatory Commission. 2009. *Guiding Opinions of the People's Bank of China and China Banking Regulatory Commission on Further Adjusting the Credit Structure to Promote the Rapid yet Steady Development of the National Economy*. March 18. www.lawinfochina.com/display.aspx?lib=law&id=7363&CGid=&EncodingName=big5.

Rajah, Roland and Leng, Alyssa. 2022. "Revising Down the Rise of China." Lowy Institute. www.lowyinstitute.org/sites/default/files/RAJAH%20LENG%2C%20Revising%20Down%20Rise%20of%20China%2C%20PDF%20v3.pdf.

Reuters. 2023. "IMF Sees Signs China Stabilizing, Says Reforms Can Boost Medium-Term Growth." September 28. www.reuters.com/world/china/imf-sees-signs-china-stabilizing-says-reforms-can-boost-medium-term-growth-2023-09-28/.

Rogoff, Kenneth, and Yuanchen Yang. 2021. "Has China's Housing Production Peaked?" *China & World Economy*, 29 (1): 1–31.

Rosen, Daniel. 2023. "How Is China's Economy Doing? Not as Well as China Says It Is." Wall Street Journal, December 6. www.wsj.com/world/china/china-economy-2023-chinese-government-62e847d0.

Rosen, Daniel, Logan Wright, Jeremy Smith, Matthew Mingey and Roland Quinn. 2024. "After the Fall: China's Economy in 2025." The Rhodium Group, December 31. https://rhg.com/research/after-the-fall-chinas-economy-in-2025/.

Rudd, Kevin. 2023. "China's Competing Ideological and Economic Policy Objectives in 2023." The Asia Society, February 16. https://asiasociety.org/policy-institute/chinas-competing-ideological-and-economic-policy-objectives-2023.

Saber, Nadya. 2018. "China Economic Outlook in Six Charts." International Monetary Fund. www.imf.org/en/News/Articles/2018/07/25/na072618-chinas-economic-outlook-in-six-charts.

Simon, Denis Fred. 1989. "China's Drive to Close the Technological Gap: S&T Reform and the Imperative to Catch Up." *China Quarterly*, 119 (September): 598–630.

Statistics Times. 2024. "Comparing United States and China by Economy." November 23. https://statisticstimes.com/economy/united-states-vs-china-economy.php.

Stewart, Heather. 2025. "China's Economy Hits 5% Growth Target but Rate among Slowest in Decades." The Guardian, January 27. www.theguardian.com/business/2025/jan/17/china-economy-hits-growth-target-but-rate-among-slowest-in-decades.

Sun, Yutao and Cong Cao. 2021. "Planning for Science: China's "Grand Experiment" and Global Implications." Humanities and Social Sciences Communications 8: n. 215. https://doi.org/10.1057/s41599-021-00895-7.

Wang, Sun Ling, Francis Tuan, Fred Gale, Agapi Somwarum and James Hansen. 2013. "China's Regional Agricultural Productivity Growth in 1985–2007: A Multilateral Comparison." *Agricultural Economics*, 44 (2): 241–251.

Wang, Tao. 2023. *Making Sense of China's Economy*. Routledge.

Weitzman, Martin 1980. "The 'Ratchet Principle' and Performance Incentives." *The Bell Journal of Economics*, 11 (1): 302–308.

World Integrated Trade Solution. n.d. (a). "China Exports by Country and Region 2012." https://wits.worldbank.org/CountryProfile/en/Country/CHN/Year/2012/TradeFlow/Export/Partner/all/Show/Partner%20Name;XPRT-TRD-VL;XPRT-PNR-SHR;/Sort/XPRT-TRD-VL/Chart/top10.

World Integrated Trade Solution. n.d. (b). "China Exports by Country and Region 2022." https://wits.worldbank.org/CountryProfile/en/Country/CHN/Year/2022/TradeFlow/Export/Partner/by-country/Show/Partner%20Name;XPRT-TRD-VL;XPRT-PRTNR-SHR;/Sort/XPRT-TRD-VL/Chart/top10.

World Bank. n.d. (a). "GDP (current US$) – China, United States." https://data.worldbank.org/indicator/NY.GDP.MKTP.CD?locations=CN-US

World Bank. n.d. (b). "GDP, PPP (current international $) – China, United States." https://data.worldbank.org/indicator/NY.GDP.MKTP.PP.CD?locations=CN-US-.

World Bank. n.d. (c). "GDP, PPP per capita (current international $) – China, United States." https://data.worldbank.org/indicator/NY.GDP.PCAP.PP.CD?locations=CN-US

World Bank. n.d. (d). "Fertility Rate, Total (births per woman) – China." https://data.worldbank.org/indicator/SP.DYN.TFRT.IN?locations=CN.

World Bank. n.d. (e). "Households and NPISHs final consumption expenditure (% of GDP) – China." https://data.worldbank.org/indicator/NE.CON.PRVT.ZS?end=2023&locations=CN&start=1990.

World Bank. n.d. (f). GDP per capita (constant 2015 US$) – China. https://data.worldbank.org/indicator/NY.GDP.PCAP.KD?locations-CN.

World Bank. n.d. (g). "GDP Growth (annual%) – China, Japan, Korea, Rep." https://data.worldbank.org/indicator/NY.GDP.MKTP.KD.ZG?end=2023&locations=CN-JP-KR&start=1990.

Wright, Logan. 2023. "Testimony before the US-China Economic and Security Review Commission, Hearing on China's Financial and Economic Challenges." August. www.uscc.gov/sites/default/files/2023-08/Logan_Wright_Testimony.pdf.

Wright, Logan. 2025. "China's Harsh Fiscal Winter." March 25. Rhodium Group. https://rhg.com/research/chinas-harsh-fiscal-winter/

Xu, Chenggang. 2011. "The Fundamental Institutions of China's Reforms and Development." *Journal of Economic Literature*, 49 (4): 1076–1151.

Xu, Chenggang. 2025. *Institutional Genes: The Origins of China's Institutions and Totalitarianism*. Cambridge University Press.

Yang, Jun. 2020. "World's 10 Highest Bridges: Guizhou Has Half." China Daily, June 12. www.chinadaily.com.cn/a/202006/12/WS5ee3424ba310834817252b85_1.html.

Yang, Carol. 2025. "Economist Michael Pettis on China's Consumption Paradox and the Pitfalls of a Trade War." March 24. www.scmp.com/economy/china-economy/article/3303369/economist-michael-pettis-chinas-consumption-paradox-and-pitfalls-trade-war

Yao, Kevin and Ellen Zhang. 2024. "China Vows to Ramp up Policy Stimulus to Spur Growth in 2025." Reuters, December 9. www.reuters.com/world/china/china-announces-first-monetary-policy-shift-since-2010-spur-growth-2024-12-09/.

Zuo, Mandy. 2025. "China's Guangdong, Missing GDP Target 3 years Running, among Slowest Economies in 2024." South China Morning Post, January 25. www.scmp.com/economy/china-economy/article/3296465/chinas-guangdong-missing-gdp-target-3-years-running-among-slowest-economies-2024.

2 China's Productivity Challenge

XIAODONG ZHU

China's economic growth has slowed significantly in recent years, with factors such as trade tensions, high debt levels, a struggling real estate sector, and an aging population being cited as possible causes. The slowdown actually began much earlier, however, with GDP growth rates trending downward since peaking in 2007 at 13 percent. This leads to the question: What long-term factors can explain China's growth slowdown?

This chapter argues that there is one key long-term factor behind China's GDP growth: productivity improvement. China's total factor productivity (TFP), which measures the aggregate production efficiency of the economy, grew at an impressive rate of over 4 percent per year between 1978 and 2007. This rate exceeds even the TFP growth rates of Hong Kong, Singapore, South Korea, and Taiwan during their own respective periods of rapid economic expansion from 1965 to 1990. As a result, China's GDP growth rate averaged 9.5 percent per year during this period. However, over the fifteen years of growth slowdown, China's TFP growth has declined considerably, averaging only 1 percent per year.[1] I show that this slowdown in productivity improvement is the main reason for China's differential GDP growth performance before and after 2007. In contrast, changes in investment rates and demographic factors play only a minor role.

After establishing the crucial role of productivity improvement in China's economic growth, this chapter examines potential contributors to this improvement, including factor reallocation, trade liberalization, migration, institutional change, and technology diffusion and innovation. Surprisingly, despite years of banking and financial market reforms, capital reallocation has had little or even negative impact on China's productivity growth. The contribution of export expansion

[1] See Brandt et al. (2022) for a survey of macro and micro evidence on China's recent productivity trends.

following China's accession to the WTO has also been limited. Rather, domestic reforms that reduced barriers to internal trade and internal migration have had a more significant impact on productivity growth. Ultimately, two factors – economic reform and decentralization that have spurred bottom-up institutional change and market-based technology diffusion and innovation aided by international trade – are the driving forces behind China's impressive productivity growth before 2007.

Unfortunately, since 2007, the Chinese government has shifted away from the bottom-up approach, instead placing greater emphasis on top-level policy design (*ding ceng she ji*) and mobilizing national resources (*ju guo ti zhi*). While this approach has achieved some short-term goals, such as the temporary growth recovery in 2010 after the global financial crisis and the rapid expansion of infrastructure projects, it has come at a significant cost to economic efficiency. The centralization of policy-making has resulted in fewer policy reforms and institutional changes initiated from below, and various top-down industrial policies aimed at boosting China's technological capabilities have resulted in significant misallocation of resources. Consequently, China's productivity has improved at a much slower pace under the new policy regime.

The final section (of the article) examines China's future growth prospects and the challenges it must overcome to achieve its goals. In the 14th Five-Year Plan (2021–2025), the Chinese government has set a target of achieving an average annual GDP growth rate of over 6 percent. However, achieving this target will be challenging if China's TFP growth remains at 1 percent per year or slower, even if the government further raises the already high investment rate. If, instead, China can increase its TFP growth rate to 3 percent, it could easily achieve the growth target for not only the 14th Five-Year Plan but also the following decade, even if the investment rate declines by half a percentage point each year. Therefore, the most important priority for China is to improve its productivity. To obtain this goal, China needs to decentralize policy-making, rely more on market competition than top-down industrial policies, and continue to engage with the global economy.

Productivity Improvement as the Driver of China's Growth

Many people have suggested that China's rapid growth between 1978 and 2007 was fueled by high and rising rates of fixed capital investment, often led by local governments and the state sector, the so-called

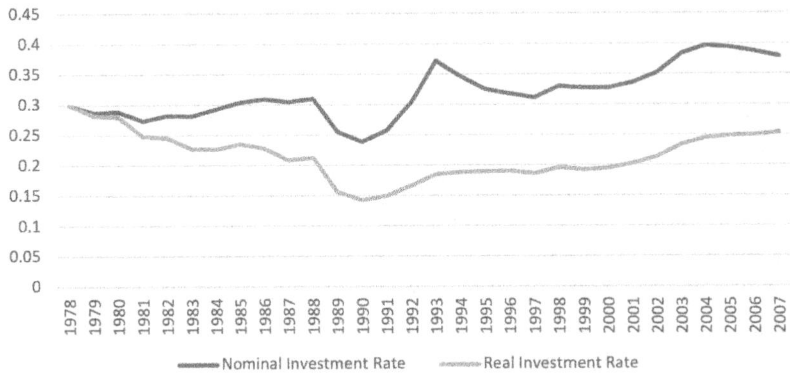

Figure 2.1 Fixed-capital investment rates

investment-driven growth model of China. This characterization of China's growth is incorrect.

Figure 2.1 shows the fixed capital investment rates of China for the period of 1978–2007. The nominal investment rate, measured as the amount spent on fixed capital formation as a percentage of nominal GDP, indeed rose from about 30 percent in 1978 to 38 percent in 2007. Before 1990, however, the nominal investment rate rose due to a rise in the costs of investment. The real investment rate, which measures the real value of investment as a percentage of real GDP after controlling for changes in the costs of investment,[2] actually declined from 30 percent to 15 percent between 1978 and 1990. Therefore, China's pre-1990 growth could not have been driven by any increase in the investment rate.

Since 1990, the real investment rate did increase from 15 percent to 25 percent. But how did this increase in the investment rate contribute to China's growth between 1990 and 2007? The answer is not much. During the period, China's GDP growth rate averaged 9.5 percent a year. Using a standard growth model, I simulate the counterfactual GDP growth rate, holding the real investment rate constant at 15 percent throughout the seventeen-year period.[3] The

[2] More specifically, the real investment rate is the ratio of fixed-capital formation to GDP, both valued using 1978 prices.

[3] The model used for simulations is the standard Solow growth model. The details of the data and simulation method are available on the author's website: www.xiaodongzhu.net.

simulation shows that, without the increase in real investment rate, the average GDP growth rate would have been reduced only slightly to 8.5 percent a year. That is, the increase in the investment rate contributed to only 1 percentage point of China's GDP growth between 1990 and 2007.

During the period, China's total employment also grew rapidly due to favorable demographic changes. According to the World Bank's estimates,[4] China's age dependence ratio (number of young and old people who are not in the labor force to the number of working-age people) declined from 0.52 in 1990 to 0.38 in 2007. Correspondingly, China's total employment grew at an average rate of 0.89 percent per year. Employment growth, however, also contributed little to China's GDP growth. Similar to the approach earlier, holding China's total employment and fixed-capital investment rate constant at their 1990 levels, China's GDP growth rate during the period would have still averaged 7.87 percent. Therefore, employment growth contributed to only 0.63 percentage points of GDP growth (7.87 percent to 8.5 percent) during this period.

What then is the main driver of China's growth during the period? Zhu (2012) argues that it is productivity growth. Between 1990 and 2007, China's TFP grew at an average rate of 4.5 percent a year. Fast TFP growth contributed to GDP growth not only directly but also indirectly by allowing capital to accumulate faster for the same rates of investment. Again, a simulation using the standard growth model shows that, if there were no TFP growth during the period, China's average GDP growth rate would have been significantly lower, at only 3.5 percentage points per year, a 6-percentage point reduction, even with the real investment rate rising from 15 percent to 25 percent. These simulation results show clearly that it is TFP growth, not the increase in the investment rate nor the employment growth, that is the main driver of China's GDP growth between 1990 and 2007.

TFP growth is important to China's GDP growth, not only in the period 1990–2007, but throughout the last four and a half decades. Figure 2.2 plots China's GDP and TFP growth rates between 1978 and 2022. As can be seen, episodes of accelerating GDP growth are invariably associated with rising TFP growth, and periods of growth

[4] The World Bank data can be found here: https://data.worldbank.org/indicator/SP.POP.DPND?end=2021&locations=CN&start=1990.

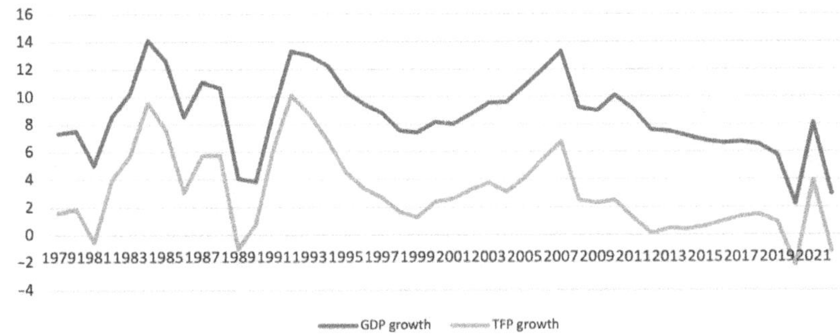

Figure 2.2 GDP growth and TFP growth in China: 1978–2022

slowdown coincide with periods of declining TFP growth. During the fast growth period of 1978–2007, China's TFP growth averaged more than 4 percent a year. In the last fifteen years of growth slowdown, on the other hand, TFP growth averaged only 1 percent.

To be sure, other factors also play a role in China's growth slowdown. China's dependence ratio has been increasing since 2008, reaching 0.45 in 2021. The aging population has caused a decline in total employment since 2015. The Chinese government's large fiscal stimulus in 2008–2009 also resulted in high debt levels, which have limited the government's ability to use fiscal and monetary policies to stimulate investment demand. China's real fixed-capital investment rate, after rising steadily for two and a half decades, has remained stable at 31 percent since 2015.

To assess the impact of these changes on China's growth slowdown, I simulate GDP growth rates between 2007 and 2022, holding total employment constant at the 2014 level and assuming the fixed-capital investment rate to increase by 0.65 percentage points per year after 2014. Figure 2.3 plots the simulated GDP growth rates under these assumptions, as well as the actual GDP growth rates. The results suggest that without the decline in employment and with continued increases in the investment rate, which would result in a nominal investment rate of over 50 percent in 2022, the average GDP growth rate would have increased by less than 0.5 percentage points.

Figure 2.3 also plots the GDP growth rates under the assumptions of 2 percent and 3 percent TFP growth, respectively. If TFP grows at 2 percent per year, the average GDP growth rate would

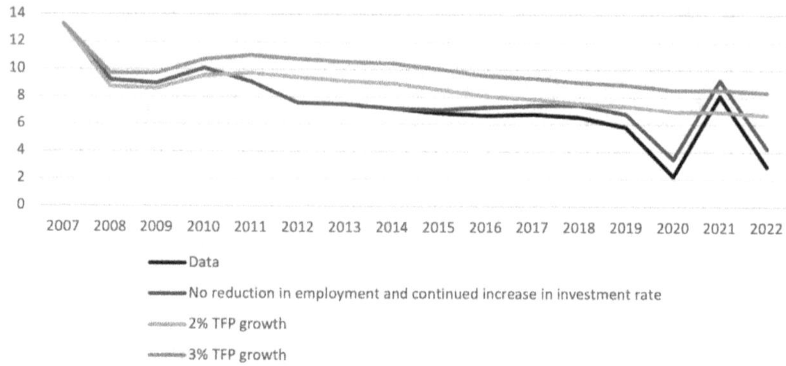

Figure 2.3 GDP growth rates: 2007–2022

have increased by 1.2 percentage points. If TFP grows even faster at 3 percent per year, the average GDP growth rate would have increased by 2.6 percentage points.

In summary, a slow pace of productivity improvement, rather than population aging or lack of investment rate increase, is the primary reason for China's relatively poor GDP growth since 2007. The following section examines the various sources of China's remarkable productivity growth between 1978 and 2007 and discusses the potential reasons for the slowdown in productivity improvement since 2007.

Sources of China's Productivity Growth

There are several potential sources of China's productivity growth, including factor reallocation, trade liberalization, migration, institutional change, and technology diffusion and innovation. I will discuss each of these sources in turn.

Agricultural Productivity Growth and Labor Reallocation

In the late 1970s, factor allocation in China was highly distorted. Around 70 percent of the labor force was employed in agriculture, and outside of agriculture, much of the employment was in the state sector and most of the capital stock was controlled by the state. Through institutional and market reforms, agricultural productivity grew at 4 percent a year between 1978 and 2007 (Zhu, 2012). The agricultural productivity growth allowed a large amount of farmers to be reallocated from agriculture to nonagriculture. This reallocation is vital for the rise of the nonstate sector in China, because most of the reallocated workers went to privately owned enterprises (POEs) and township and village enterprises (TVEs) rather than state-owned enterprises (SOEs). Since the nonstate enterprises are more productive than both agriculture and SOEs, the reallocation of labor contributed positively to aggregate TFP growth. Overall, agricultural productivity growth and the resulting labor reallocation contributed to TFP growth of 1.5 percent between 1978 and 2007, with much of the contribution concentrated in the first decade of the period, as estimated by Brandt and Zhu (2010).

Capital Reallocation

However, the reallocation of capital did not contribute substantially to China's TFP growth. Brandt, Tombe, and Zhu (2013) find that returns to capital were much lower in the state sector than in the nonstate sector, a clear indicator of capital misallocation. Although capital allocation improved in the 1980s and early 1990s through a more decentralized banking system, improvements halted after the banking and fiscal reforms in 1994. Zhu (2021) argues that both the banking reform and the fiscal reform under former premier Zhu Rongji resulted in a re-centralization of China's banking and fiscal system, making it difficult for small- and medium-sized private enterprises to obtain financing and support from banks and local governments. By 2007, the TFP loss due to capital misallocation was as high as in 1985, indicating that capital reallocation did not contribute to China's TFP growth for the entirety of 1985–2007. For the period after 2007, Bai et al. (2016), Ho et al. (2018), and Cong et al. (2019) all find that capital allocation had further deteriorated after the implementation of the central government's large fiscal stimulus in 2009. Hao et al. (2020) also find a small negative effect of cross-region capital reallocation on China's TFP growth between 2005 and 2015.

Trade Liberalization

With a declining contribution from agriculture and a negative contribution from capital reallocation, China's TFP growth slowed in the second half of the 1990s, as did its GDP growth. However, starting from 2000, a series of new reforms provided impetus to a new round of accelerating TFP growth.

During this period, the event that received the most attention was China's accession to the World Trade Organization (WTO) at the end of 2001. This move resulted in a significant reduction in China's import tariffs and eliminated uncertainty for Chinese exporters regarding the tariffs they would face when exporting to the United States.[5] The resulting international trade liberalization led to China's rapid trade expansion, eventually making it the world's largest trading nation in 2013.

What is less well known is that internal trade liberalization also occurred around the same time. In the 1990s, China had high internal trade barriers (Young, 2000; Ponce, 2005) due to local market protections, which were often related to the size of a region's state sector (Bai et al., 2004). Between 2000 and 2005, however, these internal trade barriers decreased significantly due to both the newly implemented market integration policy by the central government and the SOE reform that reduced the size of the state sector and thus local governments' incentives for local protection.

Tombe and Zhu (2019) estimate the impact of the reductions in both international and internal trade barriers on China's productivity growth between 2000 and 2005 and found that internal trade liberalization contributed to productivity growth by 2 percent per year, while international trade liberalization contributed to productivity growth by less than 1 percent per year. These results suggest that domestic reforms were more crucial than international trade expansions for China's productivity growth during this period.

Unfortunately, China's trade liberalization seems to have stalled after 2007. Hao et al. (2020) estimate the changes in trade costs of Chinese regions between 2007 and 2012. They find small increases in both internal and international trade costs for almost all regions, indicating a modest retreat from the significant trade liberalization before 2007.

[5] China had already enjoyed low tariffs on exports to the United States as a designated Most Favored Nation before its accession to the WTO, but the designation was subject to annual renewal and thus there was uncertainty regarding the potential tariffs the U.S. government might impose on Chinese exports.

Migration

During the period 2000–2005, in addition to internal trade liberalization, there had also been reforms that reduced the costs of internal migration in China. Fan (2019), Tombe and Zhu (2019), and Hao et al. (2020) all provide detailed discussions on the high migration costs posed by China's *hukou* registration system and the reforms that helped to reduce these costs. Tombe and Zhu (2019) estimate that the reduction in migration costs contributed to China's productivity growth by 1.1 percent per year between 2000 and 2005, with most of the productivity gains coming from the migration of farmers from interior regions to work in industry and services in the coastal cities of China. Productivity improvement due to reduction in migration costs is one factor that continued to contribute positively to TFP growth after 2007. Hao et al. (2020) estimate that reduction in migration costs contributed to China's productivity growth by an average of 1.2 percent a year between 2005 and 2015.

However, Hao et al. (2020) also show that, even after controlling for the contributions of trade and migration, a large residual in aggregate productivity growth remains unaccounted for. The next section argues that bottom-up institutional change and technology diffusion aided by international trade are two important sources of productivity growth in China.

Bottom-up Institutional Change

One important characteristic of many of China's successful economic reforms and institutional changes is that they are initiated from below rather than designed by the central government. The most well-known example of bottom-up institutional change is the Household Responsibility System (HRS) in agriculture. At the end of 1978, some villagers in Anhui and Sichuan provinces secretly abandoned collective farming and adopted the HRS for agricultural production, despite it being illegal to do so according to the central government's official policy at the time. The provincial leaders of the two provinces (Wan Li and Zhao Ziyang), recognizing the effectiveness of the HRS in improving agricultural productivity, allowed more villages to adopt the system instead of punishing the villagers for violating the central government's policy. The HRS then rapidly spread to other provinces, and by the end of 1981, 45 percent of villages in China had adopted the system. It was only then that the central government approved the HRS as the official policy and began implementing it nationwide.

The HRS was incredibly successful in improving agricultural productivity in China. Between 1978 and 1984, when the HRS was gradually implemented across China, the country's agricultural TFP grew at a rate of 5.62 percent per year. McMillan, Walley, and Zhu (1989) and Lin (1992) estimate that most of the TFP growth at the time could be attributed to the HRS, which generated strong positive incentive effects on farmers' efforts and input and output choices.

Bottom-up institutional change also played an important role in the reform of SOEs in urban areas. In the early 1990s, downstream industries' SOEs faced stiff competition from rapidly growing TVEs, which were not only more productive but also more adapted to market competition. Due to rigid management structures and a lack of incentives for employees, SOEs directly competing with TVEs often incurred losses.

In Zhucheng, a county-level city located in Shandong province, there were many money-losing SOEs. In a 1992 audit of 150 municipal enterprises, the city government discovered that 103 of them were losing money, and 43 were insolvent. At that time, local government fiscal revenues primarily came from the SOEs under their supervision. As a result, the SOEs' financial problems also translated into the city government's fiscal woes. In October 1992, Mayor Chen Guang of Zhucheng initiated an ownership reform. All 282 SOEs and collective enterprises in Zhucheng were restructured, with over 90 percent of the enterprises becoming joint-stock cooperatives that sold the enterprises' net assets to internal staff. Within fifteen months, the majority of the enterprises were "sold" to internal staff. The reform successfully turned many money-losing SOEs into profitable enterprises, but it also attracted national attention. Some people criticized Chen Guang for selling state-owned assets and gave him a nickname of "*Chen Mai Guang*" or "Selling-out Chen."

In 1996, Vice Premier Zhu Rongji sent a state council group to investigate the enterprise reform in Zhucheng, and later he visited Zhucheng himself and decided to adopt Chen Guang's approach for SOE reform. Between 1996 and 2000, SOE reform was carried out nationwide. The reform sold or closed many small- and medium-sized SOEs and corporatized large SOEs, reducing the state sector's share of total employment from 16 percent to 13 percent. According to Hsieh and Song (2015), the so-called grasp the large, let go of the small SOE reform contributed to about one-fifth of China's TFP growth between 1998 and 2007.

However, the downsizing of the state sector did not continue after 2007. After the global financial crisis in 2008–2009, the Chinese government has placed more emphasis on building bigger and stronger SOEs.

In a recent article, Chen, Li, and Zhu (2024) utilize a unique dataset on county-level major events to examine the formation and dissemination of major reform policies in China during the period 1976-2005. They find that policy changes from bottom-up are linked to positive TFP growth, while centrally sponsored local policy experiments are associated with higher rates of fixed-capital investment. These results provide more systematic empirical evidence on the importance of bottom-up institutional change on China's productivity growth.

Technology Diffusion

When economic reform started in the late 1970s, China was a technologically backward country at an early stage of development. It is natural then that China's technological changes in the early decades of economic reform were mainly in the form of adapting existing technologies from advanced economies rather than innovating with new technologies (Acemoglu, Aghion, and Zilibotti, 2006). This has largely remained the case, even in recent years. For example, Hsieh and Klenow (2022) find that most of China's technological advances over the 1991–2016 period were quality upgrades on existing products that were originally created in advanced economies. In contrast, during the same period, most of the US's technological changes were creating new product varieties.

Two distinct approaches to technology adoption were pursued by Chinese enterprises. SOEs often set up joint ventures with foreign enterprises, providing market access in exchange for technology blueprints. While this approach could be an effective strategy for Chinese firms to master foreign technologies quickly (Bai et al., 2020), it also reduced Chinese partner enterprises' incentives to innovate themselves (Howell, 2018).

In contrast, private enterprises in China often learn about foreign technologies through market interactions with foreign firms. By either importing foreign products or serving as sales representatives, original equipment manufacturers (OEMs), or suppliers of foreign firms, Chinese enterprises could learn about the market demand of products produced using foreign technologies, but without access to the blueprints of the foreign technologies. To imitate, they had to rely on reverse engineering, learning by doing, and trial and error, which actually helped them to develop innovation capabilities.

A good example of such enterprises is Huawei, which was founded by Ren Zhengfei in 1987 with registered capital of 21,000 CNY. The initial business of Huawei was acting as a sales agent of a Hong Kong company, selling Private Branch Exchange (PNC) systems (telephone switchboards) in China. In the early 1990s, when the Hong Kong company stopped using Huawei as its sales agent, Huawei decided to produce its own telephone switchboards. At the time, the telecommunications equipment market in China was dominated by foreign producers such as Ericsson, Siemens, Alston, NEC, and so on, and a state-controlled joint venture, Shanghai Bell. Huawei could not compete with these brand names and was forced to target lower-tier cities in rural areas. Its first self-produced switchboard model, City and Countryside 08, was sold to Yiwu County in Zhejiang Province. In the mid- to late-1990s, still unable to penetrate the market of upper-tier cities in China, Huawei started to sell its products to countries of the former Soviet Union, Africa, and Latin America. As it grew, Huawei hired IBM in 1999 as its consultant to learn how to build an integrated management system for an R&D-intensive enterprise. From its founding in 1987 to the early 2000s, Huawei received little support from the Chinese government. It was only after its impressive performance in the international market that the Chinese government viewed Huawei as a "national champion" and started to provide the company with financial support through the China Development Bank. To help Huawei further expand its export markets, the China Development Bank provided trade credits to potential buyers from developing countries.

Another example is Zhenhua Port Machinery Corporation (ZPMC), founded in 1992 by Guan Tongxian, a retired government official from China's Ministry of Transportation. At the time, all port machinery in China was imported from Germany, Japan, or Korea. Seeing the high demand for port machinery and the high costs of importing them, Mr. Guan believed that ZPMC could compete in the international market by producing these machines at a much lower cost. He was right. Through reverse engineering and imitation, he and his engineers were able to produce their first batch of port machinery in 2013 and, impressively, exported them to ports in Vancouver and Miami. ZPMC secured the exporting deals with one business innovation: promising to deliver assembled port machinery that is ready-to-use upon delivery to its customers.

This is an important competitive advantage because all other competitors in the market could only deliver parts that would need to be assembled at the customers' site, which would be costly in terms of both time and labor. ZPMC was able to gain this competitive advantage by buying and refurbishing a military ship that it found abandoned in a port near its factory. Like Huawei, ZPMC looked to global rather than domestic markets for growth. As the company grew, its product quality also improved steadily through imitation and learning by doing, and it was able to penetrate markets all over the world. By 2008, ZPMC had become one of the most successful heavy machinery companies in the world, with a remarkable 70 percent share of the global port machinery market.

However, as ZPMC became a "national champion," it was merged with a poorly performing SOE, Shanghai Port Machinery Corporation, in 2009 and became a state-controlled enterprise. In addition, the Chinese government encouraged the newly merged company to expand into one of the government's strategic areas: ocean oil exploration. Under the big fiscal stimulus plan rolled out in 2009, ZPMC made an enormous investment in building four ocean oil exploration and drilling platforms, financed through a combination of cheap credits from state-owned banks and new equity in the stock market. Unfortunately, the market for these platforms waned and ZPMC could only find buyers for two of its four platforms. The remaining two are still unsold as of today. As a result, most of the profits ZPMC generates from its core business of port machinery are now used to cover the financial losses it incurred from investing in the ocean oil exploration and drilling platforms.

The case of ZPMC offers two key lessons. First, like Huawei, ZPMC learned about the market for its product from observing foreign exports to China and, by competing in the global markets and through imitation and learning by doing, ZPMC was able to continuously upgrade its product quality and close its productivity gap with the global technology leaders in the industry. Second, the government's industrial policy distorted the enterprise's incentives and diverted it away from its core business in which it holds a clear competitive advantage in the global market.

Re-examining the Contribution of External Trade Liberalization

According to Tombe and Zhu (2019)'s estimate, the direct impact of external trade liberalization on China's productivity growth is limited.

However, as Huawei, ZPMC, and numerous other Chinese enterprises' experiences indicate, many Chinese enterprises learned and imitated foreign technologies and management practices through their market interactions with foreign companies from advanced economies. Therefore, international trade liberalization also contributed to China's growth through technology diffusion. Additionally, international trade liberalization also provided the impetus for domestic reforms. It was after China officially joined the WTO that the central government adopted a policy of promoting integrated domestic markets (Holz, 2009) and the increases in labor demand for exporting firms led some local governments to reduce their restrictions on migrant workers (Tian, 2022). Therefore, while international trade's direct effect on growth may be limited, its indirect effects, through facilitating technology diffusion and providing impetus for domestic reforms, are significant.

From Imitation to Innovation?

In recent years, the Chinese government has been placing more emphasis on indigenous innovation and promoting a transition from imitation to innovation with various industrial policies. However, the implementation of these policies has resulted in significant misallocation in R&D investments, as documented by Chen et al. (2021) and Wei et al. (2023). Furthermore, Konig et al. (2022) argue that government subsidies may encourage the wrong firms to innovate and therefore lower aggregate TFP growth: Firms that could still benefit significantly from imitation could be induced to innovate in areas they do not have a comparative advantage because of subsidies, like the ZPMC example we discussed earlier. The increasing emphasis on the role of SOEs is also not conducive to innovation. Liu, Jia, and Seamans (2023) provide evidence that SOEs lag behind private firms in robot adoption and in using robots to increase productivity because they lack incentives to make complementary investments. Finally, even without misallocation in R&D investments, it would generally be difficult to generate high TFP growth through innovation, as documented by Bloom et al. (2020) for the U.S. economy.

Summary

Taking stock, there have been four main sources of productivity growth in China: (1) labor reallocation from agriculture to nonagriculture in the early years of economic reform and rural-urban migration in more recent years, (2) internal trade liberalization, (3) bottom-up institutional change, and (4) market-based technology diffusion aided by international trade. China's recent growth slowdown is associated with a lack of further internal trade liberalization, more top-down rather than bottom-up institutional change, and more government-directed industrial policies on technology innovation rather than market-based technology diffusion.

Projecting China's GDP Growth Up to 2035

Given the importance of TFP growth, I now examine China's growth prospects under different scenarios of future TFP growth, again by using simulations from the standard growth model. For the simulation exercise, some assumptions need to be made about China's future employment and human capital growth. I assume that aggregate employment declines by half a percentage point a year due to population aging, and that the average human capital of the workforce increases by 1.3 percentage points a year, which is roughly the average human capital growth rate in China over the last ten years. We consider five different scenarios:

(1) TFP does not grow at all, and the fixed-capital investment rate increases by half a percentage point a year;
(2) TFP grows at 1 percent a year, and the fixed-capital investment rate increases by half a percentage point a year;
(3) TFP grows at 2 percent a year;
(4) TFP grows at 2 percent a year, and the fixed-capital investment rate decreases by half a percentage point a year;
(5) TFP grows at 3 percent a year, and the fixed-capital investment rate decreases by half a percentage point a year.

Figure 2.4 and Table 2.1 show the projected GDP growth rates for the period of 2023–2035 under all five scenarios. The case of zero TFP growth is the worst among the five scenarios. In this case, the aggregate production efficiency does not improve at all. Without TFP growth, the projected GDP growth rate in 2023 is only 3.76 percent, far short of the Chinese government's stated target of 5 percent. We assume that the government tries to stimulate growth by increasing the fixed-capital investment rate by half a percentage point each year,

Table 2.1 *Projected GDP growth rates for China 2023–2035*

Annual TFP growth rate	0%	1%	2%	2%	3%
Annual change in investment rate	0.50%	0.50%	0%	-0.50%	-0.05%
Year					
2023	3.76	4.76	5.76	5.76	6.76
2024	3.57	4.74	5.70	5.59	6.66
2025	3.39	4.71	5.64	5.44	6.56
2026	3.24	4.69	5.59	5.29	6.47
2027	3.09	4.67	5.54	5.16	6.38
2028	2.95	4.64	5.49	5.04	6.30
2029	2.83	4.62	5.45	4.92	6.22
2030	2.72	4.60	5.41	4.81	6.15
2031	2.61	4.57	5.37	4.71	6.08
2032	2.51	4.55	5.33	4.61	6.01
2033	2.42	4.53	5.30	4.51	5.95
2034	2.33	4.51	5.27	4.42	5.88
2035	2.25	4.48	5.24	4.34	5.82
Average	2.90	4.62	5.47	4.97	6.25

Figure 2.4 Projected GDP growth rates of China

which implies that the nominal investment rate will be more than 51 percent by 2035. Despite the increasing investment rates, the 3.7 percent GDP growth rate in 2023 cannot be sustained due to diminishing returns to capital investment. The projected GDP growth rate will fall to 2.25 percent by 2035, rendering the average projected GDP growth rate between 2023 and 2035 to be 2.9 percent.

Next, consider the case of 1 percent TFP growth, that is, the rate at which China's TFP has grown for the last fifteen years. Again, we assume that the government increases the fixed-capital investment rate by half a percentage point each year. In this case, the GDP growth rate in 2023 will be 4.76 percent, still slightly lower than the government's target of 5 percent. For the entire period of 2023–2035, the average GDP growth rate is projected to be 4.62 percent in this case.

In the third scenario, we assume that the TFP grows at 2 percent a year, and the investment rate does not increase. In this case, the GDP growth rate will be 5.76 percent in 2023, exceeding the government's target of 5 percent. The growth rate will decline only slightly in the next twelve years and still remain above 5 percent in 2035. The average GDP growth rate between 2023 and 2035 is projected to be 5.47 percent in this case.

So far, we have assumed that the fixed-capital investment rate either increases or stays constant. One plausible scenario is that the investment rate declines due to a decline in the saving rate associated with population aging, as in the experience of Japan since 1970. Assuming that TFP grows at 2 percent a year, but the investment rate declines by half a percentage point each year, the GDP growth rate will decline faster and fall to 4.34 percent by 2035. Still, the average GDP growth rate between 2023 and 2035 is projected to be 4.97 percent, close to the 5 percent target the Chinese government set for 2023.

Finally, we consider the most optimistic scenario in which TFP grows at 3 percent a year but still assume that the investment rate declines by half a percentage point each year. Then, the GDP growth rate will be 6.76 percent in 2023 and then decline slowly to 5.82 percent by 2035. For the entire period between 2023 and 2035, the average growth rate is projected to be 6.25 percent.

In summary, China's future GDP growth depends crucially on its TFP growth. Without TFP growth, China's GDP growth rate would average less than 3 percent a year over 2023–2035, even if the government increases the fixed-capital investment rate by half a percentage point each year. If TFP grows at 2 percent, however, China's GDP growth rate would still average close to 5 percent a year between 2023 and 2035, even with a declining investment rate. If TFP grows even faster, at 3 percent a year, China's GDP would grow at an average rate of over 6 percent per year between 2023 and 2035.

Conclusion

The key question concerning China's future growth should be how the nation can raise its TFP growth rate from 1 percent to 2 percent or even 3 percent. Before 2007, China's TFP growth rate averaged more than 4 percent a year because of economic reform and decentralization that resulted in constant policy and institutional changes that were often started from below. Since 2007, the Chinese government has moved away from the bottom-up approach, emphasizing more on policy design at the top and mobilizing national resources (*ju guo ti zhi*). This approach may have achieved some short-term goals, such as growth recovery in 2010 after the global financial crisis and the rapid expansion of infrastructure projects, but at great cost to economic efficiency. Shifting away from bottom-up policy reforms yielded poor TFP growth performance, averaging 1 percent a year, much lower than the 4 percent achieved prior to 2007. For China to meet its productivity challenge, it needs to go back to allow for bottom-up policy change that was so effective in generating remarkable TFP growth in the 1980s and 1990s.

References

Acemoglu, Deron, Philippe Aghion, and Fabrizio Zilibotti. 2006. "Distance to Frontier, Selection, and Economic Growth." *Journal of the European Economic Association*, 4 (1): 37–74.

Bai, Chong-En, Yingjuan Du, Zhigang Tao, and Sarah Y. Tong. 2004. "Local Protrectionism and Regional Specialization: Evidence from China's Industries." *Journal of International Economics*, 63 (2): 397–417.

Bai, Chong-En, Chang-Tai Hsieh, and Zheng Michael Song. 2016. "The Long Shadow of China's Fiscal Expansion." *Brookings Papers on Economic Activity*, 60: 309–327.

Bai, Jie, Panle Jia Barwick, Shengmao Cao, and Shanjun Li. 2020. "Quid Pro Quo, Knowledge Spillover, and Industrial Quality Upgrading: Evidence from the Chinese Auto Industry." *NBER Working Paper* No. 27644.

Bloom, Nicholas, Charles I. Jones, John Van Reenen, and Michael Webb. 2020. "Are Ideas Getting Harder to Find?" *American Economic Review*, 110 (4): 1104–1144.

Brandt, John Litwock, Elitza Mikva, Luhang Wang, and Luan Zhao. 2022. "Recent Productivity Trends in China: Evidence from Macro- and Firm-level Data." *China: An International Journal*, 20 (1): 93–113.

Brandt, Loren, Trevor Tombe, and Xiaodong Zhu. 2013. "Factor Market Distortions across Time, Space and Sectors in China." *Review of Economic Dynamics*, 16: 39–58.

Brandt, Loren, and Xiaodong Zhu. 2010. "Accounting for China's Growth," Working Papers tecipa-394, University of Toronto, Department of Economics.

Chen, Zhao, Zhikuo Liu, Juan Carlos Suarez Serrato, and Daniel Yi Xu. 2021. "Notching R&D Investment with Corporate Income Tax Cuts in China," *American Economic Review*, 111 (7): 2065–2100.

Chen, Heng, Bingjing Li, and Xiaodong Zhu. 2024. "Bottom-up Institutional Change and Growth in China." HKU Jockey Club Enterprise Sustainability Global Research Institute Paper No. 2025/013.

Cong, Lin Wiiliam, Haoyu Gao, Jacopo Ponticelli, and Xiaoguang Yang. 2019. "Credit Allocation under Economic Stimulus: Evidence from China." *Review of Financial Studies*, 32 (9): 3412–3460.

Fan, Jingting. 2019. "Internal Geography, Labor Mobility, and the Distributional Impact of Trade." *American Economic Journal: Macroeconomics*, 11 (3): 252–288.

Hao, Tongtong, Ruiqi Sun, Trevor Tombe, and Xiaodong Zhu. 2020. "The Effect of Migration Policy on Growth, Structural Change, and Regional Inequality in China." *Journal of Monetary Economics*, 113: 112–134.

Ho, Chun-Yu, Dan Li, Suhua Tian, and Xiaodong Zhu. 2018. "Policy Distortion in Credit Market: Evidence from an Economic Stimulus." Unpublished manuscript.

Holz, Carsten. 2009. "No Razor's Edge: Reexamining Alwyn Young's Evidence for Increasing Inter-Provincial Trade Barriers in China." *Review of Economics and Statistics*, 91 (3): 599–616.

Howell, Sabrina. 2018. "Joint Ventures and Technology Adoption: A Chinese Industrial Policy that Backfired." *Research Policy*, 47: 1448–1462.

Hsieh, Chang-Tai, and Pete Klenow. 2022. "Romer or Ricardo." *Unpublished Working Paper.*

Hsieh, Chang-Tai, and Zheng Michael Song. 2015. "Grasp the Large, Let Go of the Small: The Transformation of the State Sector in China." Brookings Papers on Economic Activity, Spring, 295–346.

Konig, Michael, Kjetil Storesletten, Zheng Song, and Fabrizio Zilibotti. 2022. "From Imitation to Innovation: Where Is All That Chinese R&D Going?" *Econometrica*, 90 (4): 1615–1654.

Lin, Justin Yifu. 1992. "Rural Reforms and Agricultural Growth in China." *The American Economic Review*, 82 (1): 34–51.

Liu, Qiren, Nan Jia, and Robert Seamans. 2023. "Robots at Work in China." Unpublished working paper.

McMillan, John, John Whalley, and Lijing Zhu. 1989. "The Impact of China's Economic Reforms on Agricultural Productivity Growth." *Journal of Political Economy*, 97 (4): 781–807.

Poncet, Sandra. 2005. "A Fragmented China: Measure and Determination of Chinese Domestic Market Disintegration." *Review of International Economics*, 13 (3): 409–430.

Tian, Yuan. 2024. "International Trade Liberalization and Domestic Institutional Reform: Effects of WTO Accession on Chinese Internal Migration Policy." *Review of Economics and Statistics*, 106 (3): 794–813.

Tombe, Trevor, and Xiaodong Zhu. 2019. "Trade, Migration, and Productivity: A Quantitative Analysis of China." *American Economic Review*, 109 (5): 1843–1872.

Wei, Shang-Jin, Jianhuan Xu, Ge Yin, and Xiaobo Zhang. 2023. "Mild Government Failure," Unpublished working paper.

Young, Alwyn. 2000. "Razor's Edge: Distortions and Incremental Reform in the People's Republic of China." *Quarterly Journal of Economics*, 115 (4): 1094–1135.

Zhu, Xiaodong. 2012. "Understanding China's Growth: Past, Present, and Future." *Journal of Economic Perspectives*, 26 (4): 103–124.

Zhu, Xiaodong. 2021. "The Varying Shadow of China's Banking System." *Journal of Comparative Economics*, 49 (1): 135–146.

3 Innovation in China

Drivers, Challenges, and Future Directions

KEVIN ZHENG ZHOU AND MEITONG DONG

Introduction

In March 1978, the National Science Conference was held in Beijing, during which Deng Xiaoping proposed that "science and technology (S&T) are a productive force," starting the development and reform of S&T innovation in China. At that time, China's innovation capacity was very weak, with obvious limitations in both technology and talent, as the planned economy severely demotivated individuals and enterprises from innovating. Meanwhile, Western countries had invested heavily in S&T after the Second World War, leading to the rise of new technological revolutions and fierce competition in innovation. As a result, a large gap existed between China's S&T innovation system and those of developed countries.

To bridge the gap, since 1978, the Chinese government has continuously raised the status of S&T innovation in economic development and has formulated a series of policies related to R&D funding, patent management, and talent training and attraction. Accordingly, China's S&T innovation system has gradually developed and evolved, forming a trajectory with Chinese institutional characteristics. In recent years, China as the second-largest economy in the world has shown strong aspirations to enhance its innovation capacity and move up in the global value chain. In 2021, the number of granted patents (4,601,457) was 1,522 times of that in 1986 (3,024), with an annual growth rate of 23.3 percent; the total number of R&D personnel in China in 2021 was eight times higher than that in 1991, with an average annual growth rate of 7.3 percent (National Bureau of Statistics, 2022). The intensity of R&D funding rose to 2.55 percent in 2022, surpassing the average of EU countries and reaching the level of moderately developed nations (National Innovation Survey, 2023). Now China is the world's No. 1 in terms of both total patent applications and international patent applications (WIPO, 2023).

Despite its amazing achievement, China also faces great challenges under the current complex global environment, including uncertainties stemming from the COVID-19 pandemic, risks arising from geopolitics and regional wars, and the trend toward de-globalization and decoupling. Accordingly, in this chapter, we aim to (1) summarize the trajectory and key drivers of China's innovation in the past, (2) identify the opportunities and challenges for China's innovation in the present, and (3) suggest directions for China's innovation development in the future.

In the second section "Trajectory and Drivers of Innovation in China," we examine the patent data from the State Intellectual Property Office (SIPO) of China, both at the aggregate level and in terms of distribution based on patentee sector, region, and industry. We find that government policy is a key driver of China's innovation in the past thirty-five years. China has achieved impressive growth in the number of patents, while its quality still needs improvement, as reflected in the predominance of utility model patents. In terms of patentee sector, enterprises have overtaken individuals, universities, and research institutions in domestic innovation, with innovation by private enterprises far outpacing that by state-owned enterprises (SOEs). Moreover, inward foreign direct investment (FDI) has played a crucial role in stimulating regional innovation. In addition, there is also an increasing trend in both the number of patents received from foreign patentees and the number of international patents filed by Chinese applicants.

In the third section "Challenges and Opportunities," we discuss how three highly relevant events have affected China's innovation in recent years: the Belt and Road Initiative, the Sino-U.S. trade war, and the COVID-19 pandemic. We believe that these events present both opportunities and threats for China's innovation. The Belt and Road Initiative has bolstered China's R&D cooperation with countries along the route, but it also constrains Chinese enterprises to learn from developed countries about the world's most advanced technologies. Although the combined impact of the Sino-U.S. trade war and the pandemic has imposed a large negative impact on innovation by Chinese enterprises in the short term, they are also compelling enterprises to innovate their business models and embark on the path of independent innovation.

In the section titled "Future Directions," we point out the promising fields in order to enhance China's independent innovation and maintain its global position in innovation. One is the electric vehicle battery industry, in which China is rapidly emerging as a global leader. In the future, mastering core technologies in the industry chain will help China realize the transformation from a "big auto country" to a "strong auto country." The second is the semiconductor industry. We emphasize that the Chinese government needs to increase its support for basic research and collaborative innovation between enterprises and research institutions to obtain sustainable competitive advantages. Moreover, with the rapid development of digital technologies, China's emerging and rising digital startups, represented by TikTok and Shein, should shift more attention and resources from applied innovation to basic and fundamental innovation (e.g., ChatGPT). In addition, we highlight that, in the future, government policy support alone is not sufficient for China to develop the world's most advanced knowledge and technology. Instead, open and collaborative innovation is essential for both China and other countries to achieve innovative development and mutual benefits. The final section concludes with a brief summary and a discussion of future research.

Trajectory and Drivers of Innovation in China

To provide a fine-grained account of the trajectories and drivers of innovation in China, we analyzed patent data provided by the SIPO of China. A patent is a quantified indicator of innovation and identifies the patentee, date, location, and patent category. The data were from 1986, when the Chinese patent system began to process patent applications and grants, to 2021, the latest year we had access to data.

Innovation Development in the Past Thirty-Five Years

Figure 3.1 plots the number of newly SIPO-granted patents from 1986 to 2021. Between 1986 and 2005, the number of patents granted grew moderately but steadily, from 3,024 pieces to 214,003 pieces. In addition to the continuous improvement of the patent system, the growth of patents during this period was also attributed to the increasing emphasis placed on S&T by the Chinese government. For example, in the Decision on the Reforms of the S&T System in March 1985, the Chinese government set the main task to enhance the economic orientation of the S&T system and formulated a series of laws, regulations,

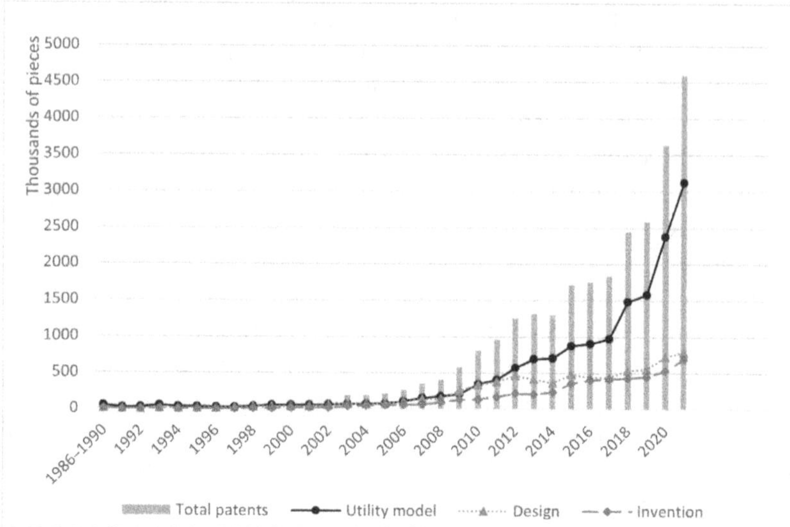

Figure 3.1 SIPO granted patents by category, 1986–2021

and policy measures on S&T funding, technology markets, and personnel management. In the Decision on Accelerating the Progress of S&T in 1995, the government put forward "revitalizing the nation through the science, technology and education" (kejiaoxingguo) and advocated for the reliance of economic development on S&T advancements. Moreover, as China progressed with its reform and opening up, the Chinese government's policy on attracting FDI greatly facilitated the increase in granted patents (Huang, 2010).

After 2006, the total number of patents granted increased dramatically, with an annual growth rate exceeding 20 percent. The year 2006 was a notable and proud year for China's innovation and intellectual property (IP) landscape. At the beginning of that year, the National Science and Technology Conference took place in Beijing, proposing the Medium- and Long-Term Plan for the Development of S&T (2006–2020), with the aim of strengthening independent innovation and building an innovative country, which serves as a milestone in the history of China's S&T development. Meanwhile, in 2006, the status and role of IP received historical recognition across various aspects of national work (China National Intellectual Property Administration, 2006). For example, in the Outline of the Eleventh Five-Year Plan for National Economic and

Social Development, the government put forward the formation of a number of internationally competitive enterprises with independent IPs and well-known brands as one of the important goals for that period. In December, the Eleventh Five-Year Plan of IP Development was completed and submitted to the State Council for approval, marking it the first IP development plan to be included in national special plans. These initiatives collectively contributed to the extensive growth of China's patents from 2006.

China's SIPO specifies three types of patents: invention, utility model, and design. Invention patent, requiring a high level of technological advancement, is the most difficult to develop and is the most rigorously examined; by contrast, utility model and design patents mainly involve incremental improvements, which require less resource investment and knowledge base and are easier to achieve.[1] Figure 3.1 shows that utility model patents accounted for the highest percentage of patents granted and invention patents had the lowest percentage. After 2012, the growth rate of design patents slightly slowed down, while invention patents witnessed a higher growth rate. It reflected that the quality of innovation had improved since the 18th Party Congress in 2012, when the government placed innovation at the forefront of national development and reinforced the innovation system.

Domestic versus Foreign Patentees

Patents granted to Chinese entities from 1986 to 2021 accounted for about 94 percent of the total patents, with Japan (2.2 percent), the USA (1.4 percent), Germany (0.6 percent), and Korea (0.6 percent) following behind (Figures 3.2 and 3.3). The share of SIPO-granted patents to foreign patentees experienced significant growth from 2001 to 2005, which was related to China's WTO accession in 2001. And since 2006, the share of foreign patents has decreased year by year, which was a result of the growing domestic patents stimulated by a series of Chinese government policies aimed at promoting domestic innovation.

[1] Invention patents are new or unique methods, processes, products, or services, whereas utility patents are improvements in terms of forms, constructions, or combinations, and design patents are simply changes in shape or color.

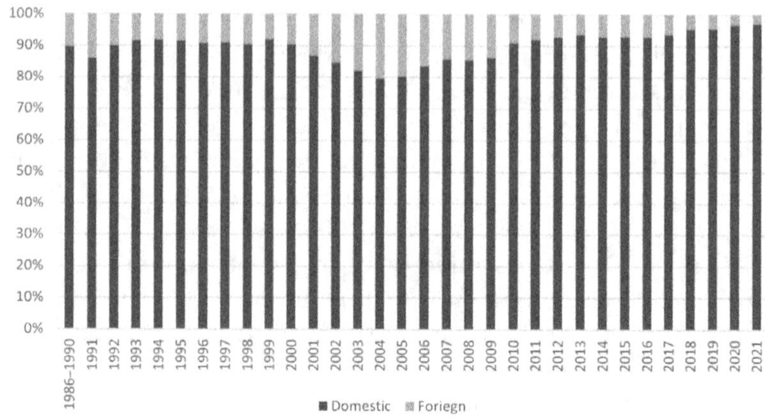

Figure 3.2 SIPO granted patents by domestic or foreign patentee, 1986–2021

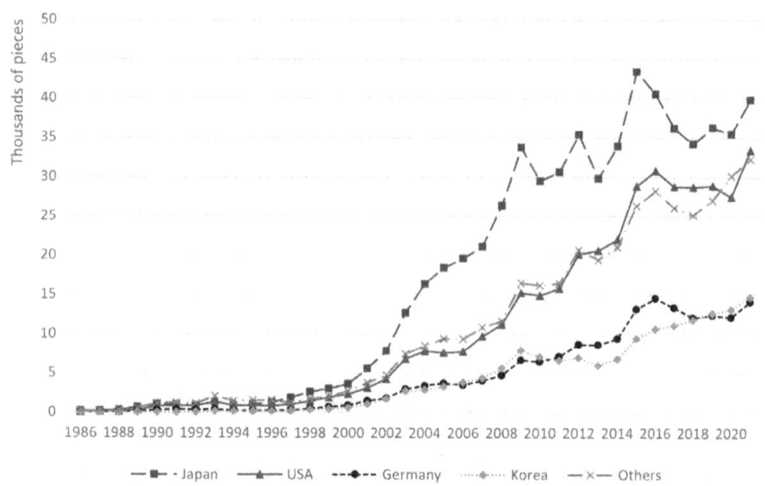

Figure 3.3 SIPO granted foreign patents by patentee country, 1986–2021

Among patents granted to foreign entities, Japan held the highest share due to its status as a "patent nation" and the importance it attached to patent applications and IP protection. Also, applying patents in China facilitated Japanese-invested firms to quickly capture the technology frontier market. Moreover, Japan's granted patents in

China were greatly affected by Sino-Japanese relations (Figure 3.3). For example, there were three significant declines in 2010, 2013, and after 2016, corresponding to the territorial dispute over the Diaoyu Islands, the appointment of Shinzo Abe as Prime Minister of Japan, and the election of Trump as President of the United States, respectively. Being the second-largest foreign source country, the USA's granted patents in China maintained a yearly upward trend until 2016, while a decline occurred since Trump was elected as president in 2017, until growth resumed in 2021. In contrast, Korea's patents granted in China maintained a growing trend in recent years, thanks to the friendly relations between China and Korea during the Moon Jae-in period (2017–2022).

Distribution of Domestic Patentee Sectors

Figure 3.4 presents the changes in the distribution of domestic patentee sectors. Prior to 2006, there was little difference in the number of granted patents across the five patentee sectors (i.e., enterprise, individual, university, scientific institute, and public institute).[2] After 2006, the growth in patent grants to enterprises and individuals significantly exceeded that of the other three sectors. Meanwhile, enterprises steadily rose to the dominant position after 2009, and in 2021, they accounted for approximately 73 percent of the total domestic granted patents in China. This trend was due to the Medium- and Long-Term Plan for the Development of S&T (2006–2020), in which the government devised detailed and actionable plans to reward domestic firms for independent innovation. However, since the assessment of innovation quality was challenging to quantify, the government tended to assess it based on the quantity of innovation. In this way, scholars find that between 2006 and 2012, some enterprises like SOEs increased the number of innovations at the expense of innovation novelty (Jia et al., 2019). They also point out that maintaining high-quality corporate and public governance can help reduce this problem.

[2] University refers to universities, colleges, or educational institutions; scientific research institution refers to non-profit research institutes, organizations, and laboratories; public institution refers to government agencies, bureaus, ministries, armies, administrations, and councils; enterprise refers to for-profit companies, firms, or factories; individual refers to individual inventor(s).

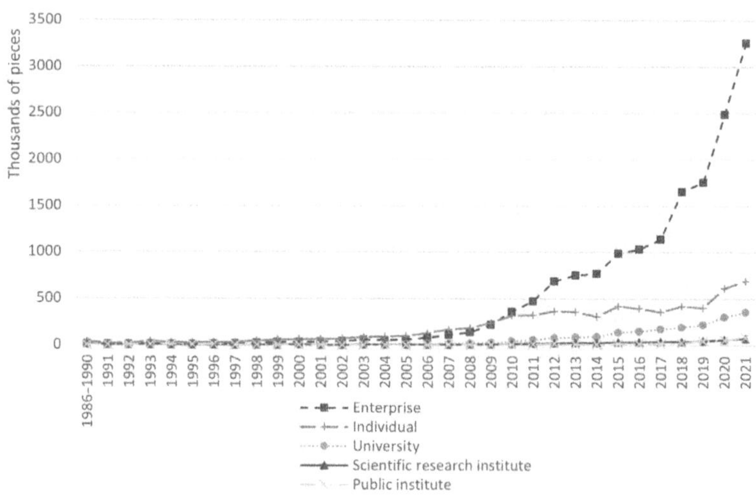

Figure 3.4 SIPO granted domestic patents by patentee sector, 1986–2021

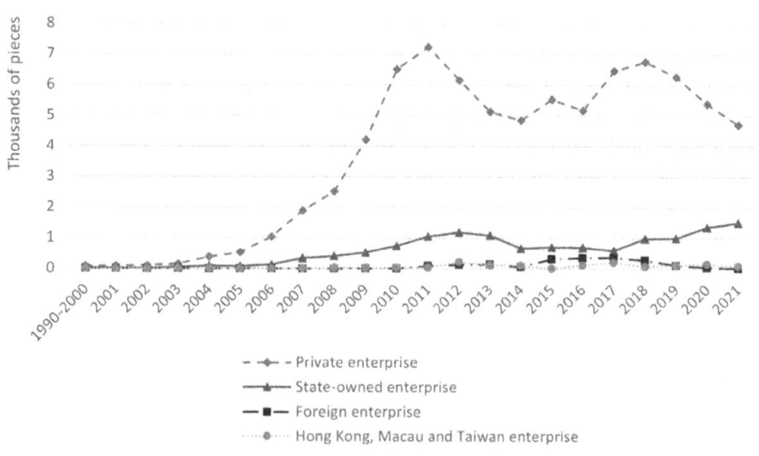

Figure 3.5 Listed firm's granted patents by ownership type, 1990–2021

To examine the distribution of patents across ownership types, we analyzed the patents granted to firms listed on the Shanghai and Shenzhen Stock Exchanges (Figure 3.5). On average, the granted patents of listed firms accounted for 1 percent of the total granted patents of all enterprises. From the Chinese Securities Market and Accounting Research (CSMAR) database, we obtained information about the ultimate controllers of listed firms and determined their ownership types accordingly. Figure 3.5 shows the increasing dominance of private enterprises, particularly between 2006 and 2011, when the annual growth rate of their granted patents was 48 percent and the number of grants accounted for about 87 percent of the patents granted to all listed firms. This suggested a fundamental shift in the contribution to Chinese innovation to the private sector as Chinese markets liberalized and government policies supported innovation of domestic firms. The years 2012–2014 witnessed a decline in granted patents by private firms, after Xi Jinping became the General Secretary of the Communist Party of China in 2012. Prior research shows that the rotation of government leaders reduces Chinese firms' incentives to innovate until the uncertainty resulting from political turnover is resolved, and such effect is more salient for private firms than SOEs (Zhang et al., 2022). After a three-year adaptation period, the number of patents granted by private enterprises gradually resumed growth starting in 2015.

From 2018 to 2021, there was a gradual decrease in the number of patents granted to both listed private and foreign firms due to the severe impact of the Sino-U.S. trade war and "state sector advances and private sector retreats" (国进民退). In contrast, the number of granted patents of listed SOEs progressively rose, reflecting the important role of the resource advantages of state ownership for firm innovation activities in the context of environmental shocks and uncertainties.

Distribution of Patents by Industry Sector

Based on International Patent Classification (IPC), we further classified the patents by industry sectors (Figure 3.6).[3] The performing

[3] Data of Figure 3.6 contained only invention and utility patents granted, as design patents do not have corresponding IPC. Performing operations and transporting include microstructural technology, railways, casting, and so on. Human necessities include agriculture, medical or veterinary science, wearing apparel, furniture, sports, and so on. Physics includes optics, computing, calculating or counting, information storage, and so on. Electricity includes basic electric elements and electric communication techniques. Mechanical engineering includes machines or engines, lighting, heating, weapons, blasting,

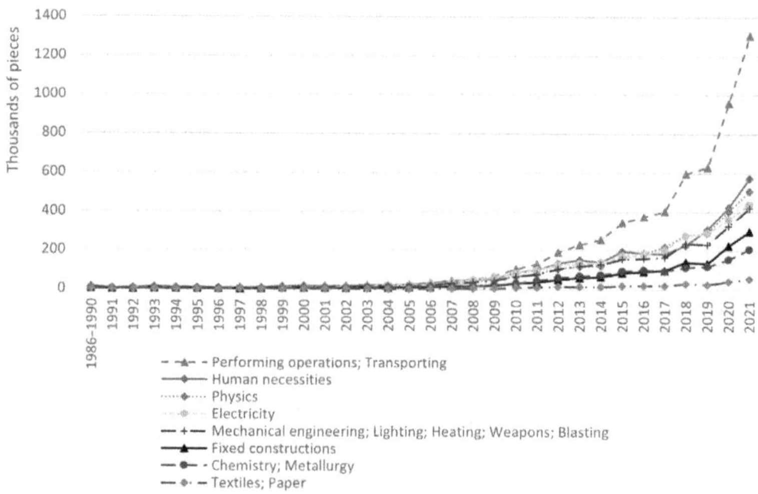

Figure 3.6 SIPO granted patents by IPC, 1986–2021

operations and transporting sector had the highest share, contributing close to 30 percent of the total granted patents. Its rapid growth appeared after 2009, which was largely due to the fast development of China's high-speed railway during this period. The Chinese government placed a strong emphasis on the development of independent technology in the field of land transportation, with a particular focus on innovation in the high-speed train sector (Genin et al., 2021). In contrast, the textiles and paper sector accounted for the lowest proportion of patents granted (1.6 percent), mainly because entities in this sector focused on manufacturing, invested less in R&D, and displayed a lower inclination toward innovation. In addition, the patent number in the human necessities sector had grown more than those in the physics and electricity sectors in the last two years and showed a continuous upward trend. This may be due to the fact that the public demand for new consumption and service models in the post-pandemic era has spawned more innovation.

and so on. Fixed constructions include building, hydraulic engineering, mining, and so on. Chemistry and metallurgy include organic chemistry, biochemistry, metallurgy, and so on. Textiles and paper include natural or man-made threads or fibers, papermaking, weaving, and so on.

Distribution of Patents by Regions

Figure 3.7 shows how innovation (i.e., granted patents) evolved over time across geographic regions.[4] In 1990, granted patents were concentrated in the coastal provinces, thanks to their higher level of economic development, greater industrial agglomeration, and more

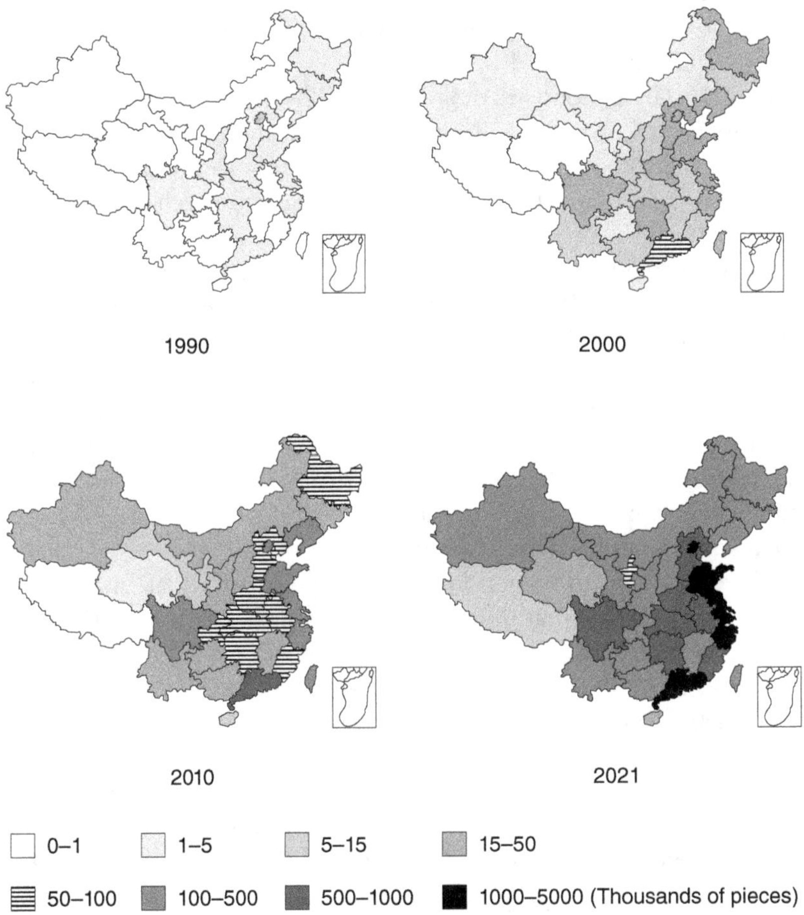

Figure 3.7 Cumulative number of granted patents by province, various years

[4] The end-of-year cumulative number of granted patents in Hong Kong in 2000, 2010, and 2021 was 7350, 25,020, and 56,987, respectively. The end-of-year cumulative number of granted patents in Macau in 2000, 2010, and 2021 was 60, 205, and 1,571, respectively.

favorable institutional environment than other regions. As the political center, Beijing led the way with 6,700 cumulative granted patents, followed by Liaoning, Jiangsu, Shandong, and Hunan. With the progression of reform and opening up, however, Guangdong, due to its proximity to Hong Kong, was exposed to more advanced technology and knowledge from all over the world, and thus its number of granted patents gradually caught up with other regions. By 2000, Guangdong's cumulative granted patent number had surpassed that of Beijing and become No. 1 in China.

By 2010, Guangdong still ranked first, followed by Zhejiang, Jiangsu, Shandong, and Shanghai. The central and western regions were also gradually catching up, reflecting China's Western Development Policy that motivated innovation capacity (firms and research institutions) to spread from the coastal regions to the central and western regions. Sichuan emerged as an innovation leader in the interior regions, ranking among the top 10, thanks to the local government's emphasis on IP protection and the higher number of local research institutions, universities, and S&T parks. From 2010 to 2021, most regions experienced steady growth in the number of granted patents, with little change in the regional distribution. The exception was Liaoning, which was concentrated in heavy industries and manufacturing; its number of granted patents grew at a slower rate, falling out of the top 10 at some point between 2010 and 2021.

The geographic distribution and changing pattern of innovation aligned closely with that of inward FDI in China. A study on China's inward FDI landscape shows that FDI was concentrated in the coastal provinces in 1997, with Guangdong leading the stock of FDI inflows (Li, 2019). Over time, the central and western regions started catching up, with Chongqing emerging as one of the major investment destinations. In contrast, FDI in the northeast provinces stagnated, with Liaoning gradually falling out of the top five after 2008. In Figure 3.8, we used data on cumulative provincial FDI inflows and granted patents up to 2021 to plot the relationship between the two. It demonstrates a positive association between regional inward FDI and innovation. As research suggests, cross-border activities such as FDI provide domestic firms opportunities to learn advanced technological knowledge from foreign counterparts, leading to spillover effects and promoting domestic innovation (Spencer, 2008). Domestic firms can observe and imitate foreign firms' advanced technologies or acquire

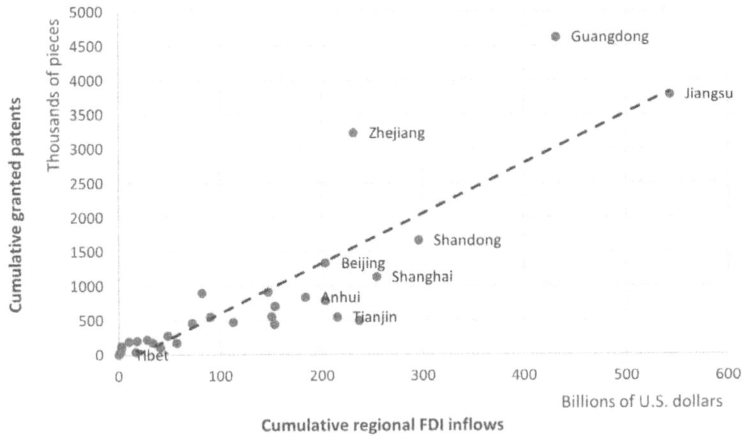

Figure 3.8 The relationship between regional inward FDI and granted patents (cumulative value by 2021)

foreign firms' knowledge by hiring their talented employees (Cheung & Ping, 2004). Therefore, the introduction of FDI was an important driver of regional innovation in China.

International Patents Granted

Figure 3.9 illustrates the change in the number of international patents granted to Chinese applicants over the past thirty-five years. In 2009, the annual number of international patents granted exceeded 1,000 pieces, and it continued to experience significant growth at an average annual rate of 32 percent over the subsequent twelve years. In 2009, the Chinese central government established a dedicated fund to support patent applications abroad and issued the Interim Measures for the Administration of Special Funds to Finance Patent Applications Abroad (SIPO, 2009). The special fund aimed to finance the relevant search and service fees paid by the domestic applicants to overseas patent offices during both the patent application and grant stages. The government support had greatly increased China's activities on international patents.

Figure 3.9 also shows the distribution of international patents granted. In addition to the SIPO of China, the world's five largest patent offices, known as the IP5, are the United States Patent and

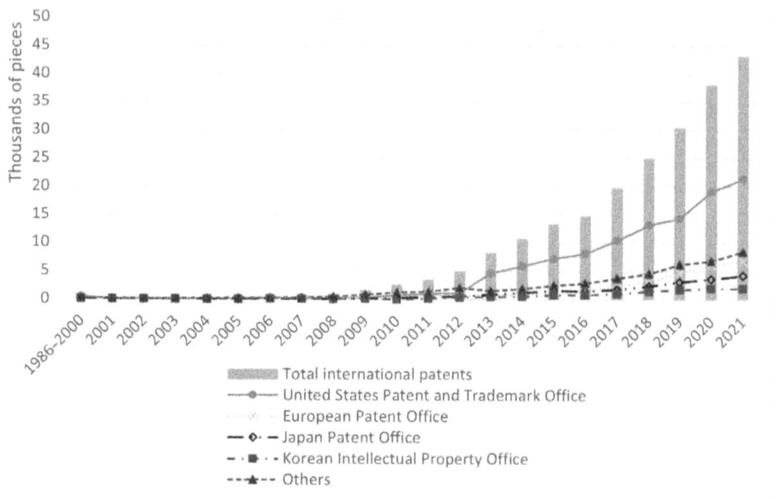

Figure 3.9 International granted patents originated from China, 1986–2021

Trademark Office (USPTO), European Patent Office (EPO), Japan Patent Office (JPO), and Korean Intellectual Property Office (KIPO). The IP5 together handle around 85 percent of the world's patent applications. For China's international patents, the highest percentage was granted by the USPTO (nearly 50 percent), followed by the EPO (13.7 percent), JPO (10.1 percent), and KIPO (5.5 percent).

A rapid increase in the number of patents granted in the USPTO occurred in 2013, coinciding with the Chinese government's increased financial support for overseas patenting in the Administrative Measures for Special Funds to Support Patent Applications to Foreign Countries introduced in 2012. Since then, the central and local governments have continued to raise subsidies, contributing to the steady growth of international patents granted by the USPTO. For example, in 2019, the Shanghai government raised the maximum annual subsidy amount for international patent applications per applicant from RMB 1 million (US$146,700) to RMB 10 million (US$1.47 million). Another important reason for the growth in international patents was the Chinese government's establishment of international patenting targets for government officials, SOEs, and universities. For instance, in March 2020, the government mandated centrally owned enterprises to double the number of U.S. and other foreign patents they hold by 2025 (SIPO, 2020). Hence, as scholars point out, subsidies and government mandates are the important part of China's massive state innovation incentives and have become effective tools for achieving innovation goals (Prud'homme & Zhang, 2019).

However, in the 2021 USPTO report on Chinese Patents and Trademarks, it notes the potential drawbacks of Chinese government subsidies for overseas patenting (USPTO, 2021). Subsidies may encourage Chinese applicants to file patent applications primarily to receive subsidies, rather than to protect an innovation. Accordingly, the commercialization of patents is often low for Chinese patentees. Government subsidies also appear to lead to strategic patenting behaviors, such as splitting a patent application into multiple applications to fulfill specific innovation criteria.

Summary

The innovation development in China since the reform and opening up exhibits the following features. First, government policy is a key driver of innovation in China. The Medium- and Long-Term Plan for the Development of S&T (2006–2020) proposed in 2006 stands as a pivotal innovation policy, and China's innovation has achieved amazing growth since then. Second, China's innovation is dominated by utility model patents, reflecting the technology gap between China and developed countries (where invention patents hold greater prominence). Third, domestic entities (vs. foreign entities) occupy a dominant percentage of patents granted by SIPO (94 percent), and Japan as the "patent nation" ranks No. 1 in terms of foreign patentees.

Fourth, for domestic patentees, enterprises dominate domestic innovation over individuals, university, and research institutions in the last decade. Among enterprises, innovation by private firms far exceeds that of SOEs and foreign enterprises. Regarding the industry distribution, the performing operations and transporting sector ranks No. 1. In terms of regional distribution, innovation has systematically spread from the coastal regions to the central and western provinces. Moreover, the geographic distribution and changing pattern of innovation largely follow that of inward FDI, reflecting that inward FDI is a crucial driver of regional innovation. Fifth, the international patents of Chinese applicants also show an increasing trend, with the USPTO granting the highest percentage and fastest growth, which reflects the effectiveness of China's policies to support overseas patenting activities.

Challenges and Opportunities

Belt and Road Initiative

In 2013, Chinese President Xi Jinping launched the Silk Road Economic Belt and the twenty-first-century Maritime Silk Road (B&R), a massive trade and infrastructure project designed to connect China with dozens of economies in Asia, Europe, Africa, and Oceania. The Silk Road Economic Belt focuses on linking China to Europe through Central and Western Asia, while the twenty-first century Maritime Silk Road connects China with Southeast Asian countries, Africa, and Europe. The B&R seeks to foster "Innovation-driven" and "High-quality Development," providing a platform for trade cooperation among enterprises from different countries and international organizations. By January 6, 2023, China had signed more than 200 documents with 151 countries and 32 international organizations to jointly build the B&R.

Collaborative innovation is always a significant objective of the B&R, particularly since the implementation of the "Belt and Road S&T Innovation Action Plan" in 2017. In the plan, the Chinese government emphasizes four actions in collaboration with the B&R countries: S&T humanities exchanges, joint laboratories, S&T park cooperation, and technology transfer. By the end of 2021, China had established S&T cooperation with 84 B&R countries, supported 1,118 joint research projects, and initiated the construction of 53 joint laboratories in fields such as agriculture, new energy, and health. For example, in 2017, the Sino-Portuguese International Joint Laboratory of Marine Biosciences was established in Shanghai, where Shanghai Ocean University and the University of Algarve jointly carry out research on marine ecosystems and polar seas. By 2021, there had been three Sino-Portuguese joint laboratories approved for establishment, covering key areas such as space marine, materials, and cultural heritage. In 2019, an international joint water-saving irrigation laboratory was established by the School of Resources and Environment of Ningxia University and Ain Shams University in Egypt. The laboratory provides 320 acres of test plots, which facilitate experiments and promote the development of smart irrigation technology. Similarly, Israel has formed agricultural cooperation with five Chinese western provinces, including Xinjiang and Gansu, and is committed to promoting advanced agricultural technologies.

The B&R initiatives have greatly facilitated innovation of Chinese firms in the B&R countries. In 2021, the number of patents filed and granted by Chinese enterprises in B&R countries was 8,596 and 4,711, representing a year-on-year increase of 29.4 percent and 15.3 percent, respectively (SIPO, 2022). Moreover, research finds that the positive impact of the B&R on firm technical innovation is more salient for non-SOEs (vs. SOEs) and nonhigh-tech firms (vs. high-tech firms), as the financial support provided by the B&R is more conducive to alleviating their financing constraints (Wu & Si, 2022).

Figure 3.10 shows the distribution of technology fields. In 2021, Chinese enterprises received the most granted patents in the field of digital communication in the B&R countries, reaching 884 pieces; computer technology (535) and electronics (298) ranked second and third, respectively. It reflects that the digital transformation and the continued spread of that global pandemic have spawned collaborative technological innovation between China and B&R countries in the sectors of digital economy and home entertainment.

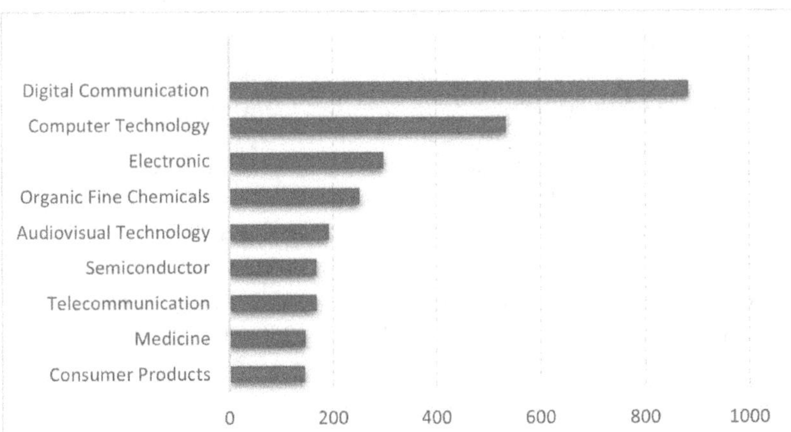

Figure 3.10 Technology field distribution of granted patents by Chinese enterprises in B&R countries in 2021 (top ten)

While the B&R brings benefits to China's innovation, particularly by accelerating innovation in the B&R regions, it may also hinder Chinese enterprises' access to advanced knowledge in leading technology fields. First, the B&R is a geostrategic initiative with political, economic, and cultural objectives. Accordingly, many B&R countries are developing countries with technological knowledge and R&D experience inferior to that of China. Research emphasizes that, when the technology gap between foreign and domestic firms is small, the potential for knowledge spillovers is limited because domestic firms learn very little from foreign firms (Zhang et al., 2010). Therefore, in the B&R context, Chinese enterprises may struggle to acquire superior knowledge for radical innovation that involves fundamental changes in technologies. Second, the B&R increases geopolitical tensions and raises mistrust in China's cooperation with some developed countries, which in turn hinders innovation. For example, Japan, which has long been a major investor in infrastructure projects in Asia for decades, sees the B&R as a measure aimed at increasing China's political influence in Eurasia. Moreover, Japan may also feel threatened by the possibility that the B&R may potentially help China strengthen its military presence along the routes. As a result, Japan's reaction to the B&R is mostly negative (Rahman, 2022). Such tense interstate relations can exacerbate mistrust and opportunity costs in international R&D cooperation and negatively affect Chinese firms' learning of advanced knowledge for major innovation.

Sino-U.S. Trade War and Technology Decoupling

The Sino-U.S. trade war began on March 22, 2018, after U.S. President Trump imposed tariffs on Chinese imports. Behind the trade war, the technology competition had already led to conflicts in the Sino-U.S. relationship. For a long time, China's technological progress had benefited from integration with developed countries, especially the United States. However, the technological dependence on the United States peaked in 2009 at the end of the financial crisis, and since then growing distrust between the two countries has threatened the Sino-U.S. relationship. In the context of the trade war, the two ecosystems are becoming increasingly separated (i.e., "decoupling"). Bremmer (2019) points out that "China has made its decision: Beijing is building a separate system of Chinese technology – its own standards, infrastructure, and supply chains – to compete with the West."

Decoupling presents both challenges and opportunities for China's innovation. In the short term, Chinese enterprises experience increased trade costs, declining profits, and financing difficulties due to uncertain trade policies. These resource constraints limit their capacity for R&D investment, resulting in a negative impact on domestic innovation. However, in the long run, trade frictions and decoupling push Chinese enterprises to enhance their incentives for independent innovation. Researchers suggest that the decline in Chinese firms' profitability and productivity reflects the costs for "reinventing the wheel" in a decoupled world; and technology decoupling forces domestic firms to innovate rather than just follow and provides a sheltered space for them to do so (Han et al., 2024).

In addition, despite China's status as the world leader in patent applications, there remains a wide innovation gap between China and developed countries. For example, innovation in the United States mainly refers to invention patents, but utility model patents occupy the largest portion in China. As a result, while China has a higher number of patents, its innovation quality is lower. Also, China's innovation efforts are predominantly centered around the improvement of products or engineering, lacking a strong emphasis on applied basic research, which serves as a crucial foundation for independent innovation. As a result, Chinese policymakers and scholars suggest that nurturing and attracting talent is the key to China's future endeavors in independent innovation.

To nurture talent, China has been increasing its spending on higher education, maintaining an average growth rate of about 10 percent since 2015. In attracting elite talent from abroad, policy support from the Chinese government has played an important role. China's Young Thousand Talents (YTT) program, for example, was established in 2010 to target outstanding young STEM scholars with generous financial support (e.g., income subsidy, start-up grants, housing subsidy). By 2017, the YTT program had made more than 3,000 offers. Research shows that, although the YTT program is less successful in recruiting top-caliber scientists, it does attract numerous high-caliber researchers and these researchers maintain high levels of productivity (Shi et al., 2023). They perform well in chemistry and life science, fueling China's independent innovation. However, in the fields of mathematics and physics, these researchers have not performed as well. Therefore, stimulation of research in basic disciplines is a top priority for the future development of China's independent innovation.

The COVID-19 Pandemic and Innovation in the Post-Pandemic Era

In early 2020, the COVID-19 pandemic suddenly broke out, which caused a public health crisis and global economic challenges. To reduce the spread of the pandemic, the Chinese government swiftly implemented various control measures such as lockdowns, self-quarantine, closure of physical shops, and transportation restrictions. People's health concerns and government measures limited market demand, cut off resource supply, and prevented employees from returning to work, resulting in disruptions to the innovation activities of enterprises and research institutions.

In the short term, COVID-19 pandemic impeded domestic innovation because it disrupted access to R&D resources and reduced R&D efficiency for most innovation entities. For example, in the early stage of the outbreak, many suppliers and service providers shut down, and basic supplies and services needed for innovation activities were in short supply or only available at a much higher price, forcing enterprises and research institutions to call off some research projects. Moreover, industrial and academic laboratories were closed, and R&D personnel could not have physical access to unique facilities and equipment. Even if some R&D projects could be carried out by remote work, working from home often placed housework responsibilities on the R&D staff, inevitably distracting them and reducing the research effectiveness. An analysis of data on Chinese listed companies for six months after the COVID-19 outbreak shows that, on average, the number of patent applications filed by each enterprise falls by 0.57 pieces during the pandemic compared to the same period in the previous year (Zhou & Dong, 2022). It is worth noting that the innovation of SOEs suffers less than that of private firms, thanks to the former's better access to R&D resources (e.g., R&D projects) and their inefficient pre-pandemic R&D, which provides more operational slack that can be used to buffer the shock of pandemic disruptions.

On the other hand, the COVID-19 has also inspired innovative ideas. As highlighted in crisis management literature, innovation enables organizations to identify and exploit new opportunities created by a changing landscape, making it the key to addressing disruptions and uncertainties (Lee et al., 2020). Crises bear the potential for new entrants to cater to new needs with innovative solutions. Accordingly, with the gradual liberalization of government prevention measures, emerging entrepreneurial opportunities have given rise to a number of startups. Established enterprises are also adapting their business models in innovative ways. For example, enterprises try to use new technology to make up for the influence of social distancing, which accelerates new technologies such as telecommuting, unmanned delivery, and smart factories. Some technology trends are becoming particularly prominent, such as online shopping and robotic delivery, tele-education, telemedicine, online entertainment, supply chain 4.0, and 5G information and communication technologies.

In particular, the COVID-19 pandemic is closely linked to the healthcare system and greatly influences innovation in the pharmaceutical sector. Vaccines and innovative drugs are the most effective means of preventing and controlling the spread of the pandemic, implying a large potential market. The Chinese government has also provided strong policy support for vaccine R&D. For example, the "14th Five-Year Plan" for the development of the pharmaceutical industry released in 2021 emphasizes the need to improve emergency R&D and production capacity for vaccines and to strengthen vaccine supply security. The broad market and policy support greatly stimulate the innovation enthusiasm of pharmaceutical enterprises. Statistics from the State Drug Administration show that by the end of February 2022, more than fifty new pandemic-related drugs had been approved to enter clinical trials in China.

Future Directions

Independent Innovation

Given the decoupling, the success of China's innovation depends critically on the development of key core technologies. Chinese enterprises realize that they cannot just engage in "imitative" and "processed" innovation; rather, they should devote efforts to reducing their dependence on key technologies of overseas competitors and enhancing their independent innovation.

Electric Vehicle Battery

The Chinese government strongly supports the development of electric vehicles, which has driven significant advances in the automotive battery technology of domestic enterprises. For example, in November 2020, the State Council promulgated the "New Energy Vehicle Industry Development Plan (2021–2035)" to promote the high-quality development of electric vehicles. In December 2021, multiple state departments jointly issued the "Notice on the Financial Subsidy Policy for the Promotion and Application of New Energy Vehicles in 2022" to further improve the subsidy policy for electric vehicles. Data from the China Association of Automobile Manufacturers shows that in 2022, China's sales volume of new energy vehicles reached nearly 6.9 million, with a year-on-year growth rate of 93.4 percent, maintaining its position as the world's No. 1 for eight consecutive years. Such achievement is possible because Chinese enterprises have mastered the core component technology of new energy vehicles, represented by the automotive battery.

Global analyst reports forecast a promising future for the automotive battery industry, with a five-fold increase in total annual demand for automotive battery packs from 2021 to 2027 (Yole Intelligence, 2022). By 2022, battery supply had been dominated by companies from Asia, such as CATL and BYD in China, Samsung SDI and LG Energy Solution in South Korea, and Panasonic in Japan. Among them, Chinese battery enterprises have experienced the fastest-growing market, capturing two-thirds of the global market share in 2022. In contrast, while Japanese and Korean battery companies such as Panasonic, LG, SK, and Samsung also have an increase in installment volume, their growth rate is much lower than that of Chinese companies, with the combined global market share of these four companies falling from about 40 percent in 2021 to 31 percent in 2022 (EV Specifications, 2022). More importantly, driven by R&D in chemistry and new materials, China's automotive battery technology continues to advance. In 2022, the energy density of domestically mass-produced automotive batteries reached 300 watt-hours/kg, which marked a world-leading breakthrough in key technologies for new energy vehicles. Thus, in the electric vehicle battery industry, China is now the global leader in terms of both technology and sales volume. In the future, China needs to cultivate more world-class leading enterprises that master the core technology of the industry chain in order to achieve the goal of moving from a "big auto country" to a "strong auto country."

Semiconductor Industry

Since the ZTE incident in 2018, the U.S. has continued its crackdown on China's semiconductor development with escalating sanction policies, which undermines the existing global semiconductor industry ecology. However, it has also made Chinese companies pay more attention to innovation and reduce their dependence on Western technologies. As a result, the domestic chip industry has entered a period of rapid development in recent years, particularly after Huawei faced sanctions. Domestic chips and semiconductors have evolved into a thriving industry, receiving strong government support and attracting investment from various capitals. For example, in the 14th Five-Year Plan, the Chinese government plans to support the development of the third-generation semiconductor industry from 2021 to 2025 in all aspects, including education, research, development, financing, and application, to achieve independent innovation. Meanwhile, the government provides substantial support for key technology segments in the semiconductor industry chain, including high-end IC design and key semiconductor equipment and materials. This has greatly facilitated the innovation of local semiconductor enterprises. Statistics show that as of September 30, 2022, there were 69,190 semiconductor patent applications worldwide in the past twelve months, with 55 percent submitted by Chinese entities (Mathys & Squire, 2023).

However, strong barriers exist for the development of semiconductor technology in China (Luo & Li, 2023). First, the basic research of semiconductors in China lags far behind that of the United States. The Ministry of Education abolished the semiconductor physics and devices program in 1997, resulting in the current scarcity of talent for basic semiconductor research. The number of laboratories and bases for basic research is also limited. Moreover, China focuses on applied research and seriously under-invests in basic research. In 2011 and 2021, the proportion of U.S. R&D investment in semiconductors accounted for 54.5 percent and 55.8 percent of the world, respectively, while this expenditure in mainland China accounted for no more than 5 percent. This leads to a gap in technological capabilities between the two countries, making it difficult for Chinese semiconductor enterprises to compete with their U.S. counterparts in the short term.

Second, China lacks collaborative innovation between companies and research institutions, which leads to a disconnect between research and practice in cutting-edge semiconductor technologies. A large number of researchers in the U.S. undertake basic research projects commissioned by companies such as Intel, Samsung, and TSMC, but China has few similar institutions to organize collaborative innovation in semiconductor research. As a result, many domestic semiconductor enterprises primarily perform process optimization based on Process Design Kit (PDK) provided by others, making it difficult to support a high level of independent innovation in the semiconductor industry. Additionally, the Sino-U.S. technology decoupling has led to international sanctions that restrict Western companies from doing business in China, making it even harder for local enterprises to gain access to the latest technologies. Given that the semiconductor industry represents the highest level of technological advances resulting from the collective efforts of multiple countries, it would be highly challenging for China to develop the entire industrial chain alone.

Digital Innovation

With the development of digital technology, China has become one of the largest digital economies in the world in a relatively short period of time. The vast array of digital technologies and their constituent digital infrastructures are embedded in the process and outcome of innovation, which greatly changes the nature and patterns of innovation. In omnichannel retail, social media, on-demand services, fintech, healthcare, supply chain, and other areas, China is developing many "China-first" innovations (McKinsey & Company, 2021). Digital innovation continues to proliferate, spanning all industries and different types of organizations and exerting a huge influence on enterprises' competitive advantages and sustainable growth. For example, Chinese companies such as Alibaba, Baidu, and Tencent are leading the development and commercialization of artificial intelligence (AI) technologies that are used in areas such as facial recognition, natural language processing, and self-driving cars.

There are also Chinese startups that thrive based on digital innovation. A prime example is ByteDance, a Chinese high-tech company that is rapidly entering overseas markets with the launch of apps like TikTok (Douyin in the Chinese market). TikTok allows people to watch, make, and share short video clips. In 2021, TikTok had been downloaded over 3 billion times globally and attracted 1.9 billion users from 150 countries. With products such as TikTok, ByteDance has been recognized as the most valuable startup in the world (Chen & Ma, 2022). TikTok is so appealing because users can watch their favorite videos directly after opening the app and scroll down to another video (usually of interest to users) in a time- and energy-saving way, without the need to choose from many videos like YouTube. Thanks to the powerful AI algorithm, TikTok can analyze the content of each video, predict the preference of each user, and then recommend highly matched video streams for users (Ma & Hu, 2021). TikTok also uses AI to continuously innovate its services on the producer (content creator) side. For example, TikTok helps producers create virtual videos through enhancement functions and provides a Duet function, which allows producers to post videos side-by-side with a video from another creator on TikTok. Moreover, with its broad user base, leveraging AI technology and talent, TikTok has the potential to enter the payment industry and delivery food industry with business model innovation.

Another example is Shein, a Chinese fast-fashion company established in 2008 that has grown rapidly since 2015, focusing on cross-border sales of clothing and operating in more than 230 countries, including the United States, Europe, and the Middle East. During the COVID-19 pandemic in 2020, restrictions on offline shopping further stimulated Shein's sales growth and Shein is now catching up with the fast-fashion giant Zara (Perri, 2023). In 2022, Shein was ranked as the fifth-largest unicorn company in the world. Shein's success results from its application of digital technologies in product design, manufacturing, and logistics. Regarding product design, Shein develops an algorithm similar to TikTok and applies it to capture and predict popular clothing trends. Shein's IT and design departments use technical tools such as Python and Google Trends Finder to collect current fashion information, including popular keywords and trend elements, and then use them as a reference for designers. With data-driven product innovation, Shein's pop-up rate is around 50 percent. Moreover, Shein has developed a digital IT management system in-house and is constantly optimizing it to improve collaboration with upstream suppliers and enhance production efficiency. In this way, Shein can launch new products and capture the emerging market rapidly.

However, Chinese companies like TikTok and Shein also face strong challenges for future development. The major reason is that they mainly do applied innovation, that is, using algorithms and AI for continuous product or service innovation, but lack basic and fundamental innovation (e.g., ChatGPT), which is the source of sustainable competitive advantages for companies. For TikTok, it has always relied on algorithms for graphic and video content distribution, but today the efficiency of the algorithms is approaching its limits, and business model innovation has largely exhausted its imagination, as reflected in TikTok's slowing-down growth. Similarly, Shein also operates at a low technical threshold. Whether it is the algorithm-based popular trend prediction, the real-time supply chain system built upon the back of Chinese factories, or the operation method with the help of social media, all of them can be copied by competitors relatively easily. Emerging AI-generated content (AIGC) technology, represented by ChatGPT, can help Chinese companies like TikTok fundamentally upgrade their technology to support the integration of massive, nonstandardized information and enable more granular personalized matching in natural language chat. Therefore, it is important for digital companies to strengthen their learning and international collaboration on fundamental innovations for long-term growth.

Policy Implications

The government and public resources have always played an important role in promoting S&T innovation in China. Since the reform and opening up, the Chinese government has first introduced FDI introduction policies to stimulate domestic innovation, then gradually introduced a series of policies that prioritize S&T innovation, and recently increased policy support for cutting-edge technology areas such as semiconductors and digital technologies. Guided by government policy, China has improved its S&T innovation system, attracted scientific researchers and fostered entrepreneurs, and promoted the development of an innovation-driven economy. The 2022 Global Innovation Index shows that China is ranked eleventh in the world, and the contribution of S&T progress to economic growth has increased from less than 40 percent in 2000 to 60 percent (WIPO, 2022).

However, the promoting role of government policy is reaching its limits, as some problems cannot be solely addressed by government support, leading to bottlenecks that restrict the future development of China's innovation. Although China ranks among the world leaders in total R&D investment, patent applications, and the number of S&T academic papers, the quality and efficiency of innovation are still low. The number of patents recognized and applied by foreign organizations is small, and the rate of patent commercialization is low. The number of general application technology innovation is high, but the core technology is still largely dependent on developed countries. For example, in China, high-end automotive automatic transmission largely relies on imports. Many medical devices, especially precision instruments, are mostly imported from Germany and Japan.

If China is to become an innovative country and a world power in S&T in the future, it should strengthen intercountry cooperation to solve these technology bottlenecks. Innovation has no national boundaries. A rational division of work is a guarantee of efficiency, so China should strengthen a multi-collaborator innovation model with different countries and entities and between research institutions and firms. Moreover, China should emphasize open innovation development by learning the most cutting-edge knowledge from all over the world. By establishing international platforms for S&T exchange and cooperation, China can improve the quality and efficiency of innovation. The Chinese government has already begun to make some efforts. For example, in 2022, Beijing Zhongguancun S&T Park released guidelines for the pilot project of the Research Fund for Senior Foreign Scholars to support foreign scientists in leading research teams in frontier areas of basic science (GuangMing Daily, 2022).

In addition, the Chinese government should actively seek resources from the international community to foster domestic innovation. For example, the government can optimize policies to support the needs of overseas talents, such as visas and education, and develop legal regulations to align with international technical and regulatory norms.

The government should also liberalize access to foreign investments and provide more opportunities for Chinese and foreign companies to collaborate through international trade shows and S&T parks. In sum, open cooperation and collaborative innovation are the inevitable paths to a win-win situation for China and other countries.

Conclusion

Through the analysis of patent data, we investigate the trajectory of China's innovation over the past thirty-five years. Driven by the government's FDI and innovation policies, Chinese innovation has achieved rapid growth, mainly attributed to the rise of Chinese enterprises, especially private enterprises. In addition, China's innovation position in the world continues to grow as it strives to catch up with developed countries. Even in the current context of high uncertainty due to technology decoupling and the COVID-19 pandemic, China still has world-leading achievements in some areas, such as electric vehicle batteries and digital startups.

However, there are also weaknesses in the development of China's innovation. China remains heavily dependent on other countries for many core technologies, often referred to as "stranglehold" technologies, which reflects China's lack of basic and fundamental research and innovation. To improve basic research, it is not enough to rely solely on the existing government policy system that mainly focuses on R&D and talent subsidy. Rather, Chinese enterprises and research institutions need more opportunities to collaborate with entities that have the most advanced technologies in the world. Therefore, the Chinese government needs to encourage cross-country cooperation and provide international collaborative research opportunities along with financial support.

By summarizing and analyzing the trajectory, drivers, and future directions of innovation in China, we provide implications for policymakers and innovative entities, mainly enterprises. For policymakers, the assessment of the patentee, regional, and industry distribution of innovation enables them to enact and adjust innovation policies to achieve balanced development across regions and industries. Moreover, we find that some aspects are overlooked in innovation policies, such as basic research and innovation quality. Accordingly, policymakers should not only emphasize innovation quantity but also improve the assessment and reward of the quality and novelty of innovation. Enterprises should understand the current opportunities and challenges of innovation to identify their competitive advantages and disadvantages and then adjust their future R&D directions to respond to the changing global landscape.

Finally, we attempt to point out three possible directions for future research on China's innovation. The first is China's IP regime. As China continues its rapid technological catch-up path and international cooperation increases, there is a growing debate on China's adherence to global IP norms (Athreye, 2020). Although China is paying more attention to IP protection, reports of industrial espionage and forced technology transfers raise concerns for technology owners about whether their innovations can be protected in China (Huang & Smith, 2019). In particular, the growth of digital technology makes imitation much easier. Thus, the inadequacy of China's IP protection system may become a major obstacle to China's technology learning from other developed countries. The second is a political perspective of China's innovation. Prior innovation research has examined the drivers of innovation from various perspectives, such as efficiency-driven economics view (e.g., R&D investment efficiency), sociological view (e.g., teamwork, cultural value), and technological view (e.g., technological development, the rise of AI). In China, as innovation is heavily shaped by the government and its policies, it is worthwhile to take a political view to examine how governmental policies and regulations affect the development of innovation. Third, we need a refined measure of innovation. While patents have long been used to indicate the degree of innovation, innovation policies in China may drive firms to apply for patents for policy implications rather than invention protection. Relatedly, foreign firms may apply for patents in China with their existing technologies from overseas, which leads to the question of whether such patents should be counted as Chinese inventions. Overall, given its unique institutional features, we call for new perspectives and refined measures to better capture innovation development in China.

References

Athreye, S. 2020. "China's Intellectual Property Regime." *Journal of International Business Policy*, 3: 58–59.

Bremmer, I. 2019. *The End of the American Order: Ian Bremmer Speech at 2019 GZERO Summit EURASIA GROUP*. www.eurasiagroup.net/live-post/end-of-american-order-ian-bremmer-2019-gzero-summit-speech

Chen, R., & Ma, R. 2022, (February 24). *How Byte Dance Became the World's Most Valuable Startup*. Harvard Business Review. https://hbr.org/2022/02/how-bytedance-became-the-worlds-most-valuable-startup

Cheung, K. Y., & Ping, L. 2004. "Spillover Effects of FDI on Innovation in China: Evidence from the Provincial Data." *China Economic Review*, 15 (1): 25–44.

China National Intellectual Property Administration. 2006. *China SIPO annual reports 2006*. https://english.cnipa.gov.cn/art/2008/4/16/art_1577_100946.html

EV Specifications. 2022. *SNE Research: Global EV battery usage for 2022*. www.evspecifications.com/en/news/f6b372e

Genin, A. L., Tan, J., & Song, J. 2021. "State Governance and Technological Innovation in Emerging Economies: State-Owned Enterprise Restructuration and Institutional Logic Dissonance in China's High-Speed Train Sector." *Journal of International Business Studies*, 52: 621–645.

GuangMing Daily. 2022. China actively promotes global S&T exchanges and cooperation. *GuangMing Daily*. www.gov.cn/xinwen/2022-11/19/content_5727817.htm (in Chinese)

Han, P., Jiang, W., & Mei, D. 2024. Mapping US-China technology decoupling, innovation, and firm performance. *Management Science*, online.

Huang, K. G. 2010. "China's Innovation Landscape." *Science*, 329 (5992): 632–633.

Huang, Y., & Smith, J. 2019. "China's Record on Intellectual Property Rights Is Getting Better and Better." *Foreign Policy*, 16, china-intellectual-property-theft-progress.

Jia, N., Huang, K. G., & Man Zhang, C. 2019. "Public Governance, Corporate Governance, and Firm Innovation: An Examination of State-Owned Enterprises." *Academy of Management Journal*, 62 (1): 220–247.

Lee, G. K., Lampel, J., & Shapira, Z. 2020. "After the Storm Has Passed: Translating Crisis Experience into Useful Knowledge." *Organization Science*, 31 (4): 1037–1051.

Li, X. 2019. "Regulating China's Inward FDI: Changes, Challenges, and the Future." In *To Get Rich Is Glorious: Challenges Facing China's Economic Reform and Opening at Forty*, edited by J. DeLisle & A. Goldstein (pp. 203–232). Brookings Institution Press.

Luo, J. W., & Li, S. S. 2023. "Strengthen the Building of Basic Reach Capacity for Semiconductor Research to Light Up the "Beacon" towards Realizing the Self-Reliance and Self-Improvement of Semiconductors."

Bulletin of Chinese Academy of Sciences, 38 (2): 187–192. doi: 10.16418/j.issn.1000-3045.20230130001, in Chinese.

Ma, Y., & Hu, Y. 2021. "Business Model Innovation and Experimentation in Transforming Economies: ByteDance and TikTok." *Management and Organization Review*, 17 (2): 382–388.

Mathys & Squire. 2023, (February 20). Semiconductor patents rise by 59% in five years to reach to record high. *Insights & events*. www.mathys-squire.com/insights-and-events/news/semiconductor-patents-rise-by-59-in-five-years-to-reach-to-record-high/

McKinsey & Company. 2021, (September 30). The Future of Digital Innovation in China. *Featured insights*. www.mckinsey.com/featured-insights/china/the-future-of-digital-innovation-in-china-megatrends-shaping-one-of-the-worlds-fastest-evolving-digital-ecosystems

National Bureau of Statistics. 2022, (September 27). *Series of reports on the achievements of economic and social development since the 18th Party Congress, Data interpretation 410A04-0502-202209-0017*. www.stats.gov.cn/xxgk/jd/sjjd2020/202209/t20220927_1888727.html (in Chinese)

National Innovation Survey. 2023, (February 22). Report on national innovation survey: China steadily ranks as the world's second largest R&D investor. *GuangMing Daily*. www.gov.cn/xinwen/2023-02/22/content_5742661.htm (in Chinese)

Perri, J. 2023, (January 4). Shein holds largest U.S. fast fashion market share. *Bloomberg Second Measure*. https://secondmeasure.com/datapoints/fast-fashion-market-share-us-consumer-spending-data-shein-hm-zara/

Prud'homme, D., & Zhang, T. 2019. *China's Intellectual Property Regime for Innovation*. Springer International Publishing.

Rahman, Z. U. 2022. "A Comprehensive Overview of China's Belt and Road Initiative and Its Implication for the Region and Beyond." *Journal of Public Affairs*, 22 (1): e2298.

Shi, D., Liu, W., & Wang, Y. 2023. "Has China's Young Thousand Talents Program Been Successful in Recruiting and Nurturing Top-Caliber Scientists?." *Science*, 379 (6627): 62–65.

SIPO. 2009. *The SIPO interprets the central financial support to overseas patent applications in 2009*. SIPO. www.gov.cn/gzdt/2009-10/22/content_1446164.htm

SIPO. 2020. *Guiding opinions on promoting the high-quality development of intellectual property work of central enterprises (Report No. 2020-15)*. www.sasac.gov.cn/n2588020/n2588072/n2591148/n2591150/c14096120/content.html

SIPO. 2022. *Briefing on intellectual property statistics*. SIPO. www.cnipa.gov.cn/module/download/down.jsp?i_ID=176009&colID=88

Spencer, J. W. 2008. "The Impact of Multinational Enterprise Strategy on Indigenous Enterprises: Horizontal Spillovers and Crowding Out In Developing Countries." *Academy of Management Review*, 33 (2): 341–361.

USPTO. 2021. *Trademarks And Patents In China: The Impact of Non-Market Factors on Filing Trends and IP Systems.* www.uspto.gov/sites/default/files/documents/USPTO-TrademarkPatentsInChina.pdf

WIPO. 2022. *The Global Innovation Index 2022.* www.wipo.int/edocs/pubdocs/en/wipo-pub-2000-2022-section1-en-gii-2022-at-a-glance-global-innovation-index-2022-15th-edition.pdf

WIPO. 2023. *Report on International Patent Applications By Origin (PCT System), International Patent Application.* www.wipo.int/export/sites/www/pressroom/en/documents/pr-2023-899-annexes.pdf#page=1

Wu, X., & Si, Y. 2022. "China's Belt and Road Initiative and Corporate Innovation." *Finance Research Letters*, 48: 103052.

Yole Intelligence. 2022, (November 17). *Automotive Battery Pack: Attractions & Improvements.* [Press releases]. www.yolegroup.com/press-release/automotive-battery-pack-attractions-improvements/

Zhang, X., Luo, W., & Xiang, D. 2022. "Political Turnover and Innovation: Evidence from China." *Journal of Chinese Political Science*, 2022: 1–25.

Zhang, Y., Li, H., Li, Y., & Zhou, L. A. 2010. "FDI Spillovers in an Emerging Market: The Role of Foreign Firms' Country Origin Diversity and Domestic Firms' Absorptive Capacity." *Strategic Management Journal*, 31 (9): 969–989.

Zhou, K. Z., & Dong, M. 2022. "COVID-19 Pandemic and Innovation of Chinese SOEs and Non-SOEs." In *Academy of Management Proceedings-Volume*, Issue 1, January 1, 2022 (p. 13262). Academy of Management.

4 When the Abundance Ends

Economic Transformation, Population Aging, and Shrinking Lifecycle Surplus in China, 2000–2020

FENG WANG, KE SHEN, AND YONG CAI

China in the last four decades has been basking in an age of abundance. Once a land where food supply could hardly catch up with population growth, entering the twenty-first century, China has ascended as a global economic powerhouse, producing enough not only for its own people but also for much of the rest of the world.

The path to prosperity in China followed that in other parts of the world earlier. It began with more abundant and higher quality food and proceeded to better clothing, new and comfortable housing, and the population enjoying leisure time such as traveling. In 1978, for instance, on average, every three people in rural China purchased only one pair of shoes.[1] By 2015, these rural Chinese manufactured and exported 3.5 billion pairs of shoes, enough to fit more than half of the entire world population.[2] With a population size less than 20 percent of the world total, Chinese consumers in 2020 purchased 35 percent of global personal luxury goods.[3] The number of privately owned vehicles per 100 urban households reached 50.1 in 2021, rising from 13.1 in 2010 and merely 0.5 in 2000.[4] In 2019, the year before the COVID-19 pandemic outbreak, 162 million overseas trips were made by Chinese for private reasons, a fivefold increase from just a decade ago.[5] Such a spectacular prosperity boom, largely unexpected and benefiting from a set of unique historical junctures, was an outcome of many opportunities and forces (Wang 2024).

[1] China Statistical Yearbook (SYB) 1981, Table 11-18.
[2] For the year 2015. SYB 2016, Table 11-7.
[3] McKinsey China Luxury Report 2019.
[4] China Statistical Yearbook 2022, Table 6-10; China Statistical Yearbook 2011, Table 10-10.
[5] China Statistical Yearbook 2011, Table 18-18, 2021, Table 17-9.

A major driving force of China's age of abundance was a demographic one: the presence of a large reservoir of young and hard-working labor, mostly living in the Chinese countryside when the economic boom began. As China ascends to its age of abundance, that reservoir has also been drying up quickly. The Malthusian dark cloud that once so heavily hovered over the Chinese landscape is now being replaced by an entirely different concern: accelerating population aging and irreversible population decline. Once a quarter or even over a third of the world population, China could see its population dwindling to less than 10 percent by the end of the current century.[6]

Population is not just a number. Human beings are social animals as well as economic actors. To gain an appreciation of the economic consequences of population change, one has to take into account two interactive forces simultaneously: population, not just the number but also age composition, and economic behaviors of the population at different ages, such as production and consumption profiles. Such an examination calls therefore for a lifecycle approach.

In this chapter, we examine how changes in labor and consumption profiles at the per capita level, combined with the shifting population age compositions, have affected national economic surplus, resulting from the difference between labor income and consumption in the last two decades. We will show how rapid economic transformations, seen in income increases and consumption changes, in combination with a favorable population age structure, generated a vast surplus in society, especially in the decade of the 2000s. We follow changes in the economic behaviors of the population over time and report how population aging, combined with shifting income and consumption patterns, is depleting that surplus by the late 2010s.

The two decades we cover in this chapter form a sharp contrast in recent Chinese economic history. The first decade of the twenty-first century registered China's fastest economic growth decade in history, with an average annual GDP growth rate of over 10 percent. In the

[6] According to the latest projections by the United Nations' Population Division. *World Population Prospect 2022* (https://population.un.org/wpp/). The UN's projection, with its median variant assumption, is that China's population will only be 7 percent of the world total by the century's end. Such a projection, of course, also subjects population growth elsewhere, especially in sub-Saharan Africa. Should population growth there be slower than projected, China's share of the world total would be higher than the projected 7 percent.

second decade, the 2010s, China entered a period of substantial and sustained slowing down in economic growth, with the annual GDP growth rate declining from 10.6 percent in 2010 to 7.8 percent in 2013 and 6 percent in 2019, prior to the COVID-19 global pandemic.[7] While income growth slowed down along with a slower-growing economy, consumption has caught up in the second decade, and it increased at a much faster pace than in the first decade. Faster growth in consumption than in labor income necessarily changes the economic surplus. Along with economic transformation, China also saw a turnaround in the path of demographic change. In the 2000s, China continued to benefit from the expanding share of working-age adults aged 15–64, rising from 70.1 percent in 2000 and reaching the peak of 74.5 percent in 2010. This share started to decline in 2011, down to 68.3 percent in 2021. In 2022, China registered its first drop in total population in six decades due mostly to sustained low fertility. Accelerating population aging, together with changes in individual economic behaviors, opens a new chapter for China in the decades to come.

Before introducing the analytical framework of lifecycle analysis, we present in the following first a brief review of the role of demographic dividend in China's economic boom. We follow this review and the introduction to our method with summary findings and comparisons of economic surplus in the first two decades of the twenty-first century. We end our chapter with a projection and discussions of the implications of future demographic change for Chinese economy and society.

From Curse to Fortune

Demography is never destiny. Yet for China, as the country moved away from its socialist planned economy systems, its population turned from a curse to a fortune. With the return of private ownership and a market-based economic system, the population was no longer planners' headaches to feed, to clothe, to house, and to provide jobs. Instead, once they regained freedom to pursue their own economic interests, the massive Chinese population seized every opportunity and improved their living standards through their ambition, initiative, ingenuity, and ultimately, hard work.

[7] China Statistical Yearbook 2021. Table 3-4.

At the root of China's economic rise however was its vast population living in the countryside, who accounted for eight in every ten Chinese as recently as in 1980. While still living largely on the margins of subsistence, China's population had already undergone a drastic improvement in health and a rapid fertility decline on the eve of its economic take-off (Lee and Wang 1999; Wang 2024). The population, especially those of the younger ages, saw not only a vast improvement in health but also in literacy. With a measured per capita income solidly in the low-income group, China by the late 1970s had both a population health and female literacy level well above those of the middle-income countries at the time (Wang et al. 2018). What China had was not just cheap labor, but good labor. Combined, improvements in health and literacy and declining fertility presented China a historical window, a window of the demographic dividend.

At the time of its economic take-off in the early 1980s, not only was China's share of the elderly population still extremely small, with less than 5 percent of the population aged 65 and over, but its fast fertility decline in the 1970s had already started to pay off. Fertility decline in China prior to the 1980s already reduced the share of the young population aged 0–14 from the high of 41 percent in 1970 to 36 percent in 1980 (United Nations 2022). The share further dropped to 29 percent by 1990, and to less than a quarter, only 24.5 percent, by 2000. What was truly opportune was that the share of the population of working ages (15–64) increased by 14 percentage points, from 59 percent in 1980 to 68 percent in 2000 and to 73 percent by 2010 (Figure 4.1). The general support ratio, expressed as the ratio between the population of working ages (15 to 64) and of the dependency ages (under 15 and over 64), remained high before the increase in the elderly population. It was 1.47 in 1980, meaning almost one and a half working-age adults support one person of dependent age. It increased to 2.69 by 2010, before declining again. In contrast to 1980, by the mid-twenty-first century the dependent population will be composed mostly of the elderly population aged 65 and over (Figure 4.1).

Instead of a curse, with a change in the economic system, China's population became a fortune, directly driving its historical economic boom. Changes in population age structure during the process of the demographic transition presented a once-in-history opportunity. This opportunity is a time window with a historically low population

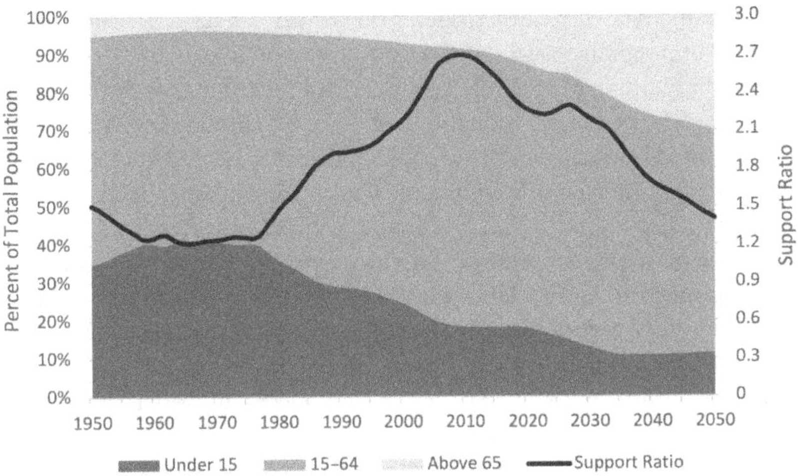

Figure 4.1 Changing population age structure and support ratio, China, 1950–2050
Data Source: WPP (2022).

dependency ratio, the ratio between population in the dependent age groups, those very young and old, and the working-age population.

China's demographic fortune can be assessed more concretely using the measure of "demographic dividend." The term "demographic dividend" is among the least understood and most abused terms in assessing the roles of population in economic changes. It is not uncommon, and understandable, that arguments are made that a large and increasing number of young people do not translate readily into a dividend. One can reasonably argue that more young people could increase the potential for more unemployment, poverty, and even social unrest.

To appreciate properly the concept of the demographic dividend, two clarifications need to be made: one conceptual and the other computational. Conceptually, demographic dividend is broadly understood as the benefits brought about by the unprecedented demographic changes in human history, which included declines in mortality, followed by fertility, and changes in population age structure (Bloom and Williamson 1998; Mason 2001; Bloom et al. 2003). Mortality reduction and improvement in health lead to a healthier population with enhanced physical and cognitive capabilities for learning and working. Reduced childbearing and childrearing cut down drastically on reproductive waste, in particular on women's bodies. Reducing the number of pregnancies from five to two, for example, could reduce the share of a woman's adult life spent on childbearing and childrearing from 70 to 14 percent, a reduction with vast economic as well as social and political implications (Lee 2003). With increased certainty in life and extended life span, the human calculus for life and social engagements has also changed in many fundamental ways (Reher 2011).

To calculate the demographic dividend properly, one needs to take into account the age-specific profiles of labor income and consumption. This is the computational definition of the demographic dividend. In this calculation, age-specific population groups need to be weighted with their corresponding labor income and consumption levels to arrive at what is known as an "effective support ratio" (Lee and Mason 2011a, 2011b). Such an approach corrects the caveat in the generally seen support ratio, which assumes all working-age adults are uniformly productive and all dependents regardless of age are homogenous consumers. The growth rate of the effective support ratio defines the demographic dividend – demographic dividend appears when the effective support ratio increases and ends when the growth rate of the effective support ratio drops below zero.

Applying this method to the Chinese case, the role of the demographic dividend in its post-socialist economic take-off is clearly evident. Calculations carried out in 2006 showed that until 2013, the growth rate of effective producers was above that of the effective consumers (Wang and Mason 2008). The effective support ratio rose continuously for the three decades after 1980, coinciding with, and contributing to, the economic boom. The demographic dividend, expressed as the growth rate of the support ratio, remained in positive territory throughout this time period. For the first two decades, this demographic dividend accounted for at least 15 percent of the increase in per capita income (Wang and Mason 2008).

The turning point of the demographic dividend for China came in 2013. It was estimated that by then the support ratio stopped increasing; the growth rate of the support ratio, which is the demographic dividend, dropped below zero. Starting in 2013, the demographic dividend entered a negative territory for China (Wang and Mason 2008). A year prior, the year 2012, indeed marked a turning point in the growth trajectory of the Chinese economy, when the growth rate in subsequent years has barely been able to pass the annual growth rate in that year, at about 8 percent.[8] The slowdown in growth rate, after an extended hyper-growth period, can trace its roots to many forces, but demography is very likely to be one of them.[9]

What China had on the eve of its economic take-off was not just a favorable age structure or the share of the population in prime working ages. China's young population was largely healthy and literate and was more than eager to take the risks to abandon a lifelong subsistence at the margins (Wang 2024). They were ready to escape the sterile social environment, an environment created under socialism that became more insufferable toward the late years of the Cultural Revolution. Without these fundamental characteristics, and in the absence of the economic opportunities made possible by the reforms later on, China's large working-age population could have indeed been a demographic curse, as feared by many. Instead of a curse, however, with reforms that brought economic opportunities, China's population generated a demographic dividend that was crucial in creating the country's historical material abundance.

Economy and Demography: A Lifecycle Approach

In all human societies, an individual's life begins and ends as a dependent. As the individual survives beyond childhood, or even into adolescent age, typically that person becomes a net producer, meaning producing more than meeting one's consumption needs. A lifecycle surplus is thus generated to finance the lifecycle deficit at the two ends of one's life span. The exact pattern of lifecycle deficit and surplus generation varies across societies. As illustrated by Lee and Mason (2011), for example, there is a strong contrast between the consumption schedule for hunter-gatherers and poor countries and the rich countries. In rich countries, heavy investment in education and substantial health care spending make child consumption and old age consumption much higher in the rich countries than in poor countries.

At dependent ages when labor income is insufficient to cover consumption, one's survival and well-being rely on two mechanisms: one is transfers from others, whether the support comes from the

8 China Statistical Yearbook 2021. Table 3-4.

9 See, for example, Eichengreen, Park, and Shin (2012) for a discussion of the forces leading to slowing down growth in fast-growing economies.

family, kin, the community, or the state. The other is asset-based reallocation, namely asset income and dissaving, which has been shown to play an important role for older adults in their sixties and a less important role for those in more advanced ages (United Nations, 2013). A lifecycle approach illustrates not only the magnitude of deficit or surplus at each age but also the mechanisms to finance the deficit or deplete the surplus at each age. The surplus, past as well as future, is not a simple equation of income minus consumption for each individual. It is an outcome of the aggregate accounts in a society, affected by the relative numbers of producers and consumers, or the population age structure.

Our empirical results in the next section of this chapter are based on analyses using the lifecycle approach, National Transfer Accounts (NTA) methodology.[10] The NTA consortium, now including 100 countries and encompassing more than 80 percent of the world's population, serves as the global platform for comparative studies on intergenerational economy. Essentially, the methodology relies on micro-level individual data from surveys to generate age profiles of labor income, consumption, transfers, asset income, and savings. Such age profiles are used to generate societal-level per capita age profiles, matching the aggregate statistics reported by each country's System of National Accounts (SNA). Together with government administrative records, the methodology further allows calculations of government transfers. The calculations result in two types of final results: per capita level lifecycle deficit or surplus and the aggregate lifecycle deficit or surplus, which is obtained via multiplying per capita level age profiles by population at each age. Lifecycle deficit, or surplus, based on the differences between consumption and labor income, is to be balanced by net transfers (public and private), asset income, and savings.[11]

Estimations of lifecycle deficit and transfers rely on both micro- and macro-level data. These age-specific profiles are constructed by relying on the aggregate labor income and consumption data from the official government statistics, distributing across ages with the age-specific labor income and consumption patterns from household surveys. The survey data for China used to produce the results in this chapter are

[10] United Nations (2013), www.ntaccounts.org/web/nta/show/NTA%20Countries.

[11] The balance equation is defined as: Consumption – Labor Income = Net Transfer + Asset Income – Saving.

from China Household Income Project surveys (for 2002 and 2007) and from the China Family Panel Studies (CFPS, for 2010, 2014, and 2018) (Xie and Hu 2014).

One main advantage of the NTA approach in comparison with other methodologies is in its consistency between micro profiles and macro aggregates. The age profiles for each component in the calculations are constructed from micro survey data and are first smoothed.[12] They are weighted by population age structure to calculate the national total, which is then adjusted proportionately to match the national macro control reported by the government. By combining micro- and macro-level data, the estimates for public transfers from household survey data for instance are in line with government fiscal spending.

The NTA approach also has the advantage of avoiding missing income and consumption based on normal household surveys, as respondents in household surveys, without the benefit of information on consumption expenditure by the government, may underreport their incomes. It also has the advantage of being able to allocate total labor income and consumption across ages to examine an entire life cycle.

Reversal of Fortune: From Surplus to Deficit

In the first two decades of the twenty-first century, China saw both the fastest economic and income growth and the beginning of a substantial downturn. Income and consumption growth, however, followed somewhat different patterns and paces. The first decade saw the fastest income growth, driven by an economic transformation featured by the birth and expansion of new economic sectors and by a massive rural-to-urban labor transfer. Income increased and standards of living improved rapidly, yet living costs remained relatively low. China's new consumption cohorts, those born after the end of China's socialist planned economic era, were yet to mature to their adult ages. Therefore, in the early years of China's economic ascendance, consumption growth among Chinese families lagged behind income growth, yielding a substantially increased surplus. At the society level, an increase in surplus

[12] The only exception is for education, as age profiles of public education transfers contain many discontinuities, which are not random but are the product of specific ages of entering and leaving schools (UNPD, 2013).

was also made possible by virtue of a favorable population age composition, when the population in the prime labor force age was abundant and the share of the elderly population remained small.

As income continued to grow and the cohorts born after China's economic transformation began reaching their adult age, a new generation of consumers arrived. Consumption increase began to outpace income growth. As a result, the accumulation of surplus started to decline. Changes in population age structure, with more people entering old age, also contributed to lifecycle surplus shrinkage at the societal level.

Changing Economy, Changing Labor Income

The decade of the 2000s was clearly the fastest income growth decade. In the eight years for which we have data to calculate labor income over the life span, using the National Transfer Accounts method, average annual income per capita (at 2002 constant prices) increased by 2.7 times, nearly threefold. Importantly, as shown in Figure 4.2, the decade also shows a very notable shift in the age pattern of labor income: the peak age of earnings, rather than following roughly a normal curve, shifted drastically toward the young: from age forty-one in 2002 to age twenty-nine in 2010.

Such a shift in the age patterns of labor income is historical, and it can be traced to China's broad economic transformations. The sharp shift of peaking age toward the young is largely due to the massive rural-to-urban, or farming-to-nonfarming, transformations. Massive rural-to-urban migration took off after the mid-1990s, when the number of rural migrants in cities shot up from 69 million in 1995 to 137 million by 2000 and further to 221 million by 2010.[13] The decade of the 2000s was also the decade that placed the share of China's urban population for the first time in its history at over 50 percent (to 50.5 percent in 2011). The earnings of hundreds of millions of migrant

[13] Note and sources: Migrants are defined as those with a rural household registration living in cities and away from their original residence for six months or more. The numbers for 1982–2009 are estimated by Chan (2012). For 2010 and later, from SYB 2019, Table 2-3. The National Statistics Bureau only provides data for 2010 and afterwards. The number published by The National Statistics Bureau for 2010, 221 million, is close to Chan's estimate, 205.6 million.

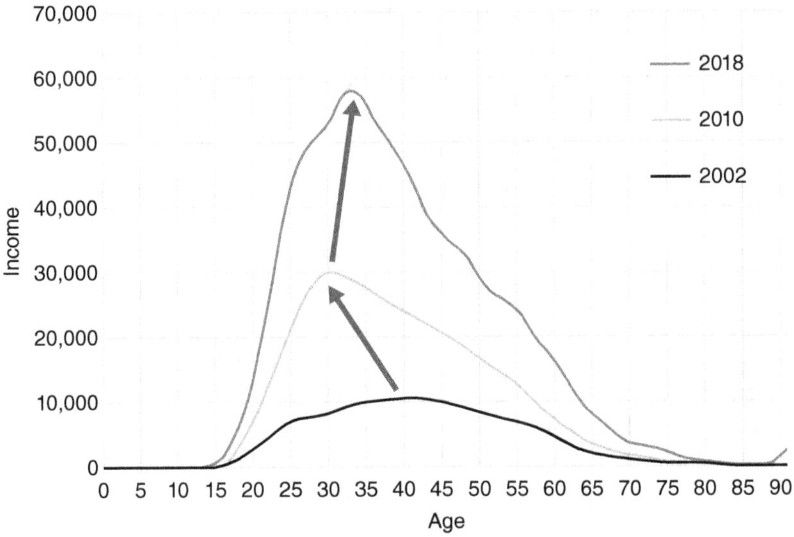

Figure 4.2 Per capita annual labor income by age, China, 2002, 2010, and 2018
Source: Calculations by authors, based on the NTA methodology, in 2002 RMB yuan.

labors, in construction, manufacturing, and services, while still substantially below those of employees of urban origin, were far higher than what they earned as farmers. Whereas the rural population of old ages and a larger share of females stayed in farming, the young predominantly moved out of the countryside by 2010. In 1990, for instance, 70 percent of males and 75 percent of females aged twenty to twenty-four were reported to be employed in the farming sector, according to China's census that year. By the decade's end, that share dropped to 36 and 41 percent, respectively. The same shift in age pattern of earnings was also happening among employees of urban origin, where young entrants to the labor market were equipped with higher education and newer skills. Following an unprecedented expansion in opportunities for higher education since 1998, college enrollments jumped from 1.08 million in 1998 to 6.57 million in 2010, benefiting in particular urban youths. A predominant share of the young workers of urban origin also entered higher-earning sectors.

Labor income growth and age profiles in the second decade of the century similarly reveal China's economic transformations in that decade. Income growth slowed down, in comparison to the decade prior, and peaking age started to move to older ages as well. In the eight years between 2010 and 2018, for which we have carried out calculations using the NTA methodology, income growth (at 2002 constant prices) registered 1.9 times, in contrast to 2.7 times in the eight years of the previous decade. Such an increase, almost doubling in eight years, is still a highly impressive record, but it was far below the record of nearly tripling in the previous decade.

Having shifted sharply to a very young age in the 2000s, the peak earning age started to shift rightward, to older ages, as shown in Figure 4.2. By 2018, peak earning age moved up from age twenty-nine in 2010 to age thirty-three in 2018. Such a shift is partly a cohort effect, as the high-earning young individuals began to age. In addition to this cohort effect, young labor market entrants in the 2010s also included those who recently attended colleges, following China's vast higher educational expansion beginning in the late 1990s. Annual enrollment in tertiary education, numbered only 0.9 million in 1995, after doubling to 2.2 million by 2000, tripled to 6.6 million by 2010.[14]

Following Abundance: Consumption Changes

Following three decades of virtually uninterrupted high growth and material abundance, by the 2010s, consumption, especially consumption by the young generation, increased sharply. As income increased and wealth accumulated, the population started to savor the fruits of their hard labor and ingenuity. There was a time lag between income increase and consumption growth. A comparison of the two decades illustrates this point, as we illustrate in Figure 4.3. In the first decade under observation, consumption measured by per capita annual consumption increased by 1.46 times between 2002 and 2010, a magnitude significantly below that in income (2.7 times). As a share of prime-age labor income (ages thirty to forty-nine), consumption was 37.2 percent in 2002, and it increased modestly, to 38.8 percent by 2010. In contrast to the 1.7 times increase in per capita labor income between 2010 and 2018, per capita consumption rose 2.7 times in the second decade of the twentieth century. As a share of prime-age labor income, consumption rose sharply, from 38.8 percent in 2010 to 49.4 percent in 2018.

[14] China Statistical Yearbook 2021, Table 21-7.

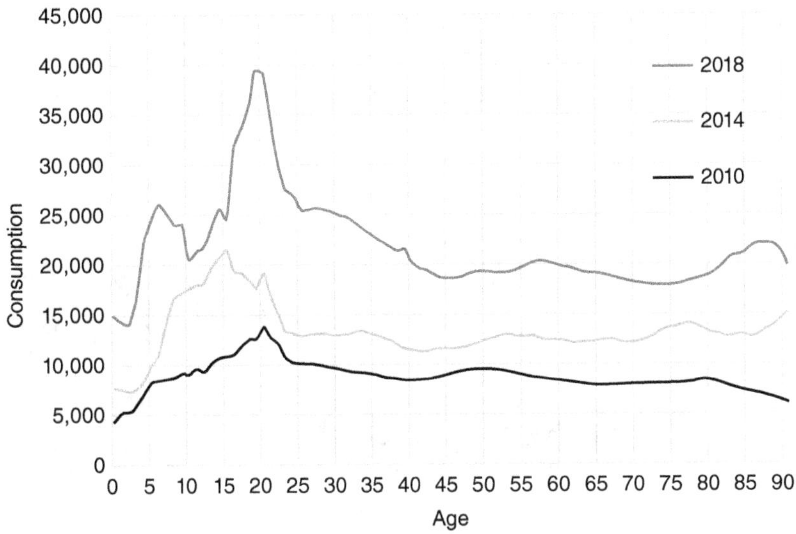

Figure 4.3 Per capita annual consumption by age, China, 2010, 2014, and 2018
Source: Calculations by authors, based on the NTA methodology, in 2002 RMB yuan.

Where and why did consumption increase in the 2010s? Our calculations of age profiles and consumption by large categories offer a window to answer this question. As shown in Figure 4.3 (top curve), whereas consumption increased across the board in all ages over the decade, the most pronounced increases are in three age ranges: pre-age 20, young adults ages between twenty-five and forty, and in the old age, especially above age eighty.

Such an increase in consumption in the 2010 can be largely accounted for by three types: education, health spending, and "others." In Figure 4.4, we plot consumption by broad types and sources (private versus public) over the lifecycle. Consumption increase among ages below twenty-five is most noticeable in education. In the compulsory educational ages, from primary to middle school (around ages 6 to 16), public expenditure makes up the major source. Public spending continues beyond age sixteen, till the mid-twenties, as higher education is also heavily supported by the government. Yet, it is clear that private educational consumption both in preschool years and in college ages are the main spending sources. Our analyses also allow us to differentiate the sources of increased consumption in older ages, which can be

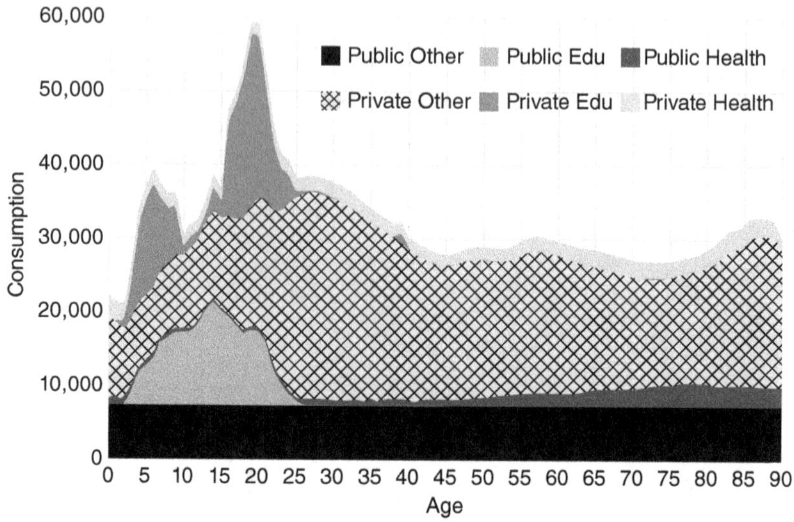

Figure 4.4 Per capita annual consumption by type and age, China, 2018
Source: Calculations by authors, based on the NTA methodology, in 2002 RMB yuan.

attributed to health care. As seen in Figure 4.4, health care is funded by both private and public sources, with public health care consumption exceeding that of the private sources after the age of sixty-five.

The bulk of the increased consumption, aside from education of the young and health care of the old, falls into the category of "other." Whereas consumption items under this category are numerous, two types of spending stand out: housing (rent or imputed rent)[15] and, for the young age cohorts, spending on transportation and personal luxury goods. Household income and consumption survey data[16] show the share of food and clothing in total household expenditure dropped from 57 percent in 1998 to 36 percent in 2021, while the share of transportation more than tripled from 4.3 percent in 1998 to 13.1 percent in 2021, and spending on housing almost doubled from 12.2 percent in 1998 to 23.4 percent in 2021.

Housing cost plays an inescapable role in increased consumption. The two decades under examination here are also the ones with

[15] In NTA construction, purchase of a house is not counted as consumption, while rent is.
[16] China Yearbook of Household Survey, 2019 and 2021.

the fastest real estate development and skyrocketing housing prices (Fang et al. 2015). By the early 2020s, with a per capita income level still far below that in high-income countries, housing cost in China reached a height that was not only higher, but multiple times higher, than in high-income countries.[17] Some of this exorbitantly high housing cost could be due to a characteristic of Chinese urbanization, namely a very large share of the urban population concentrates in megacities, driving up housing cost. It is also clearly attributable to the lack of alternative investment venues, where neither the stock market nor government-controlled banks could deliver respectable returns. Escalating housing prices create a further impression that real estate investment is a preferred venue to park the newly gained wealth and income.

China's young generation, tasting the flavor of newly accessible consumption goods, and bankrolled often by their parents, has quickly become a major source of global personal luxury goods consumption, such as brand-name cosmetics, clothing, and bags. Unlike their parents' generation, who grew up in material scarcity and who may never get used to the idea of spending on items other than those of necessity, owning luxury personal goods has become a part of personal identity for many in the young generations. With less than 20 percent of the world's total population, Chinese spending on personal luxury goods was estimated to account for 35 percent of the world's total spending in 2020, and the share was projected to grow to 40 percent by 2025. China's post-eighty generation (those born in the 1980s) made up only 43 percent of the total number of luxury goods consumers (counting together with those born in the 1970s and 1990s), but they accounted for 56 percent of all luxury spending in 2018.[18]

[17] "as of 2021, the average new urban dwelling unit in China costs 29.8 times the average income in the country. For comparison's sake, the average new urban dwelling unit In the United States costs 4.3 times the average income in the United States. In other words, housing in China averages around seven times more expensive as in the United States." "per square foot of dwelling space, Chinese housing averages 30 to 50 times as expensive as housing in the United States." www.capitalfrontiers.com/single-post/how-expensive-is-housing-in-china.

[18] McKinsey China Luxury Report 2019 (www.mckinsey.com/~/media/mckinsey/featured%20insights/china/how%20young%20chinese%20consumers%20are%20reshaping%20global%20luxury/mckinsey-china-luxury-report-2019-how-young-chinese-consumers-are-reshaping-global-luxury.pdf)

Shrinking Surplus

Two decades of shifting labor income and consumption profiles amidst continued rapid economic growth, as we document earlier, result in profound changes in the per capita profiles of lifecycle surplus. In Figure 4.5, we plot changes in per capita level lifecycle surplus (defined as income minus consumption) for 2002, 2010, and 2018. Over the two decades, as we have shown earlier, rapid income growth resulted in a substantial lifecycle surplus in the prime working ages. As peak earning age shifted to older ages in the second decade, the peak of surplus also shifted to the right, to older ages. What is notable, however, is that lifecycle deficits at the dependent ages, both young and old, increased sharply.

To fully appreciate the changes in lifecycle deficit (or surplus) at the societal level over time, we take into account the population, or population at different ages (deficit or surplus ages). The sum of the product of the population's age structure and corresponding age profile is the aggregated total of lifecycle results. In Figure 4.6, we present aggregated totals of labor income, private consumption, and

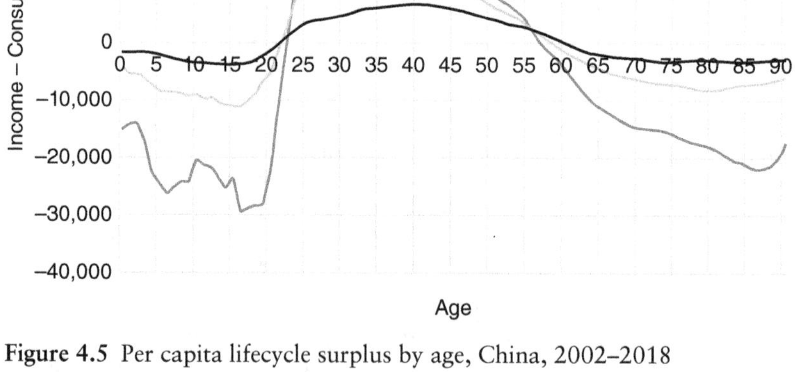

Figure 4.5 Per capita lifecycle surplus by age, China, 2002–2018
Source: Calculations by authors, based on the NTA methodology, in 2002 RMB yuan.

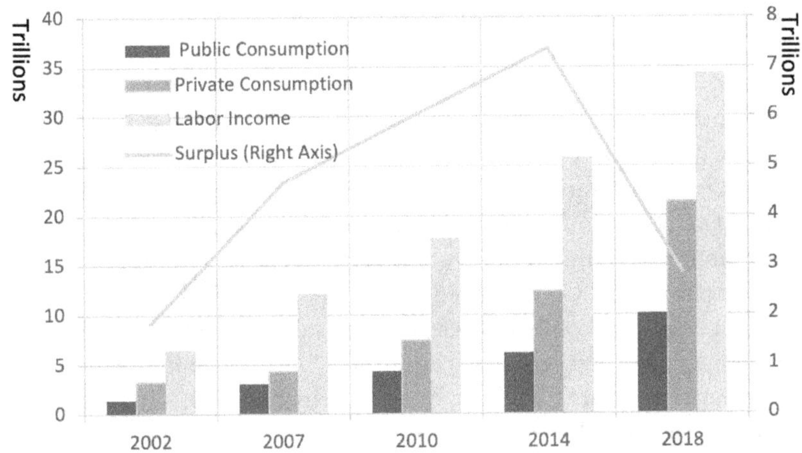

Figure 4.6 Aggregate lifecycle surplus by age, China, 2002–2018
Source: Calculations by authors, based on the NTA methodology, in 2002 RMB yuan.

public consumption for various years. The difference between labor income and consumption is defined as lifecycle surplus.

The two decades under examination reveal two rather different eras. Whereas China has been enjoying a sizable lifecycle surplus during its age of abundance, that surplus is also quickly shrinking and will soon be depleted. After taking into account the effects of the population, the aggregate lifecycle surplus results show that between 2002 and 2010, the aggregate size of the lifecycle surplus (in trillion RMB) increased by 3.3 times in eight years. As consumption growth started to outpace income growth, however, that surplus growth was slowing down, and indeed has begun to shrink. In the second decade, after increasing by only 22 percent in the four years between 2010 and 2014, it took a turn nose down, shrinking by over 60 percent between 2014 and 2018. The sharp turn was caused by a faster pace of growth in both private and public consumption than the pace of labor income increase. Between 2014 and 2018, aggregated labor income grew only 33 percent, but the growth of consumption was much faster: 65 percent for public consumption and 74 percent for private consumption. By 2018, the absolute size of aggregate lifecycle surplus was not much bigger than it was back almost two decades ago, in 2002, when the size of China's annual economic output was only less than a quarter of its size in 2018.[19]

The sharp shrinkage in the aggregate lifecycle surplus in China, as seen most directly in the second half of the 2010s, was due to two sources: changes in per capita lifecycle deficit age profiles and in population age composition. To differentiate the respective roles of these factors, we resort to a standardization and decomposition exercise. In this exercise we estimate separately what the aggregate lifecycle surplus would be had China stayed with its per capita lifecycle income/consumption age profile or age structure as of 2010 and for 2018.

Changes in the lifecycle deficit age profile, with consumption increasing faster than that in income, as shown in Figure 4.5, have a profound impact on China's shrinking lifecycle surplus at the aggregate level. Using the per capita lifecycle income/consumption age profile of 2010 and the population age structure of 2018, it would make the deficit at the dependent ages dramatically diminished due to much lower levels of consumption in 2010, and thus China's national lifecycle surplus in 2018 would have been 5.20 trillion (RMB yuan), instead of the observed 2.86 trillion, or almost twice as large. The observed difference between 2010 and 2018, 2.53 trillion, can be largely attributed to the total shrinkage magnitude in aggregate lifecycle surplus over this period, which is 1.86 trillion. In other words, in the short term, the main driving factor behind China's rapidly shrinking aggregated life cycle surplus is the swift shifts in its population's income and consumption profiles.

Population aging, at the same time, also started to exert an unmistakable impact. China's population structure aged noticeably between 2010 and 2018: the share of the population aged sixty and over increased from 13.3 to 17.2 percent, and the share of those aged sixty-five and over increased from 8.9 to 11.5 percent in just eight years. In absolute numbers, there were 66 million more individuals aged sixty and over and 44 million aged sixty-five and over in 2018 than in 2007.[20] Had China's income and consumption age profile stayed

[19] Using the World Bank source, with constant 2015 USD. China's GDP was 3.28 trillion in 2002 and 13.49 trillion in 2018 (https://data.worldbank.org/indicator/NY.GDP.MKTP.KD?locations=CN).

[20] Population age profiles used in both our calculations and in these exercises, as well as in our projections, are based on United Nations, *World Population Prospect 2022* (https://population.un.org/wpp/).

at the 2010 levels, there would be an aggregate lifecycle surplus of 3.62 trillion, instead of the observed surplus of 2.86 trillion, or about 26 percent larger. In comparison to the impact of changing lifecycle deficit age profiles, however, the impact of population aging was still much less important during this period under examination.

The impact of population aging on national lifecycle deficit will become more prominent in the decades to come. Continuing our exercises of projecting lifecycle deficit, China's lifecycle surplus, which has already been reduced sharply due to both recent changes in economic behaviors and population aging, will further shrink as the population ages. Assuming per capita lifecycle deficit profiles remain unchanged as they were in 2018, population aging alone can exhaust aggregate lifecycle surplus in less than 15 years. By 2030, the projected national lifecycle surplus will be only 0.27 trillion, or less than 10 percent of what it was in 2018. By 2050, again assuming the per capita profile of 2018 persists, the aggregate lifecycle *deficit* would reach 2.5 trillion, roughly the same size as the *surplus* in 2018.

A more detailed future scenario of China's lifecycle surplus or deficit can be seen in Figure 4.7, in which we offer two sample scenarios, based on different assumptions. Instead of measuring the aggregate lifecycle surplus in terms of nominal currency as shown in Figure 4.6, we measure lifecycle surplus at the per capita level relative to the average labor income at prime working age (thirty to forty-nine). There are two main benefits to this approach – the measure can be interpreted as per capita saving rate, and it makes cross-year comparison more robust as such a measure requires no adjustment for external factors (e.g., inflation).

China's long-term change of lifecycle deficit will be largely driven by changes in population age structure. Regardless of the assumption used for per capita lifecycle deficit profiles, population aging will drive down per capita lifecycle surplus. According to population projections of the United Nations (2022 version), China's support ratio will drop from 2.7 around 2010 to 1.2 by 2056, and to less than 1 by the end of this century (right axis). Such a precipitous drop in the support ratio would drive the overall trend in lifecycle surplus. Whether China stays at the 2010 age profile or the 2018 age profile, the lifecycle surplus would be shrinking.

Lifecycle deficit profiles can also make a major difference. The future implied by the 2010 age profile is very different from what is implied

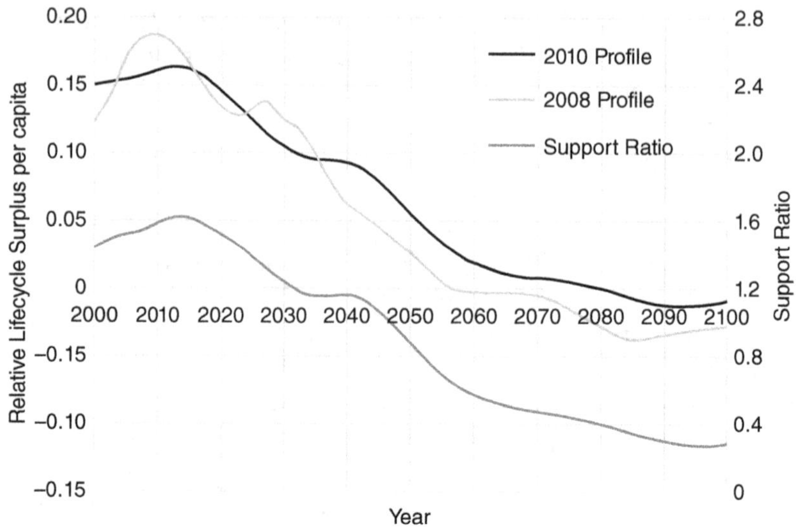

Figure 4.7 Projected support ratio and relative lifecycle surplus per capita by year
Source: Support ratio is calculated using WPP 2022. Relative lifecycle surplus per capita is defined as the ratio of per capita lifecycle surplus to the average labor income at prime working age (30–49).

by the 2018 age profile. As we have discussed, staying at the 2018 age profile would mean that China would exhaust its lifecycle surplus by the early 2030s and run an increasingly larger deficit thereafter. As a comparison, staying at the 2010 age profile means that China could retain the lifecycle surplus till the 2080s. It is doubtful, however, that China could return to its 2010 lifecycle profiles, with income increasing faster than consumption. Combined, population aging and China's new economy spell an inevitable end of the lifecycle surplus China has seen in the decades of its material abundance.

When the Abundance Ends: The Knowns and Unknowns of Population Aging

Sustained low fertility has already set China on the path of accelerating aging and population decline. By the end of this decade, according to the UN's projections, over 25 percent of China's population will be aged sixty and over. That's just a few years from now. By 2050, almost 30 percent of China's population is projected to be aged sixty-five and over. Despite calls to increase fertility, the reality is that programs and efforts at increasing fertility have almost never worked worldwide (Shen, Wang, and Cai 2020). Instead of trying to do the impossible, and indeed doing so can cause more harm than cure as women are once again targeted as birth machines, it is time to revisit and to appreciate how we got here and to embrace a new world with longer-living individuals. It is nevertheless also too premature and simplistic, if not mindless, to proclaim that population aging will "spell the end of the China century," let alone doom the world.

Population aging will certainly have profound impacts on the economy and society. The era of population-driven economic growth is ending globally. Global aging and population decline not due to wars, famines, and pandemics are both unprecedented in human history. There are hence more unknowns than knowns. Population aging may slow down global economic growth, push up public debt and fiscal pressure for governments to fund health care and pensions, and squeeze the living standards of working-age adults. Population aging, however, may also lead to increases in private assets and even higher labor productivity (Mason, Lee, and members of the NTA Network 2022).

For China, as the surplus started to shrink in the late 2010s, the need for transfers increased, and both public and private savings also started to expand, to fund lifecycle deficits. A study carried out by us suggests that, assuming China increases its social benefits generosity level by 2035 to reach the OECD's average level in 2009, not too drastic an assumption, population aging alone could double the share of pension spending as relative to GDP by 2035, to 15 percent. In the absence of rising government revenue as a share of GDP, such an increase could take up more than half of total government revenue by 2030. Pension alone could use up nearly *all* government revenue by 2050. Such changes associated with population aging may have amplified political implications for China, as the government has tied its political legitimacy to economic growth and welfare provision (Cai, Wang, and Shen 2018).

The impact of population change on the economy is by no means simple. As shown in our analyses of the lifecycle deficit using the NTA methodology, there are many moving parts. Both consumption and labor income can change in the future, as they have in the recent past. The high cost of housing, for instance, is not a measure of high living standards and is not sustainable. Sooner or later, it will have to come down. Rapid rise in the consumption of luxury goods is also likely, as seen in other recent high-growth economies, a transitional fad. Spending on health care could be made much more effective with new technologies, medicines, and especially reforms in the health care system. These are just a few examples that can affect the consumption side of the equation.

Perhaps more importantly, one can imagine similarly in numerous ways that labor productivity can increase, even if only modestly in comparison to the recent past. China's age of abundance has brought not only vastly improved physical infrastructure but also vast investment in its people, with both the public and private families spending on education, not just in young ages but also throughout life. In this sense, the consumption of education is an investment for production. Technological improvements, as well as institutional reforms such as further integrating migrants into cities, can lead to higher productivity. Current labor income age profiles, with peaking age still only at the early thirties, suggest raising retirement age now may not have the intended economic effect. But they also point to a future when labor income at older ages will rise, thus changing the calculation of lifecycle deficit.

Moreover, in this chapter we have only addressed one side of the lifecycle deficit equation, on consumption and labor income. Each entity on the other side of the equation, asset income, transfers (both in and out, and both public and private), and dissaving, can play an important role in making up the lifecycle deficit. Each entity of this equation is a moving part in the broad scheme of generational economy and can be affected by technological changes and especially by institutional reforms.

We begin this chapter with a review and reminder of how China's population turned from a curse to a fortune, starting at about four decades ago. The essence of this reminder is how institutions can make a difference. It was the abandonment of the planned-economy system and the allowance of individual freedom, economic and social, under a market- and law-based institution that made the reversal possible. As China steps into an era of slower economic growth and population decline, the same lesson still holds true.

References

Bloom, David, Canning, David, & Sevilla, Jaypee. 2003. *The Demographic Dividend: A New Perspective on the Economic Consequences of Population Change*. RAND Corporation. https://doi.org/10.7249/MR1274

Bloom, David E., & Williamson, Jeffrey G. 1998. "Demographic Transitions and Economic Miracles in Emerging Asia." *The World Bank Economic Review*, 12 (3): 419–455. https://doi.org/10.1093/wber/12.3.419

Cai, Yong, Wang, Feng, & Shen, Ke. 2018. "Fiscal Implications of Population Aging and Social Sector Expenditure in China." *Population and Development Review*, 44 (4): 811–831. www.jstor.org/stable/45174458

Eichengreen, Barry, Park, Donghyun, & Shin, Kwanho. 2012. "When Fast-growing Economies Slow Down: International Evidence and Implications for China." *Asian Economic Papers*, 11 (1): 42–87.

Fang, Hanming, Gu, Quanlin, Xiong, Wei, & Zhou, Li-An. 2015. "Demystifying the Chinese Housing Boom." In *NBER Macroeconomics Annual 2015, Volume 30*, edited by Martin Eichenbaum and Jonathan Parker (pp. 105–166). National Bureau of Economic Research, Inc. https://EconPapers.repec.org/RePEc:nbr:nberch:13595

Lee, James, & Wang, Feng. 1999. *One Quarter of Humanity: Malthusian Mythology and Chinese Realities, 1700–2000*. Harvard University Press.

Lee, Ronald. 2003. "The Demographic Transition: Three Centuries of Fundamental Change." *Journal of Economic Perspectives*, 17 (4): 167–190. https://doi.org/10.1257/089533003772034943

Lee, Ronald D., & Mason, Andrew. 2011. "Generational Economics in a Changing World." *Population and Development Review*, *37*: 115–142. www.jstor.org/stable/41762401

Lee, Ronald D., & Mason, Andrew. 2011a. "Lifecycles, Support Systems, and Generational Flows: Patterns and Change." In *Population Aging and the Generational Economy: A Global Perspective* edited by Ronald D. Lee and Andrew Mason (pp. 79–106).

Lee, Ronald, & Mason, Andrew. (Eds.). 2011b. *Population Aging and the Generational Economy: A Global Perspective*. Edward Elgar Publishing.

Mason, Andrew. 2001. Population Change and Economic Development: What Have We Learned from the East Asian Experience? *Applied Population and Policy, 1*, February.

Mason, Andrew, Lee, Ronald, & Members of the NTA Network. 2022. "Six Ways Population Change Will Affect the Global Economy." *Population and Development Review*, 48 (1): 51–73. https://doi.org/10.1111/padr.12469

Reher, David S. 2011. "Economic and Social Implications of the Demographic Transition." *Population and Development Review*, 37 (s1): 11–33. https://doi.org/10.1111/j.1728-4457.2011.00376.x

Shen, Ke, Wang, Feng, & Cai, Yong. 2020. "Government Policy and Global Fertility Change: A Reappraisal." *Asian Population Studies*, 16 (2): 145–166. https://doi.org/10.1080/17441730.2020.1757850

United Nations, Population Division. 2013. *Measuring and Analysing the Generational Economy: National Transfer Accounts Manual*. United Nations.

United Nations, Population Division. 2022. *World Population Prospects: 2022 Revision*. United Nations, New York, USA. https://population.un.org/wpp/

Wang, Feng. 2024. *China's Age of Abundance: Origins, Ascendance, and Aftermath*. Cambridge University Press.

Wang, Feng, Cai, Yong, Shen, Ke, & Gietel-Basten, S. 2018. "Is Demography Just a Numerical Exercise? Numbers, Politics, and Legacies of China's One-Child Policy." *Demography*, 55 (2): 693–719. https://doi.org/10.1007/s13524-018-0658-7

Wang, Feng, & Mason, Andrew. 2008. "The Demographic Factor in China's Transition." In *China's Great Economic Transformation*, edited by L. Brandt & T. G. Rawski (pp. 136–166). Cambridge University Press. https://doi.org/10.1017/CBO9780511754234.006

Xie, Yu, & Hu, Jingwei. 2014. "An Introduction to the China Family Panel Studies (CFPS)." *Chinese Sociological Review*, 47 (1): 3–29. https://doi.org/10.2753/CSA2162-0555470101.2014.11082908

5 Derisking Real Estate in China's Hybrid Economy

WEI XIONG

Over the past three decades, real estate has played a critical role in driving China's economic growth, with real estate investment contributing to approximately 10 percent of GDP and the real estate and construction sector accounting for over 15 percent of urban employment in recent years, for example, Rogoff and Yang (2021). But China's real estate sector is now facing a host of challenges. One of the most pressing issues is the debt problem that is plaguing many real estate firms. In 2021, Evergrande, one of the largest real estate companies in China (with a total asset of over 2.3 trillion RMB and a total debt of over 1.9 trillion RMB at the end of 2020), was on the brink of defaulting on some of its debt. This has led to concerns about the stability of the market and the broader financial system. In addition, concerns have been raised about the health of the Chinese real estate market due to drops in real estate prices, an increase in unsold housing inventory in many cities and a slowdown of the urbanization process, leading to further fears of a broader economic slowdown, for example, Glaeser et al. (2017) and Liu and Xiong (2020).

Moreover, in 2022, there have been reports of a boycott of mortgage payments by homeowners in some cities, which has put pressure on banks and further raised concerns about the financial stability of the banking sector. Finally, there are even more general concerns about China's demographics. In 2022, China's birth rate dropped below its death rate for the first time. As the population ages and the birth rate decreases, there may be a lack of long-run demand for housing, for example, Rogoff and Yang (2021). All of these challenges are adding to the uncertainty and risk not just in the Chinese economy, but also the potential contagion effects on the global economy.

To gain a better understanding of the challenges facing China's real estate market, it is important to consider it within the context of China's hybrid economy. Over the past forty years, China has adopted many features of free markets, but the government remains heavily involved in using direct and indirect measures to intervene in the economy. The Chinese economy is a mix of state-owned enterprises (SOEs) and private firms. Although private firms now account for over 70 percent of urban employment, they mostly operate in peripheral industries. On the other hand, through several rounds of SOE reforms, SOEs have become more profitable and tend to dominate strategically important industries. Moreover, the State continues to set overall direction and goals for the economy through the Five-Year Plans and other economic planning. It uses promotion and other career incentives to direct and motivate local governments and SOEs to implement its economic planning. Additionally, incentives such as tax subsidies and financial grants, regulations, and administrative orders are used to guide private firms.

Despite initial expectations that China would eventually adopt a free-market economy similar to Western countries, this outcome appears unlikely in the near future. Instead, the current Chinese leadership has affirmed its commitment to maintaining a hybrid economy that blends elements of a planned economy with those of a market economy. This hybrid economy is intended to allow the state to have a strong capacity to intervene during economic downturns and to overcome market externalities while also capitalizing on the market's economic efficiencies. See Xiong (2023) for an overview of China's hybrid economy.

The real estate sector is a vital part of China's hybrid economy, and the challenges it faces are closely tied to this structure. Figure 5.1 illustrates the hybrid structure of China's real estate sector. The government controls the supply of land, which is the primary input for real estate development, and local governments use revenue from land sales to fund infrastructure and urban development projects. Meanwhile, real estate properties are sold to households and firms in a relatively free market environment. Banks provide debt financing (either directly through bank loans or indirectly through purchasing publicly issued bonds) to all participants in the real estate sector: local governments, which often use future land sale revenues and unsold land as collateral to obtain bank loans; real estate firms, which use land holdings and unsold real estate properties as collateral to finance ongoing projects; households, which take mortgage loans to finance their housing purchases; and firms, which use real

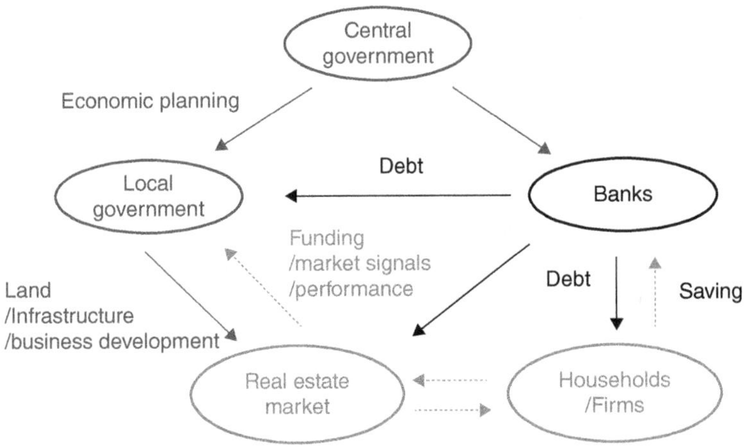

Figure 5.1 China's real estate sector

estate properties as collateral to finance their real estate purchases or other investments.

This hybrid structure allows the local government to provide infrastructure and public goods, facilitating local businesses and boosting economic growth and development. The real estate market provides feedback to the government's development plan, allowing it to respond to market signals and make informed decisions about urban development and local businesses. Moreover, the market serves as a mechanism to hold the government accountable for implementing its development plan. When this hybrid model functions optimally, state intervention and the market complement each other, balancing market externalities and promoting economic efficiency. However, if the interactions between these two forces are not appropriately managed, they may exacerbate market externalities and undermine economic efficiency.

The hybrid structure may lead to overinvestment and overleverage in China's real estate sector due to several forces. First, local governments are responsible for implementing the central government's economic and social policies, with land sales being a crucial source of fiscal funding for them. Therefore, the central government's policy agenda can significantly impact the real estate sector through its role as the financing channel of local governments, even if the policies are not directly related to real estate. Secondly, local government officials are incentivized by the central government's evaluations of their job performance, which can create short-term incentives for local governments to overinvest in infrastructure to boost local economies and overspend in projects mandated by the central government. These short-term incentives can create funding pressures that lead to incentives to boost local real estate markets so that local governments can sell more land at higher prices.

These short-term incentives are particularly concerning when local governments can use debt financing. Although the central government prohibited local governments from using debt financing before 2008 to discipline the "soft budget problem" of local governments, it granted local governments access to debt financing to implement China's massive post-crisis stimulus in 2008–2010. Since then, local governments have increasingly used debt to finance their operations. The debt financing used by local governments is typically collateralized by future land sales, land, or real estate properties and is typically in the form of bank loans and public debt directly taken by local governments or indirectly through local government financing vehicles (LGFVs).

Real estate-related debt accounts for about 25 percent of banks' assets in China, and around half of it is connected to local governments, according to Liu and Xiong (2020). Such heavy exposure of banks to the real estate sector makes it systemically important. If a real estate crash were to occur, it could lead to significant bank losses and even trigger a banking crisis. This situation creates an environment where the real estate sector is seen as "too important to fail." Therefore, both central and local governments feel pressure to provide implicit and explicit guarantees to protect the real estate sector from a potential crash. When the real estate market is under distress, the central government may adjust its macroeconomic and monetary policies and loosen mortgage requirements to support the market, while local governments may take direct measures to prevent real estate prices from falling. During real estate downturns, it is common for local governments to remove restrictions on investment home purchases. In some cases, local governments have even issued administrative orders to prohibit real estate firms from reducing residential housing prices below certain limits, as seen during the COVID-19 pandemic.

The explicit or implicit guarantees provided by the government create moral hazard and distortions in both state intervention and the market, thus providing a third channel for overinvestment and overleverage in the real estate sector. With the guarantees from the central government, local governments may be more inclined to use real estate-collateralized debt to boost their short-term performance, further exacerbating the soft-budget problem. Such short-term behaviors may prioritize real estate development over other areas of economic growth, exacerbating local governments' incentives to deliver their development plans. Furthermore, anticipating both central and local governments' incentives to protect the real estate market, real estate firms may have incentives to overbuild real estate properties, and households and nonreal estate firms may engage in reckless real estate speculation. Such speculation may distort market prices and reduce the informativeness of real estate prices as market signals. Adding these distortions together, state intervention and the market can exacerbate each other and amplify externalities in the real estate sector, ultimately jeopardizing the financial stability of the real estate sector and worsening the economic efficiency of the wider economy.

The hybrid structure of China's real estate market means that its risks are distinct from those faced by the U.S. real estate market in the mid-2000s. The decline of the U.S. real estate market in 2006 eventually led to the failure of Lehman Brothers in 2008 and a full-blown global financial crisis. Coordination failure, as identified by the seminal work of three Nobel laureates, Diamond and Dybvig (1983), on a theory of bank runs, and Bernanke (2018), on a diagnosis of the 2008 World Financial Crisis, is one of the root causes of financial crises in market economies. When some depositors rush to exit by cashing out, forced liquidation may lead to an otherwise healthy bank's failure, and the cascading effects may drag down other healthy financial institutions, leading to a system-wide financial crisis.

The Chinese government's commitment to financial stability and ability to mobilize local governments, state banks, and SOEs make a western-style debt crisis less likely. The recent example of the Evergrande crisis showed the government's determination and capacity to prevent a potential financial crisis by privately instructing local governments to sort out Evergrande's financial situation and organizing a partial bailout through state-owned banks and firms. Given the vital importance of the real estate sector to the Chinese economy, it is expected that the government will intervene to prevent a financial meltdown and mitigate a hard landing of the market in any future real estate crisis.

While government intervention can help to postpone the disruption of a financial crisis, it may not resolve the structural challenges faced by the real estate sector, which is a crucial part of the Chinese economy. A slowdown in this sector could have significant spillover effects on related industries, such as construction, manufacturing, and finance. This could lead to a decline in economic growth, job losses, and reduced consumer confidence, which could further dampen economic growth. Moreover, if the government uses too much stimulus to prop up the real estate market, it could lead to other economic problems such as misallocation of capital, inflation, and financial instability in the long run. Ultimately, the risk of the real estate sector in China is the economic growth risk, which encompasses the broader effects of a potential real estate downturn on the country's economic growth, employment, and stability.

A real estate downturn is particularly difficult for China's hybrid economy, as the country has historically relied on government-led infrastructure investments to spur economic growth during downturns. Local governments depend heavily on revenue from land sales to fund public infrastructure and social services, including the extensive COVID-19 lockdown policies. In recent years, land sales have accounted for approximately 40 percent of their total revenue. Thus, a slowdown in the real estate market not only creates substantial pressure on the economy but also limits the fiscal capacity of local governments to stimulate economic growth.

Ultimately, the path to derisk China's real estate sector is to find new growth engines for the Chinese economy. Over the past few decades, the real estate sector has been a significant contributor to China's economic growth. However, as the sector faces mounting challenges and risks, policymakers must look for new sources of growth. One proposed solution is to transform China's economy to be more driven by internal consumption rather than exports. However, this transition necessitates the bolstering of consumer confidence and enabling consumers to power the economy, which may not align seamlessly with the state-driven economic model.

In addition to finding new growth engines, policymakers must also find a new financing model for local governments, replacing the reliance on land sale revenues. This could involve exploring alternative sources of revenue for local governments, such as property taxes or other forms of taxation. However, introducing property taxes may face political resistance, as many homeowners in China have treated their properties as an investment, which makes it difficult for them to accept their properties as a basis of taxation. Imposing property taxes would also put pressure on housing prices in the short run, making it even more difficult for local governments to sell land and homeowners to increase their consumption.

The hybrid structure of the real estate sector makes it particularly vulnerable to policy risks. If the central government sets overly ambitious growth targets, local officials may be pressured to rely on land sales or debt financing to fund more infrastructure projects, exacerbating the already high leverage and debt levels of both local governments and real estate developers. This could lead to further systemic risks and worsen the economic efficiency of the economy. Moreover, the government's new policy agenda on common prosperity and other priorities, as examined by Huang (2023) and Naughton (2023), may also shift the hybrid economic system's long-standing focus away from economic growth. This redirection could further slow down growth, thereby increasing pressure on the real estate sector.

The extensive state interventions to maintain financial stability resemble the strategy of binding all boats together to weather a storm, famously employed by the northern army of Cao Cao during the renowned Battle of Chibi in the winter of 208–209 AD during the Three Kingdoms period in ancient China. However, this strategy also exposes the entire system to an unforeseen fire that could burn all boats simultaneously. In other words, if a shock were to ultimately trigger an economic collapse within the Chinese economy, the real estate sector might amplify the shock and collapse along with the economy.

Therefore, it is crucial that the central government take a prudent and sustainable approach to managing the economy and the real estate sector, prioritizing the stability and sustainability of both over short-term economic and political goals. Structural transformation toward a more consumption-driven economy, investing in new growth engines, and promoting a more balanced supply-demand relationship in the real estate sector can create a stable and sustainable economic environment that benefits all stakeholders and thus gradually reduce the risks in the real estate sector.

The Hybrid Real Estate Model

China's transformation from an agriculture-driven economy to an industry-driven economy has been accompanied by a massive wave of urbanization. As economic opportunities shifted from rural areas to cities, millions of people have migrated from the countryside to urban areas in search of better jobs and living standards. This has led to the rapid expansion of cities and the growth of new urban centers. The government has played a significant role in this process, implementing policies and investments aimed at promoting urbanization and improving the living standards of urban residents. This has included the construction of new housing and infrastructure, the development of new industries and employment opportunities, and the improvement of public services such as education and healthcare. The result has been a dramatic shift in the economic structure of China, with a growing share of the population and the economy now concentrated in urban areas. See Liu and Xiong (2020) and Rogoff and Yang (2021) for a summary of China's urbanization process.

In western economies, property tax is a commonly used funding source to pay for local government services and infrastructure. The tax is based on the estimated value of real property, including land and buildings, and is collected by the local government. The funds collected from property taxes are used to pay for a variety of services, including schools, public safety, roads and highways, parks, and other essential services. The specific uses of property tax revenue can vary from one jurisdiction to another, but it is a crucial source of funding for many western economies.

This property-tax-based funding model, as it is used in western countries, had not been a feasible option for China's urbanization. In the early stages of China's urbanization in the 1990s and 2000s, most cities were still underdeveloped and property values were relatively low, making it difficult to generate significant revenue through property taxes. Additionally, the majority of urban housing in China was owned by the government, which meant that the government could not collect property taxes from itself. Debt financing by local governments was not a viable option for funding China's urbanization in its early stages because it would have exacerbated the "soft budget constraint" problem. The "soft budget constraint" refers to the tendency of local governments to overextend their budgets without sufficient consequences, as the central government is ultimately liable for the debts of local governments. To discipline local governments and prevent them from over-extending their budgets, the central government had to restrict their use of debt financing. As a result, China has relied on other sources of revenue, such as land sales and urban maintenance and construction taxes, to fund its urbanization efforts.[1]

In particular, China has resorted to land sales as an alternative source of funding for its infrastructure development and urbanization, drawing on the experience of Hong Kong. By the Chinese constitution, the government owns all of the land, and the local government in a city can lease a parcel of land to individuals and businesses for a specified period of time. By selling such land usage rights (which are also called land sales), local governments across China have generated significant revenue to fund a wide range of infrastructure projects, including the construction of housing, roads, public transportation systems, and other essential services. The use of land sales to fund infrastructure development has been a key factor in China's rapid urbanization and economic development.

The land sales-based model of funding local government infrastructure development and urbanization in China reflects the overall structure of China's hybrid economy, which combines elements of a planned economy with elements of a market economy. By providing infrastructure often as public goods and facilitating local businesses, the government attracts investment and more immigrants from rural areas and other cities, boosting economic growth and development. Furthermore, the real estate market provides an important feedback loop to the government's development plan, allowing it to respond to market signals and make informed decisions about the allocation of resources and the development of urban areas, while also serving as a mechanism to discipline the government's efforts in implementing its development plan.

Buying a piece of land in a city is like acquiring a stake in the city's equity, as the value of the land is determined not just by the current

[1] It's useful to note that the tax-sharing reform in 1994, led by Zhu Rongji, the powerful vice premier at the time, shifted a larger proportion of the total budgetary revenue to the central government, which put even more pressure on local governments to find alternative sources of revenue for local spending.

payoff provided by the land but also by the expected future payoff. The market's willingness to pay for the land is therefore largely influenced by its expectation of the city's future development. For this reason, it is crucial for the local government to outline an ambitious development plan for the city, which helps to boost the market's valuation of the land. A convincing development plan can help to increase the confidence of the real estate market in the future infrastructure and economy of the city, even if the city currently lacks sufficient infrastructure and a booming economy. This increased confidence can allow the local government to generate a large amount of revenue based on the market's expectation of the city's future economy, which can then be used to fund the current infrastructure development.

The need for local governments to regularly sell land provides a strong incentive for them to deliver on their development plans. Failure to do so would lead to lower expectations for the future development of the city, resulting in a decreased valuation of the land and reduced revenue from land sales. This incentivizes local governments to implement their development plans efficiently and sustainably. The land sales-based funding model provides an incentive-compatible scheme for local governments to exert efforts to implement their development plans and ensure the city's sustainable and efficient development. Market prices for land and real estate properties also provide valuable information and feedback to the local government regarding their development plan. For example, higher prices for land and properties in one district relative to another district can indicate the relative strength of the development plans for the two districts, enabling the government to adjust its plans accordingly. See Xiong (2023) for more general discussions of how the market may complement the state planning by providing both incentives and information feedback to the government in China's hybrid economy.

Excesses of the Hybrid Model

In addition to the complementarity between the state and the market, the hybrid structure of China's real estate sector exposes it to potential weaknesses in China's hierarchical government system, also known as the Mandarin system. This centralized government structure is characterized by decisions made at the highest levels of the government and passed down to lower levels. As a result, the real estate market in

China is heavily influenced by policies and agendas of the central government, as well as the efficiency and incentives of local governments in implementing these policies. Song and Xiong (2023) provide a theoretical model that analyzes how career incentives of local officials within the Mandarin system may impact China's economic growth. This section explores several structural forces within the system that can contribute to the over-reliance of local governments on the real estate sector to finance their investments. This reliance is further compounded by market forces, leading to overinvestment and overleverage in the real estate sector.

The Financing Channel

Land sales are a critical source of fiscal funding for local governments, which are responsible for implementing the central government's economic and social policies. Therefore, the central government's policy agenda can significantly impact the real estate sector through its role as the financing channel of local governments, even if the policies are not directly related to real estate.

The aftermath of the 2008 global financial crisis provides a vivid example of this channel. In response to the crisis, the Chinese government launched an extensive economic stimulus package aimed at boosting growth and stabilizing the economy. The package included measures to increase infrastructure development and investment. While these measures stimulated infrastructure development, local governments primarily financed them through debt financing backed by revenue from future land sales, as they were unable to sell enough land in a short period to fund all the required projects.

Before the crisis, the central government prohibited local governments from using unauthorized debt financing to control the "soft budget constraint" problem. However, to facilitate the large-scale stimulus, the central government relaxed this restriction and allowed local governments to raise debt financing through LGFVs.[2] These companies were established by local governments for the purpose of

[2] See Bai, Hsieh, and Song (2016) for a comprehensive summary of this debt-financed stimulus. Cong et al. (2019), Chen, He, and Liu (2020), and Huang, Pagano, and Panizza (2020) provide further analysis to show that the debt incurred by local governments during the stimulus crowd out credit from banks to private firms and lead to the large expansion of shadow banking in China.

raising debt financing. Consequently, local governments borrowed trillions of RMB in bank loans, often backed by future land sale revenues. This significant increase in local governments' debt further increased their dependence on land sales for revenue and put pressure on the real estate market to perform well to generate sufficient revenue for debt repayment.

This episode highlights the possibility that to fulfill the central government's policy agenda, local governments may have to resort to not only selling more land but also utilizing land-collateralized leverage. This may result in overinvestment and overleverage in the real estate sector.

The Tournament Channel

Another factor contributing to the over-reliance of local governments on land sales and debt financing collateralized by future land sales is the economic tournament among local officials. This phenomenon refers to the competition among local officials for career advancement and promotion by boosting the local economy and improving infrastructure, as highlighted by Li and Zhou (2005), Zhou (2007), and Fang, Li, and Wu (2025). This competition can lead to a "race to the bottom" in terms of debt financing and dependence on the real estate market, as suggested by Song and Xiong (2023).

To compete with officials from other regions in the central government's performance evaluations, local officials have incentives to use debt financing backed by future land sale revenues to fund short-term infrastructure investments and improve short-term economic performance, adding pressure on the real estate market to perform well. Since local governments' ability to repay debt and fund future projects depends on revenue generated from land sales, the economic tournament among local officials can exacerbate the use of debt financing, leading to a cycle of dependence on the real estate market and increasing pressure on it to perform well.

The Central Government Guarantee Channel

The explicit or implicit guarantees provided by the government for the real estate sector may further exacerbate overinvestment and overleverage in the real estate market. The reliance of local governments on real estate-collateralized debt makes the real estate market systemically important in China. A downturn in the real estate market can have far-reaching consequences, not only for local governments in terms of a fiscal crisis but also for the banking system. According to Liu and Xiong (2020), 25 percent of banking assets in China are exposed to the real estate market, including loans made to local governments, mortgage loans to home buyers, and business loans to real estate developers. This high level of banks' exposure to the real estate sector highlights the systemic importance of the sector.

In the event of a downturn in real estate prices triggering a systemic banking crisis that significantly impacts the wider economy, there would be strong pressure on the central government to support the real estate market and prevent prices from falling. To this end, the central government has implemented a wide range of counter-cyclical policy measures to mitigate real estate market fluctuations. As Song and Xiong (2018) summarize, when the real estate market is considered overheated, the central government tends to tighten mortgage down payment requirements and raise mortgage interest rates. Conversely, when the real estate market is considered depressed, the central government tends to loosen these measures and may even use monetary policy to provide additional support. However, such interventions may undermine the usefulness of real estate prices as indicators for urban development and local economic performance.[3] Consequently, the systemic importance of the real estate sector can fundamentally alter its role as a mechanism for providing feedback and disciplining local governments.

The government's support for the real estate market, in turn, may encourage not only local governments but also real estate companies, households, and nonreal estate firms to seek risk in the real estate market. With guarantees from the central government, local governments would be more inclined to use real estate-collateralized debt to boost their short-term performance, further exacerbating their soft-budget problem. This could lead to a cycle of over-leverage and risk-taking, undermining the financial stability of the real estate market and the wider economy.

[3] Geng and Pan (2024) offer systematic evidence demonstrating that government support results in a significant premium for debt financing of state firms compared to private firms in China's credit market.

Moreover, recognizing the central government's support, other market participants would also be motivated to seek risk in the real estate sector. For example, real estate companies may become overly aggressive in their investments, taking on excessive leverage to maximize their profits. This can lead to the rapid expansion of companies like Evergrande, which had taken on a significant amount of debt to fund its expansion before its debt crisis. While this strategy may generate short-term gains, it also increases the risk of default, which can have significant consequences for the real estate sector and the broader economy.

In addition, households may also become more willing to take on debt to purchase properties, including investment homes, assuming that the government will protect them from downside risks. This can lead to a speculative frenzy in the real estate market, causing a significant increase in property prices, as analyzed by Chen and Wen (2017) and Chen et al. (2022). Moreover, nonreal estate firms may also be incentivized to enter the real estate market, diverting resources from other sectors of the economy. This can create distortions in the allocation of resources, hindering long-term economic growth, as studied by Chen et al. (2017).

Through these distortions together, the state planning and the market may also exacerbate each other, leading to increased risk-taking by market participants in the real estate sector. This, in turn, can lead to excessive leverage and a distortion in the allocation of resources, as the real estate sector becomes the primary focus of investment, diverting resources from other sectors of the economy. These outcomes can have significant long-term implications for economic growth and development.

The Real Estate Sector during the Covid Period

In this section, I provide a summary of the market dynamics of the real estate sector, with a focus on the Covid pandemic period in 2020–2022.

Land Sales

Under the Chinese constitution, land is owned by the state, and local governments are responsible for administering the use of land. Local governments regularly sell land usage rights to the market through a process known as land sales. The duration of these usage rights typically ranges from thirty years for industrial land, which is restricted for use in industrial facilities, to forty years for commercial land, which is restricted for use in commercial and business facilities, and seventy years for residential land, which is restricted for use in residential development. The revenue from land sales has contributed to about 40 percent of the fiscal budget of local governments in recent years. See the recent review by Gyourko et al. (2022) of the land-based fiscal finance in China.

Figure 5.2 provides a summary of the aggregate annual land sales from 2015 to 2022 for residential land, commercial land, and industrial land. Panel A displays the total revenue generated from land sales for the three types of land. Residential land sales account for more than 50 percent of the total land sale revenue for local governments in each of the years from 2015 to 2022. The revenue from residential land sales steadily increased from 1,047 billion RMB in 2015 to a peak of 3,625 billion RMB in 2020, before dropping to 2,564 billion RMB in 2022. Meanwhile, the revenue from commercial land sales is substantially lower than that of residential land, fluctuating between its lowest value of 631 billion RMB in 2015 and its highest value of 929 billion RMB in 2020. However, during the Covid pandemic period from 2020 to 2022, the revenue from commercial land sales dropped by 29 percent to 662 billion RMB in 2022. In contrast, the revenue from industrial land sales is the lowest among the three types of land but has increased steadily from 259 billion RMB in 2015 to 541 billion RMB in 2022. The sharp drops in the revenue generated from residential and commercial land sales during the Covid period of 2020–2022 have contributed to the fiscal distress faced by local governments.

Panel B presents the total quantity of land sales for the three types of land. Even though industrial land contributes to the lowest revenue among the three types of land, the quantity of industrial land sales is the largest. The quantity of industrial land sales has increased from 105,314 hectares in 2015 to 170,995 hectares in 2022. The quantity of commercial land sales is the lowest among the three and has fluctuated between its lowest value of 24,891 hectares in 2017 and its highest value of 32,394 hectares in 2020. During the Covid period, the quantity of commercial land sales dropped by 26 percent to 23,963

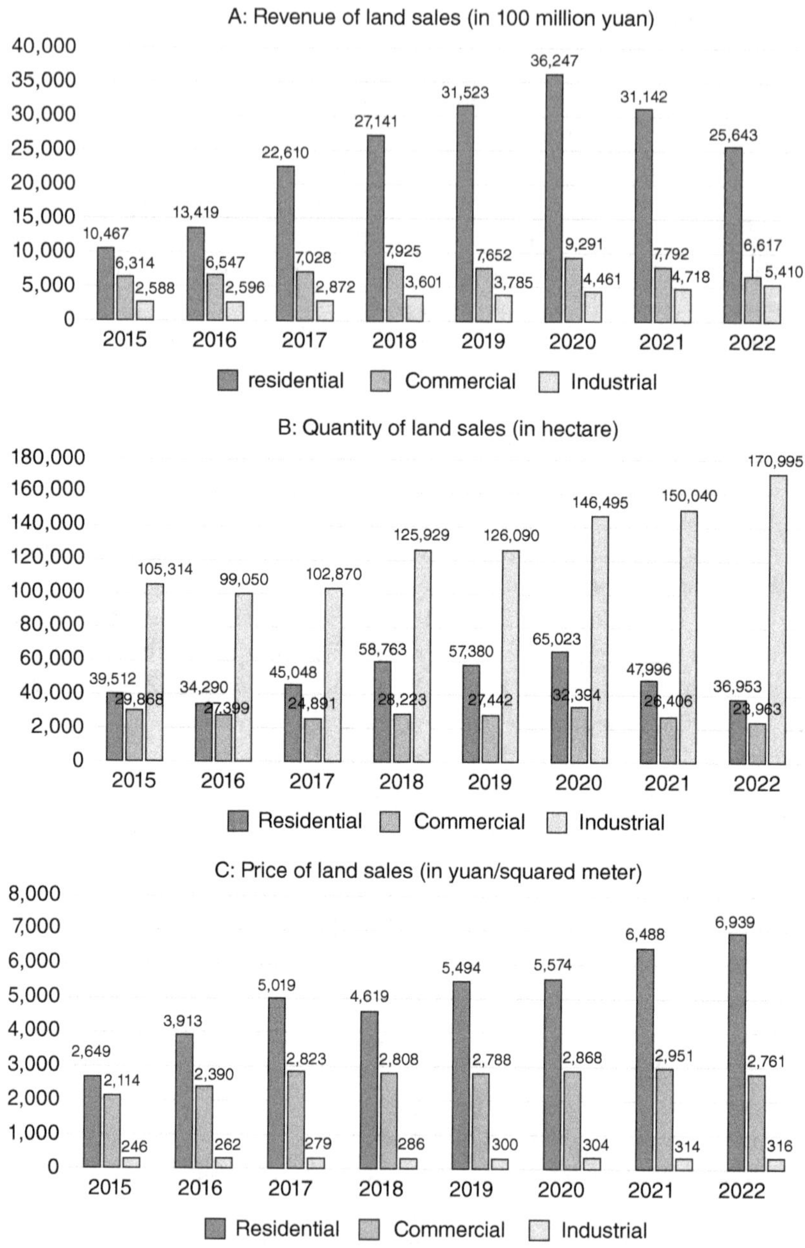

Figure 5.2 Land sales in 2015–2022
This figure reports revenue, quantity, and price of land sales from the CREIS database of China Index Academy, which collects data from local land transaction centers and the China Land Market website (www.landchina.com). The data used in this figure covers over 2,300 cities and counties across China in 2015–2022.

hectares in 2022. In contrast, the quantity of residential land sales initially increased from 39,512 hectares in 2015 to 65,023 hectares in 2020, but then dropped during the Covid period by 43 percent to 36,953 hectares in 2022.

Panel C shows the average annual prices for the three types of land, determined by the total revenue divided by the total quantity of each type of land sale. This average land sale price does not control for the difference in quality of land sold in each of the years and is thus different from a typical land price index. See Wu, Gyourko, and Deng (2012) for a widely used land price index for major cities in China. Nevertheless, the average land sale price provides a useful measure of land price change over time. Residential land is the most expensive among the three and experienced the largest price increase in 2015–2022. The average price of residential land increased from 2,649 yuan per square meter in 2015 to 6,939 yuan per square meter in 2022, representing a rise of more than 136 percent. Interestingly, even since the outbreak of the Covid pandemic in early 2020, the price of residential land has continued to rise, increasing by 27 percent from 2020 to 2022. This large increase in the average price of residential land sharply contrasts the large drop in the quantity of residential land sales during the Covid period, indicating a potential mismatch between demand and price.[4]

On the other hand, commercial land has been sold at a lower average price than residential land, ranging from 2,114 yuan per square meter in 2015 to a peak of 2,951 yuan per square meter in 2021. After reaching its peak, the price of commercial land remained relatively stable around 2,800 yuan per square meter. Meanwhile, industrial land is sold at much lower prices than residential and commercial land and has experienced a steady price increase trend over the years, with the average price rising from 246 yuan per square meter in 2015 to 316 yuan per square meter in 2022. The substantially lower prices of industrial land reflect the Chinese government's policy of discounting industrial land to subsidize industrial development, as analyzed by a recent paper of He et al. (2022).

[4] In a normal market equilibrium, an increase in price can be associated with a decrease in transaction quantity if there is a supply shortage. However, this may not be the case in China's real estate market during this period, as local governments are short of funding and thus motivated to sell more land.

Figure 5.3 provides a summary of the sales of residential land (the main source of land sale revenue to local governments) across three different tiers of cities: first-tier cities (the four largest metropolitan areas, Beijing, Shanghai, Guangzhou, and Shenzhen), second-tier cities (provincial capitals and major cities), and third-tier cities (smaller cities). Panel A shows the revenue from residential land sales. In the pre-Covid period from 2015 to 2020, the revenue from residential land sales has sharply increased for all three tiers of cities. It increased from 135 billion RMB to 354 billion RMB for the four first-tier cities, from 364 billion RMB to 1,268 billion RMB for second-tier cities, and from 548 billion to 2,003 billion for third-tier cities. However, during the Covid period, the revenue from residential land sales dropped for second-tier cities and third-tier cities, while it continued to rise for the four first-tier cities. The drop of 23 percent in the second-tier cities is substantial, while the drop of 41.5 percent in the third-tier cities is particularly large and consistent with the stress highlighted by the recent report of Rogoff and Yang (2023). In contrast, the four first-tier cities even had an increase of 18 percent from 2020 to 2022, indicating strong real estate demand in these cities despite the Covid pandemic.

Panel B shows that the quantity of residential land sales in second-tier and third-tier cities experienced significant increases prior to 2020, followed by substantial drops during the Covid period between 2020 and 2022. Specifically, there was a 42 percent drop in the quantity of residential land sales for second-tier cities and a 44 percent drop for third-tier cities during this period. Interestingly, Panel C indicates that from 2020 to 2022, the average land price in second-tier cities experienced a large increase of 33 percent, while the average land price in third-tier cities also saw a modest increase of 3.9 percent. This highlights a sharp contrast between the quantity drop and price increase in residential land sales in both second-tier and third-tier cities. This contrast again indicates a potential mismatch between demand and price.

Residential Properties

Figure 5.4 presents a summary of residential property transactions in the primary market across the three tiers of cities from 2015 to 2022. Panels A and B illustrate two measures of the quantities of residential property transactions, one by the total area of transacted properties

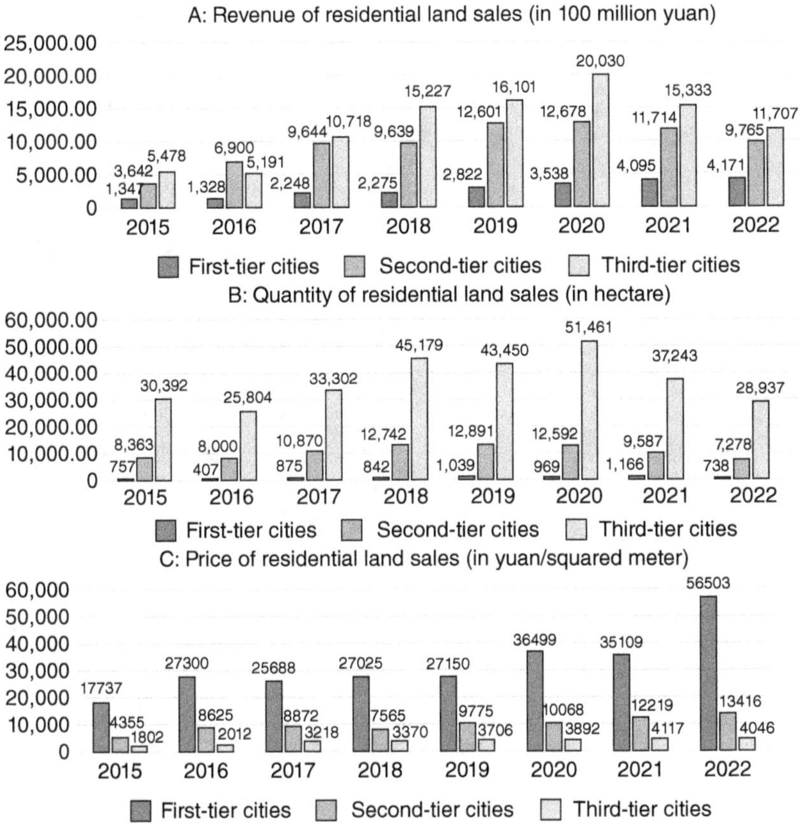

Figure 5.3 Residential land sales in three tiers of cities in 2015–2022
This figure reports revenue, quantity, and price of land sales from the CREIS database of China Index Academy, which collects data from local land transaction centers and the China Land Market website (www.landchina.com). The data covers 355 cities across China in 2015–2022. First-tier cities include four cities: Beijing, Shanghai, Guangzhou, and Shenzhen. Second-tier cities include thirty-five cities: Tianjin, Chongqing, Hangzhou, Nanjing, Wuhan, Chengdu, Suzhou, Dalian, Xiamen, Xi'an, Changsha, Ningbo, Wuxi, Fuzhou, Shenyang, Qingdao, Jinan, Nanchang, Hefei, Zhengzhou, Taiyuan, Shijiazhuang, Changchun, Harbin, Hohhot, Haikou, Nanning, Lanzhou, Kunming, Guiyang, Xining, Yinchuan, Urumqi, Wenzhou, and Sanya. Third-tier cities include the remaining 316 cities covered by the dataset, which are sometimes further classified as third- and fourth-tier cities in other reports.

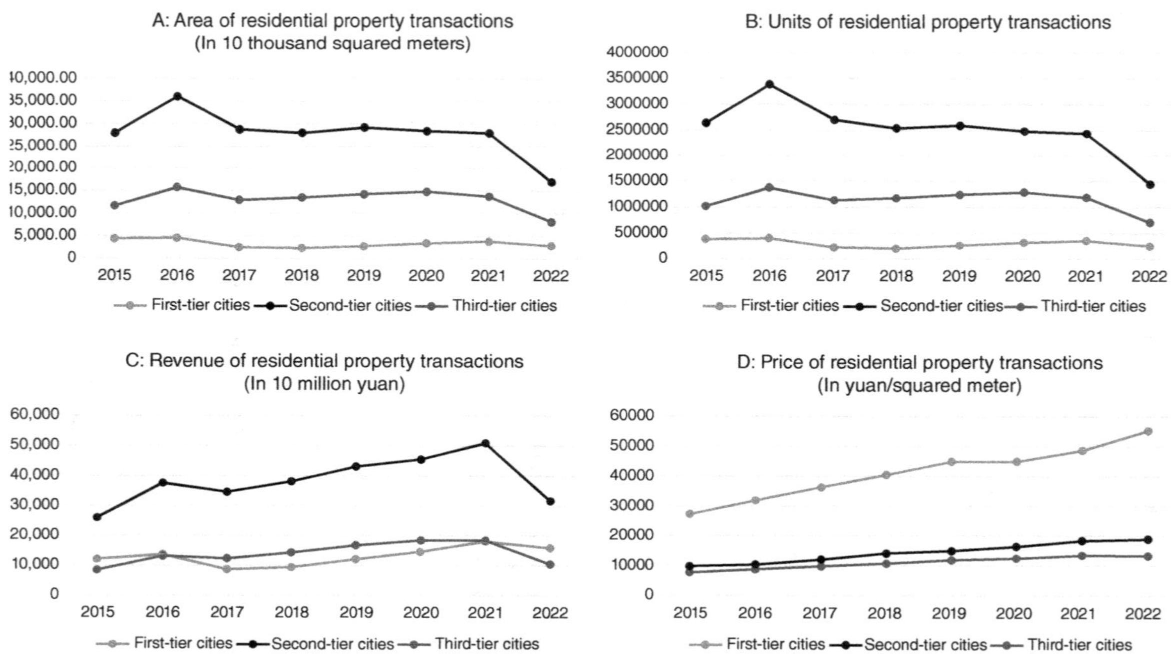

Figure 5.4 Residential property transactions across three tiers of cities in 2015–2022

This figure reports residential property transactions in the primary market from the CRIC database, which collects information from the Housing Management Bureau. The plots are based on four first-tier cities, twenty-nine second-tier cities, and thirty-six third-tier cities, which do not have any missing data in 2015–2022. The first-tier cities include Beijing, Shanghai, Guangzhou, and Shenzhen. The second-tier cities include Dalian, Fuzhou, Guiyang, Jinan, Kunming, Lanzhou, Nanchang, Nanning, Xiamen, Shenyang, Changchun, Wenzhou, Wuxi, Haikou, Xining, Sanya, Chengdu, Hangzhou, Hefei, Nanjing, Ningbo, Qingdao, Suzhou, Tianjin, Wuhan, Xian, Changsha, Zhengzhou, and Chongqing. The third-tier cities include Changzhou, Huizhou, Nantong, Quanzhou, Xuzhou, Yantai, Zhongshan, Zhuhai, Dongying, Hengyang, Huaian, Jiujiang, Langfang, Liuzhou, Luoyang, Qingyuan, Shantou, Shaoguan, Taizhou, Wuhu, Yancheng, Yueyang, Zhangzhou, Zhaoqing, Zhenjiang, Zibo, Jiangyin, Jinjiang, Kunshan, Taicang, Yixing, Guan, Xianghe, Yanjiao, Dongguan, and Foshan.

and the other by the number of units. These measures indicate that the majority of residential property transactions occurred in second-tier cities, while the least occurred in first-tier cities. During the Covid period of 2020–2022, there were significant drops in the quantities of residential property transactions across all three tiers of cities. By the area of transacted properties, the drop was 11 percent for first-tier cities, 40 percent for second-tier cities, and 45 percent for third-tier cities. By the number of transacted units, the drop was 13 percent for first-tier cities, 42 percent for second-tier cities, and 45 percent for third-tier cities.

Panel C displays the total value of residential property transactions, while Panel D shows the average price of the transacted properties measured by the total value divided by the total area of transacted properties. Interestingly, from 2020 to 2022, the total value increased by 9 percent in first-tier cities despite the 11 percent drop in the total area of transacted properties, implying that the average price increased by 22 percent. During the same period, the total value of residential property transactions dropped by 31 percent in second-tier cities and by 42 percent in third-tier cities, implying that the average price increased by 16 percent and 7 percent, respectively.

There is a consistent trend across the three tiers of cities, where despite a significant decrease in the quantity of residential property transactions during the Covid period of 2020–2022, the average price increased instead of decreasing. This sharp contrast in the quantity drop and price increase further highlights a mismatch between the demand and price of residential properties, which is in line with the previously discussed mismatch in the demand and price of residential land.

To determine if a supply shortage is causing the price increase and transaction quantity decrease, Figure 5.5 examines the ratio of housing inventory to annual sales. Panel A shows that at the national level, the ratio of inventory to sales has remained stable around 1.1 but increased to 2.1 in 2022. This suggests that it will take 2.1 years to deplete the housing inventory at the current sales rate. Panel B shows that the ratio of inventory to sales increased in 2022 across the three tiers of cities, with the largest increase in third-tier cities and the smallest increase in first-tier cities. This evidence indicates that a supply shortage may not be the cause of the price increase and transaction quantity decrease in the real estate market, as the ratio of housing inventory to sales has significantly increased in 2022.

Figure 5.5 Ratio of inventory to annual sales in 2015–2022
This figure reports inventory of residential properties in the primary market from the CREIS database. The data cover 172 cities, including the 4 first-tier cities and 35 second-tier cities defined in Figure 5.3, as well as 146 other cities. Due to missing data, the figure uses available cities for each of the years in 2015–2022.

Figure 5.6 presents the housing price index provided by the National Bureau of Statistics (NBS) of China for the seventy largest cities, which provides a measure of housing price fluctuations after controlling for the potential change in the quality of transacted properties.[5] Panel A reports the annual price increase (December to December) for primary market transactions, while Panel B reports the annual price increase for secondary market transactions.

According to the NBS housing price index, the primary market transactions in first-tier cities saw a modest price increase of 4.4 percent and 2.5 percent in 2021 and 2022, respectively, while second-tier cities experienced a price increase of 2.85 percent in 2021 and a price drop of –1.14 percent in 2022. Third-tier cities experienced a price increase of 0.93 percent in 2021 and a price drop of –3.86 percent in

[5] Fang et al. (2015) have constructed a housing price index for 120 cities in China in 2003–2013 by using an extensive dataset of mortgage loans from a state bank. Their index shows substantially larger housing appreciation in 2003–2013 than the NBS housing price index, possibly due to different controls used for housing quality.

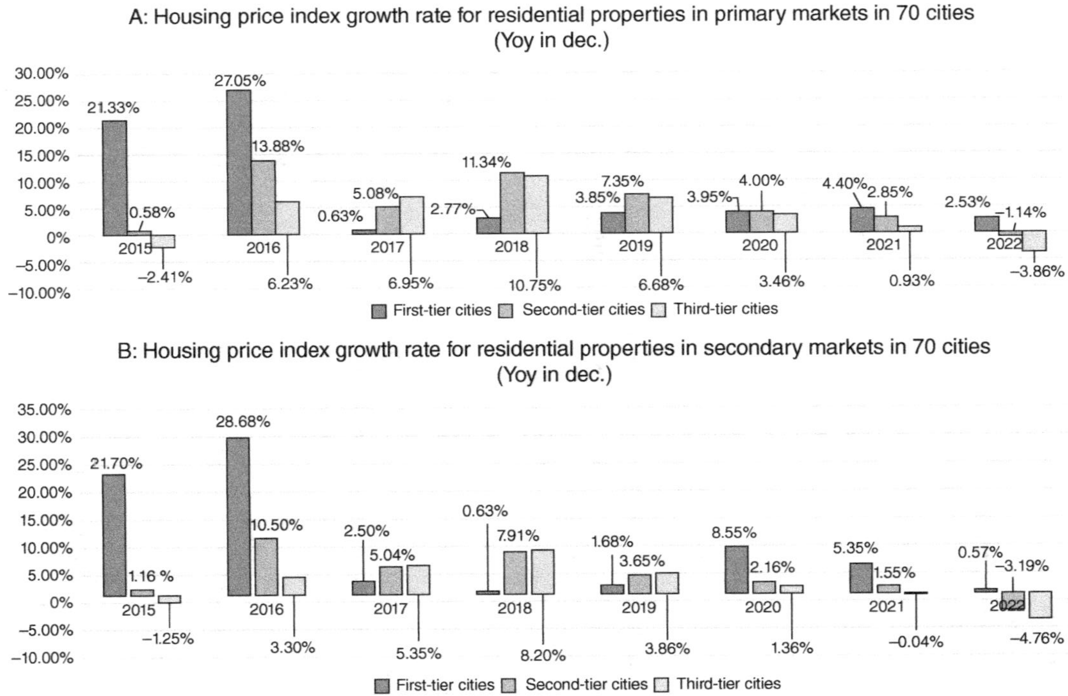

Figure 5.6 Housing price index growth rate

This figure covers the Housing Price Index provided by the NBS of China for seventy major cities. First-tier cities include Beijing, Shanghai, Guangzhou, and Shenzhen. Second-tier cities include thirty-one cities: Tianjin, Shijiazhuang, Taiyuan, Hohhot, Shenyang, Dalian, Changchun, Harbin, Nanjing, Hangzhou, Ningbo, Hefei, Fuzhou, Xiamen, Nanchang, Jinan, Qingdao, Zhengzhou, Wuhan, Changsha, Nanning, Haikou, Chongqing, Chengdu, Guiyang, Kunming, Xi'an, Lanzhou, Xining, Yinchuan, and Urumqi. Third-tier cities include thirty-five cities: Tangshan, Qinhuangdao, Baotou, Dandong, Jinzhou, Jilin, Mudanjiang, Wuxi, Xuzhou, Yangzhou, Wenzhou, Jinhua, Bengbu, Anqing, Quanzhou, Jiujiang, Ganzhou, Yantai, Jining, Luoyang, Pingdingshan, Yichang, Xiangyang, Yueyang, Changde, Shaoguan, Zhanjiang, Huizhou, Guilin, Beihai, Sanya, Luzhou, Nanchong, Zunyi, and Dali.

2022. In terms of secondary market transactions, first-tier cities experienced a price increase of 5.35 percent in 2021 and a modest increase of 0.57 percent in 2022, while second-tier cities saw a price increase of 1.55 percent in 2021 and a price drop of –3.19 percent in 2022. Third-tier cities experienced a slight price drop of –0.04 percent in 2021 and a larger price drop of –4.76 percent in 2022.

Overall, the quality controls introduced by the NBS housing price index show less price appreciation than the average price of transacted properties in first-tier cities during the Covid period of 2020–2022, almost flat prices for second-tier cities, and a modest price drop for third-tier cities.

The Risks

With the ongoing difficulties faced by the real estate sector, including many firms such as Evergrande experiencing difficulties in repaying their debt, and imbalances between oversupply of housing and insufficient demand created by the slowdown of the urbanization process and aging population, concerns have arisen regarding the potential crises and risks that could disrupt China's real estate sector. This section discusses the potential risks that may take different forms.

Will the Bubbly Real Estate Trigger a Debt Crisis in China?

The bubbly real estate prices and high leverage in China's real estate sector have drawn comparisons to the real estate market in the U.S., which also saw a combination of soaring housing prices and high leverage by subprime households, eventually leading to a full-blown financial crisis. However, it's important to note that the structure of China's real estate sector is different from that of the U.S. in the mid-2000s, making its risks distinct.

Contrary to the U.S. housing boom in the 2000s, which was propelled by a credit expansion to subprime households with minimal equity in their homes, the Chinese authorities have enforced a high down payment requirement, as emphasized by Fang et al. (2015). This substantial equity share offers a useful buffer against a modest decline in housing prices.

According to Bernanke (2018), the chairman of the Federal Reserve Board in 2008 when the crisis initially hit, the U.S. crisis was triggered by a panic run by financial market participants on various money market instruments that were tied to mortgage loans. This type of panic run is similar to runs by depositors on banks. As highlighted by the classic bank run model of Diamond and Dybvig (1983), when some depositors rush to exit by cashing out their deposits, others will also have to cash out, eventually forcing an otherwise healthy bank to fail. The cascading effects may even drag down other healthy financial institutions that either hold claims in the failed bank or assets experiencing fire sales due to the liquidation of the failed bank, leading to a system-wide financial crisis.

It's crucial to recognize that the Chinese government's strong commitment to ensuring financial stability, and its ability to mobilize local governments, state banks, and SOEs, make a western-style debt crisis less likely in China. During a panic situation, any stakeholder looking to exit would have to pass through the government, which would eventually coordinate all stakeholders to restructure their debt or equity claims to delay or even avoid costly liquidation. The recent experience with Evergrande has clearly demonstrated the government's commitment to this approach. In response to the financial distress faced by Evergrande in paying off some of its maturing debt, the central government privately instructed local governments to sort out Evergrande's financial situation and organized a partial bailout by inviting state-owned real estate firms to buy some of its properties and banks to restructure some of its debt. These measures effectively prevented a potential financial crisis triggered by Evergrande.

The government's past actions have also demonstrated its willingness to organize similar restructuring efforts for other debt-troubled real estate firms. As the real estate market remains critical to China's economy, there is little doubt that the government will intervene again in any future real estate crisis to prevent a financial meltdown.

Is There a Pending Real Estate Crash?

China's real estate market has experienced substantial growth over the past few decades, as documented by Fang et al. (2015) and Glaeser et al. (2017), with rising home prices and the piling up of housing inventory in the sector, as shown by Figures 5.4 and 5.5 in the previous section. However, the sector is facing various structural issues that may impact its future growth and stability. One of these issues is the demographic shift in China. In 2022, the birth rate dropped below the death rate for the first time, leading to a shrinking and aging population. This demographic shift will eventually lead to reduced housing demand in the long run. See Wang and Shen (2023) for a review of China's demographic change. In addition, China's urbanization process is also slowing down, adding to the reduced asset demand. As of 2022, China's urbanization rate is 65 percent, which is already close to the 80 percent level of developed countries. The annual urbanization rate has also slowed down to between 1 and 1.5 percent in recent years. As discussed by a recent IMF report of Rogoff and Yang (2022), third-tier cities face even more challenges, with a net negative migration inflow as people are migrating to first- and second-tier cities.

These structural factors have raised concerns about the potential for a real estate crash in China. The slowing down of China's urbanization process and the demographic shift could impact housing demand and put downward pressure on real estate prices. Interestingly, the NBS housing index shown in Figure 5.5 also indicates a slowing down in the growth of housing prices in 2020–2022, especially in third-tier cities.

Despite the structural factors that are putting downward pressure on China's real estate sector, it is important to note that the government is committed to preventing a potential real estate crash. A real estate crash could lead to significant losses in banks' loan portfolios, resulting in a banking crisis, as well as a crash in local governments' revenue from land sales, leading to a fiscal crisis. The Chinese government has several tools at its disposal to influence the real estate market and support demand, thus mitigating the risk of a real estate crash.

First, the People's Bank of China (PBOC) has the authority to control both interest rates and down payment requirements for mortgage loans, which directly affect home buyers' ability to finance their home purchases and thus their housing demand. In the past, the PBOC has used measures such as reducing mortgage rates and down payment requirements to support the real estate market, although it has not reduced these requirements during the COVID period.

Second, local governments have the power to regulate nonresidents' home purchases and residents' second home purchases in their cities. In the past, local governments have often used these restrictions to cool off an overheated housing market. However, in recent years, several cities have reversed some of these restrictions to stimulate housing demand.

Third, in response to the substantial downward pressures on the housing market, over twenty third-tier cities in China have implemented bans on real estate firms selling new homes at prices below certain lower limits in 2022. This type of ban on price drops directly prevents a price crash and thus avoids banks having to mark down their loan portfolios that are heavily exposed to the real estate sector.

The implementation of such bans on price drops confirms the government's commitment to stabilize the real estate market and maintain financial stability amidst mounting risks. However, some critics express concerns that such policies could interfere with the normal functioning of supply and demand dynamics, potentially hindering market efficiency and leading to misallocation of resources. These concerns are valid, as there is a sharp contrast in Figures 5.2–5.5 between increasing prices and decreasing transaction volumes in 2020–2022 for both sales of residential land and residential property transactions, indicating a mismatch between real estate prices and demand for residential land and properties.

Finally, some local governments have resorted to selling land to local SOEs and LGFVs to maintain revenue from land sales and avoid dropping land prices due to reduced demand. However, this may have led to inflated bid prices for the land purchases by these entities, potentially distorting the market and leading to misallocation of resources.

Taken together, due to China's hybrid economic structure, the government has a substantial capacity to avoid a hard landing in the real estate sector. By slowing down a real estate crash through a host of administrative orders, the government may be able to buy time to stimulate the economy, which would in turn lead to stronger demand for real estate. However, it is also important to note that some of the measures used by the government to mitigate the real estate crash, such as restrictions on price drops and selling land to local SOEs and LGFVs, may distort the market and hinder efficient resource allocation. This could make it harder for the economy to achieve sustainable long-term growth.

Economic Growth Risk

Although the Chinese government has shown a strong commitment and capacity to postpone a real estate crisis, state intervention may not address the structural challenges faced by the real estate sector. Ultimately, derisking the real estate sector depends on China maintaining its economic growth in the future. If economic growth fails to reach a necessary level, market participants may be unable to sustain high expectations of the real estate market, which are essential for maintaining real estate demand. As highlighted by Fang et al. (2015), the high housing price-to-income ratio observed in Chinese cities is heavily reliant on households' expectations of future economic growth. Conversely, if China can maintain its growth – even a modest growth rate of 4–5 percent – for the next five years, Chinese cities may gradually outgrow the high housing prices and elevated leverage.

Thus, the path to derisk China's real estate sector is to find new growth engines for the Chinese economy. In recent decades, China's real estate sector has been one of the key drivers of its economic growth, alongside the export and infrastructure sectors. However, the real estate sector is now facing increasing challenges and risks, while the other two engines have also slowed down. The export sector is uncertain due to the global trend away from globalization and tension in China–U.S. relations. Meanwhile, China has already built up a significant amount of infrastructure, especially in the eastern part of the country, reducing the demand for further development. The slowdown in the real estate sector is also limiting local governments' ability to fund new large infrastructure projects. As a result, policymakers must identify new sources of economic growth.

Shifting toward a more consumption-driven economy in China could be a solution to the current economic challenges, but it presents a major challenge in terms of stimulating domestic consumption. One of the key obstacles is the high savings rate among Chinese residents, which could be due to a lack of a strong social safety net and increasing economic uncertainty. These factors can make people hesitant to spend money and increase consumption. To encourage greater domestic consumption, policymakers will need to implement reforms that increase household incomes and improve social protections, such as healthcare and education. Additionally, promoting a more service-oriented economy with higher value-added industries could provide more opportunities for employment and income growth, which in turn can lead to higher levels of consumption. Policymakers may also introduce redistributive policies such as the common prosperity policy to further support the lower tail of the population.

Also note that a real estate downturn can have significant effects on local government fiscal budgets and their ability to stimulate the economy. Local governments heavily rely on land sales revenue, accounting for approximately 40 percent of their total revenue in recent years.[6] Thus, a slowdown in the real estate market not only creates substantial economic pressure but also limits the fiscal capacity of local governments to stimulate the economy. Policymakers must find a new financing model for local governments that does not rely solely on land sale revenues. Exploring alternative sources of revenue, such as property taxes, may be an option but may face political resistance from homeowners who view their properties as investments. Introducing property taxes could also put short-term pressure on housing prices and make it even more difficult for local governments to sell land.

Policy Risk

China's hybrid economy relies heavily on government interventions to stimulate and manage economic growth. While government intervention can help postpone a real estate crash and a full-blown debt crisis, it's important to recognize that excessive government interventions, driven by political or noneconomic considerations, may pose significant policy risks to both the real estate sector and the broader economy.

Conceptually, Brunnermeier, Sockin, and Xiong (2022) and Sockin and Xiong (2023) have developed theoretical models that illustrate how intensive government interventions in China's hybrid economy can result in noise in the government's policy-making becoming a critical factor in the macroeconomy and financial markets. This, in turn, diverts market participants' attention from acquiring information about economic fundamentals to information about noise in government policy-making, reducing the information feedback from the market to state planning and making government policy-making even more uncertain.

As discussed by Huang (2023) and Naughton (2023), in recent years, the Chinese government has begun to pursue other policy agendas

[6] See Su (2022) for a study that highlights a high fiscal multiplier of spending by local governments in China, funded by land sales, in stimulating economic growth.

in addition to economic growth, such as common prosperity, environmental protection, and better balancing against capitalists. While these agendas are important and well-justified, they may also divert the focus of the hybrid economic system away from economic growth. As explored by Song and Xiong (2023), assigning multiple tasks to local governments not only dilutes the priority of economic growth but also diminishes the efficiency of China's Mandarin system in pursuing any of the policy priorities. This, in turn, makes it even more challenging to maintain a reasonable economic growth rate, thereby exacerbating the pressure on the real estate sector.

Confronting the issue of bubbly housing prices and rising leverage in the real estate sector is a significant challenge for policymakers in China. The popular slogan "Housing for living, not for speculation" has led to the implementation of the three red line policy, aimed at tightening debt financing for real estate companies. While the slogan and policy serve a well-intentioned purpose of promoting housing affordability and ensuring financial stability in the real estate sector, they do not address the underlying structural issues faced by the sector, such as the reliance of local governments on land sales revenue to fund public infrastructure and services, as well as the reduced housing demand due to demographic changes. The timing of this policy is particularly awkward, as many real estate firms are already facing financial difficulties on the eve of a real estate downturn. The tightening of the leverage constraints may have further exacerbated the situation and contributed to the financing difficulties faced by companies like Evergrande.

There is also a concern that the central government's overly ambitious policy agenda may exacerbate the current economic conditions. In the absence of a new growth engine, setting overly ambitious growth targets can create pressure on local officials to restart the failing engine by relying on land sales or land financing to fund large-scale infrastructure projects, even when the real estate market requires time to slowly absorb its current inventory. This approach can increase leverage and debt levels for both local governments and real estate developers, further stressing an already vulnerable real estate sector.

Conclusion

China's real estate sector currently faces great challenges, such as high housing prices, elevated leverage, and increasing inventory. These challenges stem from the country's hybrid economic structure, which combines market mechanisms with extensive state interventions. Specifically, local governments' heavy reliance on land sales for funding public spending creates an environment where real estate becomes too important to fail, which in turn encourages overinvestment and overleverage in the sector. Despite the mounting pressure on real estate, the government maintains a strong commitment and the ability to delay a crisis. Ultimately, derisking real estate in China depends on the nation's economic growth. Sustaining an adequate growth rate will allow Chinese cities to outgrow high housing prices and elevated leverage.

While an imminent real estate crisis appears unlikely at this point, the extensive state interventions in China's hybrid economy also expose the real estate sector and the economy to significant policy risks. In particular, the government's strong commitment to maintaining financial stability essentially binds all boats together to weather a storm. However, this strategy also exposes the entire system to an unforeseen fire that could burn all boats simultaneously. In other words, if a shock were to ultimately trigger an economic collapse within the Chinese economy, the real estate sector might amplify the shock and collapse along with the economy.

References

Bai, Chong-En, Chang-Tai Hsieh, and Zheng Michael Song. 2016. "The Long Shadow of China's Fiscal Expansion." *Brookings Papers on Economic Activity* (Fall 2016): 129–165.

Bernanke, Ben. 2018. "The Real Effects of Disrupted Credit: Evidence from the Global Financial Crisis." *Brookings Papers on Economic Activity*, 2: 251–342.

Brunnermeier, Markus, Michael Sockin, and Wei Xiong. 2022. "China's Model of Managing the Financial System." *Review of Economic Studies*, 89: 3115–3153.

Chen, Kaiji, and Yi Wen. 2017. "The Great Housing Boom of China." *American Economic Journal: Macroeconomics*, 9 (2): 73–114.

Chen, Kaiji, Qing Wang, Tong Xu, and Tao Zha. 2022. "Impacts of LTV Policy on the Mortgage Market via Housing Speculation." Emory University Working Paper.

Chen, Ting, Laura Liu, Wei Xiong, and Li-An Zhou. 2017. "Real Estate Boom and Misallocation of Capital in China." Princeton University Working Paper.

Chen, Zhuo, Zhiguo He, and Chun Liu. 2020. "The Financing of Local Government in China: Stimulus Loan Wanes and Shadow Banking Waxes." *Journal of Financial Economics*, 137: 42–71.

Cong, Lin William, Haoyu Gao, Jacopo Ponticelli, and Xiaoguang Yang. 2019. "Credit Allocation under Economic Stimulus: Evidence from China." *Review of Financial Studies*, 32: 3412–3460.

Diamond, Douglas, and Philip H. Dybvig. 1983. "Bank Runs, Deposit Insurance, and Liquidity." *Journal of Political Economy*, 91 (3): 401–419.

Fang, Hanming, Quanlin Gu, Wei Xiong, and Li-An Zhou. 2015. "Demystifying the Chinese Housing Boom." *NBER Macroeconomics Annual*, 30: 105–166. www.jstor.org/stable/26556644.

Fang, Hanming, Ming Li, and Zenan Wu. 2025. "Tournament-Style Political Competition and Local Protectionism: Theory and Evidence from China." *Journal of Public Economics*, 248, 105421.

Geng, Zhe, and Jun Pan. 2024. "The SOE Premium and Government Support in China's Credit Market." *Journal of Finance*, 79: 3041–3103.

Glaeser, Edward, W. Huang, Yueran Ma, and Andrei Shleifer. 2017. "A Real Estate Boom with Chinese Characteristics." *Journal of Economic Perspectives*, 31: 93–116.

Gyourko, Joseph, Yang Shen, Jing Wu, and Rongjie Zhang. 2022. "Land Finance in China: Analysis and Review." *China Economic Review*, 76: 1–25.

He, Zhiguo, Scott T. Nelson, Yang Su, Anthony Lee Zhang, and Fudong Zhang. 2022. "Industrial Land Discount in China: A Public Finance Perspective." University of Chicago Working Paper.

Huang, Yasheng. 2025. "The Political Economy of Common Prosperity." In *The Arc of Chinese Economy*, Chapter 9: 239–255.

Huang, Yi, Marco Pagano, and Ugo Panizza. 2020. "Local Crowding-Out in China." *Journal of Finance*, 75: 2855–2898.

Li, Hongbin, and Li-An Zhou. 2005. "Political Turnover and Economic Performance: The Incentive Role of Personnel Control in China." *Journal of Public Economics*, 89: 1743–1762.

Liu, Chang, and Wei Xiong. 2020. "China's Real Estate Market." In *The Handbook of China's Financial System*, edited by Marlene Amstad, Guofeng Sun, and Wei Xiong, 181–207. Princeton: Princeton University Press.

Naughton, Barry. 2025. "The 'Summer of 2021' and the Trajectory of the Chinese Economic System." In *The Arc of Chinese Economy*, Chapter 10: 256–287.

Rogoff, Kenneth, and Yuanchen Yang. 2021. "Has China's Housing Production Peaked?" *China & World Economy*, 29 (1): 1–31.

Rogoff, Kenneth, and Yuanchen Yang. 2022. "A Tale of Tier 3 Cities." National Bureau of Economic Research Working Paper No. 30519.

Rogoff, Kenneth, and Yuanchen Yang. 2024. "Rethinking China's Growth". *Economic Policy*, 39 (119): 517–548.

Sockin, Michael, and Wei Xiong. 2023. "Information Discovery for Industrial Policy." Princeton University Working Paper.

Song, Zheng, and Wei Xiong. 2018. "Risks in China's Financial System." *Annual Review of Financial Economics*, 10: 261–286.

Song, Zheng, and Wei Xiong. 2023. "The Mandarin Model of Growth." Princeton University Working Paper.

Su, Yang. 2022. "Local Government Financial Constraint and Spending Multiplier in China." University of Chicago Working Paper.

Wang, Feng, Ke Shen and Yong Cai. 2025. "When the Abundance Ends: Economic Transformation, Population Aging, and Shrinking Lifecycle Surplus in China, 2000–2020." In *The Arc of Chinese Economy*, Chapter 4: 99–122.

Wu, Jing, Joseph Gyourko, and Yongheng Deng. 2012. "Evaluating Conditions in Major Chinese Housing Markets." *Regional Science and Urban Economics*, 42 (2): 531–545.

Xiong, Wei. 2023. *China's Hybrid Economy*. Manuscript.

Zhou, Li-An. 2007. Governing China's Local Officials: An Analysis of Promotion Tournament Model. *Economic Research Journal*, 36 (7): 36–50.

6 State Ownership in China
An Equity Network Perspective

JUNHUI JEFF CAI, XIAN GU, LINDA ZHAO, AND WU ZHU

Introduction

Over the past forty years, China has recorded the highest growth rates among large economies, establishing itself as the largest economy in the world in purchasing power parity (PPP) terms. Some scholars credit China's economic success to a model of "state capitalism" (e.g., Szamosszegi and Kyle, 2011; Naughton, 2018). Through strategic management of state-owned enterprises (SOEs), the government can achieve different strategic goals during different economic and social development phases. As of 2023, China has 142 business groups (including seven from Taiwan) in Fortune's Global 500 list, surpassing the U.S.'s 136, and 80 percent of the Chinese groups in the list are SOEs, so-called China's "national champions" (Lin and Milhaupt, 2013).[1]

In general, SOEs, by virtue of their privileged position vis-à-vis the state, are widely believed to enjoy favorable access to markets and resources, enabling them to pursue both economic and noneconomic goals. Privately owned enterprises (POEs), in contrast, grapple with higher external financing costs and other operational obstacles. However, abundant empirical evidence has shown that SOEs are less productive and have lower investment efficiency than non-SOEs (e.g., Allen, Qian, and Qian, 2005; Jefferson and Su, 2007; Zhu, 2012). This seems at odds with the general view that fast economic growth would be impossible when the economy is dominated by less productive SOEs, which compete for resources with more productive POEs (Hsieh and Klenow, 2009; Li, Liu, and Wang, 2015). This poses a puzzling question – how has China sustained rapid economic growth with an economy predominantly influenced by these less productive SOEs?

[1] A complete list of the Fortune Global 500 is provided here: https://fortune.com/global500/.

To answer this question, among many others related to state ownership, the very first step is to identify who are the SOEs. Existing measures are mostly based on the self-reported Annual Industrial Survey (AIS) by the National Bureau of Statistics (NBS) or the State Administration for Industry and Commerce (SAIC). Unfortunately, misreporting issues have been documented in the literature (Dollar and Wei, 2007; Hsieh and Song, 2015) and can lead to the misunderstanding of SOEs' role. In addition, these measures are either static or limited to the industrial firms that are covered by AIS.

In the chapter, we fill this gap by first introducing the first-ever comprehensive and dynamic equity ownership network, EquiNet, for all registered firms in China. This network provides granular equity ownership details, tracking changes over the years. Leveraging EquiNet, we propose a new SOE measure and compare it with the earlier-mentioned existing measures.

We construct the ownership networks using information on the dynamic firm-to-firm equity investments back to 1990 for all the registered firms in China, based on the firm registration data by SAIC.[2] This dataset records all the individual and corporate/institutional shareholders (including those not registered in China) and their corresponding equity ownership in China.[3] By the end of 2017, the ownership network covers 35 million out-of-network firms and 5.6 million in-network firms (Allen et al., 2023). Based on the ownership networks, we build SOE trees by starting from the list of SOEs provided by State-owned Assets Supervision and Administration Commissions (SASACs) and the Ministry of Finance (central, provincial, and city level) as the roots and tracing down their subsidiaries layer by layer. In this way, we are able to measure the state capital for the subsidiaries, thereby identifying SOEs and partial SOEs by setting different thresholds on state ownership stakes.

We have three sets of main findings using our new measure of SOEs. First, our SOE measure, capturing direct/indirect ownership stakes of various (central, provincial, and city) levels of government, identifies

[2] From the original firm registration database, we obtained the firm-to-firm ownership networks back to the early 1950s. We construct the ownership networks from 1990 to 2017. For more details on the equity ownership networks of all Chinese firms, see Allen et al. (2023).

[3] For the purpose of identifying SOEs in this paper, we drop individual shareholders for our analysis.

a significantly larger fraction of SOEs than the existing measures. In 2017, when we set the state ownership threshold to be 100 percent, our measure identifies 37,991 central SOEs, 36,056 provincial SOEs, and 299,665 city SOEs; when we set the threshold to be 50 percent, our measure identifies 84,904 central SOEs, 80,099 provincial SOEs, and 417,764 city SOEs. When we set the state ownership threshold to be larger than 0 percent, meaning that as long as there is any positive state ownership stake in firms, they are defined as partial SOEs and our measure identifies 1,364,601 SOEs in total.

Comparing with common definitions of ownership types in most of the prior literature that is based on the AIS,[4] we find *systematic* and *large-scale* misreporting issues based on firm registration types or state control status, the two identifiers AIS employed by existing studies to define SOEs. The misreporting issues are mainly due to two reasons: some former SOEs did not change their ownership type (from what was recorded during initial registration) after restructuring; and the absolute/relative state control from AIS is self-reported by surveyed firms.[5]

Second, state ownership shows a trend of centralization. The aggregated capital of all (partial) SOEs has climbed from 61 percent in 1999 to 85 percent in 2017, over the total capital of all the in-network firms (5.6 million), which accounts for approximately 80 percent of the total capital of all registered firms (40 million) in China. Among all SOEs, the total state capital has increased from 21 percent to 31 percent from 1999 to 2017. Suppose the threshold is 30 percent (the level of "relative control") or higher. In that case, the total capital of all firms owned by Chinese governments (SOEs) has been declining, while if setting the threshold to be 10 percent or 0 percent, the total capital of all firms owned by Chinese governments (both SOEs and partial SOEs) has been increasing from 1999 to 2017.

4 The other existing measure of SOEs, which in principle should cover the SOEs among all registered firms in China, comes from SAIC's firm registration and ownership database. More specifically, SAIC provides a firm's ownership by registration type. By comparing SAIC's database and the AIS dataset, we find the ownership types are largely consistent by registration types from these two sources. However, because of the data availability, few existing studies utilize SAIC's measure of SOEs.

5 Dollar and Wei (2007) and Hsieh and Song (2015) also document the misreporting issues and provide examples.

Third, state ownership shows both trends of decentralization ("authoritarian hierarchy") and indirect control ("ownership hierarchy") over time. The hierarchical structure of the ownership structure of Chinese firms ranges from the vertical integration of firms along the ownership trees to the top-down characteristics of policy formulation and enforcement in an authoritarian political regime (from central to local governments). Consistent with Huang et al. (2017), we also find evidence of decentralization of ownership from central to local governments: The state capital from the central government has declined, while that from provincial and city governments has increased over the years. Meanwhile, we propose a measure of hierarchical distance in the ownership networks. By constructing the hierarchical distance to governments, we find that governments tend to inject capital into firms in a more indirect way over time. More specifically, we find that the average hierarchical distance to governments along ownership trees of all SOEs has increased.

Our work contributes to and extends the existing literature on government ownership, especially on the role of SOEs in the Chinese economy. The success of the Chinese economy makes China a unique setting to study state ownership. Abundant literature investigates state ownership, privatization, and several rounds of SOE reforms in China. For example, Chen et al. (2025) examined the within-group capital transfers in 321 Chinese business groups from 2004 to 2013. They found that private business groups allocate more capital to units with better investment opportunities, while state-owned groups do the opposite. Li et al. (2011) studied whether removing market frictions improves efficiency using the share privatization process in China. Huang et al. (2017) examine the relationship between the geographic distance to governments and the likelihood of being decentralized for Chinese SOEs. Cong et al. (2019) document that state-owned banks disproportionately favor SOEs in granting loans during the economic stimulus. A good understanding of the role of state ownership in the real economy builds on an accurate measure of it. As far as we know, we are the first to propose a measure of all SOEs among all registered firms (over 40 million) in the Chinese economy. By tracing state ownership using ownership trees and reidentifying all SOEs, we provide a complete account of the state capitalism in China, which is vital to understanding the Chinese economy.

Our work also contributes to the literature on hierarchical distance in ownership. Liberti and Mian (2009) look at bank lending and find that hierarchical distance between the borrower firm and the bank branch (within the bank's hierarchy) has a more pronounced impact on the terms of the loans than physical distance. A closely related paper is Bai et al. (2021). Using the registration information for all Chinese firms, they document a hierarchy of private owners in which the largest private owners have direct equity investments from state-owned firms, and the smallest private owners do not have any ties with state owners. By using the firm-firm ownership networks, the construction of our new measure of Chinese SOEs also reflects firms' distance to different levels of the government in the organizational structure. The finding is that indirect control of the Chinese government increases, as defined by local governments' ownership via a greater hierarchy.

The remainder of the chapter is organized as follows. We first discuss the role of government ownership and SOEs in China from existing literature; then we describe the existing definition of state ownership and its misreporting issue in the AIS dataset, followed by a description of the data and sample construction; we then lay out the methodology of reidentifying SOEs in China as well as the results, before we conclude.

Chinese Model of State Ownership

Government Ownership in Firms

The role of government ownership in the economy has been puzzling. While worldwide state privatization has also proven to be successful from the early 1980s through the first years of the 2000s, the 2008's global financial crisis resulted in the resurgence of state ownership, mainly caused by market failures and government bailouts. Many governments around the world have rediscovered SOEs as useful instruments to achieve specific policy goals during economic downturn. China's emergence as a global economic power is the important factor undergirding the rise of the "state-capitalist" model in the recent decades, among others (Megginson, 2017).

A large number of studies consider privatization an effective way to improve SOE performance (e.g., Megginson et al., 1994; Megginson and Netter, 2001), as private investors have better incentives to maximize firm value than the government does. Meanwhile, other studies also find evidence that state ownership can be value-enhancing. For example, Boubakri et al. (2015) use a sample of firms from nine East Asian countries and find government-controlled firms exhibit higher market valuations than nongovernment-controlled firms. Borisova et al. (2015) find that the influence of government ownership is complex, as government imposes nonprofit-maximizing social and political objectives yet also offers implicit guarantees against default. Using evidence from forty-three countries over 1991–2010, they find government ownership is associated with a higher cost of debt during normal periods (consistent with state-induced investment distortions), while it is associated with a lower cost of debt during crises (consistent with the role of government implicit guarantees).

SOEs in China

SOEs are a distinctive type of business organization because the state is the corporate "owner." Though the state may run an SOE in the hope of earning profits, it typically also has nonfinancial objectives such as providing public goods, reducing unemployment, and so on. In China, the social responsibility of SOEs might be more important. Bearing the costs of maintaining social stability diminishes SOEs' ability to generate profits, which harms minority shareholders (Jiang and Kim, 2020). Consequently, vast literature documents the notoriously poor performance of Chinese SOEs (e.g., Bai, Lu, and Tao, 2006).

Lin and Milhaupt (2013) and Jiang and Kim (2020) provide reviews on the history of Chinese SOEs and several waves of privatization and nationalization in the recent decades. The national SOEs were carved out of ministries of the central government in the process of "corporatization," transforming government organs into joint stock companies. Crucially and in major contrast to SOEs of prior eras, corporatization has permitted the shares of SOEs to be listed on stock exchanges. As of July 2020, among all the listed firms in China, by the existing definition of SOEs, of which the government is the ultimate controlling shareholder, this group of firms accounted for 28.7 percent in firm number and 44.4 percent in total assets.[6] Obviously, many

[6] The definition of SOEs here is given by the WIND financial database, which is widely used for academic research on the Chinese listed firms. As of July 2020, there are 1,131 SOEs (out of 3,937 all listed firms) in China, including both central SOEs and local (provincial and city) SOEs.

listed SOEs, with the government as the "owner," are more accurately thought of as mixed ownership enterprises.

Many SOEs are structured as business groups under a parent holding company (organized as a special form of limited liability company [LLC]), whose only shareholder is SASAC, which was originally established in 2003.[7] To date, the largest controlling shareholder of SOEs in China is SASAC. In 2008, the *Law of the PRC on State-Owned Assets of Enterprises* (*SOE Asset Law*, henceforth) was enacted to "give full play to the leading role of the State-owned economy in the national economy." Meanwhile, the *SOE Asset Law* formally recognizes SASAC as an investor – a shareholder in the national SOEs, with both rights (control rights in both management and state assets; cash flow rights) and duties of a shareholder. Lin and Milhaupt (2013) document that the *Law* actually grants SASAC powers greater than those available to it as a shareholder under China's *Company Law*.[8] Some legal scholars discuss a unique political feature of Chinese SOEs that has been rarely seen in other economies: the monitoring of SOEs by the Party-state which comingles the Chinese Communist Party (CCP) and the CCP-controlled government (e.g., Wang, 2014).[9]

Because of the close ties to the governments, Chinese SOEs enjoy a large amount of cheaper loans from state-owned banks (Lin and Tan, 1999). This phenomenon is particularly significant after 2008's global financial crisis when the government launched the massive stimulus plan to boost the economy (Cong et al., 2019). Connections to the government can also bring subsidies, favorable tax treatment, and industrial license approvals, all of which are called government's "helping hands" in Shleifer and Vishny (1998). Prior studies have provided strong evidence that after privatization of listed SOEs, stock prices decline as investors fear the loss of government's helping hands

[7] SASAC is a ministerial-level agency, and so are the most important SOEs under its supervision (Lin and Milhaupt, 2012).

[8] For example, apart from control rights and cash flow rights, SASAC also has personnel power over SOEs. There are two parallel personnel systems in Chinese SOEs: the regular corporate system and the party system. The top executives in major Chinese SOEs are appointed and evaluated by the Party and SASAC. In addition, SASAC also rotates senior corporate and party leaders among business groups.

[9] The latest round of SOE reform in 2016–2017 has stipulated that party leadership should be incorporated in SOEs' corporate bylaws. For more details: www.sasac.gov.cn/n2588030/n2588919/c4615614/content.html (in Chinese).

(Calomiris, Fisman and Wang, 2010)[10]. Harrison et al. (2019) find that even though SOEs have been partially privatized, compared to those purely private firms with no government ownership, they are still favored by cheaper bank loans and government subsidies. In addition to these preferential conditions in financing and operations, national SOEs under SASAC supervision are exempt from enforcement of Anti-trust Law, which regulates the alliances/mergers and acquisitions between business groups (Lin and Milhaupt, 2013).

Ownership and Its Misreporting

Existing Definition of Ownership

The definition of ownership of Chinese firms in most of the existing studies comes from the AIS published by China's NBS. AIS covers industrial firms with annual sales over RMB 5 million (about US$800K) before 2010 and over RMB 20 million after 2010 as well as all SOEs across industries based on its own definition. In AIS, there are three variables that are widely used to define ownership: registration type (*dengji zhuce leixing*), controlling shareholder type (*qiye konggu qingkuang*), and state capital (*guojia ziben*).

- Registration type distinguishes twenty-three exhaustive ownership types and can be categorized into one of the seven basic groups: state-owned, collectively owned, privately owned, limited-liability corporation, share-holding firms, Hong Kong-Macau-Taiwan owned, and foreign owned.
- Controlling shareholder type distinguishes the type of controlling shareholder as state-owned (absolute/relative state control)[11], collectively owned, privately owned, Hong Kong-Macau-Taiwan owned, and foreign owned. A firm is state-controlled if its controlling shareholder is a state-owned firm.
- State capital reports the share of paid-in capital owned directly by the state.

10 In addition to the existing state ownership, Calomiris, Fisman, and Wang (2010) also find that companies managed by former government officials have positive abnormal stock returns, suggesting personal political connections can substitute for state ownership.

11 Before 2005, absolute and relative state control were distinguished.

Firm's registration type or state control is commonly used to identify SOEs. However, both ways reveal inconsistencies. First, some former SOEs do not change their registered ownership type after ownership restructuring. This has also been documented by Dollar and Wei (2007), who found that the ownership defined by registration type is not reliable as there are serious mismatches between firms' actual and notional (registered) ownership due to the rapid changes in the economy.[12] In their own sample of firms (a total of 12,400 firms), 169 firms (out of a total of 1,122) registered as SOEs and 208 firms (out of a total of 869) registered as collectives are already wholly domestic private firms by the time of their survey. Hsieh and Song (2015) find that a large number of firms directly or indirectly controlled by SASAC are legally registered as private firms; meanwhile, some privately owned firms may use SASAC to mask their ownership stake for certain reasons, therefore these firms appear to be SOEs based on their registration type. One example they provided is a company named Chongqing International Trust, a firm legally owned by the local government of Chongqing according to its registration type, whereas in fact it was privately owned by a crony of the Party Secretary of Chongqing at that time.

Second, the absolute/relative state control from AIS is also self-reported by reporting firms. Doctrine 81 by SASAC of the State Council in 1994 stipulates that there are two types of state controlling (as controlling shareholder): absolute controlling if the state owns above 50 percent of equity; relative controlling if the state owns above 30 percent but below 50 percent of equity.[13] In both cases, the state must be the largest shareholder. Consistently, AIS provides such information, that is, whether a firm is in absolute/relative state control, though it is self-reported by reporting firms. Some existing studies use this definition. For example, Huang et al. (2017) define SOEs by relative state control with the state ownership exceeding 30 percent from AIS.

[12] In order to address the concerns of ownership definition, Dollar and Wei (2007) conduct their own survey for ownership type with two different questions: first, the ownership type according to the current firm registration form; second, breaking down ownership shares by owners' types (state, collective, legal person, private individual, and foreign investors).

[13] In Doctrine 81 by SASAC of the State Council in 1994, it also states that when calculating state ownership, we should not only aggregate the ownership by different entities but only consider ownership by each entity separately. The full document (in Chinese) can be found here: www.sasac.gov.cn/n2588025/n2588119/c2689970/content.html

Misreporting Issues in Annual Industrial Survey (AIS)

In addition to registration type and state-control type, AIS also provides subcategories of paid-in capital, including state capital.[14] Hsieh and Song (2015) use state capital with state control to define state-owned firms.[15] Here we use the information of state capital to examine the definition of state ownership by registration type. We find significant misreporting issues.

To illustrate, we focus on a subsample of firms reported as wholly SOEs in at least one year over the sample period of AIS from 1999 to 2013.[16] By definition, wholly SOEs are firms fully owned by central or local governments, and hence, in principle, all the paid-in capital should come from the governments. However, we find significant misalignment between these two items. Table 6.1 reports the confusion matrix of the reported wholly SOEs and the contribution of state capital. Panel A presents the matrix of reported wholly SOEs and zero state capital contribution. We find that some firms are reported as wholly SOEs, but the contribution of state capital is zero percentage which contradicts the definition of wholly SOEs. Specifically, out of 19,872 firm-year observations of wholly SOEs, 6,067 observations (30.5 percent) have zero percentage of state capital. Panel B presents a matrix of reported wholly SOEs and full-state-capital contribution, where we find significant inconsistency to a similar extent. Out of 17,450 firm-year observations with 100 percent contribution of state capital, 6,286 observations (36.0 percent) are not reported as wholly SOEs.

By checking firms' registration types over the years in the AIS sample period, we also find a large number of firms change their registered ownership types while there is no change in shareholders as well as their equity holdings. To illustrate, a firm named *Jiangsu Nanjing Tianfang Clothing Ltd. Co.*, located in Jiangsu Province, changed its registered ownership type from other limited companies to wholly SOE in 2008 and 2009, and then changed back to other limited companies again in

[14] The subcategories of paid-in capital include state capital, collective capital, legal person capital, individual capital, HMT capital, and foreign capital.

[15] In Hsieh and Song (2015), a firm is defined as state-owned "when the share of registered capital held directly by the state exceeds or equals 50 percent or when the state is reported as the controlling shareholder."

[16] In AIS, wholly SOEs (*Guo You Du Zi*) by registration type are numbered 151 in subcategories.

Table 6.1 ***Misreporting: Comparison between wholly SOE and state capital***

Panel A: Confusion matrix: Reported wholly SOEs and state capital (0%)

	% of State Capital = 0%		
Wholly SOE	False	True	Firm-year obs.
False	9,118	6,930	16,048
True	13,805	6,067	19,872
Firm-year obs.	22,923	12,997	35,920

Panel B: Confusion matrix: Reported wholly SOEs and state capital (100%)

	% of State Capital = 100%		
Wholly SOE	False	True	Firm-year obs.
False	9,762	6,286	16,048
True	8,708	11,164	19,872
Firm-year obs.	18,470	17,450	35,920

This table reports the confusion matrix between wholly SOEs and proportion of state capital (either 0 percent or 100 percent) to reflect the inconsistency from different items in the AIS data.

2010, and then again to wholly SOE in 2011. Over the survey period, this firm is solely invested in by a wholly provincial SOE (named *Jiangsu Fangyuan Holding Co.*) owned by the Jiangsu provincial government.

Data Integration and Sample Construction

Data Description

Our data comes from multiple sources. The first is the Firm Registration and Ownership Database, which originated from China's SAIC. This database contains two parts of information. One is firm basic information, such as firm name and code, registration date, registration capital, firm status (e.g., existing, bankrupt), ownership type, industry, and location. Firms in this database can be traced back to as early as 1950. The number of all the registered firms is up to 90 million as of 2017, including individual businesses (self-employed businesses). Meanwhile, SAIC also provides detailed information of shareholders, including the names of shareholders and their holdings back from 1950. Each update of shareholders records the time of update, names of shareholders, and the change of holdings (the investment amount and share percentage) before and after the updates. Finally, the logout dataset records the dates and reasons of firms' exit.

In order to compare firms' ownership types, we also retrieve related information from the AIS published by China's NBS, and then match it with the SAIC registration and ownership database. AIS covers industrial firms with annual sales over RMB 5 million (about US$800K) before 2010 and over RMB 20 million after 2010, as well as all SOEs in China. Matching these two datasets allows us to have a panel dataset of industrial firms and SOEs with financial information from 1999 to 2013.

Capital and State Ownership in China

Registered Capital and Paid-in Capital

According to Chinese *Company Law* (1994; 2005), registered capital is the capital that all shareholders commit to invest when the firm is registered at SAIC, while paid-in capital is the capital that all shareholders actually invested in firms. Before 2014, firm registration in China was based on the "paid-in" system, meaning that registered capital had to be fully paid in within the first two years after the firm was registered at SAIC. The *Company Law* (2014) further changed the old "paid-in" system to the "subscription" system, meaning that registered capital might be different from the actual paid-in capital within a certain period, but at the end, registered capital still needs to be realized.

In addition to registered capital, shareholders and their ownership are also required to be recorded at SAIC. For LLCs, all the shareholders and their holding changes need to be recorded; for incorporated companies, all the original shareholders and their holdings need to be recorded, while there is no mandatory requirement that changes of holdings afterwards have to be reported. However, shareholders are motivated to be registered at SAIC to get government endorsement. By checking the sample of AIS firms, for which we have access to both registered and paid-in capital, we do not observe significant differences between these two. The actual paid-in capital by each shareholder represents cash flow rights and voting rights of shareholders.

State Ownership

SOEs/POEs can be identified in two ways in AIS. One is through registration type, which gives the details of the ownership type upon registration at SAIC: whether the firm is a wholly SOEs, SOEs, a collectively owned enterprises, a privately owned enterprises (POE), and so on. The other is through an item "absolute/relative state control," which gives the identification of SOEs if the state ownership is above 30 percent (relative state control) or 50 percent (absolute state control). Meanwhile, AIS also provides the proportion of state capital in paid-in capital for each firm, which could be used to calculate the state ownership as well. However, as we document in the previous section, we find significant inconsistency of SOEs identified using different definitions.

An accurate measure of state ownership should be able to capture the total state capital in firms. We propose a measure of state ownership, which we calculate from the ownership trees constructed based on the firm-to-firm equity ownership networks of all registered firms in China. The measure of state ownership can capture the direct/indirect ownership by various levels of government. Using the information on state ownership stakes, we are able to identify SOEs (or partial SOEs) by setting different thresholds of ownership when tracing SOEs along the ownership trees.

Equity Ownership Network and Reidentifying SOEs

In this section, we delve deep into the construction of our dynamic equity ownership network, based on which we build the SOE ownership trees. Through the SOE ownership trees, we provide a new SOE measure and reidentify SOEs across different state ownership thresholds and government levels (central, provincial, and local). Compared with the existing measures, we discover a notably larger pool of SOEs. Our analysis reveals a trend of centralization in state ownership – both the state capital and the total capital of SOEs have increased across the years. Moreover, we discover parallel trends in state ownership, showing both decentralization and indirect control over time.

Constructing Dynamic Equity Ownership Network

Our equity ownership network consists of firms as nodes and investment amounts/shares as edges. Figure 6.1 visualizes the two-level subtree of the equity ownership network of a significant SOE in China.[17] To construct the dynamic ownership network, on a high level, we first construct the up-to-date equity network from the shareholder dataset and then trace back the historical equity networks using the change records and the logout datasets. The major challenge of constructing the historical networks is twofold. First, the 28 million shareholding change records[18] are in text format and they need to be converted into a structured format such as a table so as to trace back the historical equity network year by year. Second, the shareholder names are inconsistently formatted (e.g., Apple Corps vs. Apple Inc.) and could have changed. We adopt word-embedding techniques to extract common structures of firm names and change records. We then design text parsing and preprocessing routines to clean and stem firm names and develop a stage-wise matching algorithm.

We now describe our construction procedure in detail. To construct the current equity holding network, we use both the shareholder dataset and the operating status provided in the basic information dataset. The shareholder dataset provides the current shareholders with their corresponding equity investment amounts and shares of all firms, including firms that have exited. To separate firms that have exited along with their corresponding investment relationships from the current equity network, we exclude firms with operating statuses that are neither "operating" nor "surviving."

To construct the historical equity holding networks, we backtrack from the current network using the preprocessed change records year by year. The change records contain the before and after shares and investment amount for each investor-investee pair if there is a change in year t. If a holder exits, the after-change share and investment amount will be 0 percent and zero RMB. We further incorporate the

[17] This is just an example of a subnetwork for the purpose of illustration, so we did not plot the networks including the ultimate controlling shareholder.

[18] In the original SAIC data, there are in total 175 million records of changes in firm names, registration capital, board members, and so on.

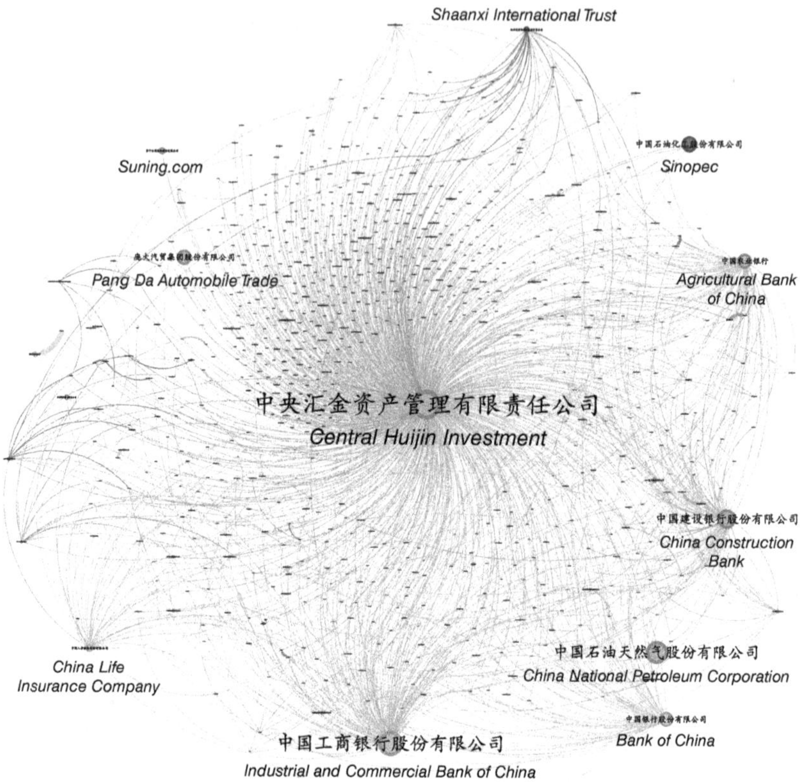

Figure 6.1 Network visualization of Central Huijin Investment, a significant SOE, in China

This figure visualizes the equity ownership network of the 2-layer sub-network of Central Huijin Investment, a significant SOE in China. There are 857 firms in the 2-layer sub-network, out of 80,000 affiliated firms in the whole network of Central Huijin Investment. The nodes represent firms/institutions as investors/investees. The node size represents the eigenvector centrality (Jackson, 2010) throughout the entire equity ownership network. The edges represent equity investment flows among firms/institutions. The arrows represent the investment direction, from investors to investees.

logout information so that if a firm exits, we will include the firm during the backtracking procedure starting from the year of exit. We backtrack the shareholding structure of each firm until the year when the firm was established.

Building Ownership Trees and Searching Algorithm

Based on the firm-to-firm equity ownership networks, we then build ownership trees, in order to reidentify all SOEs in the Chinese economy. We use the searching algorithm as following:

i. Locate firms directly controlled by the central government in the whole network over years, use them as the roots of the ownership trees, and build the trees based on the firm-to-firm connections from the ownership networks. We then trace firms owned by roots by setting different thresholds of ownership (100 percent, 50 percent, 30 percent, 10 percent, >0 percent). We use a consistent threshold throughout the searching process. At the central government level, we consider firms directly controlled by the SASAC of the State Council, by the Ministry of Finance ("*Cai Zheng Bu*") and other related government departments. We handcollect the list of firms (127 firms in total) from the websites of various departments of the central government.
ii. Locate firms 100 percent directly owned by provincial governments in the networks, and then use them as the roots to grow the trees. We then trace firms owned by provincial governments by setting the same thresholds of ownership (100 percent, 50 percent, 30 percent, 10 percent, and 0 percent). At the provincial government level, we consider firms 100 percent directly owned by the SASAC of the provincial governments, the Department of Finance ("*Cai Zheng Ting*") and other related provincial government departments. We hand collect the list of 850 provincial-government-owned firms from websites of provincial governments (and their departments) and use them as root firms.
iii. In a similar manner as step ii), locate firms 100 percent directly owned by city governments in the networks (247,736 firms in total), and use them as the roots to grow the trees. Given there are a large number of firms owned by city governments, instead of starting from a list collected from government websites, we use keywords of SASAC of city governments and related city government departments to search in the SAIC database to identify the root firms. Then, we trace firms owned by city governments by setting the same thresholds (100 percent, 50 percent, 30 percent, 10 percent, and 0 percent).

When using 100 percent as the threshold of ownership to trace SOEs along the trees, the firms we identify are apparently wholly SOEs (whole SOEs). We define the firms we identify as SOEs when using 100 percent, 50 percent, or 30 percent as the threshold of ownership, given the definition of absolute/relative state control by SASAC. We define firms as partially SOEs (partial SOEs) when using 10 percent or >0 percent as the threshold, to differentiate them from SOEs.

Panel A of Figure 6.2 illustrates the 10 percent ownership tree of the CITIC Group. Panel B of Figure 6.2 overviews the 100 percent ownership trees of the central government.

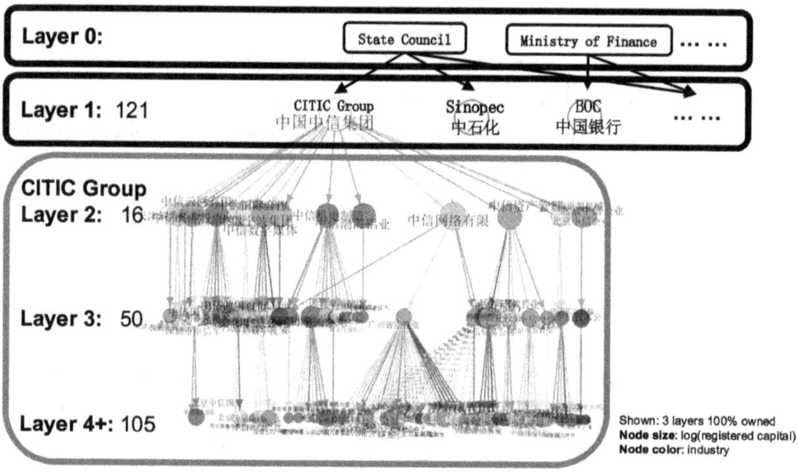

Figure 6.2 Illustration of our searching algorithm to build the ownership tree
Panel A: Building the ownership tree of CITIC Group

This figure shows how we build the ownership tree of CITIC Group using our searching algorithm with a 100 percent threshold. Layer 0 includes all departments of the central government, for example, SASAC of the State Council, the Ministry of Finance ("Cai Zheng Bu"), and other related government departments. Layer 1 includes all the firms directly controlled by the central government, including the CITIC Group, our focal firm of this figure. Using our equity network, we trace firms wholly owned by the CITIC Group and construct Layer 2. We then trace firms wholly owned by firms in Layer 2 and construct Layer 3. We iterate this process until this equity chain ends. The tree spanned by the CITIC Group is shown in the gray box. Only three layers from the CITIC Group are shown here with each node size scaled according to each firm's registration capital.

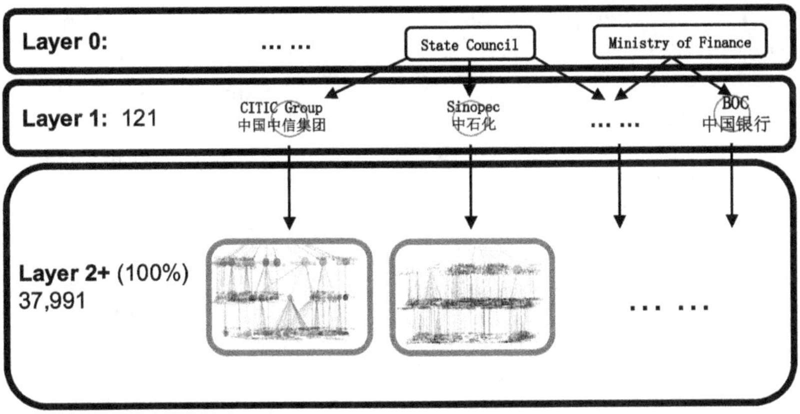

Figure 6.2 (cont.)
Panel B: Central government wholly owned ownership tree

This figure overviews the ownership trees wholly owned by the central government built by our searching algorithms. Layer 0 includes all departments of the central government, for example, SASAC of the State Council, the Ministry of Finance ("Cai Zheng Bu"), and other related government departments. Layer 1 includes all the firms directly controlled by the central government, for example, the CITIC Group and Sinopec as shown. Using our equity network, we trace firms that are ultimately 100 percent owned by Layer-1 firms.

Reidentifying SOEs

Using the search algorithm earlier, we trace all SOEs in the Chinese economy. Table 6.2 reports the SOEs that we identify using ownership trees layer by layer. In Panel A, we set the threshold to be 100 percent: in other words, from the roots of the ownership trees, we trace firms that are 100 percent owned by the last layer of firms in the trees to be SOEs. We identify 37,991 SOEs wholly owned by the central government (i.e., central SOEs), 36,056 SOEs wholly owned by provincial governments (i.e., provincial SOEs), and 299,665 SOEs wholly owned by city/county-level governments (i.e., city SOEs). At the central and provincial government level, we find the most SOEs in the third to fourth layers, while at the city/county government level, we find the most SOEs in the first and second layers. Central SOEs and provincial SOEs tend to have larger average registered capital

Table 6.2 *Re-identify state-owned enterprises (SOEs): Layer by layer using ownership trees by 2017*

Panel A: Summary of SOEs layer by layer in ownership trees (threshold = 100%)

Step	Layer	Avg_Reg cap (RMB mn)	Avg_Firm age	Firm number
Total				*37,991*
1st step	1	63,606.06	21.04	127
1st step	2	4,822.69	15.97	4,301
1st step	3	187.38	15.28	13,587
1st step	4	68.26	15.89	11,869
1st step	5	55.28	15.56	5,835
1st step	6	53.26	12.38	1,597
1st step	7	57.85	9.20	450
1st step	8	55.10	8.86	175
1st step	9	31.89	14.00	46
1st step	10+	11.58	13.25	4
Total				*36,056*
2nd step	1	3,838.17	15.19	850
2nd step	2	449.85	14.33	8,658
2nd step	3	101.81	15.37	14,213
2nd step	4	54.76	15.88	8,731
2nd step	5	32.06	17.12	2,600
2nd step	6	21.76	17.04	655
2nd step	7	17.56	11.41	283
2nd step	8	14.43	8.68	54
2nd step	9	3.50	1.67	12
2nd step	10+	–	–	0
Total				*299,665*
3rd step	1	56.48	19.91	247,736
3rd step	2	42.11	14.64	36,875
3rd step	3	32.63	13.06	11,185
3rd step	4	26.16	11.30	2,904
3rd step	5	34.63	9.31	607
3rd step	6	35.42	5.96	154
3rd step	7	65.75	4.44	108
3rd step	8	12.22	2.72	74
3rd step	9	10.46	1.00	22
3rd step	10+	–	–	0

Table 6.2 *(cont.)*

Panel B: Summary of SOEs layer by layer in ownership trees (threshold = 50%)

Step	Layer	Avg_Reg cap (RMB mn)	Avg_Firm age	Firm number
Total				*84,904*
1st step	1	74,421.36	20.87	155
1st step	2	3,526.30	13.75	6,700
1st step	3	317.46	13.14	24,946
1st step	4	178.62	13.59	26,736
1st step	5	112.44	12.63	15,809
1st step	6	105.76	10.65	5,957
1st step	7	91.44	8.10	2,032
1st step	8	101.86	5.63	1,124
1st step	9	14.12	4.14	985
1st step	10+	101.17	5.26	460
Total				*80,099*
2nd step	1	4,196.99	15.81	1,014
2nd step	2	521.47	13.14	13,087
2nd step	3	163.82	13.10	28,865
2nd step	4	123.54	12.90	21,792
2nd step	5	78.38	12.98	8,676
2nd step	6	52.62	10.98	4,169
2nd step	7	88.76	9.01	1,739
2nd step	8	123.61	8.94	322
2nd step	9	82.01	9.23	114
2nd step	10+	88.04	6.72	321
Total				*417,764*
3rd step	1	72.89	18.77	301,500
3rd step	2	65.60	13.06	71,002
3rd step	3	71.00	11.41	29,627
3rd step	4	131.23	10.08	10,043
3rd step	5	81.21	7.50	3,509
3rd step	6	54.92	5.82	906
3rd step	7	38.41	6.38	439
3rd step	8	462.10	5.28	308
3rd step	9	100.22	4.07	262
3rd step	10+	16.13	2.52	168

Table 6.2 *(cont.)*

Panel C: Summary of SOEs layer by layer in ownership trees (threshold = 30%)

Step	Layer	Avg_Reg cap (RMB mn)	Avg_Firm age	Firm number
Total				*116,972*
1st step	1	76,193.32	20.89	157
1st step	2	2,905.32	12.67	8,558
1st step	3	353.01	12.16	32,406
1st step	4	183.01	12.45	36,218
1st step	5	105.66	11.61	22,298
1st step	6	109.55	9.63	9,240
1st step	7	118.66	7.38	3,752
1st step	8	354.54	5.47	1,764
1st step	9	237.99	4.84	811
1st step	10+	136.84	3.63	1,768
Total				*113,336*
2nd step	1	4,163.32	15.73	1,023
2nd step	2	563.18	12.60	15,576
2nd step	3	195.05	12.28	38,121
2nd step	4	130.18	11.84	31,125
2nd step	5	96.66	11.64	14,649
2nd step	6	79.98	11.05	6,795
2nd step	7	94.27	10.62	3,444
2nd step	8	59.62	7.56	1,548
2nd step	9	74.82	7.51	453
2nd step	10+	72.29	7.45	602
Total				*489,872*
3rd step	1	86.07	18.17	328,221
3rd step	2	80.96	12.20	92,492
3rd step	3	81.63	10.54	42,720
3rd step	4	114.54	8.96	16,130
3rd step	5	78.58	6.88	6,504
3rd step	6	54.94	5.68	2,150
3rd step	7	51.63	4.56	916
3rd step	8	126.61	5.47	363
3rd step	9	49.52	3.77	250
3rd step	10+	1,263.03	3.26	126

Table 6.2 (*cont.*)

Panel D: Summary of partial SOEs layer by layer in ownership trees (threshold = 10%)

Step	Layer	Avg_Reg cap (RMB mn)	Avg_Firm age	Firm number
Total				*185,579*
1st step	1	76,591.02	20.63	163
1st step	2	2,477.75	11.87	11,078
1st step	3	419.96	11.31	43,182
1st step	4	203.97	11.25	53,659
1st step	5	112.11	10.43	36,445
1st step	6	131.53	8.08	19,550
1st step	7	137.20	6.65	9,704
1st step	8	145.34	5.73	5,636
1st step	9	184.22	5.56	2,651
1st step	10+	120.00	3.97	3,511
Total				*168,166*
2nd step	1	4,092.47	15.56	1,002
2nd step	2	721.15	12.17	18,021
2nd step	3	266.81	11.79	48,255
2nd step	4	159.71	11.07	46,234
2nd step	5	132.82	10.21	25,742
2nd step	6	132.30	8.67	13,764
2nd step	7	89.52	6.59	6,832
2nd step	8	73.43	5.08	3,287
2nd step	9	58.79	5.26	1,804
2nd step	10+	42.22	5.75	3,225
Total				*614,789*
3rd step	1	107.58	17.54	360,319
3rd step	2	108.51	11.52	121,630
3rd step	3	114.22	9.56	68,071
3rd step	4	107.68	8.00	32,667
3rd step	5	82.94	6.68	15,575
3rd step	6	80.81	5.56	7,559
3rd step	7	63.27	6.36	4,332
3rd step	8	59.55	6.61	2,266
3rd step	9	163.04	5.23	962
3rd step	10+	57.11	4.08	1,408

Table 6.2 (*cont.*)

Panel E: Summary of partial SOEs layer by layer in ownership trees (threshold = 0%)

Step	Layer	Avg_Reg cap (RMB mn)	Avg_Firm age	Firm number
Total				*303,559*
1st step	1	75,386.92	20.29	169
1st step	2	2,528.91	11.69	13,377
1st step	3	489.31	10.81	55,950
1st step	4	217.66	10.33	77,519
1st step	5	141.04	8.97	62,616
1st step	6	115.36	7.11	40,741
1st step	7	132.86	5.57	24,920
1st step	8	80.51	4.92	14,239
1st step	9	97.25	4.52	7,504
1st step	10+	86.40	4.25	6,524
Total				*282,570*
2nd step	1	4,162.77	15.49	971
2nd step	2	841.27	12.20	20,052
2nd step	3	340.80	11.41	59,001
2nd step	4	229.94	10.34	65,590
2nd step	5	179.08	8.79	50,142
2nd step	6	125.45	6.50	35,288
2nd step	7	151.92	5.10	22,549
2nd step	8	94.14	4.81	12,409
2nd step	9	174.38	4.53	7,394
2nd step	10+	105.43	5.75	9,174
Total				*778,472*
3rd step	1	135.09	17.14	388,266
3rd step	2	175.10	11.01	155,714
3rd step	3	123.67	8.67	108,558
3rd step	4	81.78	6.96	65,748
3rd step	5	91.75	6.28	31,740
3rd step	6	1,204.08	5.51	15,398
3rd step	7	108.64	5.44	7,630
3rd step	8	92.66	5.43	3,185
3rd step	9	81.48	6.02	1,254
3rd step	10+	51.67	8.99	979

Table 6.2 (*cont.*)

This table reports the results of the reidentification of the SOEs in the Chinese economy using ownership trees. We follow this search algorithm to identify SOEs: In the first step, we start from the firms directly controlled by the SASAC of the State Council and by the Ministry of Finance ("*Cai Zheng Bu*"), which are used as roots. We then trace all firms directly or indirectly (we set a consistent threshold throughout the process) controlled by this group of firms; in the second step, we start from the firms 100 percent directly owned by the provincial SASAC or Department of Finance ("*Cai Zheng Ting*"), and other related departments of provincial governments, and trace all firms directly or indirectly owned by this group of firms; in the third step, we start from firms that are 100 percent directly controlled by local governments (at the city or county level) and trace all firms directly or indirectly owned by this group of firms. We impose various thresholds of ownership (100 percent, 50 percent, 30 percent, 10 percent, and 0 percent) to identify (*partial*) SOEs along the ownership trees. In Panel A, we set the threshold to be 100 percent, meaning that in each step if the firms are owned 100 percent by the state, then they are defined as *SOEs* (i.e., wholly SOEs); in Panel B, we set the threshold to be 50 percent, meaning that in each step if the firms are owned 50 percent by the state, then they are defined as *SOEs*; in Panel C, we set the threshold to be 30 percent to define *SOEs*; in Panel D, we set the threshold to be 10 percent to define *SOEs*; and in Panel E, we set the threshold to be 0, meaning that as long as the firms have state capital (larger than 0 percent), then they are defined as *SOEs*. Note that in order to calculate firm age, firms established prior to 1950 are set to be established in 1950. *Avg_Rep cap* denotes the average registered capital of the SOEs identified in each layer and step. *Avg_Firm age* denotes the average firm age of SOEs identified in each layer and step, *Firm number* denotes the number of SOEs identified in each layer and step. Note that if information of share percentage is missing, then we treat as *zero* holding.

when they are closer to the roots of the ownership trees (and also closer to the governments in the ownership networks), while city SOEs have relatively similar registered capital in different layers of the ownership trees.

Panel B reports the SOEs that we identify when setting the threshold to be 50 percent. We find 84,904 central SOEs, 80,099 provincial SOEs, and 417,764 city SOEs. Consistently, we find central SOEs and provincial SOEs tend to have larger firm size (in terms of average registered capital) when they are closer to the governments. Panel C reports the SOEs when using 30 percent as the threshold; Panels D and E report the partial SOEs when using 10 percent or 0 percent as the threshold. When we impose lower thresholds, the difference in firm size among different layers shrinks. This suggests that firms with a higher percentage of state capital tend to have a larger firm size.

Table 6.3 reports the summary statistics of the SOEs that we identify using ownership trees. In Panel A, we see the threshold to be 100 percent. For central SOEs, the mean value of registered capital is 81.1 billion RMB, and the median value of registered capital of central SOEs is 524 million RMB. For provincial SOEs, the mean registered capital is 25.2 billion RMB, and the median registered capital is 580.5 million RMB. For city SOEs, the mean registered capital is 5.3 billion RMB, and the median is 87 million RMB. However, the average firm age shows a different pattern. The average firm age of central SOEs is 15.4 years; that of provincial SOEs is 15.4 years; and that of city SOEs is 18.9 years. Overall, central SOEs have the largest firm size, followed by provincial SOEs and city SOEs, while they all have fairly similar average firm ages. In Panels B, C, D, and E, we set the threshold to be 50 percent, 30 percent, 10 percent, and 0 percent, respectively, and we find consistent results.

Panel A of Table 6.4 compares the proposed and existing definitions of SOEs. Panel A compared the number of SOEs identified using ownership trees and using registration type in SAIC. In SAIC,

Table 6.3 *Summary statistics of SOEs identified by our proposed measure*

Panel A: SOEs: Threshold = 100%

Variable	Obs.	Mean	Std. Dev.	Min	25%	50%	75%	Max
First step: Central SOEs (by SASAC of the State Council; Ministry of Finance)								
Reg cap (RMB mn)	35,635	81,096	1.553e+06	0	50	524	5,000	1.550e+08
Firm age	37,564	15.39	9.939	0	6	16	24	67
Second step: Provincial SOEs (100% owned by provincial governments)								
Reg cap (RMB mn)	34,693	25,161	198,126	0	75	580.5	4,360	1.100e+07
Firm age	35,588	15.35	10.91	0	5	15	24	67
Third step: Additional 100% state-owned companies by local city or county governments								
Reg cap (RMB mn)	284,803	5,344	57,637	0	22	87	644	9.872e+06
Firm age	288,784	18.86	10.39	0	11	21	25	67

Table 6.3 (*cont.*)

Panel B: SOEs: Threshold = 50%

Variable	Obs.	Mean	Std. Dev.	Min	25%	50%	75%	Max
First step: Central SOEs (by SASAC of the State Council; Ministry of Finance)								
Reg cap (RMB mn)	80,838	58,001	1.255e+06	0	100	1,000	5,795	1.550e+08
Firm age	84,097	12.71	9.637	0	4	12	20	67
Second step: Provincial SOEs (100% owned by provincial governments)								
Reg cap (RMB mn)	77,492	24,174	197,155	0	100	800	5,000	1.990e+07
Firm age	79,255	12.82	10.05	0	4	12	21	67
Third step: Additional 100% state-controlled companies by local city or county governments								
Reg cap (RMB mn)	399,819	7,320	128,896	0	30	109.5	1,000	6.690e+07
Firm age	405,714	16.87	10.43	0	8	18	24	67

Panel C: SOEs: Threshold = 30%

Variable	Obs.	Mean	Std. Dev.	Min	25%	50%	75%	Max
First step: Central SOEs (by SASAC of the State Council; Ministry of Finance)								
Reg cap (RMB mn)	111,990	50,119	1.078e+06	0	100	1,000	7,000	1.550e+08
Firm age	115,928	11.56	9.415	0	3	10	19	67
Second step: Provincial SOEs (100% owned by provincial governments)								
Reg cap (RMB mn)	109,915	23,571	191,383	0	100	1,000	5,000	1.990e+07
Firm age	112,259	11.91	9.730	0	3	10	19	67
Third step: Additional 100% state-controlled companies by local city or county governments								
Reg cap (RMB mn)	470,466	8,565	161,197	0	40	170	1,246	6.690e+07
Firm age	477,284	15.78	10.50	0	6	17	24	67

Table 6.3 *(cont.)*

Panel D: SOEs: Threshold = 10%

Variable	Obs.	Mean	Std. Dev.	Min	25%	50%	75%	Max
First step: Central SOEs (by SASAC of the State Council; Ministry of Finance)								
Reg cap (RMB mn)	179,118	41,813	868,864	0	150	1,000	7,720	1.550e+08
Firm age	184,073	10.18	9.073	0	2	8	17	67
Second step: Provincial SOEs (100% owned by provincial governments)								
Reg cap (RMB mn)	163,298	25,842	225,222	0	111	1,000	5,250	4.130e+07
Firm age	166,570	10.62	9.355	0	2	8	18	67
Third step: Additional 100% state-controlled companies by local city or county governments								
Reg cap (RMB mn)	592,954	10,703	178,088	0	50	242	2,000	6.690e+07
Firm age	601,306	14.32	10.46	0	4	15	23	67

Panel E: SOEs: Threshold = 0%

Variable	Obs.	Mean	Std. Dev.	Min	25%	50%	75%	Max
First step: Central SOEs (by SASAC of the State Council; Ministry of Finance)								
Reg cap (RMB mn)	293,972	35,803	707,448	0	170.4	1,000	7,496	1.550e+08
Firm age	301,231	8.851	8.636	0	2	6	15	67
Second step: Provincial SOEs (100% owned by provincial governments)								
Reg cap (RMB mn)	274,709	26,926	280,898	0	148	1,000	5,958	6.690e+07
Firm age	280,217	8.988	8.823	0	2	6	15	67
Third step: Additional 100% state-controlled companies by local city or county governments								
Reg cap (RMB mn)	752,147	15,582	1.954e+06	0	50	380	2,740	1.680e+09
Firm age	763,603	12.96	10.34	0	3	12	22	67

This table reports the summary statistics of the SOEs that we identify using ownership trees.

by registration type, there are in total 391,490 SOEs, while by our definition, if setting the threshold above 50 percent (either 100 percent or 50 percent), there are in total 539,238 SOEs. Undoubtedly, these are SOEs absolutely controlled by the governments. By the threshold of 30 percent, which, according to the rules by SASAC, is the definition of "relative state control," we identify in total 628,554 SOEs. If we define SOEs as long as there is state capital in them, we identify in total 866,757 million SOEs, among which 238,203 (=866,757 – 628,554) are partial SOEs (with a proportion of state capital above 0 percent and below 30 percent). In short, we find a significant difference between the two definitions.

Panel B of Table 6.4 reports the discrepancy of SOEs by the measure of setting the ownership threshold to be 30 percent and the exiting measure by registration type from SAIC. Our proposed measure identifies 628,544 SOEs, while the existing measure of SOEs from SAIC identifies 391,490 SOEs in total. Only 167,544 firms are SOEs under both definitions, which are 26.7 percent of all SOEs by the measure and 42.8 percent of all SOEs by the SAIC measure.[19]

State Capital in Aggregation

Then we examine the total capital of all SOEs as well as the total state capital in the Chinese economy. Panel A plots the proportion of the aggregated capital of all SOEs identified using our algorithms over the total capital of all in-network firms (5.6 million) among all registered firms in the Chinese economy from 1999 to 2017, using different ownership thresholds. By 2017, there were 35 million out-of-network firms and 5.6 million in-network firms in the ownership networks for the Chinese economy. In-network firms are those that are either investing in other firms or being invested in by others; out-of-network firms are those neither investing in others nor being invested in by others (Allen et al., 2023). By 2017, the total registered capital of all the in-network firms accounted for approximately 80 percent of the total capital of all the registered firms in China.

The figure shows the aggregated capital of all SOEs (and partial SOEs using larger than 0 percent as the threshold) has increased from

[19] We have discovered a similar discrepancy between our SOE measure and that of the AIS.

Table 6.4 *Comparison of the proposed and existing definitions of SOEs: 2017*

Panel A: Comparing number of SOEs[a]

	Revised SOEs					Existing measure of SOEs in SAIC
	100%	50%	30%	10%	0%	
Central SOEs	37,991	84,904	116,972	185,579	303,559	
Provincial SOEs	36,056	80,099	113,336	168,166	282,570	
City SOEs	299,665	417,764	489,872	614,789	778,472	
Total	362,693	539,238	628,554	743,821	866,757	391,490

Panel B: Discrepancy of SOEs by the proposed/existing measure[b]

	Revised SOEs	Revised non-SOEs	Total existing SOEs
Existing SOEs	167,544	223,946	391,490
Existing non-SOEs	461,010	4,487,593	4,948,603
Total revised SOEs	628,554	4,711,539	5,340,093

[a] This table compares the number of SOEs by the proposed definition of SOEs and by the existing definition of SOEs according to registration type in SAIC. Please note some SOEs are at the intersections of central SOEs, provincial SOEs, and city SOEs, based on our search algorithm and identification strategy. The total number of SOEs according to the proposed measure here reports the actual total number of SOEs taking into consideration the potential double-counting issue.

[b] This table reports the intersection as well as the total number of SOEs by the proposed (ownership threshold set to be 30 percent) and existing measure. Our proposed measure identifies 628,544 SOEs, while the existing measure of SOEs by registration type from SAIC identifies 391,490 SOEs in total. Only 167,544 firms (26.7 percent of the total revised SOEs) are SOEs under both definitions.

60.6 percent in 1999 to 85.3 percent in 2017, while that of wholly SOEs has reduced from 41.0 percent in 1999 to 25.4 percent in 2017. Overall, if setting 30 percent or higher than 30 percent as the threshold, the total capital of all SOEs has been declining, while if setting 10 percent or 0 percent as the threshold, the total capital of all SOEs has been increasing from 1999 to 2017. We further calculate the state

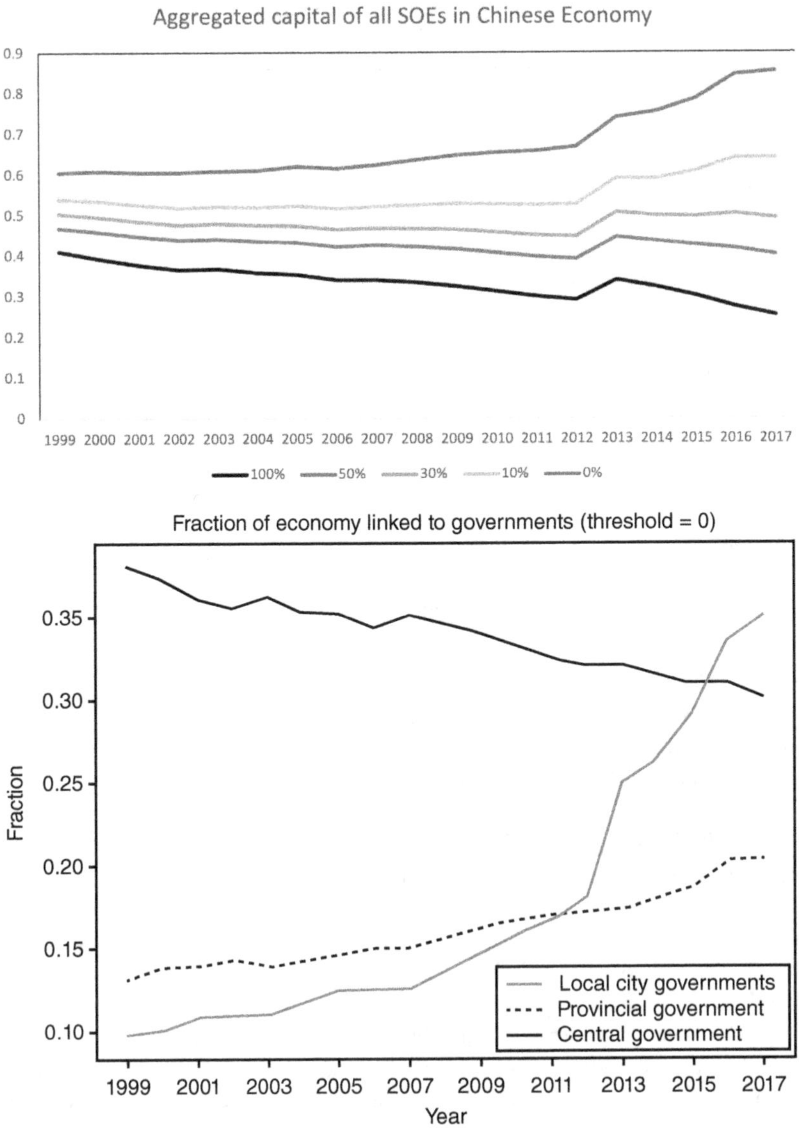

Figure 6.3 Total capital of SOEs and total state capital in Chinese economy
Panel A: Total capital of all SOEs: Different ownership thresholds

This figure plots the proportion of the aggregated capital of all SOEs (and partial SOEs) over total capital in the Chinese economy from 1999 to 2017. We first trace all firms (SOEs) *in the whole economy* directly or indirectly invested by various levels of government along the ownership trees by setting multiple ownership thresholds to be 0 percent, 10 percent, 30 percent, 50 percent, and 100 percent, and then calculate the proportion of total registered capital of all SOEs over total registered capital of all in-network firms (5.6 million) that are connected to other firms in the equity ownership networks in China.

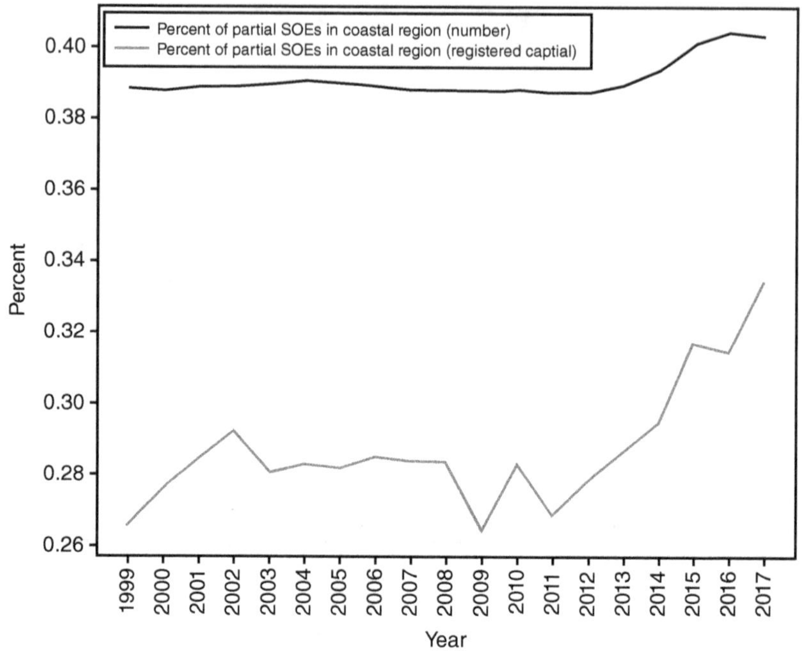

Figure 6.3 (cont.)

The figure shows that if setting the threshold being 30 percent or higher than 30 percent, the total capital of all SOEs has been declining, while if setting the threshold being 10 percent or 0 percent, the total capital of all SOEs has been increasing from 1999 to 2017

Panel B: Total capital of all SOEs and partial SOEs (ownership threshold 0 percent): Central and local governments

This figure plots the total capital of all SOEs and partial SOEs owned by various levels of government (central, provincial, and city governments) when setting the ownership threshold being 0 percent. We first trace all firms *in the whole economy* directly or indirectly invested in by various levels of government along the ownership trees (by setting the threshold of ownership to be 0 percent), and then calculate the proportion of total registered capital of all SOEs and partial SOEs over the total registered capital of all in-network firms (5.6 million) in China. The figure shows that the capital of SOEs in the whole economy by local governments has been increasing continuously, while the capital of SOEs by the central government has been declining from 1999 to 2017.

Panel C: Geographic distribution of SOEs: Coastal areas versus noncoastal areas

This figure plots the geographic distribution of SOEs (defined by the ownership threshold of 0 percent) in coastal regions versus noncoastal regions. Coastal regions include Shanghai, Shandong, Zhejiang, Jiangsu, Fujian, Guangdong, and Hainan; noncoastal regions include the rest of mainland China. Black line represents the percentage of SOEs (and partial SOEs) in coastal regions in terms of the number of firms; the gray line represents the percentage of SOEs (and partial SOEs) in coastal regions in terms of registered capital.

capital in all SOEs based on the proportions of state ownership: It has increased from 21.0 percent in 1999 to 30.8 percent in 2017.

Panel B plots the total capital of all SOEs (and partial SOEs) owned by central, provincial, and city governments over the total capital of all registered firms when using the threshold of 0 percent. The figure shows that the proportion of central government capital has been declining from 37 percent in 1999 to 31 percent in 2017, while that of local governments has been increasing continuously (especially that of provincial government, increasing from 9 percent in 1999 to 35 percent in 2017). Panel C plots the geographical distribution (coastal vs. noncoastal areas) of SOEs. The percentage of SOEs in coastal areas has been rising compared to that in noncoastal areas after 2011, both in terms of firm number and registered capital, suggesting a growing state ownership in coastal areas in recent years.

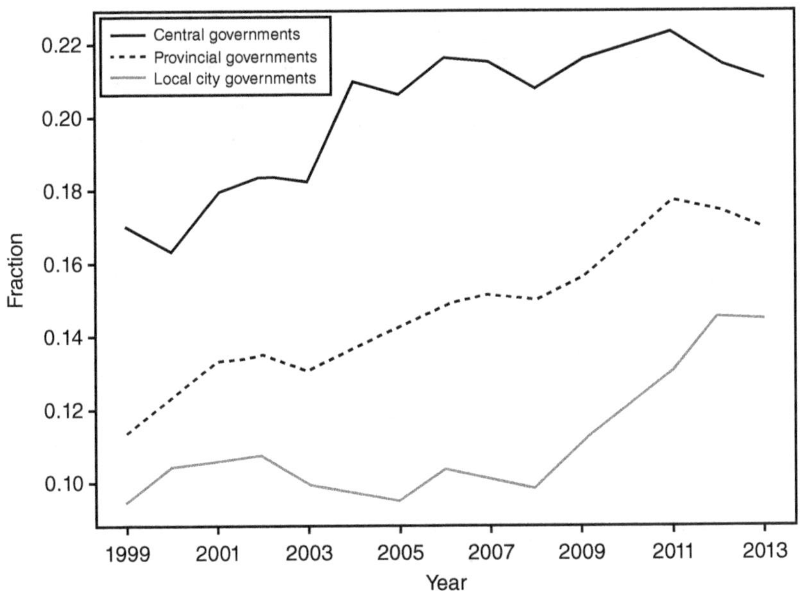

Figure 6.4 State assets in aggregation: Matched with AIS sample
This figure plots the total assets owned by the governments (central, provincial, and city governments), using the sample of industrial firms matched with AIS data. We first trace the firms directly/indirectly invested in by governments along the ownership trees and then calculate the assets owned by governments according to their proportion of equity ownership over the total assets of these firms. The figure shows the state-owned assets have been increasing for central, provincial, and city governments from 1999 to 2013.

Figure 6.4 plots the aggregate state assets owned by central, provincial, and city governments, using the group of firms, that is, industrial firms in the AIS dataset, over the years from 1999 to 2017. Note that only through the AIS dataset do we have access to firms' financial information. In order to obtain this, we calculate the assets owned by governments according to their equity holding in the firms that they have invested in. The figure shows that the proportion of state assets over total assets of the AIS firms has been rising for all levels of government. Figures 6.3 and 6.4 together suggest that governments are investing in a large number of firms while the average holding in firms is declining; meanwhile, the central government is investing in firms with a larger scale of assets in recent years.

Figure 6.5 plots the state capital in firms directly invested by central, provincial, and city governments, over the years from 1999 to 2017.

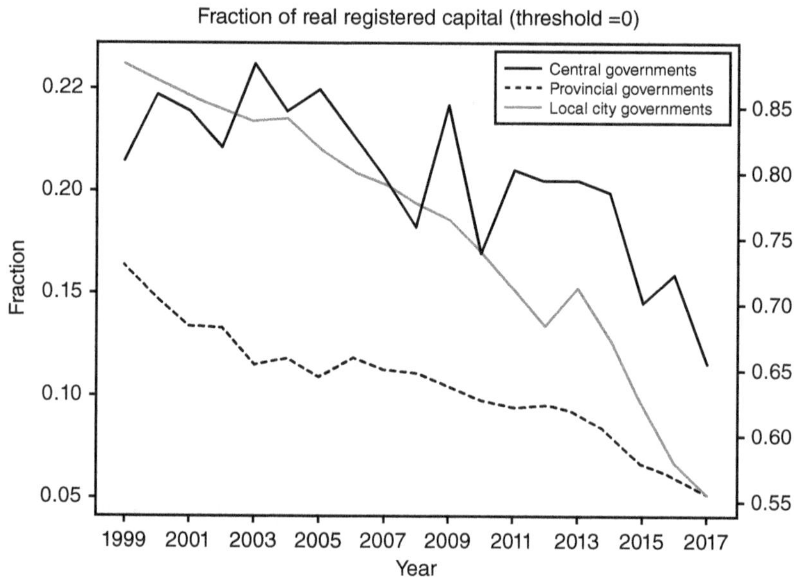

Figure 6.5 State capital in firms directly invested by governments
This figure plots the proportion of state capital in firms directly invested in by central, provincial, and city governments. The left Y-axis stands for the proportion of state capital in firms directly invested by central and provincial governments; the right Y-axis stands for the proportion of state capital in firms directly invested by city governments. This figure shows that the proportion of state capital in firms directly invested by governments has been decreasing from 1999 to 2017.

In other words, we only consider firms in the next layer to governments along the ownership trees. The left Y-axis stands for the proportion of state capital in firms directly invested by central and provincial governments; the right Y-axis stands for that by city governments. The figure shows that all levels of government capital have been declining in the last two decades. Overall, Figure 6.5 suggests that while keeping the stake in firms, the central government is changing from direct investment to remote investment.

Conclusion

Understanding SOEs is key to studying the Chinese economy. In this paper, we propose a new measure of Chinese SOEs (and partial SOEs) based on equity ownership networks of all registered firms in China (over 40 million), which cleans up the mysteries of other self-report measures. By capturing direct/indirect ownership by various (central, provincial, and city) levels of government, our measure identifies a significantly larger number of SOEs than the existing measure: if taking 30 percent as the ownership threshold to be SOEs, the criteria of relative state control by SASAC, our measure covers 89 percent more SOEs; if taking 50 percent as the ownership threshold to be SOEs, the criteria of absolute state control by SASAC, our measure covers 5 percent more SOEs. Our new measure of Chinese SOEs provides a rich vein of future studies on the role of government in the Chinese economy.

References

Allen, F., J. Cai, X. Gu, J. Qian, L. Zhao, W. Zhu. 2023. *Ownership Network and Firm Growth: What Can Forty Million Companies Tell about the Chinese Economy?* Imperial College Working Paper.

Allen, F., J. Qian, and M. Qian. 2005. "Law, Finance, and Economic Growth in China." *Journal of Financial Economics*, 77: 57–116.

Bai, C., J. Lu and Z. Tao. 2006. "The Multitask Theory of State Enterprise Reform: Empirical Evidence from China." *American Economic Review*, 96: 353–357.

Bai, C., C. Hsieh, Z. Song and X. Wang. 2021. Special Deals from Special Investors: The Rise of State-Connected Private Owners in China. Working paper.

Boubakri, N., V. Fotak, K. Holland, W. Megginson. 2015. "Government Ownership and the Cost of Debt: Evidence from Government Investments in Publicly Traded Firms." *Journal of Financial Economics*, 118: 168–191.

Borisova, G., V. Fotak, K. Holland, W. L. Megginson. 2015. "Government Ownership and the Cost of Debt: Evidence from Government Investments in Publicly Traded Firms." *Journal of Financial Economics*, 118 (1): 168–191, ISSN 0304-405X, https://doi.org/10.1016/j.jfineco.2015.06.011.

Calomiris, C., R. Fisman, Y. Wang. 2010. "Profiting from Government Stakes in a Command Economy: Evidence from Chinese Asset Sales." *Journal of Financial Economics*, 96: 399–412.

Chen, D., D. Jiang, A. Ljungqvist, H. Lu and M. Zhou. 2025. "State Capitalism vs. Private Enterprise." SSRN Working Paper: https://papers.ssrn.com/sol3/papers.cfm?abstract_id=2562201

Cong, L., H. Gao, J. Ponticelli, and X. Yang. 2019. "Credit Allocation Under Economic Stimulus: Evidence from China." *Review of Financial Studies*, 32(9): 3412–3460.

Dollar, D. and S. Wei. 2007. "Das (Wasted) Kapital: Firm Ownership and Investment Efficiency in China." NBER Working Paper No. 13103.

Harrison, A., M. Meyer, P. Wang, L. Zhao and M. Zhao. 2019. Can A Tiger Change Its Stripes? Reform of Chinese State-Owned Enterprises in the Penumbra of the State. NBER Working Paper No. 25475.

Hsieh, C. and P. Klenow. 2009. "Misallocation and Manufacturing TFP in China and India." *Quarterly Journal of Economics*, 124: 1403–1448.

Hsieh, C. and Z. Song. 2015. "Grasp the Large, Let Go of the Small: The Transformation of the State Sector in China." NBER Working Paper No 21006.

Huang, Z., L. Li, G. Ma and L. Xu, 2017. "Hayek, Local Information and Commanding Heights: Decentralizing State-Owned Enterprises in China." *American Economic Review*, 107 (8): 2455–2478.

Jackson, M. 2010. *Social and Economic Networks*. Princeton University Press.

Jefferson, G. and J. Su. 2007. "Privatization and Restructuring in China: Evidence from Shareholding Ownership, 1995–2001." *Journal of Comparative Economics*, 34, 146–166.

Jiang, F., and K. Kim. 2020. "Corporate Governance in China: A Survey." *Review of Finance*, 24 (4): 733–772.

Li, K., T. Wang, Y. Cheung, and P. Jiang. 2011. "Privatization and Risk Sharing: Evidence from the Split Share Structure Reform in China." *Review of Financial Studies*, 24 (7): 2499–2525.

Li, X., X. Liu and Y. Wang. 2015. "A Model of China's State Capitalism." HKUST Working Paper: https://iems.ust.hk/assets/publications/working-papers-2015/iemswp2015-12.pdf

Liberti, J. and A. Mian. 2009. "Estimating the Effect of Hierarchies on Information Use." *Review of Financial Studies*, 22 (10): 4057–4090.

Lin, L. and C. Milhaupt. 2013. "We Are (National) Champions: Understanding the Mechanisms of State Capitalism in China." *Stanford Law Review*, 65 (4): 6970759.

Lin, K. and G. Tan. 1999. "Political Burdens, Accountability, and the Soft Budget Constraint." *American Economic Review*, 89: 426–431.

Megginson, W. 2017. "Privatization, State Capitalism, and State Ownership of Business in the 21st Century." *Foundation and Trends in Finance*, 11 (1–2): 1–153.

Megginson, W., R, Nash, and M. Randenborgh. 1994. "The Financial and Operating Performance of Newly Privatized Firms: An International Empirical Analysis." *Journal of Finance*, 49 (2): 403–452.

Megginson, W., and J. Netter. 2001. "From State to Market: A Survey of Empirical Studies on Privatization." *Journal of Economic Literature*, 39: 321–389.

Naughton, B. 2018. "State Enterprise Reform Today." In *China's 40 Years of Reform and Development, 1978–2018*, edited by Ross Garnaut, Ligang Song, and Cai Fang. ANU Press.

Shleifer, A. and R. Vishny. 1998. *The Grabbing Hand: Government Pathologies and Their Cures*. Harvard University Press.

Szamosszegi, A. and K. Cole, 2011. "An Analysis of State-Owned Enterprises and State Capitalism in China." US-China Economic and Security Review Commission.

Wang, J. 2014. "The Political Logic of Corporate Governance in China's State-owned Enterprises." *Cornell International Law Journal*, 47: 631–669.

Zhu, X. 2012. "Understanding China's Growth: Past, Present, and Future." *Journal of Economic Perspective*, 26(4): 103–124.

7 China's Journey in Embracing Economic Openness
Four Perspectives

SHANG-JIN WEI AND XINDING YU

Introduction

The Chinese economy in the 1960s and much of the 1970s was as detached from the world economy as North Korea is today. The country did not do many exports or imports and had virtually no foreign-owned firms operating on its soil. That changed with Deng Xiaoping's reform starting in 1978. Importantly, China's move toward a "normal economy" is set against the background of a world economy that is broadly receptive to reintegrating China.

Fast forward to today, while China is now deeply integrated in the world economy, several developments have raised the question of whether the country could again "decouple" or "be decoupled" from the world economy. First, the U.S.–China tension seems to take the form of the U.S. taking a series of steps to decouple itself from China by not buying certain products from China, rejecting attempts by Chinese firms to invest in the U.S., and imposing a ban on exports of semiconductors and other U.S. products that are key components in Chinese production, especially of the dual-use varieties. Second, China is also taking steps to reduce its dependence on the world economy, especially the U.S. economy, both as a key supplier of inputs and as a key market for its output. The "dual circulation strategy," announced by the Chinese government in 2020, is billed by the country as a "new development paradigm." While the substance of the paradigm in practice is not yet clear, one possible interpretation is a systematic strategy to progressively delink itself from the world economy. Third, the general world economic environment appears to be becoming less hospitable to international flows of goods, services, capital, and people. For example, the dispute settlement mechanism of the World Trade Organization (WTO) has been made unfunctional. Industrial policies have been more openly embraced by many economies in ways that often include a decoupling component in the name of greater resilience. Such developments may not aim exclusively at China but affect China's degree of international integration nonetheless.

In this chapter, we analyze China's journey in embracing economic openness with four perspectives. First, while it is clear that China in the 1980s was climbing out of a self-imposed economic isolation, the question is whether China has eventually overshot its trade openness, as some of its trading partners appear to think. Second, since the Chinese authorities have expressed a desire since 2006 to increase the "quality" of its openness, we will seek a way to quantify the evolution of the "quality" of China's trade. In particular, we measure the sophistication level of China's export bundle and track its evolution over time. Third, as China's integration in the world economy includes cross-border direct investment in addition to raising trade openness, we also propose a broad measure of openness that incorporates the roles of both trade openness and FDI openness in the country's overall value-added creation.

By estimating a "normal" level of trade openness based on other countries' experiences, we characterize China's trade openness since the start of the reform period by three phases. The first period, from 1978 to 1992, is a phase of **progressive correction of a below-the-norm trade openness.** The second period, from 1992 to 2006, is a phase of **progressive expansion of an above-the-norm trade openness.** The third period, from 2006 to 2021, is a phase of **progressive reduction of an above-the-norm trade openness.** Interestingly, the level of China's trade openness today is approximately "at the norm," that is, consistent with what one would have predicted based on cross-country experience. It will therefore be interesting to see whether its trade openness going forward will stay at the norm, fall below it, or go back to surge above it.

While trade openness is measured by exports plus imports, politicians, media, and sometimes economists also pay special attention to exports minus imports, that is, a country's trade balance. After a period of near balance in the first decade of the reform era, a persistent trade surplus started to emerge in China's trade account in the mid-1990s. The trade surplus became especially large after the country joined the WTO in 2001 and was a point of contention with the United States. While exchange rate manipulation – making the value of the RMB artificially low through deliberate interventions in the foreign exchange market – is commonly argued as the main reason for

China's persistent trade surplus, we note a number of structural factors that cause China's savings rate to be greater than its investment could produce the observed surplus. This includes imperfections in its financial system that cause non-state-owned firms to save more than they otherwise would (Song, Storesletten, and Zilibotti, 2011) and a competitive savings motive by Chinese households triggered by an unbalanced sex ratio in the dating and marriage cohorts (Wei and Zhang, 2011; Du and Wei, 2013). It is also worth noting that the unilateral trade liberalization taken by China in the lead-up to its WTO accession and especially after its WTO membership can also generate a rise in its trade surplus. The last result seems counterintuitive on the surface. In partial equilibrium, one might think that China's trade reforms, by lowering import barriers and thus raising imports, should reduce its trade surplus. But this partial equilibrium intuition does not hold in the general equilibrium. As Ju, Shi, and Wei (2016) show, for a labor-abundant country like China, a trade reform means a disproportionate increase in the imports of capital-intensive goods, which has the effect of putting downward pressure on the domestic return to capital. This is essentially the Stolper–Samuelson effect in a dynamic model. To restore the equilibrium, the exports of labor-intensive products not only would rise but also would have to increase by a greater amount than the imports. This leads to an enlargement of China's trade surplus.

We estimate the sophistication of a country's export bundle based on the implied income level of the exporting countries that are typically associated with such a bundle. This has been computed by Wang and Wei (2010) for China during 1996–2005. The methodology follows that of Hausman, Rodrik, and Wang (2007). We find that the sophistication level of China's export bundle was below an international norm before 2006 and has surged above the norm after 2006. In other words, the country was playing a catch-up game in its export (and production) sophistication before 2006, and the progress is palpable as reflected in the post-2006 data. This evolution is consistent with the rising education and skill level of the Chinese labor force, the rising capability of Chinese firms, and possibly the expanding role of foreign multinational firms in China's production and exports.

For a broader indicator of economic openness that incorporates both openness to FDI and trade openness, we adopt a newly developed framework for value-added accounting in Wang, Wei, Yu, and Zhu (2022). The key innovation of that framework is to incorporate the role of foreign-invested firms not only in their direct exporting activities but also in their sales in the local market and in supporting domestic firms' production. The share of broadly defined openness as a share of China's GDP is about 50 percent higher than looking at the export activities alone. Interestingly, the broadly defined economic openness measure also peaked around 2006. By 2019, the latest year for which the relevant data are available, while it is much lower than its peak years, it is still higher than those of the next two largest developing countries (India and Brazil) or those of the two largest developed countries (the United States and Japan).

Institutional Background: Dual Circulation

On May 14, 2020, the meeting of the Standing Committee of the Politburo of the Central Committee emphasized the need to "deepen the supply-side structural reform, fully leverage the advantages of China's super-large-scale market and domestic demand potential, and build a new development paradigm in which the domestic and international circulations reinforce each other."[1] The phrase "dual circulation" has been used since as shorthand for this "new development paradigm." Indeed, "dual circulation" has been reiterated in various high-level meetings. For example, on October 16, 2022, President Xi emphasized once again in the report of the 20th National Congress of the Communist Party of China (CPC) that China should adhere to high-level opening-up and accelerate the establishment of a new development paradigm with domestic circulation as the mainstay, and with domestic and international circulations reinforcing each other.

There are multiple ways to interpret the "dual circulation strategy." As a first interpretation, China may decide to become more inward-looking and wish to reduce its dependence on external markets and production factors. Both the Economist (2020) and Financial Times (2021) appear to believe so, with article titles such as "China's 'dual-circulation' strategy means relying less on foreigners" and "China turns inward."

As a second interpretation, the strategy does not signal any weakening of the international circulation but will strengthen the previously

[1] Web link: http://news.cctv.com/2020/05/14/ARTIWKrhQJAEbhvzszg QIZ84200514.shtml

weak "internal circulation" by eliminating within-country production and trade barriers among different regions within China. Interregional barriers in China have been documented by Young (2000, QJE) and Amiti & Javorcik (2008, JDE).

As a third interpretation, the "dual circulation strategy" might represent no substantive change in any policy. After all, the Chinese economy always has a "dual circulation." So the "dual circulation strategy" could simply be a continuation and strengthening of China's existing economic policies, rather than a policy shift.

To understand the future direction of China's policy toward economic openness, it is useful to understand the journey it has taken.

Evolving Trade Openness Relative to an International Norm

Figure 7.1 presents China's ratio of total trade (exports + imports) to GDP from 1952 to 2022. The ratio was on the order of 10 percent before Deng Xiaoping's economic revolution in 1978. After Deng's "Southern Tour Speech" in 1992, the trade/GDP ratio started to rise rapidly and peaked at 64.2 percent in 2006. The decline from the peak is almost as spectacular. After 15 years since the peak, the trade/GDP ratio has declined to a level close to 30 percent.

One intriguing question is why the trade openness fell after 2006. Did the Chinese policies become less open after 2006? Or was the initial rise in the trade openness in the years leading up to 2006

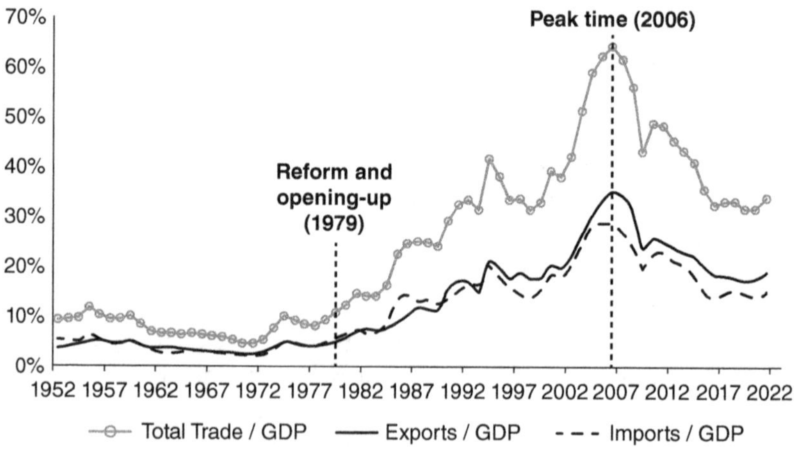

Figure 7.1 China's trade openness, 1952–2021

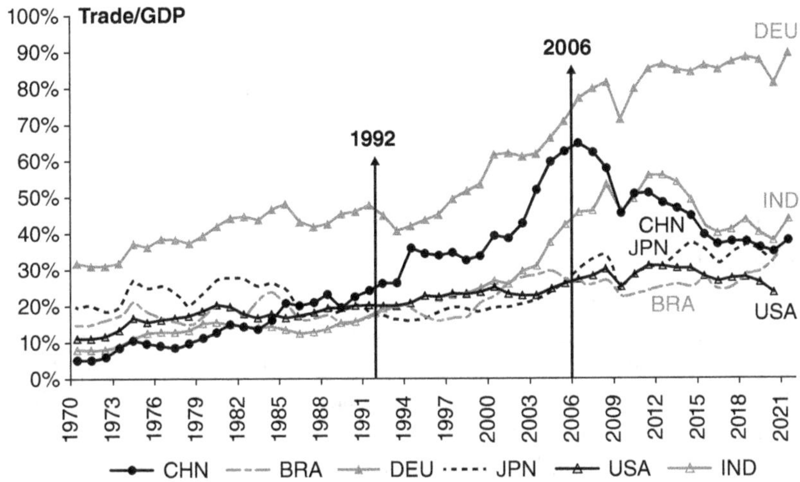

Figure 7.2 International comparison of the degree of economic openness

abnormal and does the decline in the trade openness represent a return to a more normal level? One noteworthy policy document that took effect in 2006 is the 11th Five-Year Plan, which for the first time proposed to pay attention to the "quality of trade" as opposed to just "quantity of trade."

To provide a comparison between China and other large economies, Figure 7.2 adds the time series of trade openness of the three largest developed countries (the United States, Japan, and Germany) and the next two largest developing countries (India and Brazil). None of these countries shows a turning point at or around 2006. An ocular inspection suggests that although China's trade openness declines after 2006, it is possible that it is "regressing to the mean." That is, perhaps its pre-2006 trade openness was "too high," and the post-2006 was simply converging toward some international norm.

We construct a simple regression-based "international norm" for trade openness as a function of economic size and level of development:

$$lnOpenness_{it} = \beta_0 + \beta_1 lnGDPPC_{it} + \beta_2 lnGDP_{it} + \gamma_t + \varepsilon_{it}$$

where, $lnOpenness_{it}$ represents the ratio of total trade/GDP for country i in year t, $lnGDPPC_{it}$ and $lnGDP_{it}$ represent log per capita GDP and log GDP, respectively, γ_t represents the time fixed effect to account for common global factors.

We estimate the coefficients using a sample of all economies covered by the World Bank WDI database except for China, and thereby obtain a general relationship between a country's trade openness as a log-linear function of its economic size and level of economic development. Based on China's actual GDP and per capita GDP in a given year, we can predict what the "normal trade openness" for China would be in that year. By comparing China's actual trade openness with the predicted level, we can see whether the country is trading at, above, or below the predicted level (see Figure 7.3).

Using the model-predicted "normal trade openness," we may characterize the time series of China's trade openness by three phases. The 1980–1992 period is a phase of **progressive correction of a below-the-norm trade openness.** This is not surprising since the country was climbing out of a self-imposed economic isolation. The second period, from 1992 to 2006, is a phase of **progressive expansion of an above-the-norm trade openness.** It may not entirely be a coincidence that this phase started in 1992, a year in which paramount leader Deng Xiaoping was giving a big push to market-oriented reforms. This period also corresponds to an emergence of a large and persistent trade surplus, which we will comment on in the next section. The third period, from 2006 to 2021, is a phase of

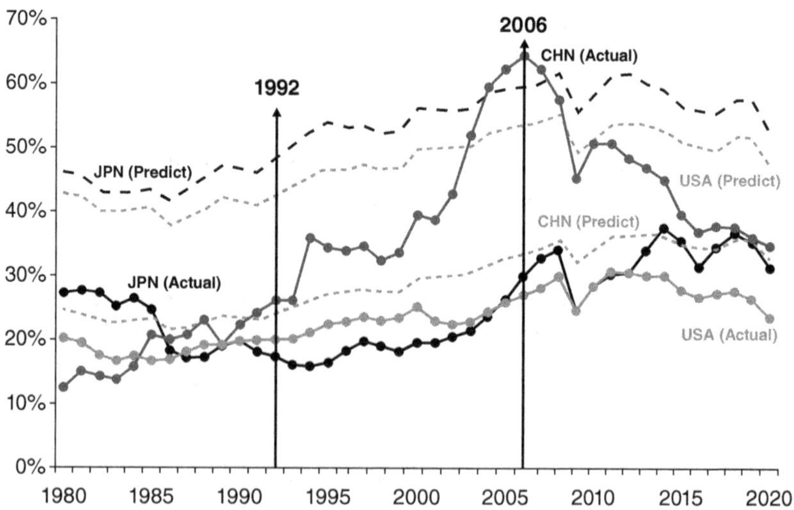

Figure 7.3 The actual and expected levels of economic openness

progressive reduction of an above-the-norm trade openness. Perhaps it is not coincidental that this phase started in 2006, which was the year in which the Chinese government started to talk about a need to improve the quality of trade.

Interestingly, the level of China's trade openness today is only slightly higher than what one would have predicted based on cross-country experience. In other words, at least up to now, there is no evidence that China is turning more inward than other countries at a similar level of development. It will therefore be interesting to see whether its trade openness going forward will stay at the international norm, fall below the norm, or go back to surge above the norm.

Trade Imbalances

Besides total trade (i.e., exports + imports), China's trade balance (i.e., exports − imports) also often attracts international attention. From Figure 7.4, one can see a persistent trade surplus started to open up in the mid-1990s, and the trade surplus widened further following China's accession to the WTO. By 2005, China's trade surplus reached 7 percent of its GDP, which is one of the highest in the world. On the surface, this seems puzzling as much of the Chinese trade reform is unilateral liberalization, that is, China reducing trade barriers unilaterally without necessarily seeking or succeeding in

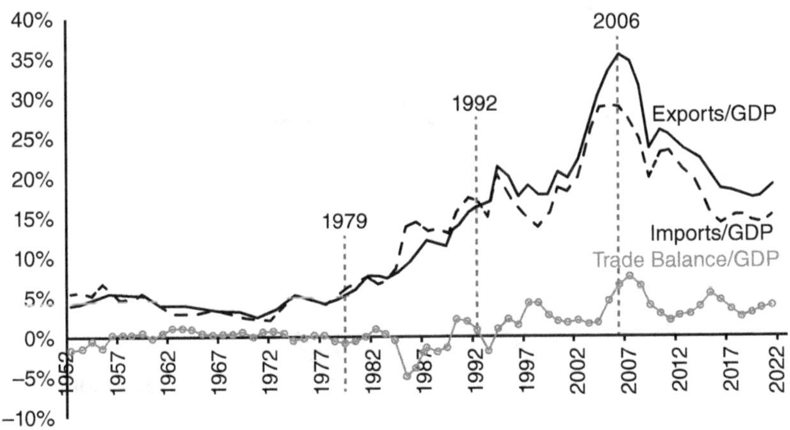

Figure 7.4 China's trade imbalance

getting partner countries to reciprocate with their reforms. If China increases its imports, should the country start to have an increase in trade deficit or at least a reduction in trade surplus?

One possibility is exchange rate manipulation, a theory pushed hard by some. But a country's trade balance also reflects its savings and investment imbalance. By now, we know that China's high corporate savings rate is partly driven up by imperfections in its financial system (Song, Storesletten, and Zilibotti, 2011) and its high household savings is partly driven up by a sex ratio imbalance (Wei and Zhang, 2011; and Du and Wei, 2013).

As we study economic openness, it may be especially interesting to reflect on another alternative explanation: unilateral trade liberalization by a labor-abundant country such as China should be expected to see a rise in the trade surplus. This is the explanation provided by Ju, Shi, and Wei (2021). As shown in Figure 7.5, before 2001, China's average tariff rate was as high as 14 percent but declined in phases to a more modest 5 percent by 2004 and stayed that low afterwards. At the same time, China's current account surplus was not significant in the year before China joined the WTO but started to rise noticeably afterward until 2007 when it began to fall.

As this appears counterintuitive on the surface, we must reflect on its logic. This analysis goes beyond the traditional "partial equilibrium" framework and reveals a "general equilibrium" link between trade liberalization policies and current account imbalances.

Under the traditional partial equilibrium framework, a reduction in a country's trade barriers (such as import tariffs) leads to an increase

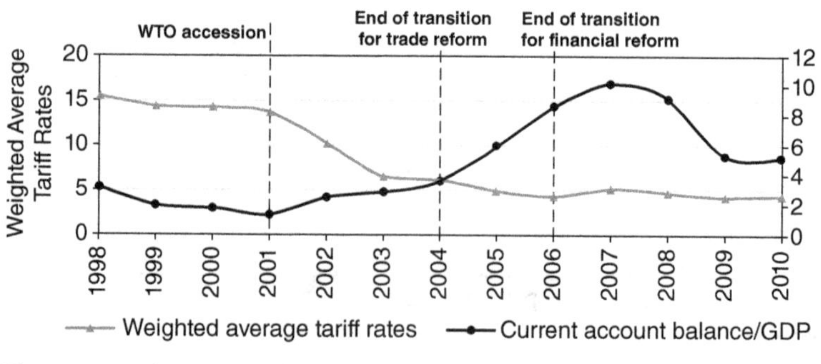

Figure 7.5 Chinese tariff rates and current account during 1998–2010
Source: Figure 1 in Ju, Shi, and Wei (2021).

in its imports, thereby reducing the current account surplus of the importing country and improving the current account deficit of the exporting country. However, a general equilibrium perspective can lead to a completely different conclusion: for labor-abundant countries, a reduction in import barriers can actually increase their current account surplus, while capital-abundant countries may experience a current account deficit.

The economic logic behind this is as follows: suppose the importing country is a labor-abundant country. With trade liberalization, the importing country's trade barriers (such as import tariffs) decrease, leading to an increase in imports, specifically more capital-intensive products. The reduction of import trade barriers (tariffs) leads to a decrease in the price of imported products. According to the Stolper–Samuelson theorem in the Heckscher–Ohlin model, the decrease in the price of imported products leads to a decrease in the price of the "capital" factor used intensively in the production of imported products, namely the interest rate. The decrease in the domestic interest rate means that the domestic capital return is lower than the foreign capital return. To reestablish the equilibrium, there would be a capital outflow, which is realized by having an increase in exports relative to imports, resulting in a current account surplus for the country.

Evolving "Quality of Exports"

Since "quality of trade" has been emphasized by the Chinese government in recent years, we examine one measure of "trade quality," which is "export sophistication" proposed by Hausmann, Hwang, and Rodrik (2007). The indicator attempts to characterize the technological complexity of a country as implied by its export bundle.

Using global bilateral trade data from UNCOMTRADE, we first estimate the level of technological complexity for each traded good (at the six-digit HS level), based on the idea that if a product is exported mostly by developed countries, it is likely to have a relatively high technological sophistication. This is expressed mathematically as

$$PRODY_k = \sum_j \frac{(x_{jk} / X_j)}{\sum_j (x_{jk} / X_j)} Y_j$$

where $PRODY_k$ represents the technological complexity of product k, x_{jk}/X_j represents the share of product k in country j's exports, and Y_j represents the per capita GDP of country j. Therefore, the concept of technological complexity of product k can be intuitively understood as the weighted average GDP per capita of the countries that export product k globally.

The export sophistication of country j (EXPY) is then defined as the weighted average of the implied per capita incomes of all products in its export bundle. This is calculated using the share of each product in the country's export basket (measured by export value) as weights:

$$EXPY_j = \sum_k \left(\frac{x_{jk}}{X_j} \right) PRODY_k$$

In Figure 7.6, we report China's export sophistication index and compare it to other developing countries in the G20 (Brazil, Indonesia, India, Mexico, and Russia). Before 2006, China's export sophistication was approximately similar to other large developing countries. But since 2006, it has surged above other developing countries, and

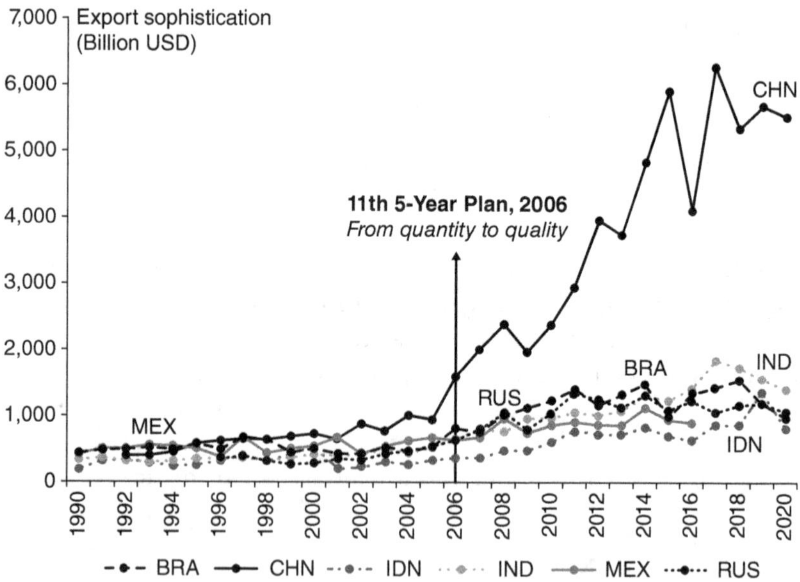

Figure 7.6 Export sophistication of China and other large developing countries

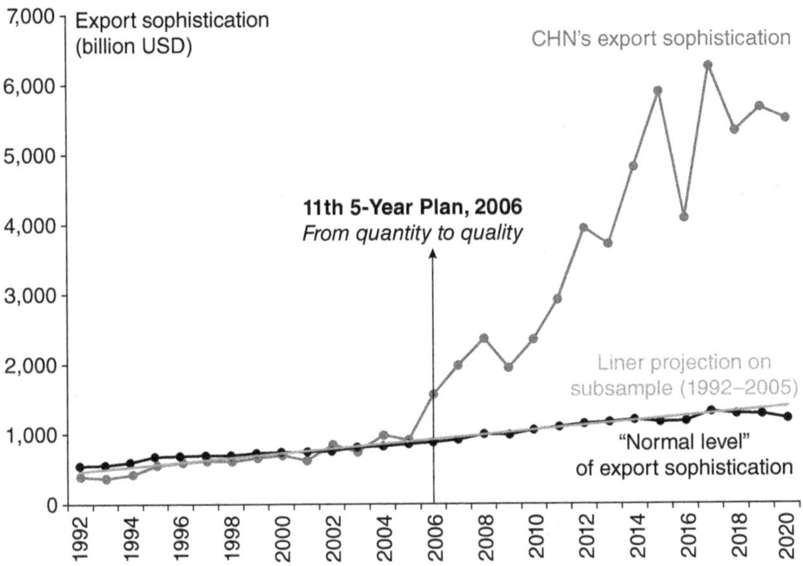

Figure 7.7 Changes in China's export sophistication

the gap appears to have widened over time until it stabilizes at a relatively high level in the most recent years.

Using a method similar to the estimation of "Normal Openness" in the previous section, we can estimate a "normal level" of export sophistication based on economic size and level of development using cross-country data that excludes China. In Figure 7.7, we compare China's actual export sophistication with the model-predicted norm, and see a similar pattern.

These patterns are consistent with the findings in the literature. In particular, using data up to 2006, Hausmann et al. (2007) found that China's export technological complexity was significantly higher than expected relative to its current GDP level, and the gap between China and developed countries was still narrowing. Rodrik (2006) also suggested that China's export structure was comparable to countries that are three times its income level. Similarly, Wang and Wei (2010) concluded that the complexity of China's export products is relatively high compared to its economic level, indicating that China has some competitiveness in high-tech and knowledge-intensive industries.

By extending the data by another decade, we show that China's export sophistication has stayed above the model-predicted norm. Going forward, it will be interesting to see if the U.S. CHIPS and Science Act, Inflation Reduction Act, entity lists, and other measures that are designed to hobble Chinese technological advances in several technology areas will result in a decline in China's export sophistication.

A Broader Indicator of Economic Openness

An important aspect of economic openness is inward foreign direct investment, which produces and sells in the host country and also contributes to the host country's overall exports. The trade/GDP ratio does not fully capture this aspect of openness.

Figure 7.8 presents the time series of annual new inward FDI as a share of GDP from 1980 to 2022. The inward FDI into the country started essentially from zero in 1980, rose steadily throughout the 1980s, and accelerated after Deng Xiaoping's proreform "southern tour" speech in 1992, reaching about 6 percent of GDP that year. From 1996 to 2004, new inflow of FDI as a share of FDI exhibited a gradual moderation, although it stabilized around 4.5 percent during 2005–2006. Since 2006, inward FDI as a share of FDI has declined progressively to about 1.5 percent a year now.

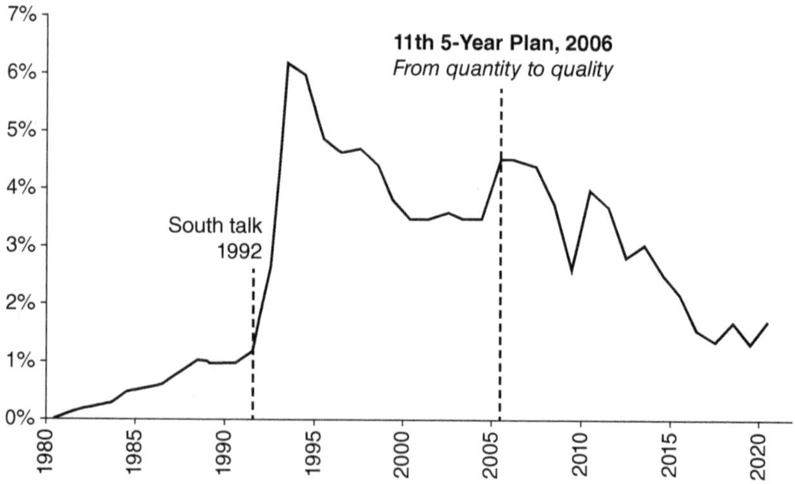

Figure 7.8 China's FDI to GDP ratio

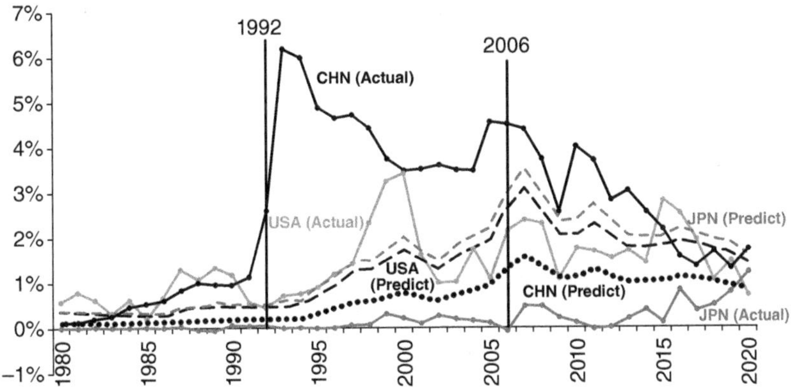

Figure 7.9 The actual and expected levels of inward FDI to GDP ratio

Once again, we estimate the "Norm Level" of the FDI-to-GDP ratio corresponding to China's economic development level. As shown in Figure 7.9, we observe again that the decline in China's dependence on FDI is also a phase in the process from an "over-the-norm" level to a more normal level.

We propose a broad indicator of economic openness that incorporates the role of FDI in domestic value production. The measure is based on the value-added accounting framework developed by Wang, Wei, Yu, and Zhu (2022) that incorporates both within- and cross-country supply chains, and importantly takes into account the presence of foreign firms in an economy.

Based on this decomposition framework, a country's value added can be disaggregated into four categories (see Table 7.1): (1) Local economic activities – value added that is produced without the participation of foreign invested enterprises (FIEs) and is eventually directly absorbed in the local market; (2) trade-related value – export value added that is produced without the participation of MNEs; (3) FDI-related but locally absorbed value creation – value added that is produced with the participation of MNEs but is directly absorbed in the local market; (4) value added related to both FIEs and exports – exported value added that is produced with the participation of MNEs.

By this accounting framework, "FDI-related" or "FDI and Trade-related" value-added creation can be further divided into three types of

Table 7.1 *Forward-linkage decomposition framework for identifying the "open economy" portion in GDP*

	Value added that is produced and consumed locally	Exported in the form of final goods or intermediate goods
D-D	Local Economic Activities (VA_D)	Open Economic Activities (Trade-Related, VA_T)
D-F F-D F-F	Open Economic Activities (FDI-related, VA_I)	Open Economic Activities (Trade and FDI-Related, VA_TI)

organizational forms: "Foreign-Foreign" (F-F), "Foreign-Domestic" (F-D), and "Domestic-Foreign" (D-F), enabling the distinction of the economic role of multinational corporations in the host country. (1) Foreign-Foreign (F-F): MNEs use the host country as a platform to collaborate with other MNEs, with no production connection to domestic firms in the host country. (2) Foreign-Domestic (F-D): MNEs serve as upstream intermediate goods suppliers, serving the downstream production of domestic firms in the host country. (3) Domestic-Foreign enterprise (D-F): MNEs serve as upstream intermediate goods suppliers, serving the downstream production of domestic firms in the host country. With this information, a broad degree of economic openness can be defined as

$$\text{Broader Indicator of Economic Openness} = \frac{\text{VA}_\text{T} + \text{VA}_\text{I} + \text{VA}_\text{TI}}{\text{GDP}}.$$

Similarly, from a "backward decomposition," we can also calculate the portion of value added in a country's final goods output that is related to local FIEs, international trade, or both.

We reexamine the evolution in China's economic openness with the two broader measures and compare them with the traditional indicator of trade-to-GDP ratio. As value-added decomposition requires the use of cross-border input–output tables, which are only available for 2000–2019, our analysis is limited to the same period. To ensure comparability of the results, the trade-to-GDP ratio is also computed based on the same ICIO table, whose numbers differ slightly from Figure 7.10.

In Figure 7.10, the two graphs in the first row show China's exports and imports in a share of GDP, whereas the two graphs in the second row trace the broad measures. Notably, the broad indicator of economic openness for China has risen to a level that is above both the largest developed economies (the United States, Japan, and Germany) and the largest developing countries (India and Brazil) in the early 2000s.

In Figure 7.11, both the broad indicators and the traditional trade-to-GDP were "above-the-norm" level before 2006 but started to

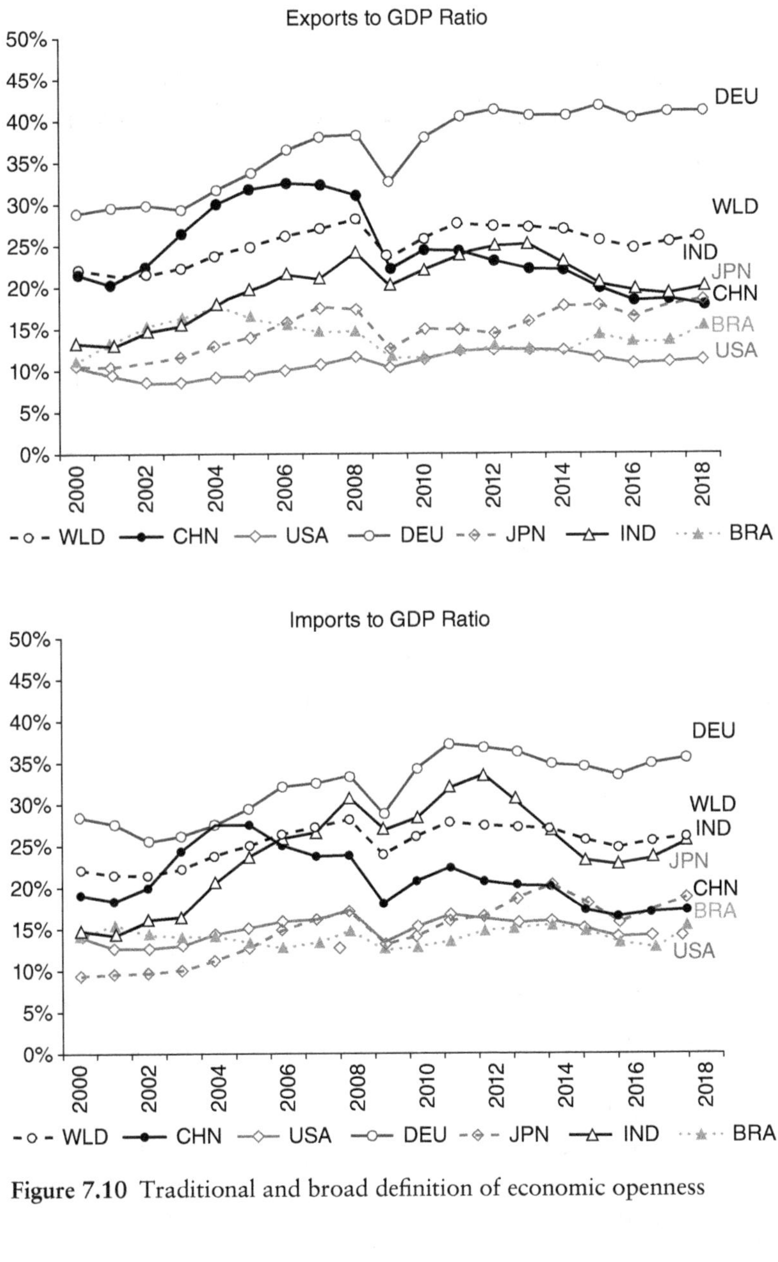

Figure 7.10 Traditional and broad definition of economic openness

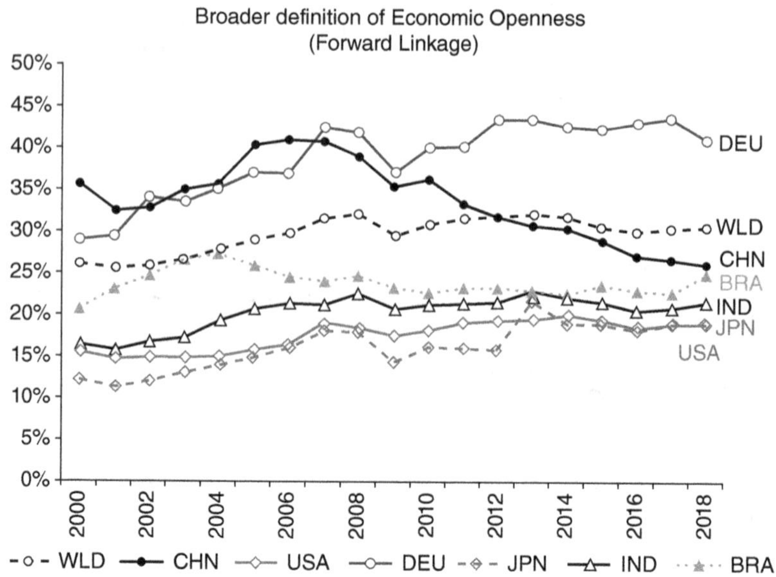

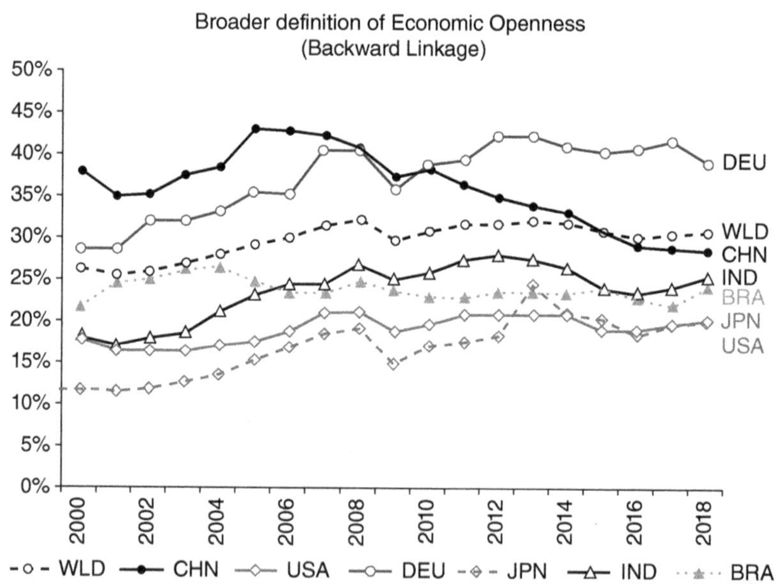

Figure 7.10 (cont.)

decline afterward, reaching a level similar to most other large economies by 2013. Some structural transformation has taken place (Figure 7.12). In particular, the D-F type activities – foreign firms in China

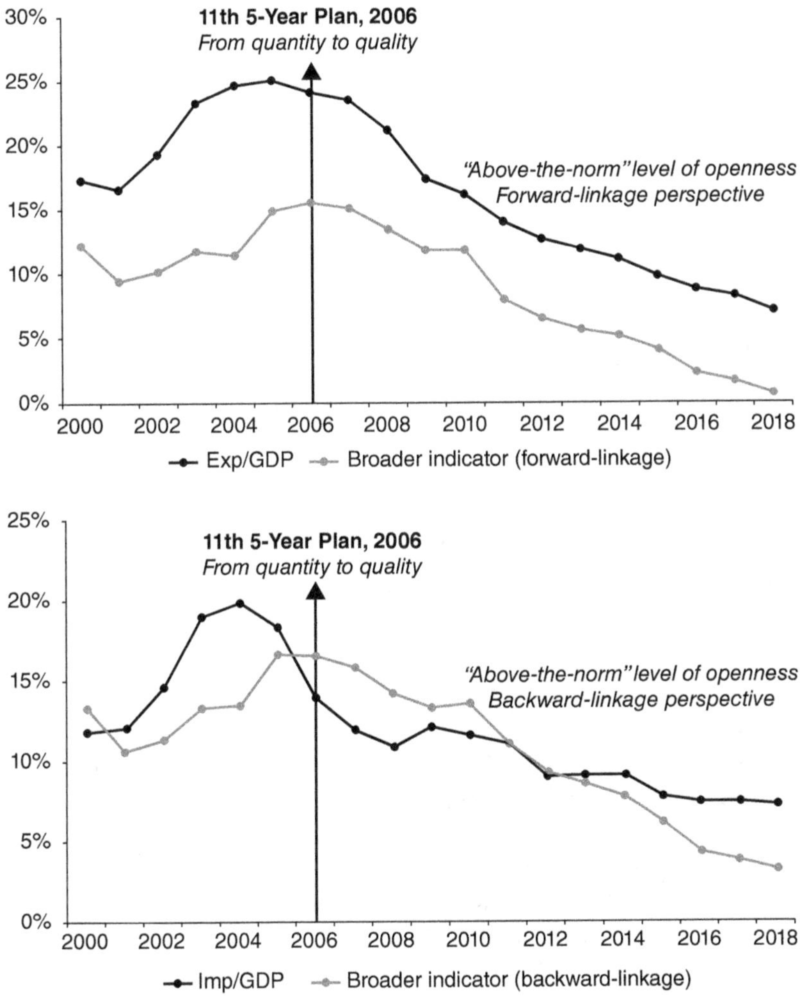

Figure 7.11 China's "above-the-norm" level of economic openness

buying inputs from Chinese firms – have risen in relative importance, while the F-D type – foreign firms in China supplying intermediate inputs to Chinese firms – and the F-F type – foreign firms in China supplying inputs to other foreign firms – have correspondingly declined in relative importance. These patterns may reflect rising capabilities of local Chinese firms in producing intermediate inputs for both other Chinese firms and foreign firms in China, replacing some of the upstream production activities that used to be carried out by multinational firms in China.

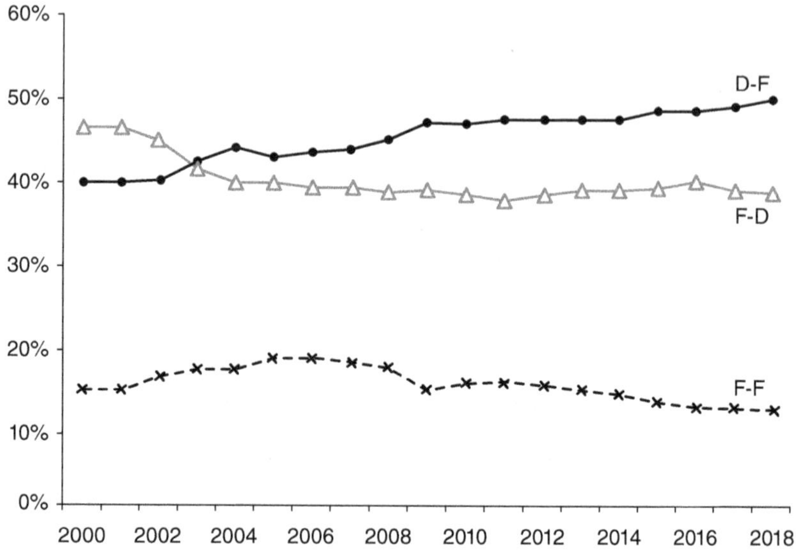

Figure 7.12 Different types of FDI-related value-added activities

Conclusion

We have reviewed China's journey to embracing economic openness with a view toward both "quality" and "quantity" of openness. In terms of trade openness measured by the ratio of total trade to GDP, the country has experienced three phases: a correction of a below-the-norm trade openness from 1980 to 1992, a progressive expansion of an above-the-norm openness from 1992 to 2006, and a progressive reduction of the above-the-norm openness. In terms of trade balance, we see the emergence of a large and persistent trade surplus from 1992 to 2006. These data patterns are likely related to each other. It is precisely the large trade surplus during 1992–2006 that has produced a steady stream of international pressure for China to reduce the trade surplus through a revaluation of the RMB, additional trade reforms, and other means. Indeed, the Chinese authorities started to talk about paying attention to the "quality of trade" and deemphasize the "quantity of trade" in their five-year plans. The Chinese central bank also introduced an exchange rate reform that effectively allowed an appreciation of the RMB. All of these factors may have contributed to a turnaround in the measured trade openness.

Consistent with these developments, China's export sophistication index started around 2006 to surge ahead to a level that is above what one would have predicted based on other countries' experience. The bundle of goods that China produces and exports looks increasingly like what is produced by a much richer country, consistent with a rise in domestic skill level.

A broader index of economic openness that incorporates both FDI-related value-added activities and trade-related activities exhibits a 50 percent higher level of openness than looking at trade-related activities alone. While we can only compute such measures for the 2000–2018 period, we see similar patterns nonetheless. In particular, by the early 2000s, China's broad indicator of economic openness was already above those of other large developed and developing economies. Since 2006, we see a gradual reduction in the above-the-norm openness.

There are many bumps in the roads ahead, including the geopolitical tensions, realignment of FDI in response to the rising wages in China, previous Covid lockdowns, U.S. policies aimed at reducing the technological capabilities of the Chinese, and China's own policy choices under the rubric of a "dual circulation strategy." Whether China's economic openness will stay at the international norm, fall below it, or surge above it will affect not only Chinese households and firms but also the rest of the world.

References

Amiti, M. and Javorcik, B. S., 2008. "Trade Costs and Location of Foreign Firms in China." *Journal of Development Economics*, 85 (1–2): 129–149.

Du, Q. and Wei, S. J., 2013."A Theory of the Competitive Saving Motive." *Journal of International Economics*, 91 (2): 275–289.

Hausmann, R., Hwang, J., and Rodrik, D. 2007. "What You Export Matters." *Journal of Economic Growth*, 12 (1): 1–25.

Ju, J., Shi, K. and Wei, S. J., 2021. "Trade Reforms and Current Account Imbalances." *Journal of International Economics*, 131: 103451.

Rodrik, D., 2006. "What's So Special about China's Exports?" *China & World Economy*, 14 (5): 1–19.

Song, Z., Storesletten, K., and Zilibotti, F. 2011. "Growing Like China." *American Economic Review*, 101 (1): 196–233.

Wei, S. J., and Zhang, X. 2011. "The Competitive Saving Motive: Evidence from Rising Sex Ratios and Savings Rates in China." *Journal of Political Economy*, 119 (3): 511–564. https://doi.org/10.1086/660887.

Wang, Z., and Wei, S. J. 2010. What Accounts for the Rising Sophistication of China's Exports? (No. w16500). National Bureau of Economic Research.

Wang, Y., Wei, S. J., Yu, X., and Zhu, K. 2022. "MNEs' Activities Measurements and Value-Added Tracing in GVCs." *Economic Research Journal*, (3): 136–154.

Young, A. 2000. "Gold into Base Metals: Productivity Growth in the People's Republic of China during the Reform Period." *The Quarterly Journal of Economics*, 115 (2): 389–416.

Appendix: Official statements on economic opening in Five-Year Plans

	The #th Five-Year Plan	Expressions in the Five-Year Plan
Emphasis on "planning"	Six (1981–1985)	统一计划、统一政策 Follow the principles of "unified planning and unified policies"
Emphasis on "scale" From the one-sided emphasis on exports to the promotion of balanced development of imports and exports.	Seven (1986–1990)	坚持进一步对外开放，在努力增加出口收汇的同时，节约使用各种外汇。 Further open up to the outside world, strive to increase export earnings, and at the same time save the use of various foreign currencies.
	Eight (1991–1995)	坚定不移地推进改革开放。进一步发展出口贸易，在坚持外汇收支平衡的前提下，适当增加进口。 Continued to advance reform and opening up. Further develop export trade, and under the premise of adhering to the balance of payments, appropriately increase imports.
	Nine (1996–2000)	扩大对外开放程度，提高对外开放水平。改革进口体制，提高出口竞争力。 Expand our degree of openness and elevate the level of opening-up, reform the import regime, and enhance our export competitiveness.
	Ten (2001–2005)	推动全方位、多层次、宽领域的对外开放。 Promote all-round, multi-tiered, and wide-ranging opening up to the outside world.

	The #th Five-Year Plan	Expressions in the Five-Year Plan
Emphasis on "quality and balance"	Eleven (2006–2010)	促进对外贸易由数量增加为主向质量提高为主转变。 We will promote the transformation of foreign trade from a focus on increasing quantity to improving quality as the main objective.
	Twelve (2011–2015)	推动外贸发展从规模扩张向质量效益提高转变、从成本优势向综合竞争优势转变。 Promote the shift of foreign trade from expanding scale to improving quality and efficiency, and from pursuing cost advantage to enhancing overall competitiveness.
	Thirteen (2016–2020)	奉行互利共赢的开放战略，坚持内外需协调 Pursue an opening-up strategy of mutual benefit, and adhere to the coordinated development of domestic and international demands.
	Fourteen (2021–2025)	加快构建以国内大循环为主体、国内国际双循环相互促进的新发展格局 Accelerating the establishment of a new development paradigm with domestic circulation as the mainstay, and with domestic and international circulations reinforcing each other.

8 *RMB Internalization and Digitization*

BIN WEI AND VIVIAN ZHANWEI YUE

Introduction

China's economy, which trails only that of the United States, has undergone a miraculous expansion over the past several decades. Since its accession to the World Trade Organization (WTO) in 2001, China has occupied the position of the world's leading exporter, a status that it has retained since 2009. However, the international prominence of the Renminbi (RMB), which is the official currency of China, has not yet reached the same level as that of its thriving economy.

The Chinese government initiated RMB internationalization in the mid-2000s, aiming to promote the use of the Chinese currency beyond China's borders for international trade, investment, and financial transactions. It has taken a number of steps in recent years to elevate the RMB to the ranks of elite currencies, such as the U.S. dollar, the euro, the Japanese yen, and the British pound sterling, by enhancing its global usage. The designation of the RMB as an official reserve currency by the International Monetary Fund (IMF) in 2015 is a significant milestone in its rise to global prominence.

Due to the Chinese government's endeavors to internationalize the RMB, many countries, including some of China's largest trading partners, have started to settle their trade transactions in RMB, and financial institutions around the world are increasingly offering RMB-denominated products and services. For example, cross-border trade settlement in RMB has expanded substantially from a minuscule level in 2009 to nearly 8 trillion RMB in 2021, accounting for about 20 percent of China's total external trade (comprising both exports and imports). On the other hand, China has established bilateral currency swap agreements with forty central banks or monetary authorities between 2009 and 2022, totaling approximately 3 trillion RMB notional amounts.

Despite such significant progress in RMB internationalization, there is still a long way to go before it can rival the dominance of the U.S.

dollar in the international monetary system. For example, the U.S. dollar is dominant in terms of its turnover in foreign exchange markets, accounting for nearly 90 percent of all turnovers in the last two decades, whereas the RMB accounted for about 7 percent in 2022. For the RMB to become a serious competitor to the U.S. dollar as a "safe haven" currency, China will need to undertake broader reforms of its institutional framework in addition to other market-oriented reforms.

More recently, the People's Bank of China (PBOC), the central bank of China, has been exploring the possibility of issuing a digital version of the RMB. This initiative, commonly known as "RMB digitalization," refers to the process of transforming the Chinese currency into a digital form, allowing it to be transacted, stored, and traded electronically. This transformation is part of China's broader efforts to modernize its financial system and move toward a more cashless economy.

At the forefront of this digitalization effort, the PBOC launched a pilot program for its digital currency in 2020. The digital currency is called Digital Currency Electronic Payment (DCEP), and it is designed to function like physical currency, allowing for peer-to-peer transactions without the need for intermediaries.

The introduction of RMB digitalization has significant implications for businesses and consumers alike. It provides greater convenience and security in making transactions, reduces the need for physical currency, and promotes financial inclusion by making it easier for people without bank accounts to participate in the economy.

Moreover, RMB digitalization has the potential to enhance China's position in the global financial system. As the use of digital currencies becomes more widespread, China's digital RMB could become an attractive option for cross-border transactions and trade settlements. Yet, there is still a long way to go before the RMB can challenge the dominance of the U.S. dollar as the world's reserve currency.

Overall, internationalization and digitalization are important developments in the global financial system and have significant implications for businesses and investors around the world. However, there remain several challenges China faces in its endeavors. One such challenge lies in the lack of convertibility of the RMB, particularly with regard to capital account transactions, making it difficult for foreign companies and investors to possess and utilize the RMB in cross-border transactions. Moreover, to garner the confidence of foreign businesses and investors on a global scale, more profound reforms within China's institutional framework are imperative for its currency to attain the esteemed "safe-haven" status. Similar to CBDCs in general, concerns regarding privacy, data security, and the potential exploitation of digital RMB for money laundering and other illicit activities pose serious considerations in China's effort to digitalize its currency.

RMB Internationalization

The internationalization of the RMB refers to the process of increasing the use of the RMB as a global currency. This includes promoting the use of RMB in international trade, investment, and financial transactions, as well as making it more widely available as a currency for foreign exchange reserves and debt issuance. The goal of RMB internationalization is to increase the role and influence of the RMB in the global financial system. An increasingly important RMB also helps reduce China's dependence on the U.S. dollar as the dominant international currency.

Motives

There are several important reasons for the Chinese government to internationalize the RMB. First, internationalizing the RMB helps reduce the dependence on the U.S. dollar as the dominant international currency. This would make the Chinese economy less vulnerable to fluctuations in the value of the dollar.

Second, by internationalizing the RMB, China hopes to increase its role and influence in the global financial system, making it more attractive to investors and traders. This would also improve China's economic and political influence on the global stage. Greater use of the RMB in international trade and investment could help Chinese companies access new markets, increase exports, and stimulate domestic economic growth.

China wants to elevate its currency to the ranks of other major currencies in the global financial system, namely the U.S. dollar (USD), the euro (EUR), the Japanese yen (JPY), and the British pound sterling (GBP). Guo et al. (2020) look at the internationalization path of these currencies and provide a historical perspective for the internationalization of the RMB. Chinese leaders want to boost the profile of the RMB as a reserve currency, as the status of the reserve currency represents the perception of security and resilience of the issuing country.

Recent Progress

In this subsection, we summarize the recent progress of RMB internalization along the dimensions of its functions as a unit of account, a medium of exchange, and a store of value. The process of RMB internationalization is a gradual and ongoing one, with the Chinese government taking measured steps to promote the use of its currency on the global stage. Roughly speaking, the RMB internationalization has evolved over several stages:

- Pre-2009: This was the period before the global financial crisis when the RMB was largely an onshore currency, and its use was primarily restricted to China.
- 2009–2015: This stage saw the initial steps towards RMB internationalization, with the PBOC allowing selected companies to settle their trade in RMB. The PBOC also signed a number of currency swap agreements with other central banks, which helped to promote the use of RMB in cross-border transactions.
- 2015–2016: In this stage, the PBOC announced the launch of the China International Payment System (CIPS), a cross-border payment system that allows the use of RMB in international transactions. The IMF also included the RMB in its basket of reserve currencies, known as the Special Drawing Right (SDR).
- 2017–2019: During this period, the use of RMB in global trade and investment continued to grow, with more countries accepting RMB as a settlement currency. The PBOC also allowed foreign investors greater access to China's domestic financial markets through programs such as the Bond Connect and Stock Connect.
- 2020–present: Currently, the RMB continues to gain acceptance as an international currency with increasing use in trade, investment, and global finance. China is also promoting the use of digital RMB, which is expected to further facilitate cross-border transactions and boost RMB internationalization.

In light of the key developments above, RMB internationalization was more policy-driven before 2015, focusing more on payments and clearings, and since then it has become more market-driven, focusing more on the investment function of the RMB.

Medium of exchange

The progress of RMB internationalization as a medium of exchange has been steady, and the currency still faces significant challenges in this regard. A medium of exchange is a currency that is used to buy and sell goods and services, and the wide adoption of a currency as a medium of exchange is critical to its internationalization.

Cross-border RMB settlement of trade and direct investment. Given China's tremendous trade volumes, promoting greater use of the RMB in settling cross-border trade and investment transactions constitutes an important step towards the internationalization of the currency.

In Figure 8.1, we plot the RMB settlement of the goods trade (dark gray bars) and the trade of cross-border services and other items (light gray bars) in trillion RMB under the current account between 2010 and 2021. Following the launch of the pilot program of RMB settlement of cross-border trade transactions in July 2009, cross-border trade settlement in RMB expanded substantially from 2.56 billion RMB in 2009 to more than 7 trillion RMB in 2015, when the RMB was accepted for inclusion into the IMF's SDR basket.

The PBOC published the breakdown of RMB settlement transactions into imports and exports for the first couple of years after the

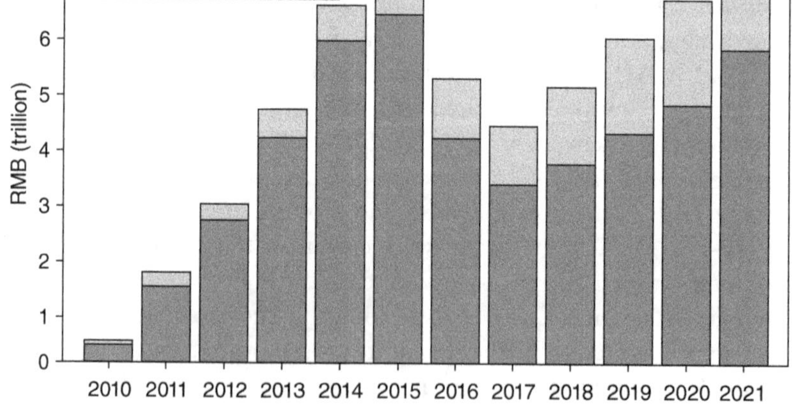

Figure 8.1 RMB settlement under the current account
Note: This figure plots the RMB settlement of goods trade (dark gray bars) and cross-border services trade and other items (light gray bars) in trillion RMB under the current account between 2010 and 2021. Source: PBOC.

RMB trade settlement was initiated but stopped publishing such disaggregated data shortly after. The available data on the breakdown suggest that most of the RMB trade settlements in the early 2010s involved payments by Chinese importers in RMB, which allowed foreign exporters to obtain the currency that was otherwise difficult to acquire.

Such a one-sided pattern of RMB settlement transactions is consistent with the appreciationary pressure on the currency back then. As the RMB began to slide towards a depreciationary path around 2014, interest in settling trade transactions with RMB dwindled. Consequently, the volume of RMB settlement declined to 4.3 trillion RMB in 2017, only to recover to nearly 8 trillion RMB in 2021 amidst the strong economic climate, representing approximately 20 percent of China's entire external trade (comprising exports and imports).

On the other hand, the RMB settlement of cross-border direct investment has seen a similar rise since 2010, when the pilot program of RMB settlement on foreign direct investment (FDI) was first launched. In particular, the volume of ODI-related (FDI-related) RMB settlement soared to 1.6 (4.2) trillion RMB in 2021 (see Figure 8.2).

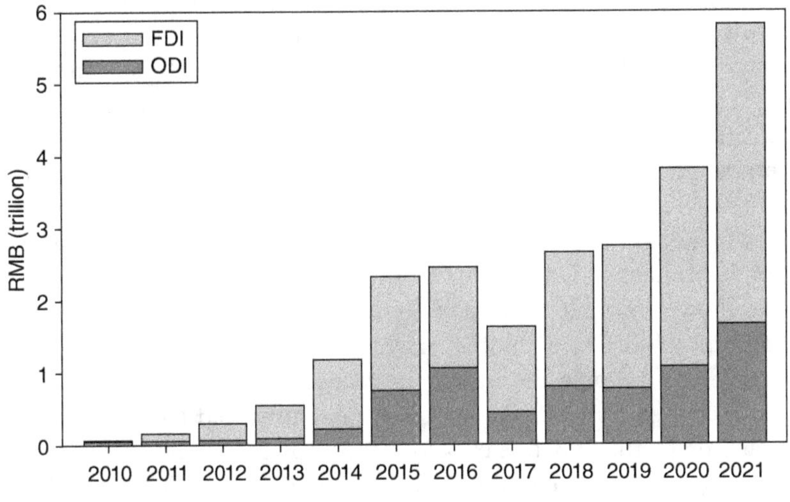

Figure 8.2 RMB settlement of cross-border direct investment
Note: This figure plots the RMB settlement of cross-border outward direct investment (ODI, dark gray) and foreign direct investment (FDI, light gray) in trillions of RMB between 2010 and 2021. Source: PBOC.

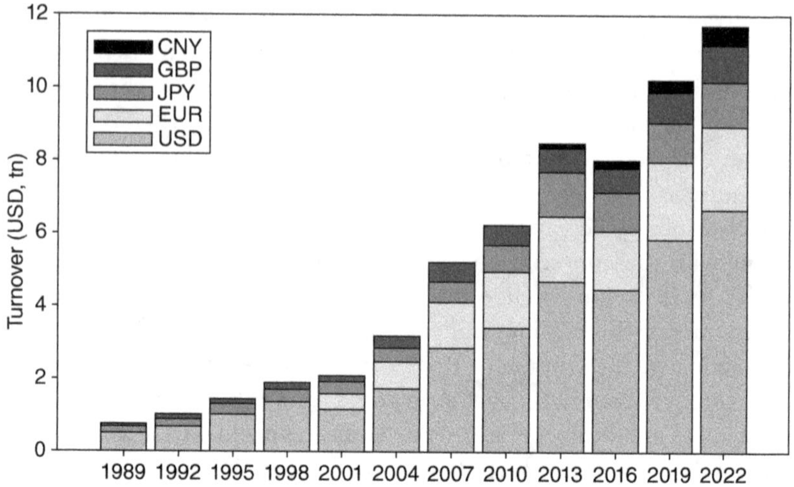

Figure 8.3 Average daily turnover of major currencies
Note: This figure plots the average daily turnover of USD, EUR, JPY, GBP, and CNY in global foreign exchange markets between 1989 and 2022, represented by light gray, silver gray, medium gray, charcoal gray, and black, respectively. Source: BIS's Triennial Central Bank Survey of Foreign Exchange and OTC Derivatives Markets.

Foreign exchange transactions. The pace of the RMB internationalization also depends on the use of the currency in foreign exchange transactions. The Bank for International Settlements (BIS) conducts the Triennial Central Bank Survey of Foreign Exchange and OTC Derivatives Markets, a survey of central banks around the world once every three years on foreign exchange market turnover, derivatives markets, etc. According to the survey, the average daily turnover of RMB in global foreign exchange markets increased from zero to more than 500 billion USD between 2001 and 2022 (see Figure 8.3).

As shown in Table 8.1, the daily turnover of RMB accounted for 7 percent of the total global amount and surpassed AUD, CAD, and CHF to become the fifth most traded currency. Although foreign exchange transactions in RMB have advanced to a significant extent, they still remain far below those of the traditional reserve currencies. For example, the U.S. dollar is dominant in terms of its turnover in foreign exchange markets, accounting for nearly 90 percent (of 200 percent, as each transaction involves two currencies and is thus counted twice) of all turnover in the last two decades. The

Table 8.1 *Shares of daily foreign exchange turnover of major currencies (%)*

Year	USD	EUR	JPY	GBP	CNY
2001	89.8	37.9	23.5	13.1	0
2004	88.0	37.4	20.8	16.5	0.1
2007	85.6	37.0	17.2	14.9	0.5
2010	84.8	39.0	19.0	12.9	0.9
2013	87.0	33.4	23.1	11.8	2.2
2016	87.6	31.4	21.6	12.8	4.0
2019	88.3	32.3	16.8	12.8	4.3
2022	88.4	30.5	16.7	12.9	7.0

Note: This table reports the shares of daily turnover of major currencies in foreign exchange markets in percentages between 2001 and 2022. Source: BIS's Triennial Central Bank Survey of Foreign Exchange and OTC Derivatives Markets.

four major reserve currencies (the dollar, the euro, the yen, and the pound sterling) together account for about 150 percent of the total turnover in 2022.

Currency swap agreements. China has also established bilateral currency swap agreements with a number of countries, which allow direct RMB settlements in trade and investment transactions.

Figure 8.4 plots the cumulative amount of newly signed RMB swaps (gray-shaded area, left axis) in trillion RMB and the total number of newly signed agreements (black line, right axis) between 2009 and 2022. As shown in the figure, a total of forty swap line agreements were signed in that period with a total notional amount of nearly 3 trillion RMB. Most of the swap line agreements were signed before 2015, with a significant slowdown after the RMB was included in the SDR's currency basket in 2016.

Figure 8.5 plots the forty central banks that signed bilateral RMB currency swaps with the PBOC between 2009 and 2022 on the World Map. The size of each circle corresponds to the amount of each swap agreement at initialization. The largest such arrangement is with the European Central Bank, for 350 billion RMB, signed in October 2013. The PBOC's arrangements with the Hong Kong Monetary Authority, the Bank of Australia, the Bank of England, the Bank of Canada, and the Bank of Japan are the second largest, for 200 billion

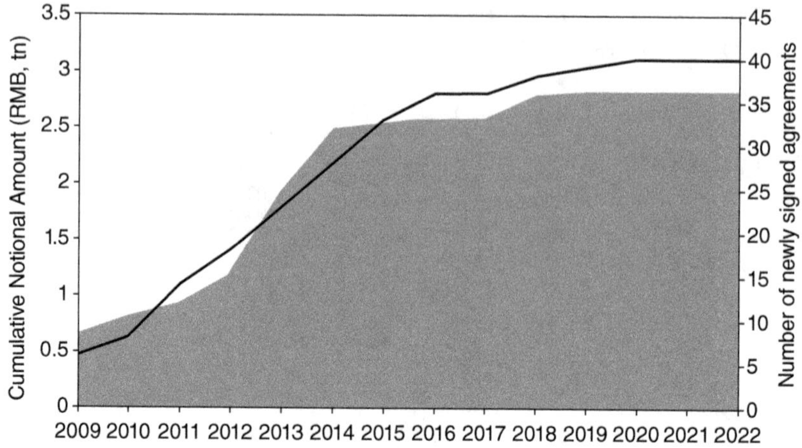

Figure 8.4 RMB currency swaps
Note: This figure plots the cumulative amount of newly signed RMB swaps (gray-shaded area, left axis) in trillion RMB and the total number of newly signed agreements (black line, right axis) between 2009 and 2022. Source: PBOC.

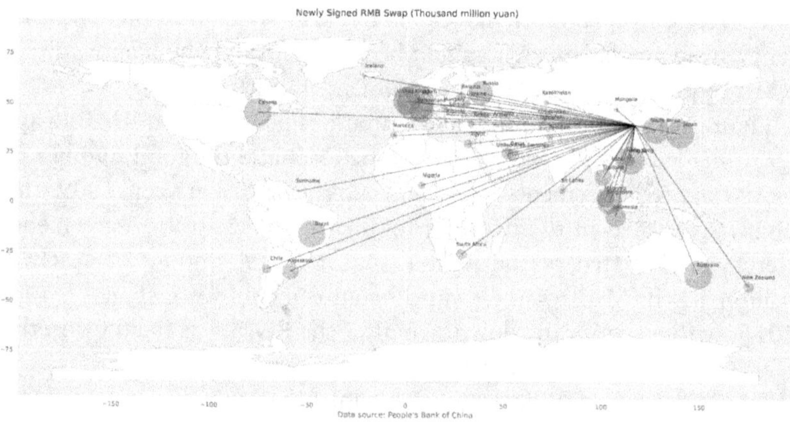

Figure 8.5 Map of RMB currency swap arrangements
Note: This figure plots the forty central banks that signed bilateral RMB currency swaps with the PBOC between 2009 and 2022 in the world map. The size of each circle is proportional to the amount of the swap agreement. Source: PBOC.

RMB. The Bank of England was the first central bank in the G7 to sign a swap agreement with the PBOC, signed in June 2013, with the goal of making London an important offshore center for RMB-denominated activity.

Perks et al. (2021) discuss the history and evolution of bilateral swap lines, which are agreements between two central banks to exchange their respective currencies in times of need. It provides an overview of the use of swap lines during the global financial crisis of 2008–2009 and the COVID-19 pandemic in 2020. The paper highlights the benefits of swap lines in stabilizing financial markets during times of stress and recommends further cooperation and coordination among central banks to strengthen the swap network and enhance its effectiveness in managing crises.

Bahaj and Reis (2022) argue that the swap lines helped trigger a jumpstart of the RMB as an international currency for payments. Specifically, they show that for a typical country that signed a swap line agreement with the PBOC, the use of the RMB was little prior to the agreement but started to increase significantly afterwards. They argue that such policies can start the internationalization status of a currency because the choices of the currency of working capital and sales invoicing complement each other.

Belt and Road Initiative. To further promote trade and investment between China and countries in Asia, Europe, and Africa, China launched a development strategy in 2013 also known as the "One Belt One Road" initiative (BRI). The BRI involves the construction of various infrastructure projects, such as roads, railways, ports, and pipelines, to connect countries and regions along the route. Despite some criticism that China uses the initiative to expand its influence and increase its geopolitical power, the BRI has been gaining momentum, with more and more countries participating in the initiative. The former governor of the PBOC, Zhou (2017), emphasized that China could collaborate with relevant countries to increase the use of RMB in investments and financing, thus promoting internationalization of RMB. Internationalization of the RMB would benefit trade and investment along the BRI route because it can mitigate exchange losses, reduce capital and transaction costs, and serve as a powerful driver for BRI development. By conducting a top-level design for RMB internationalization and cooperating with relevant countries, China can further strengthen the role of RMB in these regions.

Store of value

The progress of internationalization of the RMB as a value store has been slow but steady in the past few years. An important development is the inclusion of the RMB in the Special Drawing Rights (SDR) basket of the IMF in 2016, alongside the U.S. dollar, euro, yen, and pound sterling. This move recognized the RMB as an international currency and gave it greater legitimacy and visibility on the global stage.

The inclusion of the RMB in the IMF's SDR basket was approved on November 30, 2015, marking a milestone in the internationalization of the Chinese currency. The inclusion became effective on October 1, 2016, and the RMB joined the U.S. dollar, euro, Japanese yen, and British pound as a fifth currency in the SDR basket. As such, the RMB was recognized as another major reserve currency and was given greater legitimacy and visibility on the global stage. Its weight in the SDR basket has increased from the initial level of 10.9–12.3 percent since August 2022 (see Figure 8.6).

Since the RMB's inclusion in the SDR basket, its use as an international reserve currency has increased. According to the IMF, the RMB's share of global foreign exchange reserves held by central banks increased from 1.1 percent in 2015 to 2.2 percent in 2020. The RMB has also become more widely used in international trade and investment, with its share of global payments and settlements increasing steadily in recent years.

According to the IMF's database on official foreign exchange reserve composition (COFER), total foreign reserves in RMB amounted to approximately 300 billion USD in 2022 Q3, more than triple the amount reported in 2016 Q4 when the database began to report official reserves in RMB after its inclusion in the SDR basket (see Figure 8.7). As shown in Table 8.2, almost 3 percent of the foreign reserves of all COFER-reporting countries were in RMB at 2022 Q3, a substantial increase from approximately 1 percent at the end of 2016. Although the share of total foreign reserves in USD has dropped from 65 percent to about 60 percent during the same period between 2016 and 2022, the USD is still the dominant reserve currency.

One of the key initiatives has been the establishment of offshore RMB centers in major financial centers around the world, such as London, Hong Kong, and Singapore. These centers allow foreign companies and investors to hold and transact in RMB without having

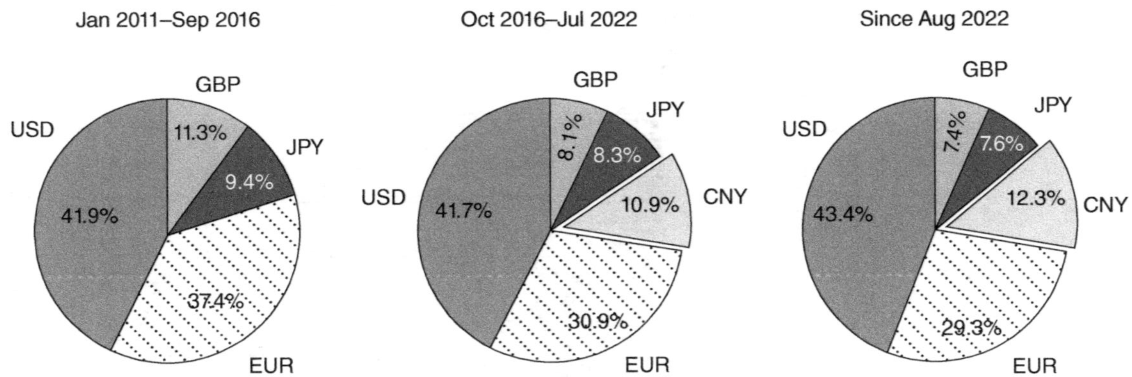

Figure 8.6 SDR basket

Note: This figure plots the composition of the SDR basket since 2011, consisting of USD, EUR, JPY, GBP, and CNY depicted by charcoal gray, white striped, dark gray, medium gray, and light gray segments in the pie chart, respectively. Source: IMF.

Table 8.2 *Shares of foreign reserves in major currencies (%)*

Year	USD	EUR	JPY	GBP	CNY
2016	65.4	19.1	4.0	4.3	1.1
2017	62.7	20.2	4.9	4.5	1.2
2018	61.8	20.7	5.2	4.4	1.9
2019	60.7	20.6	5.9	4.6	1.9
2020	58.9	21.3	6.0	4.7	2.3
2021	58.8	20.6	5.5	4.8	2.8
2022	59.8	19.7	5.3	4.6	2.8

Note: This table reports the shares of total foreign reserves of COFER-reporting countries in major currencies, namely, USD, EUR, JPY, GBR, and CNY, between 2016 and 2022. Source: IMF's COFER Database.

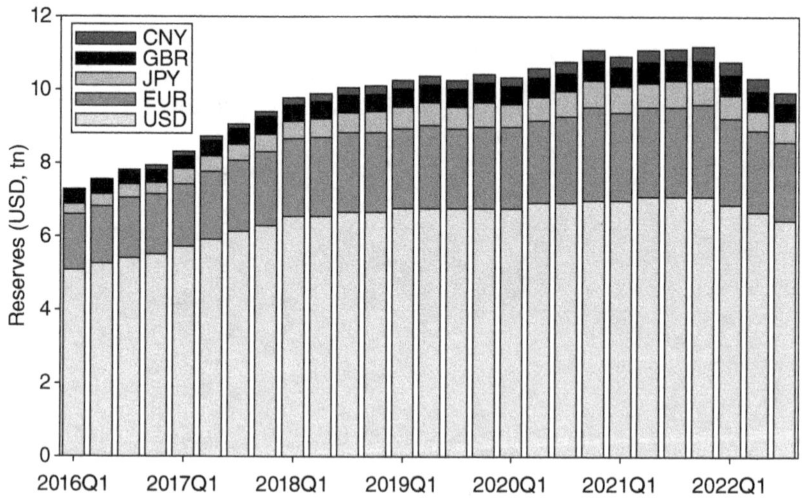

Figure 8.7 Total foreign reserves in major currencies
Note: This figure plots the total foreign reserves of COFER-reporting countries in major currencies, namely, USD, EUR, JPY, GBP, and CNY, between 2016 and 2022, represented by silver gray, medium gray, light gray, black, and charcoal gray bars, respectively. Source: IMF's COFER Database.

to go through the Chinese mainland, thus reducing transaction costs and increasing the attractiveness of the RMB as a store of value.

Another major development is the gradual opening of China's financial markets to foreign investors. The Qualified Foreign Institutional

Investor (QFII) scheme enables institutional investors who meet specific criteria to participate in the PRC equities and bond markets. QFIIs can invest in these markets under this transitional arrangement. Through platforms such as Bond Direct, foreign investors now invest in 3.2 trillion foreign holdings of RMB bonds. The monthly trading volume of RMB bonds reaches RMB 744 billion.

However, despite these efforts, the RMB is still not widely accepted as a reserve currency by central banks and is not yet a major component of international trade settlements. As a result, its use as a store of value remains limited compared to the U.S. dollar and other major currencies.

Unit of account

The progress of RMB internationalization as a unit of account has been slower than its progress as a store of value. A unit of account is a currency that is used to measure the value of goods, services, assets, and liabilities in an economy. As part of China's broader efforts to promote the use of the RMB as a unit of account, in March 2018, China launched its first RMB-denominated crude oil futures contract on the Shanghai International Energy Exchange, which is the first futures listed on China's mainland to overseas investors. By providing a new pricing mechanism for crude oil in RMB, China is seeking to reduce the influence of the U.S. dollar on the global energy market and increase the use of its own currency in international trade. Overall, the use of the RMB as a unit of account remains limited.

Challenges and Prospects

Although the Chinese government has taken steps to promote the use of the RMB on the global stage, the currency is still not widely accepted in international transactions. One major obstacle is the lack of convertibility of the RMB, particularly for capital account transactions. This makes it difficult for foreign businesses and investors to hold and use RMB in cross-border transactions. Currently, China's exchange rate policy is characterized by a "two-pillar" policy, as shown in Jermann et al. (2022), aiming to balance exchange rate flexibility and RMB index stability via market and stability pillars. For the RMB to become an important reserve currency, suitable reforms would be needed to make its exchange rate policy more market-driven.

Another challenge is the lack of trust in the Chinese financial system. Investors and companies may be reluctant to use the RMB as a medium of exchange if they are not confident in the reliability of Chinese economic data and the stability of its financial system. Examining the history of the rise of the British pound and the U.S. dollar, some researchers point out that an open financial market is key for a country's currency to become widely used on international markets. Because China's capital account is not fully liberalized, it becomes the main roadblock for the RMB to become an international reserve currency (Frankel, 2011). Eichengreen et al. (2022) argue that the RMB has the potential to gain its importance as an international currency with the assistance of import financing, debt payments, payment infrastructures, currency swap lines, and offshore markets. Clayton et al. (2022) argue that China's gradualistic approach – gradually allowing flightier foreign investors into its domestic bond market – is a good one to build a reputation as an international currency issuer.

Lastly, whether the RMB becomes a serious competitor to the U.S. dollar depends on whether it is seen as a "safe-haven" currency. A safe-haven currency, for example, the U.S. dollar, is one to which investors turn during turbulent times. If China is not perceived as a safe haven, it is unlikely that the RMB will account for a substantial portion of global foreign exchange reserves, even if it may become a significant reserve currency. As noted by Prasad (2016), a country seeking the safe-haven status "must have a sound institutional framework – including an independent judiciary, an open and democratic government, and robust public institutions (especially a credible central bank) – to earn the trust of foreign investors." Therefore, he argues that "for the RMB to become a safe haven currency, however, China will have to undertake broader reforms of its institutional framework that would ultimately alter its political, legal, and public institutions."

RMB Digitalization

The digital yuan, also known as the digital renminbi (e-CNY) or DCEP, is a centralized digital currency issued by the PBOC. China is a pioneer in digital currency, and the RMB digitalization has been an important issue for policymakers and researchers.

China has been a leader in digital payment. AliPay and WeChatPay are the major digital payment platforms. These platforms are mobile payment solutions that allow users to make digital payments for various goods and services through their smartphones. Alipay and WeChatPay are privately operated digital payment platforms, primarily used for consumer transactions within their ecosystems. They are operated by private companies and are subject to relevant regulations, but they are not directly controlled by the government or central bank. Yet the development of these digital payment platforms makes the introduction of CBDC easier to accept by households in China.

Main Features of CBDCs

A central bank digital currency (CBDC) is a digital version of a country's national currency that is issued and backed by the central bank. It is similar to traditional physical currency, but it exists in a digital form and can be stored and transferred electronically. CBDCs are designed to coexist with physical currency and bank deposits rather than replace them.

CBDCs can take several forms. Some countries are exploring the creation of digital versions of their existing physical currency, while others are looking at creating new digital currencies that are distinct from their existing currency.

CBDCs, if designed with caution, may have the potential to provide greater durability, safety, accessibility, and affordability compared to private digital currencies. This is particularly evident in contrast to unsecured cryptocurrencies, which are inherently unpredictable. Kiff et al. (2020) conduct a comprehensive research survey that examines key considerations around CBDC.

The Progress of RMB Digitalization

The idea of a digital RMB has been around for several years. In 2014, the PBOC began to investigate the feasibility of a digital currency. In November 2020, the PBOC announced that it had completed the "top-level design" of the DCEP system and that it was ready to move to the next stage of development.

The top-level design of China's DCEP system, as stated by the PBOC, is a two-tier system, consisting of the central bank and commercial banks. The PBOC acts as the issuer and regulator of DCEP, and will maintain the digital currency accounts of commercial banks and also has the responsibility of issuing and destroying DCEP. Commercial banks will be responsible for the distribution and circulation of DCEP and will also be responsible for maintaining the digital currency accounts of individuals and organizations.

The DCEP has a similar denomination as the paper money and will have the same legal status as the Renminbi. The DCEP will have the same rights and obligations as cash and will be protected by the same laws and regulations. The e-CNY is designed to be a more efficient and secure way to make payments than traditional cash or credit cards. It can be used to make payments online or in-store and can also be used to send and receive money between individuals.

The DCEP is based on blockchain technology and is designed to be fully compatible with existing payment systems, which will allow it to be used in various scenarios such as retail payments, cross-border trade, and public transportation systems. It is also designed to be interoperable with other digital currencies and foreign currencies, which will allow it to be used in cross-border trade and investment.

It is worth noting that the DCEP is designed to be a controllable and anonymous system, which will allow the central bank to have more direct oversight of transactions and reduce the risks of financial crimes such as money laundering and the financing of illegal activities. DCEP also grants central banks access to data stored by intermediaries.

The Chinese government has been actively promoting the development of DCEP and has tested it in several pilot cities such as Shenzhen, Suzhou, and Chengdu. In 2016, the PBOC launched a pilot program in Shenzhen to test a digital yuan. It is believed that a small amount of the DCEP has been issued in these pilot tests. The DCEP has also been used in a number of pilot projects, including public transportation systems, retail payments, and cross-border trade. The pilot program was successful, and in 2019, the PBOC announced that it would launch a national digital yuan. It is also reported that the PBOC has been testing the DCEP in a closed-loop system, meaning that the DCEP is only being used in a limited number of scenarios and is not yet in circulation among the general public. The DCEP continues to progress with more than 100 million individual users and billions of yuan in transactions.

The DCEP is, however, still in the testing phase, and it is hard to say how successful it will be. The PBOC has not yet officially announced the amount of DCEP that has been issued. Despite some indications that the DCEP is making progress, there are still some challenges that need to be addressed, such as regulatory and legal frameworks, technical issues, and international coordination. Overall, China's CBDC project is considered to be one of the most advanced in the world, and it has the potential to become a global leader in the field, but it is still too early to say how successful it will be.

Implications for China

China's interest in the development of a digital RMB is motivated by a number of factors, including the desire to increase the efficiency of its payment system. With a CBDC, payments could be made faster, cheaper, and more secure by reducing the need for intermediaries such as banks. This could significantly increase the speed of transactions, reduce transaction costs, and improve the overall payment experience for consumers and businesses. The resulting more streamlined payment system is better able to meet the needs of consumers and businesses. In addition, a CBDC could provide increased financial inclusion for those who are unbanked or underbanked, as it would provide a low-cost and accessible payment system.

Another potential benefit of a CBDC for China is the ability to reduce the risks of financial crime, such as money laundering and financing of illegal activities. By providing the central bank with more direct oversight of transactions, a CBDC could reduce the risks of financial crime and increase the transparency of financial transactions. The traceability and transparency of a CBDC could make it easier for law enforcement agencies to identify and prevent financial crimes, providing a significant benefit to society.

A CBDC could also improve monetary policy by providing the PBOC with new tools to control interest rates and the money supply. This could enable the PBOC to better implement monetary policy, which could help stabilize the economy, reduce the risks of inflation and deflation, and ensure financial stability in the long term.

Moreover, the issuance of a CBDC would increase China's control over the financial system, which could help reduce the risks of systemic financial crises. This would enable the Chinese government to better manage the financial system and respond to economic shocks, which could help promote stability and growth. Direct control of the central bank over the payment system would allow for more effective regulation and oversight, reducing the risks of financial instability.

Finally, a CBDC could promote the internationalization of the RMB by increasing its global usage and decreasing the dominance of the U.S. dollar in the international financial system. This could help to reduce China's dependence on the U.S. dollar and increase its influence in the global economy.

Challenges and Prospects

The development of a CBDC by China has the potential to offer a range of benefits, including increased efficiency, reduced financial crime, enhanced monetary policy, increased control over the financial system, and the promotion of internationalization of the RMB. These potential benefits could have significant implications for China's economy and its role in the global financial system.

Although the potential benefits of CBDCs are significant, there are also a number of concerns that must be addressed. One of the main concerns is the potential impact on the banking system. CBDCs could potentially reduce the demand for bank deposits and change the money multiplier, which could have implications for the stability of the banking system. The introduction of CBDCs could also lead to a crowding-out effect on bank deposits, which could reduce the availability of credit and potentially harm the economy. Finally, it is not clear whether CBDCs make it possible for policies of negative interest rates by giving negative returns to cash.

Recent literature studies how the introduction of a CBDC affects the economy in which both currency and bank deposits are used in exchange [Williamson (2022) and Keister and Sanches (2023), Agur and Dell'Ariccia (2022)]. There is an important policy trade-off: while a digital currency tends to improve efficiency in exchange, it can also crowd out bank deposits, increase banks' funding costs, and decrease investment. The design of DCEP in China aims to mitigate such policy trade-offs. China currently does not pay interest on CBDC holdings. The reason is to limit CBDC's competition with bank deposits. If there is no interest, CBDC can still be attractive as a payment means, even when its attractiveness as a store of value diminishes. However, only time can tell the real impact of CBDC on the Chinese economy after a full-scale implementation of the DCEP in China.

Privacy and data security are also important considerations. CBDCs could potentially enable the central bank to monitor all transactions, raising concerns about the privacy and security of personal financial information. Wang (2021) shows that a fully cash-like CBDC design could also increase tax evasion. It will be important to ensure that appropriate data protection measures are in place to safeguard the privacy of individuals. However, as discussed in Schilling (2019), a complete record of transactions attached to user identities leads to its own challenges, in particular around cybersecurity, with the potential for the central bank to become an attractive "honeypot" of data for hackers.

Another concern is the potential for money laundering and the financing of illegal activities. CBDCs could make it easier for criminals to conduct transactions without detection, which could undermine the integrity of the financial system. This highlights the need for strong measures to counter money laundering and counter-terrorism financing alongside the development of CBDCs.

In general, the development of CBDCs is an area of active research and experimentation, with many important questions that still need to be answered. Auer et al. (2021) surveyed the growing literature on CBDCs on the various issues related to operational architectures, technologies, and privacy, and the implications for the financial system, financial stability, and monetary policy. As CBDCs continue to evolve, it will be important to address these concerns and questions to ensure that the benefits of CBDCs are realized while minimizing potential risks.

Prospects of RMB Internationalization

Impact of Digital RMB on the Internationalization of RMB

If the DCEP system is utilized on an international scale, it could streamline cross-border RMB payments for companies that import or export from China. This could minimize currency exchange costs and risks by eliminating the need for the U.S. dollar as an intermediary currency. DCEP's cost-effective nature has the potential to break through the current entrenched network characteristics of the global currency system, which often still relies on the U.S. dollar even when third currencies could be exchanged directly into RMB. Furthermore, DCEP could be integrated into broader digitization programs for trade with China.

At the same time, we cannot ignore the profound challenges posed by the macroprudential aspects of cross-border utilization of CBDC. Adverse macroeconomic implications, such as increased currency substitution and vulnerability to financial shocks, are possible as retail CBDC becomes available across borders.

The PBOC is also exploring how retail CBDC, such as e-CNY, can be used for cross-border payments and has partnered with the BIS Innovation Hub and other national central banks in the multi-CBDC Bridge project, an experimental CBDC arrangement that uses distributed ledger technology (DLT) to facilitate cross-border payments.

The PBOC states three principles for their ongoing work on cross-border payments for CBDC. The first is the principle of "no disruption," which in practice means avoiding negative spillovers on the Chinese economy and that of other nations, such as significant currency substitution. The second rule is that any CBDC cross-border payments system must comply with the rules and regulations of all connected countries, including capital flow management measures. In addition, according to the PBOC, information flows between countries should be improved to help authorities counter the illicit use of money, including tax evasion. According to the third rule, cross-border payments should involve interoperability between domestic CBDCs or between domestic CBDCs and incumbent payment systems rather than a single CBDC used for transactions on both sides of the border. The PBOC thus prefers a system in which domestic CBDCs are converted to other currencies as payments cross borders.

Moreover, individuals in other countries could also use DCEP for common payments and transactions, especially in developing countries with underdeveloped financial infrastructures or unstable currencies. DCEP could function as an alternative to local currency and provide digital payments to remote areas and unbanked populations. As the number of unbanked adults globally is significant, especially in developing countries, DCEP's accessibility could be particularly attractive in these regions. Nations entwined in intimate ties with China or hosting a significant influx of Chinese tourists may likewise embrace DCEP. Across numerous Asian and African countries, cross-border payment activities involving the Chinese RMB are already on the rise, while Chinese electronic payment enterprises like Ant Financial and Tencent are extending their presence in burgeoning markets.

Furthermore, DCEP could potentially provide an efficient and possibly more economical alternative to the SWIFT payments system used for most international transactions between financial institutions. China may also partially relax its capital control based on DCEP. Wei (2023) remarked that DCEP can facilitate partial capital account liberalization without formally removing capital controls because PBOC can control the types of financial investors using DCEP.

However, China's digital RMB is not a fast track to internationalization of the currency. Some proponents contend that the digital RMB introduces a novel and sophisticated payment framework capable of posing a challenge to the supremacy of the U.S. dollar because of the innovative technology and standards used to create the digital currency. These claims may be exaggerated. The digital RMB is primarily intended for domestic retail transactions and is still in its experimental phase. Although the PBOC has conducted trials for cross-border transactions using the digital RMB, these efforts have been limited to the Beijing 2022 Winter Olympics.

Latest Developments and the Future of RMB Internationalization

The Ukraine–Russia war that began in 2022 caused escalating geopolitical tensions. In particular, in 2022, the European Union and other Western countries imposed sanctions on Russia, including a SWIFT ban on some Russian banks, aiming to weaken Russia's economy by hindering their access to the SWIFT financial system. These recent changes in geopolitical factors may play a role in China's RMB internationalization. Some countries could find the U.S. dollar more appealing as a safe-haven currency, potentially slowing the RMB's internationalization. On the other hand, China may accelerate efforts to promote the RMB as an alternative to reduce reliance on the dollar-dominated financial system amid possible sanctions. Furthermore, changes in global commodity markets could increase the demand for using the RMB in energy trade, bolstering its internationalization. Monitoring these developments is essential to understanding the RMB's evolving role in the global monetary system.

For example, the acceptance of RMB in settlements between Russia and countries in Asia, Africa, and Latin America demonstrates its growing global presence. With Russia already holding 17 percent of its foreign reserves in yuan as of July 2023 and the RMB becoming the third most demanded on the Moscow Exchange, the RMB's role as a reserve currency is solidifying. As China's partnerships with countries like Brazil and the Association of Southeast Asian Nations (ASEAN) strengthen, the RMB's position on the global stage is set to grow even stronger.

The global ascendancy of the RMB holds the promise of presenting a formidable challenge to the preeminent stature of the U.S. dollar within the global financial realm. However, it remains unclear to what extent the RMB can emerge as a potent alternative to the dollar in the coming years. The RMB still has a long way to go before it can truly compete with the dollar as a global reserve currency. Although the RMB has gained in popularity as a trade and investment currency, it still has a relatively low share of global currency reserves and is not widely used in international transactions.

Another obstacle is that the Chinese government still maintains strict controls over the exchange rate and capital flows of the RMB, which limits its attractiveness as a global currency. The RMB is also not fully convertible, and the Chinese financial markets are not fully open; these factors make it harder for the RMB to be used as an alternative to the U.S. dollar. Jermann et al. (2022) provide a detailed analysis of the two-pillar policy for the RMB. Based on the monetary model for the RMB in Jermann et al. (2022), the two-pillar policy emerges endogenously as an optimal response of the government, which faces the key trade-offs between exchange rate flexibility and current account stability.

According to Eichengreen et al. (2022), it is possible for China to achieve the internationalization of the RMB even if there is no complete financial liberalization. The RMB could potentially have a more significant international role, particularly as a form of central bank reserves. China's path is crucially based on the fast-growing use of RMB in voicing and settling China's foreign trade and payments. China's policy in developing offshore RMB markets and central bank swap lines thus plays a major role.

The timing for RMB's full internationalization is not straightforward; it necessitates robust mechanisms to manage capital flow volatility and financial market turbulence. The establishment of supporting institutions is crucial for this process, and patience may prove to be a virtue. It is possible that the RMB might become a reserve currency within a specific bloc of countries if the global economy continues along the path of separate economic blocs. However, if the RMB does achieve major international reserve currency status, it may be more attributable to the U.S. abusing the dollar's "exorbitant privilege" and its repercussions (e.g., sanctions, irresponsible monetary policies) rather than solely to China's efforts toward internationalization. Moreover, potential trade fragmentation could lead to fragmented internationalization of the RMB, where it plays a vital role in selected markets despite the USD retaining its dominant global currency status.

It is unlikely that China's approach would result in the dominance of the RMB. Instead, it might possibly lead to a multipolar world where major currencies, such as the dollar, euro, and renminbi, coexist. Therefore, it is likely that the internationalization of RMB will continue to grow in the future, but it will not pose a significant threat to the U.S. dollar as the dominant global currency in the short term. However, it is worth keeping an eye on developments in the internationalization of the RMB and its potential impact on the global monetary system.

References

Agur, I., Ari, A. and Dell'Ariccia, G. 2022. "Designing Central Bank Digital Currencies." *Journal of Monetary Economics*, 125: 62–79.

Auer, R., Frost, J., Gambacorta, L., Monnet, C., Rice, T., and Shin, H. S. 2021. "Central Bank Digital Currencies: Motives, Economic Implications and the Research Frontier." *BIS Working Paper*, No 976.

Bahaj, S. and Reis, R. 2022. "Jumpstarting an International Currency." *London School of Economics Working Paper*, 20/104.

Clayton, C., Dos Santos, A., Maggiori, M., and Schregger, J. 2022. "Internationalizing Like China." *NBER Working Paper, 30336.*

Eichengreen, B., Macaire, C., Mehl, A., Monnet, E., and Naef, A. 2022. "Is Capital Account Convertibility Required for the Renminbi to Acquire Reserve Currency Status?" *CEPR Discussion Paper, DP17498.*

Frankel, J. 2011. "The Rise of the Renminbi as International Currency: Historical Precedents." *VoxEU.org*, October 10. https://cepr.org/voxeu/columns/rise-renminbi-international-currency-historical-precedents.

Guo, K., Jiang, N., Qi, F., and Zhao, Y. 2020. "RMB Internationalization: Past, Present, and Prospect." In *The Handbook of China's Financial System*, edited by Marlene Amstad, Guofeng Sun and Wei Xiong, 229–251.

Jermann, U., Wei, B., and Yue, V. 2022. "The Two-Pillar Policy for the RMB." *The Journal of Finance*, 77: 3093–3140.

Keister, T. and Sanches, D. 2023. "Should Central Banks Issue Digital Currency?" *Review of Economic Studies*, 90: 404–431.

Kiff, J., Alwazir, J., Davidovic, S., Farias, A., Khan, A., Khiaonarong, T., Malaika, M., Monroe, H., Sugimoto, N., Tourpe, H., and Zhou, P. 2020. "A Survey of Research on Retail Central Bank Digital Currency." *IMF Working Paper, 20/104.*

Perks, M., Yao, Y., Shin, J., and Tokuoka, K. 2021. "Evolution of Bilateral Swap Lines." *IMF Working Paper, No.* 2021/210.

Prasad, E. S. 2016. *Gaining Currency: The Rise of the Renminbi.* Oxford University Press.

Schilling, L. 2019. "Risks Involved with CBDC: On Cash, Privacy and Information Centralization." mimeo.

Wang, Z. 2021. "Tax Compliance, Payment Choice, and Central Bank Digital Currency." mimeo.

Wei, S.-J. 2023. "A Reality Check for the RMB." *Project Syndicate.*

Williamson, S. 2022. "Central Bank Digital Currency: Welfare and Policy Implications." *Journal of Political Economy*, 130: 2829–2861.

Zhou, X. 2017. "Belt and Road." China Finance. Remarks by Governor Zhou Xiaochuan at the Thematic Session on Financial Connectivity during the Belt and Road Forum for International Cooperation, May 24, 2017. www.cips.com.cn/cipsenmobile/2017-10/26/article_20231125120726617l3.html

9 *The Political Economy of Common Prosperity*

YASHENG HUANG

In August 2021, when Xi Jinping proclaimed his common prosperity program, he could have touted common prosperity as a substantial policy accomplishment under his watch rather than as a future policy challenge facing his leadership. If we go with the official statistics (as reproduced by the World Bank), in 2012 when he succeeded Hu Jintao as the General Secretary of the Chinese Communist Party (CCP), the Gini index of China stood at 42.2. By 2019, it declined to 38.2, reverting China, within a short span of seven years, to the Gini index prevailing in the mid-1990s.

But that was not what Xi Jinping did. Instead of resting on his laurels, he doubled down on the equalization rhetoric and portrayed the common prosperity as a dire challenge that required a radical pivot in policy approach. Unlike the previous approaches that relied on tax policies, Xi focused on the microeconomic side of the equation and adopted firm-specific and ownership-specific approaches. He singled out the corporate sector, more specifically, the private corporate sector, as both a target and a solution to his common prosperity goal.

This chapter speculates that this policy pivot was highly unusual, and it proposes a political economy framing as a way to make sense of this policy development. It is not clear that targeting the private sector – while leaving China's vast state sector intact – is a straightforward solution to tackle a problem that we conventionally would label as an income inequality problem. It is also surprising that such a radical approach was adopted at a time when income inequality – as conventionally measured – was already on its declining trajectory.

I propose that a more plausible objective – or a truer effect – of the common prosperity was to realign a different imbalance altogether: to correct what Xi Jinping viewed as a persistent imbalance between the power of the state and the power of private capital. The private capital was felt to have held too much power and was beginning to pose as a threat to his sense of political control and ideological legitimacy. Common prosperity is a way to cut the corporate sector to its appropriate role, size, and place. A related rationale is that forcing the corporate sector to take on a social role has the auxiliary twin benefits of regaining some of the lost ground the state has ceded and providing some relief to the state as a sole provider of public services.

This approach has a distinct stamp of Xi Jinping. First, it should be noted that his common prosperity is not about creating a welfare state. In fact, doctrinally Xi is strongly opposed to the notion of a welfare state. In a speech he gave in 2021, he remarked, "Even in the future when we have reached a higher level of development ... we still must not aim too high or go overboard with social security, and steer clear of the idleness-breeding trap of welfarism." China is nowhere near a welfare state. The transfer income as a proportion of the total household income is small. An approach that shifted burdens of social welfare by an edict of the state to the corporate sector is superficially consistent with his antiwelfare stance.

Second, during the first two terms, China's tax burdens declined, and that reduction was accompanied by a mild improvement in Gini. That was an approach favored by Li Keqiang, China's premier between 2013 and 2023, who often advocated tax reductions to small businesses as a way to grow the economy and to achieve equity.[1] The policy did deliver, probably because the beneficiaries of these tax cuts – small-scale single proprietors – are on the lower end of China's income distribution.

But these accomplishments were achieved at a price – political or psychological – to Xi's overall visions. Xi favors a big-push approach. He has embarked upon a number of extraordinarily expensive policy programs, such as building Xiong'an city, the Belt and Road Initiative, "Made in China 2025," and so on. A tax-centric policy approach could be viewed as undesirable as it diluted state resources to welfare spending as opposed to the grandiose policy programs that he cherished. In addition, tax reductions, by weakening the state as a claimant to income, can be viewed as inimical to Xi's larger objectives of maintaining a strong state.[2] Shifting the burdens of social balancing

[1] Also see this report by CNN: www.cnn.com/2022/01/06/economy/china-economy-li-keqiang-tax-cuts-intl-hnk/index.html

[2] Also see Wu (n.d.).

can help him, again according to his perspective, rebalance power in favor of the state.

I will lay out this admittedly speculative argument in this short chapter. I will begin with a factual account of Xi's common prosperity program and the broad contextual background against which that program was proclaimed and enacted. Then I will propose a political economy framing of the common prosperity, a framing that explains the program as a rebalancing act among three actors in an economy – the state, the capital, and the household sector. The unusual feature of this program is that it does not directly address the imbalances among the households but addresses the sectoral imbalances among these three actors. The last section concludes with some broad implications of this way of narrating the common prosperity program.

The Contexts

The fact that China has a high level of income inequality is not disputed. According to the official source provided by the National Bureau of Statistics (NBS), the All-China Gini peaked in 2008, at 0.491, but independent scholars have produced estimates that are substantially higher than those provided by the NBS. Gan Li, director of the China Household Finance Survey at Chengdu's Southwestern University of Finance and Economics, estimates that the All-China Gini in 2010 was 0.61. In contrast, the NBS estimate for 2010 is only 0.481. Another independent academic, Li Wei, a sociologist at the Chinese Academy of Social Sciences, estimated Gini in 2008 to be 0.54, compared to NBS's 0.491.[3]

Even if we take the official figure at its face value, China has one of the world's most skewed income distributions. In his 2011 paper "*A Comparative Perspective on Poverty Reduction in Brazil, China, and India*," Martin Ravallion of the World Bank calculated that China's Gini coefficient was rising at a trend rate of 7 percent per decade. In 1981, China began with the lowest Gini compared with Brazil and India. By 1993, China surpassed India, and by 2005, its Gini index stood at 0.415 compared with 0.334 for India. This disparity has

[3] See the news report on the various Gini estimates by independent academics in www.bloomberg.com/news/2012-12-09/china-s-wealth-gap-soars-as-xi-pledges-to-narrow-income-divide.html.

persisted, although it has since narrowed. In 2019, China's Gini stood at 0.382, whereas for India it was 0.357.

Ravallion (2011) predicted in his paper that if China continued on that trend, it would reach Brazil's level by 2025. (It should be noted that the unofficial estimate for China already puts China in a similar range of income inequality as Brazil as early as 2010.) But China's Gini was detrended abruptly. It reached its peak in 2010 and then it started a steep decline. By 2019, the latest year for which data are available, China's Gini was significantly below that of Brazil (0.382 vs. 0.535). Unless this is a statistical reversion rather than a real economic one, it is a remarkable achievement the CCP was able to accomplish within such a short span of time.

The Common Prosperity Program

This is the background against which Xi Jinping's common-prosperity program was proclaimed. The official rationale is quite conventional and straightforward: It seeks to achieve common prosperity for all Chinese citizens by promoting equitable economic growth and addressing income inequality. The program is seen as a continuation of Xi's "Chinese Dream" of national rejuvenation and aims to build a "modern socialist country" by 2035. According to various media reports, the program includes a range of measures, including:

1. Regarding economic development, the aim is to even out imbalances between regions, business sectors, and small and large enterprises. Regional development, for example, could be better balanced by fiscal transfers. In business, solutions would include faster monopoly reforms and closer coordination between the finance and property sectors and the rest of the economy.
2. Making delivery of public services more equal would be of particular benefit to low-income groups in terms of education, social security, and other forms of aid, such as improvements in housing supply.
3. Income inequality would be addressed in part by tax changes focused on those deemed to earn excessively high incomes. These would include changes to personal income tax (income derived from capital is currently subject to a separate flat tax rate) and to property and consumption taxes.

4. Measures for expanding the middle-income group include improvements in higher education, better training and higher wages for skilled workers, lower tax, and other benefits for small business owners and the self-employed, help for migrant workers, and salary increases for low-level public-sector employees.
5. Rural land reform, together with increased agricultural productivity and infrastructure investment, would lead to higher rural incomes.

In addition to regulatory campaigns such as these, common prosperity policies involve investments and incentives to address development and quality of life issues. For example, the Chinese government is embarking on a rural revitalization campaign to improve conditions in rural areas, encouraging industrial transfer to less-developed regions, and pursuing carbon neutrality.

Targeting Private Capital

These are fairly conventional and orthodox policy measures, and they represent a high degree of continuity from the previous leadership of Hu Jintao. But the common prosperity program is not known just for these measures, and it is not clear whether these are the most important elements of the program. The departure of the common prosperity program is that the program aimed directly at the private capital as the headline component of the program and at the "excess profits" in the private sector.

According to reports prepared by China Briefing, Xi Jinping enacted a series of regulatory crackdowns and overhauls, all under the mantra of common prosperity.[4] These include crackdowns in a number of sectors of the economy, all dominated by private capital.

Private Education Sector

The Chinese government launched a regulatory crackdown on private education companies in July 2021 to tackle excessive profits and the widening education gap in the country. The crackdown led to the

[4] Also see the report published by the Brookings Institute: www.brookings.edu/articles/assessing-chinas-common-prosperity-campaign/

suspension of after-school tutoring services for core subjects such as mathematics and science, during weekends and holidays. The government also barred companies from raising capital through stock markets or foreign investment. As a result, many private education companies saw a significant drop in their stock prices, with (New Oriental) some losing up to 90 percent of their market value. According to reports, the regulatory measures resulted in a loss of jobs for millions of teachers and employees in the private education sector.

According to consultancy firm Macquarie Research, it projected the private education industry to reach RMB 1.17 trillion (US$183 billion) by 2023, but the new restrictions jeopardize its prospects. China's New Oriental dismissed 60,000 employees and saw operating income plunge by 80 percent after Beijing enforced new sweeping rules on the country's private education industry that barred for-profit tutoring last year, according to its founder. New Oriental, consequently, has seen its market value sink by 90 percent since the rules were announced according to news reports by Reuters.

On the Video Game Industry for Gaming Addiction Among Children

To address gaming addiction among children, the Chinese government introduced a series of regulatory measures on the video game industry in August 2021. The measures include limiting the amount of time minors can spend playing online games to three hours per week and prohibiting online gaming between 10 PM and 8 AM. The government also imposed restrictions on the release of new online games, which required companies to undergo a strict approval process before launching new titles. The regulatory measures caused a significant drop in the share prices of major gaming companies, and many smaller game studios were forced to shut down. According to reports, the regulatory crackdown resulted in a loss of jobs for thousands of employees in the gaming industry.

About 62.5 percent of Chinese minors often play games online, and 13.2 percent of underage mobile game users play mobile games for more than two hours a day on working days, according to state media. In August 2021, China had forbidden under-18s from playing video games for more than three hours a week, a stringent social intervention that it said was needed to pull the plug on a growing addiction to what it once described as "spiritual opium." These measures immediately registered an impact. During the license suspension, about 14,000 video gaming-related firms – including those involved in merchandising, advertising, and publishing – closed their businesses, according to business registry firm Tianyancha.

Entertainment Industry for "Improper" Content

In the mainland Chinese entertainment industry, a star's level of success is only partly measured by standard metrics such as how much money their films make at the box office or how many people tune in to their TV show. However, in this industry, increasingly, gaining high-profile corporate sponsorships and merchandising by the social media stars have become more important income-generating opportunities. "Fans flaunt the number of sponsorships their idols have; the biggest stars have lucrative corporate partnerships, with some holding over 30 or 40 brand contracts at once." One 2019 estimate found China's "fan economy," in which fans support their idols by buying their advertising products and consuming their media, could be worth up to 90 billion RMB ($13 billion), according to an article in Vox. The CCP launched a sweeping crackdown on this merchandising business model by targeting and curtailing the fan economy.

On Tech Companies for Exploitation of Platform Workers and Use of Algorithms

The Chinese government launched regulatory measures in 2021 to tackle the exploitation of platform workers and the exploitative use of algorithms by tech companies. The measures required tech companies to provide better protection and benefits to platform workers, such as social security, insurance, and minimum wages. The measures also required tech companies to be more transparent about their algorithms and to avoid using algorithms to discriminate against certain groups of people. The regulatory measures resulted in increased costs for tech companies and a loss of jobs for some platform workers who were not able to meet the new requirements.

According to reports prepared by China Briefing, China's top court has ruled that the controversial "996" overtime work policy – that is, working from 9 AM to 9 PM, 6 days a week – is illegal, taking aim at the excessive working hours commonly practiced at Chinese Internet technology companies. In one case, "a worker at a parcel delivery company was fired after refusing to work overtime under the company's '996' policy. The worker applied for labor dispute arbitration and the arbitration committee ordered the company to compensate the worker RMB 8,000 (US$1,238)." On December 31, 2021, the Cybersecurity Administration of China (CAC), China's internet watchdog, "passed the Internet Information Service Algorithm Recommendation Management Regulations, a new set of regulations that rein in the use – and misuse – of recommendation algorithms."

The crackdown poses a threat to the way that China's tech sector has historically organized its business – using capital to subsidize aggressive market shares – and has potentially serious consequences for wider investor confidence. Last year, Alibaba was fined a "record-breaking $2.75 billion for antitrust violations," while the IPO of its fintech arm, Ant Group, was canceled. Under China's regulations, "violators who refuse to correct issues or whose actions have had serious consequences are liable for fines of between RMB 10,000 (US$1,568) and RMB 100,000 (US$15,688)," which is an insignificant amount for large technology companies. However, as many of the regulations overlap with those outlined in other legislation, some cases could culminate in much larger fines. In addition, public naming and shaming tactics, such as putting a company on an "undesirable entity" list, would seriously damage the reputation of Chinese high-tech companies.

The Political Economy of Common Prosperity

The official mantra of the common prosperity is to improve income distribution, but, as noted earlier, China managed to bring down its Gini index without the crippling crackdowns on the private sector. In light of the progress China has made, it is puzzling that Xi chose to go way beyond the conventional policy measures that seemed to have already delivered a degree of common prosperity.

One possibility is that the declining Gini value is statistical rather than real. As noted before, the estimates by independent scholars put China at a much higher level of income inequality compared with the impression conveyed by the official estimates. The likely reason for the difference between these alternative estimates and the estimates by NBS results from the differences in the sampling frames. As Gan Li pointed out, NBS' surveys under-sample households at the low-income spectrum and the households at the high-income spectrum, which leads to biased estimates. It should be noted that NBS has never made available its survey data and that it has not disclosed refusal rates by the respondents, a standard disclosure in any survey research. By contrast, the disclosure by Professor Gan Li is detailed and it is plausible that China's real income distribution is far more skewed than the ones conveyed by the estimates by the NBS.[5]

That said, we should distinguish between the factors affecting the level estimates and the factors affecting the trend estimates of Gini. The level estimates are heavily influenced by the sampling frame of the NBS household surveys that probably oversampled those households clustered in the middle of the income distribution. However, conditional on the same problematic sampling frame, the trend estimates can still convey meaningful information (or at least they can be more reliable than the level estimates). It is possible that by the time the common prosperity was enacted, China faced a less daunting problem of income distribution than in the previous decades. But the rhetoric and the dramatic pivot of the common prosperity program are curiously unsuggestive of these policy achievements.

Is the common prosperity program a correct course of policy actions for China? One could argue that by the time the common prosperity program was enacted, the problem of interhousehold income inequality had been ameliorated. It is thus plausible to conjecture that the common prosperity program was designed to solve a different problem altogether – it is a political economy problem, not narrowly a socioeconomic one, of solving an intersectoral problem. Specifically, it is a program designed to rebalance the relationship between the capital sector and the two other sectors of Chinese society, the government and the household sectors.

Does China have an oversized capital sector? Let's first look at this question from the perspective of the household sector. Data do show that China's labor share of GDP experienced a sharp decline as the Chinese economy took off. A 2009 paper by Li Daokui, an economist

[5] It should be noted that an independent research project, the China Household Income Project (CHIP), has produced Gini estimates far closer to the estimates by NBS. However, CHIP follows the sampling frame of NBS.

at Tsinghua University, and his coauthors shows that the labor share of China's GDP declined from 53 percent in 1990 to 48 percent in 2005. In that paper, Li et al. (2009) noted that China had one of the lowest labor shares of GDP in the world. Major economies had a labor share varying usually between the 60 and 80 percent range.

Why China's labor share of the GDP declined is debated among economists. Chinese economists often invoke the so-called Lewis turning point to explain China's declining labor share of GDP.[6] Lewis' turning point refers to an idea first proposed by the Nobel Prize-winning economist W. Arthur Lewis that in an urban–rural dual economy, wages tend to stagnate during the transition period when a large proportion of labor moves from agriculture to industry.[7] This is known as the dual-sector growth model in development economics.

This is debatable. The dual-sector growth model predicts a stagnation of absolute wage level, not a stagnation of wage or labor income relative to GDP. The reasoning is simple. Once a large quantity of labor moved from low-productivity agriculture to high-productivity industry, even though there is no change in the absolute level of industrial wage, the labor share of the GDP has to rise as the higher-paying industrial jobs replace the lower-paying agricultural earnings. Other economists point to institutional factors such as the hukou system, which in effect depressed the wage bargaining power of the labor migrants, reinforcing the wage stagnation of a dual-sector economy postulated by Lewis.

Whatever the underlying dynamics that drove down the labor share of the GDP around 2008 and 2009, the Chinese labor share began to rise. A plausible explanation is the enactment of the 2008 Labor Law that enforced stronger wage protection for Chinese workers. The demographics were another factor. China's population growth slowed down dramatically. In 2012, for the first time in a very long period, the number of the Chinese working-age population, defined as those between fifteen and fifty-nine years old, decreased by 0.6 percent from last year.[8] This trend continued into the Xi Jinping era. In 2022, for the first time since the early 1960s, China reported a negative population

[6] See, for example, Yao (2014).
[7] See Lewis (1954).
[8] "中国劳动力人口首次下降人口红利拐点显现," 财经凤凰网. Accessed September 22, 2019. http://finance.ifeng.com/news/macro/20130224/7694587.shtml.

growth rate. In other words, these developments, either singularly or combinatorically, would generate an organic improvement of China's labor share of GDP.

The shrinking and small labor share of GDP is a real problem, not the least of which is a serious imbalance of China's macroeconomic structure. However, it is not clear that by the time of the proclamation of the common prosperity program, the problem was still as serious as it was before. Official data indicate that under Xi Jinping, China improved both the interhousehold income distribution and stemmed the slide of households' share of the GDP.

If we go with the official data, China began to stabilize and even slowly increased the labor share of the GDP since 2008 or so. China's labor share peaked at 60–61 percent in the early 2000s, fell to 55 percent from 2008 to 2011, and then recovered to 59 percent by 2015. India's labor share, historically higher than China's, bottomed out at 48 percent in 2006–2007 and recovered to 52 percent by 2016 (University of Groningen and University of California, Davis, 2025a and 2025b). These data suggest that China was working to stem the declining labor share of the GDP in the pre-common prosperity era and that India's efforts to increase the labor share were less effective. It is likely that the policy program that reversed China's Gini was also responsible for reversing the decline of China's labor share of the GDP. The 2008 Labor Law could have contributed to this development just as demographic dynamics could have raised the bargaining power of the labor sector.

A rational course of action would be to continue with that policy package that delivered this result rather than engineering a major policy turn, but Xi surprised us again. He rewrote the script, and he chose to directly target the corporate sector with a policy approach that amounted to curtailing the private capital share of the GDP. He did not target the state capital share of the GDP, which is probably substantial. (The reason is that the SOEs dominate the capital-intensive sector of the Chinese economy.) This policy pivot is more consistent with a desire to rebalance the relationship between the private capital and government sectors. In other words, despite its nomenclature, the common prosperity has relatively little to do with the common citizens; it is about putting the private corporate sector in its appropriate place.

The primary claimant to income in any economy is the household sector. Capital and government are secondary claimants. Capitalists claim their share through profit retentions and the government claims its share through taxation. One mechanism through which China's labor share of the GDP has risen is that the government has ceded a small share of its income through tax cuts. One crude measure is tax revenue as a share of GDP. Among the three countries often compared with each other, China, India, and Brazil, China has the lowest share. In 2018, China's share stood at 9.1 percent compared with Brazil's 13.9 percent and India's 12 percent. Also, over time, China's share, although fluctuating, tended to fluctuate in a downward direction. During the Hu Jintao era, that share fluctuated around 8.5–10 percent, whereas during the Xi era, that share fluctuated around 8–9 percent. Another measure is the tax rate, a measure in the World Development Indicators database labeled as "Taxes on income, profits and capital gains." Among these three countries, China has by far the lowest rate. For India, that rate hovered around the mid-40s, whereas for Brazil, it was around the mid-20s. Under Hu Jintao, that rate typically prevailed at high-20s, but under Xi Jinping, the rate fell drastically, to the high-10s.

This by no means suggests that the Chinese state was losing in an absolute sense. The Chinese state has access to the dividend flows from the SOEs and revenues of the land transactions, rendering its dependency on tax revenues less important. But tax concessions also matter. They matter in a fiscal sense, but they also matter politically. Tax concessions empowered both the corporate and the household sectors in ways that make it difficult to ascertain the identity of the primary beneficiary. It is plausible, given the magnitude of the tax concessions and the seemingly miniscule gains the household sector garnered, that the capital has captured a significant share of the tax concessions. The labor share of the GDP rose, yes, but it rose by a small amount. During the first ten years of Xi Jinping, the household sector did not lose, but its gains were relatively modest, suggesting that the majority of the benefits from the government's tax concessions accrued to the corporate sector. Reversing those gains to the corporate sector is probably a more plausible and more direct motivation behind the common prosperity program.

Assessing Its Long-Term Implications

Will the common-prosperity program work? To answer this question, it is critically important to define what constitutes having worked.

The program is not primarily about income distribution or redistribution within the household sector, so its impact on Gini is uncertain. It is also not about an income redistribution from the corporate sector to the household sector; at least it is not about that redistribution of a significant size. It is about regaining some of the felt lost ground the state has ceded to the corporate sector and it is about reaffirming or reasserting the control right of the state over the corporate sector.

The reason for my skepticism of a real common prosperity effect of this approach is that the headline numbers are often misleading. Under the common prosperity program, a number of Chinese companies pledged a huge amount of capital to address challenges such as income inequality and rural development. According to press reports, Tencent, a high-tech firm, agreed to donate US$15 billion to social aid as the government stepped up its scrutiny of the company. Other high-tech firms, Alibaba, Pinduoduo, JD, and Meituan, have made similar pledges. These are sizable pledges, but in an economy the size of China, these pledges are unlikely to fundamentally alter the income distribution patterns among the Chinese households.

Pinduoduo unveiled its 10 billion RMB ($1.57 billion) agriculture program to "face and address critical needs in the agricultural sector and rural areas." The initiative is all-encompassing, including possible equity funding for agritech startups and grants for fundamental research and talent training. The program won't be profit-driven, the company promised, and all profit from the second quarter and "any potential profits in future quarters would be allocated to the initiative." Some see Pinduoduo's investment in agriculture as an effort to alleviate rural poverty and thus a response to Beijing's call for "common prosperity."

JD.com took a different approach. On November 22, 2022, JD.com announced that it would "cut the salaries of more than 2,000 senior managers by 10–20 percent next year to help pay for improved benefits for other staff amid the government's 'common prosperity' drive to reduce income inequality" according to a report by Reuters. Chinese tech giant Alibaba, which has seen its global profile rise in recent years, has now pledged to invest $15.5 billion to help promote shared prosperity in China and has set up a special task force led by its CEO, Zhang Yong. "Later, it will also set up a 20 billion RMB ($2.91 billion) 'common prosperity development fund,'" according to the media report, subsequently confirmed by the company.

As large as these sums of money are for a single company, they are modest and insignificant for a country the size of China, whether measured in terms of its GDP or population. Or relative to tax policies and the government's own antipoverty programs. But there are symbolic and political connotations. The ultra-rich Chinese billionaires have been brought to their knees in the context of many other actions Xi Jinping has enacted to put the private sector in its designated place. Just a few days before the biggest initial public offering (IPO) ever in history, the IPO of Ant Group, a fintech subsidiary of Alibaba, Xi cancelled the scheduled stock debut. Jack Ma was often viewed by others, and he probably made the error of viewing himself, as politically untouchable. Not so. The usually visible and outspoken Jack Ma then completely disappeared from public view. The collective silence of China's most prominent billionaires is the mission accomplished on the part of the Common Prosperity program.

The question is, "What are the broad economic and political costs of this rebalancing approach?" The economic costs are substantial in the form of dented incentives of Chinese entrepreneurs and the increase of fear and insecurity among the Chinese entrepreneurial elites. Unless there was a coincidental rise of conscience among Chinese high-tech billionaires, the simultaneity of their charity pledges indicates coercion in the background. A coerced redistribution undermines private incentives and wealth accumulation on the part of the ultra-rich but also on the part of China's middle-class shareholders. A detail of the large donation pledges made by Alibaba, Tencent, and other high-tech firms is that the donations are funded by company funds, that is, by investors' money. Not surprisingly, the announcements of these donations were followed by declines in stock prices. The destruction of the capital gains was then followed by layoffs in the high-tech sector, undermining income gains of the Chinese professional labor force. Overnight, an entire sector of the Chinese economy, private tutorial services, was wiped out, and, with a stroke of a pen, millions of good-paying and middle-class jobs and income-earning opportunities were eliminated.

The corporate donations are more optics than substance. In a country of 1.4 billion people, they do not come close to offsetting the lost income gains that would result from an economic slowdown. In other words, the modest static benefits of income redistribution will be completely offset or overwhelmed by the detrimental dynamics that weaken confidence and attenuate incentives. The negative effects on employment and income generation overshadow any positive effects of income redistribution.

A long-term cost of the common-prosperity program is an additional shock that will accentuate the secular economic slowdown that is already well in place. That slowdown, more than any hoped-for upsides that can be gained with the common prosperity program, will be detrimental to both the common prosperity in a real and operational sense and to China's long-term stability.

A bigger economic pie, rather than any particular partitions of that pie, has been a panacea to many ills. It palliates labor, capital, and the state and alleviates distributional conflicts. Distributional tensions have been manageable, even with China's extraordinarily high level of Gini index. It was Martin Whyte (2010) who first debunked the notion that China was on the cusp of a social volcano of unrests and instabilities because of the widening income gap between the rich and the poor. His survey data show that the Chinese respondents had a higher tolerance of income inequality than many scholars assumed. However, it is important to note the larger context of his findings. His book was published in 2010, and the findings were based on data from an earlier time when economic growth was still robust. The social volcano did not erupt because the effect of the absolute income gains bested the effect of the relative income gains.

Economic growth produces absolute income gains. The political dynamics among three actors of the economy, the state, the capitalists, and the household, are very different under an expanding economy compared with a shrinking economy. During the reform era, the declining labor share of income did not translate into a social volcano because that decline is politically and psychologically palatable when there are still absolute income gains. Historically, the state and the capital reaped an outsized benefit through rapid income gains and through a shift of income distribution in their favor.

Absolute income gains are critical to political stability.[9] An economic downturn changes the political calculus. It exacerbates both types of instabilities. A smaller size of an economic pie increases distributional conflicts among elites and between elites and nonelites. These conflicts are difficult to manage in any circumstances but are even more fraught when politics has become less rule-based, power struggles are

[9] See the empirical classic by Alesina and Perotti (1996).

more intense, information to decision-makers is more distortionary, and an unbridled autocrat is overly confident. The single biggest threat to Xi's stewardship of the third term is mishandling of the economy. Complexities and uncertainties, rather than persistence, are on the rise.

A shrinking economy makes absolute income gains impossible. In that scenario, the only way to appease the household sector – so that it remains politically pliable – is to engineer an income shift in its favor. As noted, during the early reign of Xi Jinping, the state did exactly that: it cut taxes, but cutting taxes disempowered the state, a situation inimical to the preferences of Xi Jinping. In this scenario of low growth, capital becomes vulnerable, and further predations on the capital reinforce the growth slowdown. The common prosperity program, executed through shaming Chinese capitalists and through a tertiary income redistribution funded by massive and apparently coerced charity donations, is fundamentally predatory and, like all predatory actions, is economically and socially unproductive in terms of its long-run effects.

References

Alesina, Alberto, and Roberto Perotti. 1996. "Income Distribution, Political Instability, and Investment." *European Economic Review*, 40(6): 1203–1228.

Lewis, W. Arthur. 1954. "Economic Development with Unlimited Supplies of Labour." *The Manchester School*, 22 (2): 139–191. https://doi.org/10.1111/j.1467-9957.1954.tb00021.x

Li, David Daokui, Liu Linlin, and Wang Hongling. 2009. "Changes in the Labor Share of GDP: A U-shaped Curve." *Social Sciences in China*, 30 (4): 131–153.

Ravallion, Martin. 2011. "A Comparative Perspective on Poverty Reduction in Brazil, China, and India." *The World Bank Research Observer*, 26 (1): 71–104. https://doi.org/10.1093/wbro/lkp031

University of Groningen and University of California, Davis. 2025a. "Share of Labour Compensation in GDP at Current National Prices for China [LABSHPCNA156NRUG]." Retrieved from FRED, Federal Reserve Bank of St. Louis. https://fred.stlouisfed.org/series/LABSHPCNA156NRUG. May 22, 2025.

University of Groningen and University of California, Davis. 2025b. "Share of Labour Compensation in GDP at Current National Prices for India [LABSHPINA156NRUG]." Retrieved from FRED, Federal Reserve Bank of St. Louis. https://fred.stlouisfed.org/series/LABSHPINA156NRUG. May 22, 2025.

Whyte, Martin, 2010. *Myth of the Social Volcano: Perceptions of Inequality and Distributive Injustice in Contemporary China*. Stanford University Press.

Wu, Guoguang. n.d. "For Xi Jinping, the Economy Is No Longer the Priority." *Journal of Democracy*. Retrieved July 14, 2023 (www.journalofdemocracy.org/for-xi-jinping-the-economy-is-no-longer-the-priority/).

Yao, Yang. 2014. "The Lewis Turning Point: Is There a Labour Shortage in China?" In *The Oxford Companion to the Economics of China*, edited by S. Fan, R. Kanbur, S.-J. Wei, and X. Zhang. Oxford University Press.

10 The "Summer of 2021" and the Trajectory of China's Economic System

BARRY NAUGHTON

The events of summer 2021 were abrupt and surprising but they also amplified tendencies that were already apparent in the longer-term trajectory of China's economic system. A series of dramatic policy actions by Xi Jinping that summer reshaped China's political environment. Xi took a series of regulatory measures that drastically hobbled some of China's biggest and most dynamic private companies; he resurrected "common prosperity" as a key regime goal and slogan; and he laid the groundwork for his continuing personal dominance of the Chinese Communist Party, formalized at its Twentieth Congress in October of 2022. These actions had obvious political significance; the purpose of this chapter, however, is to use the specific events of 2021 to better understand the trajectory of the Chinese *economic* system and the implications for assessing that economic system today. The thesis is that the events of 2021 marked a point of no return and signaled the crystallization of a qualitatively different economic system. We expect that this new institutional setup will display systematically different economic outcomes and performance from the previous economic system.

It has long been clear that the contemporary Chinese economic system is on a very different path from the sustained market liberalization that distinguished the 1978 through 2005 era. Gradually increasing government intervention and "steerage" has been a feature of the past almost twenty years, since about 2006. Within this trajectory, the summer of 2021 was an episode of extraordinary importance. It was not a "turning point" – since the general direction of China's evolution was already clear – but it was a significant "culminating point" in which the system abruptly went through a change of state. That is, we can select this period as the time when a cumulative set of institutional changes came together to create a new type of economic system.

The first section of this paper provides a quick resume of the events of Summer 2021, emphasizing the regulatory crackdown, which has long been recognized as the most surprising and public part of the period. Abrupt new rules imposed heavy costs and significant new constraints on many of China's most important and successful private businesses. The second section describes the dramatically expanded menu of policy objectives that was announced at the same time, which government officials, businesses, and ordinary people were and are expected to follow. The third section is the heart of the chapter, analyzing how these changes affected the overall economic system. Coming on top of a decade of incremental change, these key events catalyzed a shift to a new set of rules for economic decision-making, that is, a new economic system. In essence, until recently, the reform-era Chinese economic system had been one in which economic decision-making was broadly distributed, with high-powered incentives that gave unambiguous priority to economic growth and profit-making activity. The qualitative shift triggered by the summer of 2021 actions was to a system in which economic decision-making authority was less decentralized and considerably more constrained than before, and in which decision-makers were expected to juggle a basket of competing objectives, of which economic growth was only one. Basic theory tells us the first system should be one of high-powered incentives for economic growth, along with strong credibility and relative policy stability. The new system, by contrast, should have less powerful incentives and should have low policy credibility but be capable of high decisiveness. It is therefore likely that the emerging economic system should be less efficient because of a combination of weaker incentives, policy instability, and inappropriate and costly policy objectives.

The argument about the nature of the economic system naturally leads to two additional questions, each concerning a dimension of China's economic system where significant change seems to have occurred in 2021. First, given the complex, competing objectives that began to guide Chinese policymaking, have the policy instruments introduced by the Chinese government been appropriately targeted to the goals envisioned? Second, have policymakers been able to ensure that information flows in the economy provide the feedback needed about the impact of policy on the performance of the economy? The initial answer to both these questions is "no." This answer reinforces the expectation that there will be negative economic consequences from systemic change. The final section argues that through the end of 2024, the behavior of policymakers and the response of economic decision-makers have been consistent with the predictions of this chapter. Especially since the end of the Twentieth Party Congress in October 2022 and the collapse of the "zero COVID" lockdown the next month, policymaking has displayed the inconsistency and lack of credibility anticipated, and the performance of the economy has seemingly been well below potential. There are reasons to believe that the Chinese economy has moved onto a less dynamic and less efficient trajectory in the wake of changes implemented in the summer of 2021.

The Regulatory Crackdown of the Summer of 2021

The events concentrated in the "summer of 2021" began to unfold about a year earlier. Two events were especially important. In August 2020, Chinese regulators introduced a tough new set of rules for Chinese real estate developers, known as the "three red lines." These required every real estate firm to maintain a debt/asset ratio below 70 percent and hit targets for net debt and short-term liabilities as well. Firms were told to come into compliance quickly, by the end of September, which was remarkable since only nine of China's top thirty real estate firms were in full compliance, and eight violated two or more of the three red lines (Bloomberg, 2020). Financial stress appeared immediately in the real estate sector, and one of China's largest real estate firms, Evergrande, tipped into a long-running crisis that resulted in default in December 2021 and a U.S. bankruptcy filing in August 2023. The new policies signaled a much tougher government line toward the real estate industry, touching off a slow-rolling real estate crisis that remains unresolved as of the end of 2024, more than four years later. Moreover, it quickly became clear that this was the opening salvo of a more general offensive against highly leveraged business empires. At the December 2020 Economics Work Conference, a criticism of the "disorderly expansion of capital" was launched, and during 2021, this became a recurrent theme of policymakers (Lu and Zhou, 2020).

The second event occurred after a speech that Jack Ma, founder and chairman of Alibaba, made in Shanghai on October 24, 2020. Ma's light-hearted speech poked fun at China's financial regulators for being too conservative, and the banks for having a "pawn-shop mentality," because of their insistence that private businesses provide tangible collateral to qualify for loans. Ma's criticisms were not particularly cutting, but they were astonishingly poorly timed. Ant Financial, a subsidiary of Alibaba, was being spun out from the parent firm and was set to launch its initial public offering (IPO) in Shanghai and Hong Kong only two weeks later (November 5, 2020). The IPO was expected to raise $34.5 billion, which would have made it the biggest IPO in history and given Ant roughly the same valuation as JPMorgan, the world's most valuable financial firm. Moreover, Ant was going to do this without recourse to U.S. capital markets, planning a dual listing on the Shanghai and Hong Kong stock markets (Chen 2020). Jack Ma was set to become one of the world's richest men – while also retaining control of Ant – so it would be understandable if he felt on top of the world at that moment. However, since Ant's business had been built on making small loans without much collateral, and since financial regulators had up until that point allowed Ant to grow without impediment, Ma's criticisms might also have seemed a little churlish. They might even have been interpreted as a boast that he had prevailed over stodgy bureaucrats and regulators.

Nobody was prepared for what happened next. On November 3, 2020, Ant's IPO was abruptly suspended, and Ant was subjected to a thorough review of business practices, licenses, and regulatory compliance, and the company's business scope was dramatically scaled back. Credit, payments, and savings divisions were separated and placed under direct supervision by the People's Bank of China, with provisions that limited their profitability, pricing power, and ability to cross-sell. Moreover, Jack Ma was forced to give up the controlling interest in Ant he would have had if the IPO had gone through.[1] Despite these concessions, Ant's IPO has never been resumed.

Yet Alibaba's troubles were just beginning. On December 22, 2020, Alibaba and the other big internet companies (Tencent, Jingdong, Meituan, Pinduoduo, and Didi) were summoned by the State Administration of Market Regulation (SAMR) and informed of the "Nine Prohibitions." The Nine Prohibitions were designed to control market manipulation and collusion, but they gave regulators enormous discretionary control: it was forbidden to sell goods below cost,

[1] Jack Ma agreed in January 2023 to an ownership restructuring of Ant that included him reducing his stake to 6.2 percent of voting rights, eliminating his previous, highly controversial, 50.5 percent controlling stake.

price discriminate, achieve unfair market dominance, or "illegally" collect consumers' personal information (SAMR, 2020a, 2020b; NDRC, 2021). Regulators are reported to have interpreted these provisions strictly as forbidding the cross-subsidization of new internet businesses by existing profitable businesses, such as online gaming.

Nor did regulators hesitate to enforce these provisions: in April 2021, Alibaba was hit with a massive $2.8 billion fine for antitrust violations and subjected to a wide range of additional regulatory actions. This was astonishingly fast action for China's notoriously slow-moving anti-monopoly authorities. Abrupt imposition of huge penalties marked the true beginning of the "summer of 2021." Punitive regulatory actions followed in quick succession. In July, Chinese regulators took a series of abrupt regulatory actions that cut in half the value of the start-up darling Didi, "China's Uber," just days *after* its listing on the New York Stock Exchange. Two weeks later, the Chinese Ministry of Education suddenly required virtually all private tutoring firms to convert to nonprofit entities, effectively destroying a $100 billion industry. For good measure, the edict banned weekend teaching, hiring foreign teachers outside the country, or teaching school curricula to children under six.

In August, the official Xinhua News Agency announced that regulators would step up oversight of how online media employ algorithms to share and promote content. Effective algorithms are the key competitive advantage of ByteDance (the owner of TikTok in the U.S. and Douyin in China), as well as other successful online content providers such as Kuaishou. Exactly how (or even whether) the state can manage algorithms is unclear, but this was certainly the logical next step in the broad crackdown on Internet businesses. By this time, it was impossible to ignore the fact that regulatory crackdowns had targeted virtually every star of China's internet economy, and the actions began to be labeled a "regulatory storm" (see Table 10.1 for a summary). These Internet giants had all grown up outside the purview of China's policymakers and were in businesses that did not compete with state-owned enterprises (SOEs). They had long been embraced as national champions that exemplified China's technological dynamism and had faced a friendly and permissive regulatory environment. Didi, for example, had been assisted by the Chinese government in easing Uber out of China, thereby establishing a virtual national monopoly. Now the government's approach suddenly changed.

Table 10.1 ***The regulatory storm: Major milestones***

Beginning of crackdown	Target company	Official rationale	Outcome
November 2020	Ant Financial = Fintech	Financial RiskControl of Payments Network	IPO Cancelled; Ongoing Regulatory Reform
April 2021	Alibaba = eCommerce	Antitrust Violations	$2.8 billion fine; Ongoing Antitrust Campaign
July 2021	Didi Chuxing = Ridehailing	Data Security	Suspension of downloads; Regulatory crackdown; Massive losses
July 2021	New Oriental, all = Private Education	Reduce Social Burdens; Social Equity	Abolish For-Profit Status; Limit Weekend Classes and Foreign Teachers and Material
July 2021	Meituan = Food delivery	Social Equity	Guidelines for Gig Workers
August 2021	Tencent = eCommerce, gaming	Social Morality	Gaming targeted; Outcomes Uncertain

There were plausible regulatory rationales for nearly every facet of this crackdown. Ant Financial, for example, had built its enormous financial empire on the basis of a single consumer banking license from the city of Chongqing, and several of its financial activities operated in grey areas, even loopholes, in the financial regulatory framework. There were abuses in the private education sector and monopolistic behavior by many online businesses. However, it would have been entirely possible to implement regulatory changes through a gradual and deliberate approach. Instead, Xi Jinping chose to launch a multi-faceted political campaign that was massively costly to Chinese businesses and households. The losses at Alibaba – including the fall in market capitalization of Alibaba and the reduced valuations accorded to Ant Financial – have been calculated at $850 billion through the summer of 2023 (Chen and Zhang, 2023). It has been a staggering comedown for what was once one of the world's most valuable firms.

The Multiplication of Policy Objectives

In the summer of 2021, China's leaders not only intervened in the business economy in unprecedented fashion, they also enunciated a raft of new policy objectives as the rationale for doing so. The most striking was a new emphasis on "common prosperity" (see Huang in this volume), but the overall effect was to commit the Chinese government to a dozen high-priority policy goals. This new multi-objective policy framework is a dramatic shift from the situation prevailing through most of the reform era. For decades, there had been an apparent social consensus on the importance of economic growth. The drive of Chinese households for economic betterment; the conviction of intellectuals that market reforms were essential for economic development; and the desire of national leaders to grow the economy in order to achieve national power and greatness all fit together seamlessly. Policymakers had stressed GDP growth as the paramount goal, pushed for market-oriented reforms as a secondary goal precisely because those reforms were seen as essential to sustained growth, and prioritized GDP growth as the foundation for national security and other long-term goals. By the summer of 2021, this had completely changed. We look first at the new goals and then put them in the context of changing priorities.

New Headline Commitments

The Chinese Communist Party, as part of its governance style, continuously provides society with goals and slogans, preserving initiative in the hands of party officials and maintaining a favorable propaganda environment. Several new high-priority goals were introduced in the summer of 2021 and subsequently dominated official media. From this virtual blizzard of new objectives, we can select five as most important:

1. **Common Prosperity:** "Common prosperity" was highly promoted but vaguely defined and severely hedged. Xi Jinping called for a reduction in income and consumption disparities to a "reasonable level" by mid-century. In the same speech, Xi Jinping warned citizens that China's budgetary capabilities were limited, and that welfare dependency was, in any case, a bad thing (Xi Jinping 2021b; Xinhua 2021). Other speeches linked common prosperity to

equalization of social welfare benefits and anti-poverty campaigns. Common prosperity is a high-priority goal with imprecise contents.

2. **Stemming Demographic Decline:** Demographic anxieties have been rising in China since the abandonment of the "one child policy" in 2015, which was not followed by a sustained increase in births. The summer of 2021 saw the emergence of something like panic in relation to China's demographic trends, and China adopted a new "three-child" policy and began measures to actively encourage additional births. A top-level policy document expressed alarm and made some eye-popping commitments: "By 2025, China will establish a policy system that actively supports birth." Tellingly, one of the objectives cited was to "maintain the advantage of cheap human resources, in order to respond to complex global challenges." (CCP and State Council 2021). That this concern is specifically related to industrial development is confirmed by policies to increase the share of children going into vocational high schools, removing them earlier from the college preparation track. In other words, policies are designed to ensure an abundant, low-cost supply of skilled labor to China's industry, and the Chinese government would like Chinese women to contribute to this effort by having more babies.
3. **Cultural "Self-Strengthening":** The summer of 2021 witnessed the introduction of a cluster of culture-related policies designed to make Chinese society "tougher." Xi Jinping repeatedly emphasized the word "struggle" as a key feature of new China's culture and Communist Party morality. Gender inevitably played a role: "unmanly" male pop stars were castigated, and women were reassured that homemakers and child bearers were fully satisfactory roles for new women (Li, 2021, 2022).
4. **Priority to the Real Economy:** From 2021, China has made it clear that it supports "hardware" and not "software." The criticisms of Alibaba and Tencent were not limited to specific abuses but rather reflected a broader devaluing of the internet-based virtual economy. Throughout 2021, official media stressed a general policy that the maintenance of a strong manufacturing base is intrinsically more valuable than growth of the net-based service economy. A "German-style" industrial development path was sometimes claimed as superior to an "American-style" internet-based development path.

5. **Information Security:** The Chinese government introduced comprehensive controls over all Chinese data, including, for the first time, rules on data privacy. The government wants to make sure that foreigners cannot compromise Chinese security by accessing Chinese data. Chinese companies will also not be allowed substantial, independent control over data: that is allowed only to the Chinese government. This includes consumer data and financial data and increasingly will include algorithms controlled by companies. Data is part of information, which is a Communist Party monopoly, and the digital age calls for even more stringent controls.

Old Goals Reformulated: Leaning Away from Growth

The introduction of new policy objectives in the summer of 2021 was not a bolt from the blue, but rather the culmination of a process under way for over a decade. In China from the 1980s through the 2000s, economic growth had been *the* top priority objective. While other objectives, such as environmental protection and social security, had been addressed from time to time, it was understood that if they were in conflict with economic development, the economy should take precedence. GDP growth was the keystone, far more important than any other policy objective. After the turn of the century, a moderate displacement of the "growth at all costs" orientation of the 1990s took place. Goals that were potentially competing with growth began to receive attention. Rudimentary national health insurance and social security programs were established. The fight against pollution was taken seriously for the first time. Initially, these policy objectives were compatible with China's growth orientation. In the first place, human capital investments and social insurance protection are surely complementary with growth, and demand for these government services inevitably increased as China reached middle-income levels. Moreover, the introduction of new policies was generally cautious, and with attention given to establishing separate funding mechanisms and providing new regulatory agencies. An example is rural health insurance, where initially very modest contributions from households and government were gradually increased to provide basic protection. Earlier, I called this ambitious but basically market-compatible approach "grand steerage" (Naughton, 2020).

Similarly, when the Chinese government began a gradual move into industrial policy, from 2006, it provided a steadily expanding array of incentives for producers to move into emerging and high-technology industries. Growing subsidies paid entry and start-up costs in targeted industries. Procurement and mild protectionism were used to support immature industries and businesses. Crucially, these new policy objectives were, for about a decade, approached in ways that were fundamentally compatible with growing China's market economy. New "government guidance funds" were set up, and credit priority for targeted industries was established. Alternately stated, the first decade of China's industrial policy was carried out through a state-sponsored venture capital industry that was layered on top of the market economy. The mechanisms were expensive, but not highly distortionary (Naughton, 2021). Moreover, new industries were typically open to a range of entrants, with the government often only "picking winners" after a strong competitor had emerged. The choice of "national champions" was not a hurried process, and the "venture capital state" was happy to finance successful private firms and treat them as "national champions." The Chinese government was gambling the people's money on the long-run growth of the economy, but in the meantime, it did relatively little to distort or impede the underlying operation and growth of China's market economy. This was to change after 2020.

National security considerations became increasingly important from the very beginning of Xi Jinping's administration in 2012–2013. Xi Jinping has paired national security and economic development as two equally essential counterparts. Indeed, he has in some respects reversed the received relationship between the two, considering security as an essential prerequisite for development, instead of seeing development as the basis for security. Security has been progressively knit into economic decision-making at all levels (Cheung, 2022). The process was sustained and incremental, but a milestone came in 2020, when – in the wake of COVID and an intensifying trade and technology conflict with the United States – Xi Jinping introduced the "new development paradigm (新发展格局)," which explicitly called for the recognition of many types of security (food security, energy security, political and ideological security, and many more) as equal counterparts to growth in China's development strategy.

Thus, the steadily increasing weight given to goals like high technology development and national security was becoming increasingly difficult to harmonize with ordinary economic growth. Then, in 2020–2021, policymakers for the first time introduced macroeconomic goals that explicitly went against the organic evolution of the economy that would have occurred in the absence of intervention. That is, economic planners began to articulate a vision of the economy that actually went *against* the kind of structural changes that one would normally anticipate as part of the economic development process. For example, in the Fourteenth Five-Year Plan, officially issued in March 2021, Chinese policymakers committed to much more aggressively interventionist macrostructural economic objectives. In the plan, policymakers sought to (a) maintain a high rate of investment, abandoning efforts to "rebalance" the economy; (b) prevent the decline of manufacturing as a share of Gross Domestic Product; and (c) establish science and technology self-sufficiency (NPC 2021). With these three targets, Chinese leaders began to take a stand against peaceful *economic* evolution, defined as deindustrialization, shrinkage of the labor force and population, and a shift toward household consumption of services. Chinese policymakers have determined, in essence, that they have the power to shape markets in the way that they want, and perhaps even have the obligation to do so. Thus, the summer of 2021 came immediately upon the heels of the dethroning of economic growth as the primary objective, and after the *hierarchy* of objectives had already begun to shift. Thus, the insistence in 2021 that diverse decision-makers respect all the new government policies was established on a broad foundation of steadily expanding policy objectives.

Pluralization of Objectives: Conclusion

The balance between proliferating policy objectives and the goal of economic growth changed dramatically in the summer of 2021. In the first place, the abrupt way in which certain new objectives were raised, and the sudden mobilization of the propaganda apparatus behind these goals signaled an intensification of Xi Jinping's campaign-like style of governance and a further downgrading of ordinary economic incentives. Second, the willingness of the government to impose massive costs on wealth-holders in China was unprecedented. In the earlier "grand steerage" approach to government guidance, it was understood that government would pick up the costs when it chose to shape China's development trajectory. But from the summer of 2021, China's leaders began to impose some of those costs on private actors. This clearly showed a subordination of economic growth – which after all inevitably produces wealth – to other political goals. The moves against private education and internet platforms destroyed financial assets, which are nothing more than the current value of future revenues. Chinese leaders in the earlier reform era sometimes imposed costs and destroyed businesses, but these were fairly rare events. In 2021, Xi Jinping destroyed an entire industry – private tutoring – simply because he did not value the outputs from that industry even though the market was willing to pay for it. The kneecapping of Alibaba and Tencent was qualitatively no different. These events provided a dramatic punctuation to an evolutionary process whose trajectory had already begun to become clear.

Features of the New System

The expansion of government authority and the multiplication of policy objectives are bound to have an important effect on the entire economic system, particularly because they are so obviously mutually reinforcing. In this section, we draw back and attempt to look at the economic system as a whole: the network of institutions and rules that determine *how* and *by whom* economic decisions are made.

The Distribution of Economic Decision-Making

"Who makes economic decisions?" is the most fundamental question of any economic system. In the pre-reform "command economy," economic decisions were made almost entirely by government officials, either at the central or the local level. Economic reform after 1978 opened up the economy to millions of new economic decision-makers. Indeed, it is reasonable to view the entire reform era in China (1978–2006) as a gradual movement towards a system in which economic decision-making authority was steadily dispersed to a broad range of actors. Beginning with farmers, rural enterprises, and village corporations, and then expanding to urban private and state-owned businesses, expansion of decision-making authority was a fundamental trend. Indeed, deconcentration of authority was one of the main lessons that Deng Xiaoping drew from the Cultural Revolution era. Thus, even within the bureaucratic state-run economy, steps were taken to insulate economic decision-making from constant political interventions. In ordinary situations, the government, and specifically the Premier, is generally in charge of economic decision-making (and not the Communist Party). A panoply of regulatory and government management institutions was created. SOEs, for their part, were converted to the "factory manager responsibility system" in the 1980s in order to ensure that the enterprise manager with the biggest stake in firm operations and profitability would be the ultimate decision-maker.

Alongside this expansion of decision-making authority was the systematic introduction of high-powered incentives for government officials and SOEs. Local officials were rewarded for economic growth. They were assigned performance indicators tied to GDP growth and fiscal revenue growth. When they hit their targets, they were given short-term bonuses and income supplements for hitting economic targets. Even more crucially, their odds of promotion were substantially greater if they presided over successful economic performance. In addition, they benefited from growth because of the multiple ways it enriched constituents and, perhaps, family members. Thus, it is not simply that there was a broad social consensus in favor of growth: specific concrete incentives were structured to be high-powered and aligned with growth (Naughton, 2008). Since government bureaucracies typically have to balance off multiple tasks, and high-powered incentives draw effort from lesser priorities, such high-powered incentives are quite unusual (Holmstrom and Milgrom, 1991). Government and enterprises were both given profit incentives that mobilized them as active participants in the transition to a market economy. As shown in later sections, these elements of decentralization were decisively reversed in the system crystalized in the summer of 2021.

Reconciliation and Rupture with Capitalism

In the previous reform era, along with the decentralization and incentivization of decision-making in the bureaucracy, by far the most consequential change was the massive expansion of the private, market-oriented business sector, where it was accepted that actors would be profit-oriented and self-interested. The CCP, famously, was born as an armed revolutionary party, and its reconciliation with the market economy and a capitalist class was transformative. In 2001, Jiang Zemin introduced the "Three Represents" to make clear that elites, including capitalist elites, deserved to be Party members. Most observers thought this was a permanent peace and the reconciliation was at the center of a Chinese reputation for pragmatism that underpinned its global reputation at the beginning of the twenty-first century. Perhaps the single most surprising occurrence of the summer of 2021, then, was the extent of the break between the CCP and China's capitalists. A note of disdain, even derision, entered into official media comments on capitalist businessmen for the first time since the Cultural Revolution (Li, 2021, 2022; White, McMorrow, and Yu, 2022).

During the reform era, many sectors were opened up to private firms and quickly dominated by them. Those sectors still dominated by state-owned firms, most importantly finance and utilities, were frequently those that would be highly regulated in developed market economies, so state ownership could be seen as an alternative to regulation. Regulatory reforms were often associated with the entry of new private firms. Entry was allowed until something broke (as in, for example, the case of peer-to-peer lending, which led to some massive losses), and then regulation was tightened as the mess was cleaned up afterwards. The general direction was an evolution toward greater private participation and relatively light-touch regulation.

The summer of 2021 was a dramatic change from these reform era trends. Beginning in 2020, the rhetoric against "disorderly expansion of capital," for example, was expanded beyond a handful of egregious highflyers to a wide range of respected businesses.[2] Any firm that tried to leverage success in one line of business into other sectors was potentially a target. During the summer of 2021, this changed attitude manifested broadly in government actions and party media. Of course, it is not the case that private businesses were abolished or nationalized. Rather, there was a subtle but unmistakable constriction of their decision-making authority and an emphasis that their profit-seeking activity had to be subordinate to greater political goals.

[2] There had been hints of this change a few years earlier. From December 2016 through 2017, a general de-leveraging campaign began with a crackdown on "insurance" products that were thinly disguised investment and fundraising vehicles. The campaign then expanded to the dismantling of four highly leveraged conglomerates that had dominated Chinese outbound investment during the previous two years: Wanda, Anbang Insurance, Fosun, and Hainan Airlines. However, it appeared that the target firms were egregious offenders, quite different from ordinary legitimate businesses.

Creeping Controls on Private Business Decision-Making

The gradual state constriction of the legitimate scope of private business decision-making can be illustrated by the example of Alibaba. Of course, Alibaba can hardly be considered "typical," since it was the central target of several of the most important initiatives of the summer of 2021. Yet while Alibaba is atypical, it is hard to overstate the centrality of Alibaba in the economic and social development of China in recent decades. Alibaba's online marketplace, Taobao, provides an astonishing variety of inexpensive goods that have hugely expanded the real income of Chinese people, to say nothing of providing millions with the sheer delight of hunting for and acquiring bargains. Moreover, Alibaba was the outcome of many of the things that made reforms successful in China for over thirty years: a start-up in an uncharted sector, Alibaba got advice and early funding from international venture capitalists, and ultimately listed on the New York Stock Exchange. From this process, Alibaba generated enormous wealth, some of which accrued to foreigners but most of which enriched Chinese (Erisman, 2015).

Most important, Alibaba seemed to have naturally convergent interests with government policymakers and had been widely viewed as a "national champion" and a partner of the government in multiple initiatives. This includes "Smart Cities," in which Alibaba's hometown of Hangzhou is a global front-runner. Alibaba provides much of the soft technology that runs the "Digital Silk Road" initiative that is part of the "Belt and Road Initiative": the Chinese government loans money and builds physical infrastructure, while Alibaba brings valuable commercial applications (Cramer-Flood and Boland, 2023). Perhaps most important, Ali developed formidable technological capabilities. While Alibaba is not a hardware firm, it has developed substantial capabilities in data management and many kinds of critical software, including artificial intelligence. Today, Ali Cloud is a rapidly growing and profitable business filling a fundamental role in China's information infrastructure. Ultimately, many assumed that China would continue to support and nurture Alibaba since it was one of the few actors – anywhere in the world – with the heft to potentially rival U.S. internet giants such as Google, Facebook, and Amazon.

Despite its demonstrated achievements and strategic importance, Xi Jinping presided over a multi-dimensional interference in Alibaba's business decision-making that affected every aspect of its operations. Three dimensions can illustrate the point:

1. **Business model.** The "Nine Prohibitions" announced at the end of 2020 went deep into the internal decision-making and business strategy of internet platforms. The rules are designed to limit the scope of internet platforms such as Alibaba and Tencent, preventing them from cross-subsidizing new markets from profits of old markets – indeed not allowing them to sell "below cost" at all, except in certain approved types of clearance sales. Use of customer data to engage in price discrimination was forbidden. These orders were followed by the proposed "voluntary" break-up of Alibaba into six separate divisions, which would make it much easier for the government to control or support specific business lines.
2. **Research strategy.** Alibaba and other firms were criticized for investing too much in soft skills and capabilities, and not enough in basic research and cultivation of scientific talent. One semi-official article claimed,

   > some of the domestic large-scale internet companies have not invested their funds in basic scientific research but rather focused on competition for user traffic and 'last-mile applications.' In the long term, these practices do not benefit the country's technological progress and long-term development ... Internet giants with massive data and advanced algorithms should play a greater role in original and fundamental technological innovation. (Lu and Zhou, 2020)

3. **Compulsory charity.** The main internet companies were told to "proactively take on greater social responsibility" (SAMR 2020b). Alibaba and Tencent got the message, and each pledged 100 billion yuan (about $15 billion) to common prosperity efforts. Of course, each strategized their donations to support their business models: Alibaba, for example, contributed substantial sums for connecting villages to the internet, which gives the village more efficient sales outlets and connects consumers to Taobao.

No individual element of these interventions is necessarily disastrous, and most could be imposed fairly through a set of new regulations. But it is quite clear that the initiatives of the summer of 2021 went far beyond that, and a firm like Alibaba is now expected to incorporate politically determined objectives into their decision-making at every point and completely conform their business models to state demands. The impact of this is clear: Alibaba's market capitalization peaked on October 21, 2020, at $838 billion, making it one of the most valuable companies in the world. At the end of 2024, Alibaba's market value was under $200 billion, and it was the sixty-fourth most valuable company in the world.

It is not appropriate to think of the summer of 2021 as having been primarily a "regulatory storm," or a new Chinese-style regulatory regime (Zhang and Gong, 2023). Regulation implies a set of arm's-length principles that apply to the firm and others like it. However, the multi-dimensionality of the demands made on Alibaba shows that the objective is instead to generate an ongoing responsiveness to a variety of policy objectives, which can in turn be constantly updated or changed by policymakers. It is more useful to think of this as a change in the decision-maker's objective function and decision criteria, rather than a change in the regulatory framework. Firms are expected to be constantly looking over their shoulders for policymakers' approval, reinstating a kind of dependence and "petty tutelage" that characterized the firm under the command economy.

Re-Politicization of State-Owned Enterprises

By the summer of 2021, Xi Jinping had been steadily altering the decision-making environment of SOEs for a decade, insisting they follow political dictates and Communist Party guidance. The "factory manager responsibility system" that had been in place for more than thirty years was discarded, and the top position of the Party Secretary was reinstated. Party committees now dominate the strategic decision-making process in SOEs by initiating discussion, and party secretaries chair the board of directors that makes all final decisions (Naughton and Boland, 2023; Leutert and Eaton, 2021). These changes in the internal governance system had been explicitly designed to facilitate the transmission of noneconomic tasks to the enterprise leadership and make SOEs willing to take on noneconomic tasks. In the summer of 2021, these types of extra-economic objectives were widely applied to private businesses as well, in a clear break with previous practice.

SOEs have already been fully reorganized to accommodate the new decision-making criteria. While this process has gone much farther with respect to SOEs than it has for private firms, it is worth seeing how the new objectives are described for SOEs. In 2001, when China entered the World Trade Organization, it accepted an article in its accession protocol that promised that SOEs would be governed "solely by commercial objectives." This obviously no longer applies. The head of SASAC, the body that controls central SOEs, recently declared that SOEs have:

> "Three roles" of technological innovation, sector control, and security support.... Technological innovation is fundamental.... Sector control is crucial, and we must actively cultivate leading enterprises in the value chain, accelerate the building of a modern industrial system that is independent, secure, reliable, and competitive.... Security support is the bottom line, focusing on key areas and enhancing the resilience of the industrial chain (Zhang, 2023)

And more generally:

> Whatever General Secretary Xi Jinping requires, whatever the Party Center arranges, whatever the nation needs, central SOEs must resolutely move in that direction (Zhang, 2023).

Thus, throughout the system, but to different degrees in different areas, a new economic calculus has been introduced.

Principles of Decision-Making

If economic growth is no longer the dominant objective, than what is? Xi Jinping has, in fact, given very clear answers to this question. Precisely because there are many different criteria that must be considered, decision-makers of all stripes must handle the trade-offs properly. In Xi Jinping's framework, this means that everything is politics: "Reform, development, and stability; domestic and foreign affairs and national defense; party, state or military governance, everything is political, and nothing can be separated from politics.... The more complex the situation and the more arduous the task, the more we must adhere to the Party's overall leadership" (Xi, 2021a).

Xi's speech was on his "new economic development concept," so it referred specifically to economics-related trade-offs. In a system-level decision-making framework, this means that government and party officials maintain a high level of discretion at all times and that they are not rule-bound. Then, according to the proper spirit and prevailing policy line, they make "correct" decisions that balance off multi-dimensional considerations.

Xi Jinping regards this balancing of objectives as a high expression of the art of politics. For example, in the speech just quoted, Xi goes on to urge comprehensively paying attention to both development and security, while in other venues, Xi calls for dialectically uniting openness and self-reliance, and so forth. In this conception, everything is politics, with clear implications for the functioning of the economic incentives faced by local government officials, in particular. In the past, they were instructed to maximize economic growth, subject to a few constraints. This is no longer the case. The incentive system for local officials might now be described as, "You will be judged on your success in balancing or juggling a constantly changing set of policy objectives; you must be especially sensitive to the most recent priorities of the leader, while avoiding standing out for violating anything." Clearly, this is incompatible with a system in which high-powered incentives are created for economic growth, in which big rewards are provided for the most successful. To varying degrees, this shift in incentive systems is visible throughout the Chinese system, and during the summer of 2021, it was made clear that Xi had many different objectives, and that they applied to private as well as state firms.

Overall Features of the Economic System

How have the changes described in the previous sections affected the Chinese economic system as a whole? In the first place, the trend towards a wider distribution of economic decision-making has been halted, and significantly reversed. It is not that the number of decision-makers has been reduced, rather that the scope of autonomy has been reduced for all decision-makers. All decision-makers have been commanded to "think politically" and incorporate regime-designated goals into their decision-making calculus. Private firms have been brought into the same political orbit as SOEs, albeit not completely. Government agencies that once aspired to independence in policymaking and regulation have now been clearly told that their decisions should be governed by the same set of political trade-offs. A more generalized and homogeneous set of evaluation criteria has been diffused throughout the economy, and decision-makers must allocate effort among multiple tasks required by their superiors (Cf. Holmstrom and Milgrom, 1991).

This new reality inevitably reduces the power of economic incentives. Private firms see more immediate limits to disruptive business plans: it pays to be more cautious. Data is particularly sensitive: you must be careful what you do with your customers' data. Conspicuous profitability might attract attention, in an environment in which private firms are supposed to proactively contribute to regime goals. In the new environment, private firms should be more cautious, and perhaps aim for a lower profile. For SOEs, the shift is even greater. SOEs need not just pay attention to some social responsibility goals, as might have been the case fifteen years ago; they are now expected to lead the implementation of many regime goals, including technological dominance and control of supply chains. It is clear that the big SOEs are expected to lead such policies *not* because they contribute to profitability, but because the profits they earn in other markets give them resources that can be harnessed to state goals. This reality clearly diminishes the strength of incentives to maximize profit and productivity.

The changes in incentives for government officials are complementary to those for enterprises. Local officials are no longer incentivized predominantly to grow their local economies: they must perform in terms of technological self-reliance and common prosperity, to say nothing of social order and conformity. De facto, success indicators have been altered to include more objectives (this is the point of Xi's remarks discussed in the previous section). Clearly, the old idea of a promotion "tournament," in which successful growth contributed to political advancement, is dead. None of the top leaders promoted at the Twentieth Party Congress presided over economically successful provinces. Without these additional high-powered incentives, while local officials will still want to see local economic growth, they no longer have the additional incentives to work especially hard and take extraordinary risks to promote growth. It is reasonable to conclude that the incentives to support economic growth are significantly weaker in the Chinese economic system that crystallized in the summer of 2021.

An additional feature of the new Chinese economic system is that policy can be very quickly altered. This is because the system has already been reorganized to permit decision-makers at all levels to quickly conform to top-level policy dictates. There are literally no formal "veto points" in the system that could obstruct a change in policy direction. This type of system can be expected to lack credibility (or consistency), but to have high flexibility (or decisiveness). In other words, decisions can be made quickly and carried out promptly, but decision makers have no way to assure audiences that any current (or announced) policy will be maintained or systematically applied (Tsebelis, 2003; MacIntyre, 2001). The new Chinese economic system, in other words, should exhibit lower credibility for any given policy orientation. This is an additional reason why the characterization of the summer of 2021 as a "regulatory storm" is inadequate. In fact, the changes in the incentive system amount to a kind of deregulation of the economic system. Clearly enunciated regulatory principles are actually less important, because any regulation can be changed at any moment. It is not so much adherence to the letter of the regulation as it is maintaining good relations with the regulator that keeps the business out of trouble.

In conclusion, a simple look at system-level features reveals a transition in a relatively short period of time from one type of economic system to another with significantly different features. The "old," reform-era economic system was one in which economic decision-making authority was highly distributed, and many decision-makers, especially private businesses, experienced relatively few constraints in their pursuit of profit. The distribution of power was not just a fact, but also a trend, as steady decentralization and reduction of constraints occurred from the beginning through the 2000s. This trend stalled in the mid-2000s and was replaced by, at first, a modest trend towards a new level of politicization, which then steadily grew. The summer of 2021 was critical as an expansion of this pattern in public and private businesses. Thus, a new system crystalized in 2021: a system in which decision-making is always constrained, at every level, and in all types of business units, by the need to maintain fealty to political objectives that are potentially fickle. We expect this system to have weaker incentives and less credibility. Does it? Before we can address this, we need to examine two more dimensions.

Adequacy of Instruments: The Clumsy Instruments of Common Prosperity

Modern societies regularly balance a multiplicity of goals. Personal freedom and opportunity must be balanced with the need to protect individuals who suffer economic and personal shocks. In general, economists rely on the idea that the trade-offs involved in competing objectives require that there be as many instruments as there are policy objectives, an idea often called the Tinbergen principle. If Chinese policymakers were introducing new instruments effectively targeted at each of the new policy objectives they advance, we would not worry much about the conflict between economic efficiency and proliferating noneconomic goals. However, this does not seem to be the case. None of the goals enunciated in 2021 were targeted with effective instruments; for example, how does one stem demographic decline? In particular, there is a relatively large mismatch between the rhetoric of common prosperity, for example, and the policy instruments that have actually been introduced to move in that direction.

The core meaning of "common prosperity" is to reduce income inequality. Yet the actual policy measures taken have been inappropriate and even irrelevant. In the first place, the experience of every other country has been that tax and welfare reform is the fundamental policy instrument that lowers income inequality. OECD countries on average reduce their pre-tax Ginis from 0.41 to a post-tax-and-benefit Gini of 0.31 (according to OECD data), and even the United States, despite its bad reputation for income inequality, reduces its pre-tax Gini from 0.47 to 0.39 (OECD 2021). Yet China's fiscal system scarcely reduces household income inequality at all, according to numerous studies. Despite this obvious need, fiscal reforms have been utterly stalled in China since 2014, and Xi Jinping's sudden emphasis on common prosperity has not been accompanied by any discernible effort to resume fiscal and tax reforms. This major shortcoming represents a major mismatch between goals and instruments as far as common prosperity is concerned.

The policies that *have* been enacted in the name of common prosperity have instead generally been punitive policies targeted at privileged groups. Compulsory charity has been the most obvious part, such as the contributions by Alibaba and Tencent discussed above. Perhaps even more peculiar have been Xi Jinping's efforts to cap high incomes within the state sector in the name of common prosperity. This initiative actually dates back to 2014: When the complex reforms of SOEs laid out in the fall 2013 Third Plenum got off to a slow start, Xi Jinping suddenly passed a resolution imposing a salary cap for SOE executives as part of "SOE reform." The initiative then faded out until suddenly gaining impetus in the summer of 2021. Foreign investment banks were warned that the approval of their domestic operations would be influenced by the "excessive" salaries they pay their executives. Since

2021, the pressure has been maintained. Officials in the financial regulatory system previously earned high salaries but were cut back to bureaucratic-scale salaries, as their organizations were redefined as government departments. State-run securities firms and investment banks have reduced top salaries up to 40 percent. And an anti-corruption drive in the financial sector that began shortly after 2021 continued unabated through 2024 (Bloomberg, 2024a). These actions are sometimes popular with ordinary people, but it is difficult to see how they contribute meaningfully to common prosperity: there seems to be a spectacular mismatch between objectives and instruments.

Information Flows

A crucial feature of any economic system is the nature of the information flows on which decision-makers at all levels rely. Despite the politicization of the Chinese economic system, China starts in an advantageous position. The information flows in the Chinese system are those produced by a robust market economy. In this sense, China is utterly different from a Soviet-style command economy system, in which planners labored often without market prices of any kind, and instead relied on deeply misleading quantitative indicators of mispriced goods. By contrast, China has developed efficient market pricing mechanisms for most goods and is also deeply integrated with world markets and the prices that they produce and publicize.

Moreover, policymakers have repeatedly reaffirmed their commitment to the general idea of the market economy. Despite this favorable starting position, the recent systemic changes have negative implications. This is most obvious for state enterprises. During the first decade of the century, SOEs were instructed to focus on profit and increased value of capital. It was relatively easy for the state owners to monitor their performance, and profitability increased rapidly. As SOEs are given more responsibilities, it is increasingly difficult to monitor their performance. Did profitability decrease – as it did after 2007 – because SOEs were following instructions and diverting effort to social goals? Or did it decrease because SOE managers reduced effort and enjoyed a quieter life because of their stronger political position? It is nearly impossible for public owners (or ourselves) to make this determination, because the information flows available are no longer as informative as they were before.

Moreover, there are additional worrisome signs about the quality of information flows. Four aspects that warrant concern:

1. Government industrial policies have expanded to cover so many different high-technology sectors, with multiple overlapping preferential policies; it has become impossible for anyone (including policymakers) to know what the net effect is on any particular sector. Self-reliance policies include hidden protectionist measures that support import-substitution projects; these impose costs on downstream sectors, which are supposedly also high priority. China is simultaneously investing in sectors with revealed comparative advantage and also "strengthening weak links" in the technology chain, which means investing in activities that have in the past revealed low returns and lack of competitive advantage. It is almost impossible to price out these countervailing effects.
2. Government interventions in capital markets have stepped up, meaning that the signals provided by those markets are increasingly unreliable. During 2023, new IPOs on China's stock market surged, even while the overall market stagnated. This surprising phenomenon is largely explained by the fact that most listings have been small, specialized technology firms explicitly "green lit" by China's regulators, while other consumer-facing firms are excluded (Lockett and Leng, 2023). In mid-2024, such IPOs suddenly dried up. Capital market signals are increasingly distorted, as investors both follow and evade government policy dictates.
3. There is less competition between state firms and private businesses, which was one of the dynamic ways the economy responded to legacy inefficiencies. Ant Financial was set to provide competition for state banks in its original IPO plan but has now been fenced off in regulatory terms. Initially, Alibaba grew in a completely new sector of the economy, so there wasn't much competition with state firms; now, after the crackdown, policymakers are ensuring there won't be competition in finance or information infrastructure. This absence of competition clearly threatens to silence a crucial source of information about the effectiveness of various initiatives.
4. Policymakers have been increasingly vocal about the need for "positive energy" and have tried to shut down negative and critical economic commentary in China. Clearly this distorts the information available, both to the public and to leaders themselves.

These create the danger that the quality of real economic information in China has been degrading substantially since the summer of 2021. Policymakers lose access to some of the feedback that might allow them to halt or correct unsuccessful policies. It may also deprive private businesses of the ability to craft diverse, independent business strategies based on their access to good information. If the quality of information continues to degrade, the efficiency of the new economic system is also likely to decline.

Implications for Economic Performance

Preceding sections have argued that gradual changes in the decision-making structure in China crystallized into a new type of economic system in the summer of 2021 that is substantially different from the reform era system that preceded it. This section asks what the implications for economic performance are likely to be for these systemic changes. In fact, the implications are overwhelmingly negative. At the most immediate level, the diversion of effort into noneconomic objectives – cultural self-confidence, a pro-fertility environment, demonstrative but ineffective measures to support common prosperity, scientific self-reliance, and the list goes on – inevitably implies less effective attainment of economic goals. The productivity growth of the economy should slow.

More interesting are the system-level effects. At the grass roots, the immediate implication is that decision-makers throughout the system have weaker incentives to invest effort in economic growth or push for pro-growth policies. It is not simply that growth has been demoted as a regime goal, but rather that incentive systems have been systematically restructured to short-circuit the channels through which growth priority was transmitted to actual decision-makers. The channels through which decision-makers were rewarded for delivering growth have been constricted, and the system has returned to a multi-task principal-agent relationship, which is typical of bureaucracies and typically displays low-powered incentives. This is most obvious for local government officials (this follows immediately from our preceding discussions). However, it is also true for business decision-makers, including executives at SOEs and private businesses. For SOEs, the events of 2021 simply dramatized the important changes that had been taking place in corporate governance in previous years. These have been underlined in 2022–2023 by a series of programmatic requirements for all central government SOEs: They are required to have plans for peak carbon emissions, for social responsibility, and for leading economy-wide technological transformation and overcoming technological bottlenecks (Naughton and Boland, 2023).

For private firms, of course, the picture is more modulated. Private businesses still want to grow and make profits. However, in the new system, the pursuit of profits must inevitably give greater attention to government policy mandates. Companies will invest more in influence activities and try to ensure consistency between their private opportunities and public policy goals by bargaining for leniency and special treatment. By contrast, the potential returns from radical, disruptive business ideas have been reduced. This diversion of effort amplifies the weaker incentives overall for profit and growth.

The policy failure to create new appropriate instruments directly reinforces the negative incentive effect of the new institutions. It will be difficult or impossible to segregate the new goals and delegate their attainment to specialized decision-makers. Instead, new goals without targeted instruments – decarbonization, breaking technology bottlenecks, and social equity – will inevitably be added to the multi-objective incentive system at the enterprise level. This, of course, adds complexity to the multiple trade-offs that firm managers have to make and will contribute to the reduced attention given to productivity, profitability, and growth.

We should also expect policymaking to become less effective. Policymakers are getting less accurate information from SOEs and (through capital markets) from private firms as well. Simultaneously, policymakers have become more ambitious in their desire to shape the economy. Economic and technological objectives have become increasingly ambitious and concrete, imposing tangible targets for economic structure, technology, and (indirectly) import substitution. Because of their complexity, it is difficult for policymakers and private decision-makers to decide whether the effects of different policies are reinforcing, neutralizing, or merely overlapping.

Yet while policymakers have worse information for shaping policies, they also face fewer veto points that constrain their choice of policy. They are free to change policies at will – they can be more decisive – but that means they have no way to convey to economic actors the credibility and stability of their policies. That means policy implementation will be more difficult, more costly, and more time-consuming. Policymakers have weaker information, fewer constraints, and grander ambitions. We expect, then, that policy effectiveness will generally decline.

The implications of system-level changes for economic performance are quite negative because they overlap and reinforce each other. While it is easy to predict the direction, it is hard to estimate the scale of these effects. Institutional efficiency is just one part of overall efficiency, which will be strongly influenced by the future trajectory of technology and the global economy. Diversion of resources into non-economic and inappropriate objectives; weaker incentives at the grass roots level; and less effective policymaking: for these reasons we expect the summer of 2021 to be followed by sustained underperformance.

Conclusion: Since the Twentieth Party Congress

Since the Twentieth Congress of the Chinese Communist Party, in October 2022, the Chinese economy has been struck by a series of surprising events and is generally seen to have been underperforming. To be sure, the performance of the Chinese economy in 2022–2024 was strongly affected by external events. Most important, the multi-year recession in the housing market has seriously eroded household wealth and reduced activity in the largest single sector of the economy. The collapse of the Zero COVID policy caused additional economic disruption. Finally, the impact of weak demand and slower growth had a big impact on household expectations, operating in particular through the weak labor market. These powerful external and structural factors explain a lot of the underperformance of the Chinese economy since 2022.

Yet it is impossible to ignore the fact that many of the negative phenomena in the Chinese economy are consistent with – and were probably exacerbated by – the systemic shifts described in this chapter. These events are generally consistent with the predictions of this paper (the first draft of which was written during 2021). We have already noted that the housing downturn was triggered by the abrupt imposition of new regulatory standards in 2020–2021. It is estimated that the housing recession caused the destruction of 500,000 jobs between 2021 and 2023. The crackdown on Alibaba, Baidu, and Tencent caused them to shed 63,000 jobs since the crackdowns (Bloomberg 2024a). Laid-off tutors and private teachers account for hundreds of thousands of other lost jobs. The 2021 crackdown bears some direct responsibility for the downturn in the labor market and in household expectations.

Sluggish growth implies that the economy has continued to underperform in terms of total factor productivity (TFP) growth. Despite continued high investment rates – concentrated in state-owned firms, infrastructure projects, and massive inflows into high-technology industrial investment – growth in GDP remains sluggish. Prices as measured by the GDP deflator declined through 2023 and 2024. China's sluggish recovery from lockdown at the end of 2022 has been striking. Although it would be reckless to attribute this underperformance to the weaker incentive environment created by the summer of 2021 measures, it is certainly consistent with the predictions made on the basis of those systemic changes. Future research may be able to clarify the relative contributions of external shocks and changes in institutional and systemic efficiency.

In the area of effective policymaking, it is possible to be much more definitive in the evaluation. The credibility of Chinese economic policymakers has been unusually low in recent years. The zero COVID policy was repeatedly and aggressively reaffirmed by policymakers throughout the first ten months of 2022, and then abruptly and completely abandoned within six weeks of the Party Congress. Policymakers have struggled without success to restore policy credibility in two areas directly related to economic performance: first, reconciliation with private businesses, and second, convincing the market that policymakers would produce an effective stimulus program to provide adequate aggregate demand.

Chinese policymakers since 2022 have made repeated efforts to reassure private businesses that their contribution to China's development is valued, yet these efforts have had limited impact. The culmination was perhaps Premier Li Qiang's meeting with the heads of major Internet businesses on July 12, 2023. He reassured them that the crackdown was over and praised a number of specific contributions each of the firms had made to China's technological development (Zhang, 2023). Within a couple of weeks, a top-level document on supporting the development of the private sector was issued (CCP and State Council 2023). Moreover, a close reading of the policy document revealed that it included little more than promises made in similar earlier documents on the private sector, which had been broken in 2021; and that the Premier was praising private firms (solely) for the actions they have taken that were consistent with state objectives, and not necessarily being given any wider scope for pursuing their own interests. In the months following the meeting, the share prices of these companies did not rebound, and the campaign of reassurance dwindled. As noted earlier, through the end of 2024, the market capitalization of Alibaba in particular has never recovered its pre-2021 value.

Similarly, the Chinese government has repeatedly rolled out stimulus initiatives in the years since the summer of 2021. These measures have included reductions of interest rates, special credit facilities, restructuring of local government debts, and fiscal stimulus. So far, none of these efforts have been perceived as adequate, or even credible. Only an injection of funds specifically targeted at the stock market in September 2024 had some effect in stemming a decline in that market. Even then, there was evidence that the policy was abruptly thrown together over a three-day period (Bloomberg, 2024b). Once again, the problems are related to a lack of policy credibility. Top Chinese policymakers meet every December to set the main economic policy themes for the following year. Meeting in December 2022, policymakers set "expanding domestic demand" as the top priority. The next year, in December 2023, expanding demand was demoted to third place after two key large-scale industrial policy programs, despite the fact that aggregate demand was still clearly below that warranted by potential growth. Then in December 2024, expanding domestic demand – and specifically consumption demand – was returned to first place in the annual exercise. Such a pattern is hardly going to restore policy credibility. Indeed, if policy is adopted and retracted at will, no reassurance of policy continuity will be credible. The obvious decline in policy effectiveness in China shows that some of the predicted systemic effects of the summer of 2021 do indeed seem to be present. In that sense, China is still struggling with the systemic legacy of the events of the summer of 2021.

References

Bloomberg News. 2020. "What China's Three Red Lines Mean for Property Firms." October 8, 2020. www.bloomberg.com/news/articles/2020-10-08/what-china-s-three-red-lines-mean-for-property-firms-quicktake

Bloomberg News. 2024a. "Xi Unleashes a Crisis for Millions of China's Best-Paid Workers." September 18, 2024. www.bloomberg.com/news/features/2024-09-18/china-risks-deflationary-spiral-as-xi-reshapes-economy-cracks-down-on-workers

Bloomberg News. 2024b. "Xi's Economic Adrenaline Shot Is Only Buying China a Little Time." September 24, 2024. www.bloomberg.com/news/features/2024-09-24/china-s-sweeping-stimulus-package-buys-economy-time-but-won-t-end-slump

CCP Center and State Council. 2021. "Decision on Optimizing Birth Policy and Achieving Long-term Balanced Population Development [in Chinese]." Xinhua News, July 20, 2021. www.gov.cn/zhengce/2021-07/20/content_5626190.htm

CCP Center and State Council. 2023. "Opinions on Accelerating the Healthy Development of the Private Economy." July 19, 2023. www.gov.cn/zhengce/202307/content_6893055.htm

Chen, Lulu Yilun. 2020. "Jack Ma's Ant Set to Raise $35 Billion in Biggest-Ever IPO." Bloomberg, October 26, 2020. www.bloomberg.com/news/articles/2020-10-26/jack-ma-s-ant-raises-about-34-5-billion-from-asian-ipos

Chen, Lulu Yilun and Jane Zhang. 2023. "Jack Ma's Clash with Beijing Costs Ant, Alibaba $850 Billion." Bloomberg, July 9, 2023. www.bloomberg.com/news/articles/2023-07-09/jack-ma-s-clash-with-beijing-costs-ant-alibaba-850-billion

Cheung, Tai Ming. 2022. *Innovate to Dominate: The Rise of the Chinese Techno-Security State*. Cornell University Press, pp. 51–82.

Cramer-Flood, Ethan and Briana Boland. 2023. "CCP Inc. in Malaysia: How State Capitalism Supports and Constrains China's Tech Giants." In *CCP Inc.: The Reshaping of China's State Capitalist System*. Washington, DC: CSIS, 2023.

Erisman, Porter. 2015. *Alibaba's World: How a Remarkable Chinese Company is Changing the Face of Global Business*. Palgrave Macmillan.

Holmstrom, Bengt and Paul Milgrom. 1991. "Multitask Principal-Agent Analyses: Incentive Contracts, Asset Ownership, and Job Design." *Journal of Law, Economics, & Organization*, 7: 24–52.

Leutert, Wendy Leutert and Sarah Eaton. 2021. "Deepening Not Departure: Xi Jinping's Governance of China's State-owned Economy." *The China Quarterly*, 248: 200–221.

Li, Guangman. 2021. 李光满. "Everyone Can Feel it – A Profound Change is Occurring." Li Guangman Freezing Point Commentary. August 29, 2021. www.politics.people.com.cn/n1/2021/0829/c1001-32211523.html

Li, Guangnam. 2022. 李光满 "My Year-End 2021 Review: A Vigorous Debate Around My 'A Profound Change is Occurring,'" Kunlun Policy Network, January 1, 2022. www.kunlunce.com/ssjj/guojipinglun/2022-01-01/157852.html

Lockett, Hudson and Cheng Leng. 2023. "How Xi Jinping is Taking Control of China's Stock Market." *Financial Times*, September 21, 2023. www.ft.com/content/f9c864c1-6cd4-405e-aa4b-d0b5e2ec6535

Lu, Min and Zhou Lin. 2020. 陆敏周琳. "Reading the Spirit of the Central Economic Work Conference: Preventing the Disorderly Expansion of Capital." *Economics Daily* 经济日报. December 27, 2020. www.gov.cn/xinwen/2020-12/27/content_5573663.htm

MacIntyre, Andrew. 2001. "Institutions and Investors: The Politics of the Economic Crisis in Southeast Asia." *International Organization*, 55 (1): 81–122.

Naughton, Barry. 2008. "Market Economy, Hierarchy and Single Party Rule." In *Market and Socialism: In the Light of the Experiences of China and Vietnam*. IEA Conference Volume, edited by Janos Kornai and Yingyi Qian. Macmillan, 135–161.

Naughton, Barry. 2020. "Grand Steerage." In *Fateful Decisions: Choices That Will Shape China's Future*, edited by Thomas Fingar and Jean C. Oi. Stanford University Press, 53–83.

Naughton, Barry. 2021. *The Rise of China's Industrial Policy, 1978-2020*. Boulder: Lynne Rienner. PDF available for download through Universidad Nacional Autónoma de México CECHIMEX, at www.economia.unam.mx/cechimex/index.php/en/publications

Naughton, Barry and Briana Boland. 2023. "CCP, Inc.: The Reshaping of China's State Capitalist System." A Report of the Freeman Chair in China Studies. Washington, DC: Center for Strategic and International Studies, January 2023. www.csis.org/analysis/ccp-inc-reshaping-chinas-state-capitalist-system

NDRC 2021. National Development and Reform Commission and eight other ministries, "Several Opinions on Promoting the Standardized, Healthy and Sustained Development of the Platform Economy." December 24, 2021. www.ndrc.gov.cn/xxgk/zcfb/tz/202201/t20220119_1312326_ext.html

NPC 2021. National People's Congress. "Outline of the PRC 14th Five Year Plan for Economic and Social Development and Long-rang Targets for 2035." March 12, 2021. www.gov.cn/xinwen/2021-03/13/content_5592681.htm

OECD 2021. "Income redistribution." in *Government at a Glance 2021*, Paris: OECD Publishing, 2021. https://doi.org/10.1787/637b3a40-en

Olcott, Eleanor and Wang Xueqiao. 2024. "How China Has 'Throttled' its Private Sector." *Financial Times*, September 11, 2024. www.ft.com/content/1e9e7544-974c-4662-a901-d30c4ab56eb7

Ren, Shuli. 2021. "How Xi's Four Pillars of Regulation Will Reshape China's Big Tech." *Bloomberg*, July 26, 2021. www.bloomberg.com/opinion/articles/2021-07-26/xi-s-four-pillars-of-regulation-will-change-the-way-big-tech-works-in-china

Ren, Shuli. 2022. "If You Think China Cares about Investors, Think Again." *Bloomberg*, June 12, 2022. www.bloomberg.com/opinion/articles/2022-06-10/if-you-think-china-cares-about-investors-think-again

SAMR 2020a. State Administration for Market Regulation. "Guidelines for Anti-Monopoly Guidelines in the Platform Economy Area" (Public Consultation Draft). November 10, 2020. https://web.archive.org/web/20201110142317/www.samr.gov.cn/hd/zjdc/202011/P020201109757564420041.docx

SAMR 2020b. State Administration for Market Regulation. "'Nine Prohibitions' Released: Two Ministries Summon Six Major Internet Giants for a Meeting." Nanfang Dushibao. December 22, 2020. https://m.mp.oeeee.com/a/BAAFRD000020201222399763.html

Tsebelis, George. 2003. *Veto Players: How Political Institutions Work*. Princeton University Press.

White, Edward, Ryan McMorrow and Sun Yu. 2022. "China Inc Unconvinced Xi Jinping's Regulatory Storm is Over." *Financial Times*, March 17, 2022. www.ft.com/content/27a3e58c-eadc-4796-8798-b37bdf19298f

Xi, Jinping. 2021a. "The Entire Party Must Completely, Correctly, and Comprehensively Implement the New Development Concept." January 28, 2021. Printed in *Qiushi*求是2022: 16, www.qstheory.cn/dukan/qs/2022-08/15/c_1128913644.htm

Xi, Jinping. 2021b. "Realistically Promote Common Prosperity." 扎实推动共同富裕. August 17, 2021, at Finance and Economic Meeting. *Qiushi* 求是. 2021: 20. www.qstheory.cn/dukan/qs/2021-10/15/c_1127959365.htm.

Xinhua News 2021. "Xi Jinping Chairs the Finance and Economics Commission Meeting, Advocates High Quality Development and Common Prosperity." August 17, 2021. www.xinhuanet.com/politics/leaders/2021-08/17/c_1127770343.htm

Zhang, Youyi and Sen Gong. 2023. "A Recent Regulatory Storm in China: Theoretical Interpretations and Applicability." *Asian Review of Political Economy* (2023) 2:1. Https://doi.org/10.1007/s44216-023-00011-3

Zhang, Yuzhuo. 2023. 张玉卓. "Write a new Chapter in the Story of Central State Enterprises Propelling Chinese-style Modernization." Xuexi Shibao学习时报 August 7, 2023. http://ztjy.people.cn/n1/2023/0807/c457340-40051719.html

Zhang, Lillian. 2023. "Alibaba, Tencent and Meituan Praised by Beijing for Helping China's Tech Progress in New Sign of Attitude Change." *South China Morning Post*. July 12, 2023. www.scmp.com/tech/big-tech/article/3227421/alibaba-tencent-and-meituan-praised-beijing-helping-chinas-tech-progress-new-sign-attitude-change

11 *China's Coming Era of Slow Growth*

WILLIAM H. OVERHOLT

Summary

The best way to understand China's present and future is that the Chinese reform era emulated the "Little Dragons," South Korea, Taiwan, and (to a lesser degree) Singapore. The little dragons were initially run by ruthless hierarchical politics and highly centralized economic management, guided by Marxist-Leninist ideas. Mobilized by fear of imminent national catastrophe, they focused on economic growth, informed by egalitarian efforts to ensure the broadest social support. They typically experienced a generation of growth at nearly a 10 percent annual rate, then a crisis of success brought on by emerging social complexity, bursting of economic bubbles, exhaustion of the early drivers of growth, and a financial squeeze of the government and government-associated companies. They responded to social complexity by moving to more market-oriented economics and politics, at the cost of the old hierarchical, centralized institutions. The generation of 10 percent growth gave way to a period of 7 percent growth and then declined to a relatively stable 3 percent. Through this process they achieved high incomes, high technology, and high domestic stability.

Emulating the little dragons, China has had its generation of 10 percent growth and is now in the era of crisis of success with lower growth. By 2030 or before, its potential growth will have declined to around 3 percent. However, instead of accommodating social complexity by moving to more market-dominated economics and politics, China is fighting the complexity revolution. Instead of sacrificing the interests of Party and state-affiliated firms to the pressures of a more complex society, China is prioritizing Party over society. This entails security policies that hamper economic growth, create a chronic fear of instability, and likely jeopardize its goal to become the world's leading economy and geopolitical power.

Introductory Note

The invitations to contribute to this symposium challenged participants to reflect on two alternate views of China's economic prospects: those who project its exceptional growth indefinitely into the future, like one William Overholt, and those who take a more skeptical view. The optimistic outlook was presumably based on my 1993 book, *The Rise of China: How Economic Reform Is Creating a New Superpower*. The forecast that China would become a superpower based on exceptional economic growth caused by post-Mao reforms has been fulfilled and is a present reality. However, I have never argued that rapid growth will extend indefinitely into the future.

In fact, with that forecast fulfilled, I published another book, *China's Crisis of Success*, in 2018, contradicting the then-consensus expectation that China's progress would remain superior for decades. *China's Crisis of Success* argued that China was headed into a period of difficulty characterized by rising expressions of discontent, concerns about state capture, financial crises among big state-connected companies, a state financial squeeze, and suppressed but very broad elite disgruntlement. This too has been happening. Demonstrations rose by an order of magnitude compared with the beginning of this century to the point where an embarrassed Beijing stopped publishing the statistics. Conglomerates like Anbang, Fosun, HNA, and Wanda; asset managers Huarong, Cinda, and Great Wall; much of the property sector; and many others experienced financial crises.[1] Alibaba and others were clipped and their leaders were sidelined for criticizing (trying to capture) government policies. The financial problems of local governments cumulated into an overall squeeze on government finances. This

[1] When I speak of government-linked companies, that includes most big companies in China, not just state enterprises. Big private property companies get big because of Party or government support; nobody gets a big parcel of land and building permits and other licenses without a Party connection. A conglomerate like HNA gets its funding and its support for deals from Party bosses. Like the nominally private Korean chaebol, which under Park Chung Hee were much more tightly government-controlled than today's Chinese state enterprises, their government links are the foundation of their success story.

pattern of developments was in the 2018 book. Subsequently, I have emphasized the coming economic slowdown in multiple articles.[2]

Thinking about Patterns of Growth

How does one make longer-run forecasts like this? I ask the reader's indulgence in an extended discussion of one way of approaching this, with examples of how I've used it. Econometric models have limited applicability because, in fast-growing economies, the economic structures change so fast and politics is so crucial. Likewise, because of the interaction of politics and economics, studies based in either of today's highly siloed economics and political science have limited value. Single-country specialists often miss what's coming, as China specialists generally did in the 1980s and early 1990s, because the insights come from observing international patterns of comparative development. However, these skills become invaluable and irreplaceable after one has a broader framework within which to exploit them.

Parenthetically, I must add that a great deal of contemporary political economy analysis is actively misleading because so much is based on a conceptually misguided focus on trying to discern broad differences between democratic and authoritarian systems – a whole literature that is effectively based on the assumption that Singapore and Somalia, South Korea and the Democratic Republic of the Congo, or, alternatively, the U.S. and the Philippines, comprise groups that share common characteristics.

What is useful is the developmental construct, a concept pioneered by Harold Lasswell.[3] Most countries fit into broad patterns of political-economic development or non-development. In a career based heavily on risk analysis, I have used such patterns mostly to discern patterns that lead to crises.[4] For instance, in a number of post-colonial African

[2] For instance, see "Thinking Through the China Hype," The International Economy, Summer 2022, http://international-economy.com/TIE_Su22_Overholt.pdf; and "Xi Jinping Won't Enjoy His Third Term," Global Asia Vol. 17, No. 4, December 2022, www.globalasia.org/v17no4/feature/xi-jinping-wont-enjoy-his-third-term_william-h-overholt

[3] For an elaboration of Lasswell's concept, more refined than Lasswell's own articulations, see Heinz Eulau (1986, pp. 328-334).

[4] For some of these patterns, see Overholt (1982), 66ff. The comments above reflect my own history. After Brzezinski moved to Washington in 1977, I took over from him a lecture gig speaking to bankers about politics and markets. One day I got a call from a bank that specialized in cross-border lending: "Senior management has noticed that you've been able to predict crises like the Iranian revolution years in advance whereas our economists can only predict

countries, a government run by an urban elite of officials, intellectuals, and military officers suppressed food prices in order to help their urban constituents. This led to food shortages and rural discontent, leading the government, in the interest of stability, to guarantee prices paid to farmers. Combined, these policies entailed large and increasing government budget deficits, leading the government to borrow from abroad and later to a crisis when it couldn't service the foreign debt. Often the resultant financial crisis led to political upheaval. The inexorable financial outcome of this model did not appear in standard economic analyses of foreign reserve adequacy, debt service ratios, and the like until it was too late. If one understood the construct (or model or template), one could then use standard (mainly economic and historical) tools to build useful scenarios with specific timelines.

Closer to home for Asia specialists is a construct or model of what I call peasant democracy. Here the Philippines exemplifies the construct.[5] At independence, the Philippines was ahead of every other developing country in every measure of development except railroads (because it is a nation of islands). In peasant democracies, the institutions of U.S.-style free elections and court system have quite different consequences than in a middle-class society. In a peasant society, the vast majority of the population lacks the resources for effective political participation; they don't have the wherewithal to organize in support of their interests and they have no money to donate to politicians. Elections then are a game within a tiny elite. Landlord groups compete and bring along their respective peasant clients, but, whichever group wins, the fundamental policies are the same: superb universities for the elite, poor education for the rest; superb hospitals for the elite, poor healthcare for the rest. Because the elite knows it will dominate, it is complacent. It doesn't give any priority to hiring the best people

them when they're already happening. We'd like to talk to you about forming a new risk analysis group." That group came to be perceived as the leader in the field, so Euromoney commissioned me to write the first book about political risk analysis. The availability of Lasswellian frameworks actually enhanced the value of professional economists and the use of them expanded. In contrast, an early 1980s wave of hiring political risk analysts quickly receded because academic political science provided few useful tools and those (Gini index/political discontent) were heavily borrowed from economics and employed crudely. The obsessive but futile effort to discern broad differences between democratic and authoritarian systems in meritocracy, long-range planning, growth rates...has ensured that much of contemporary political science continues to be irrelevant, not to mention wrong.

[5] This brief sketch of a model adapts the findings in Overholt (2017).

for efficient outcomes. It doesn't rapidly build infrastructure and it doesn't assess the taxes that would be necessary to pay for good infrastructure and broad public services. There is no sense of urgency to eliminate poverty. Rural development is neglected and comprehensive land reform is impossible; no democracy except Costa Rica has ever done an effective land reform. A complex Western court system – the Philippines had by far the most sophisticated judicial system in the developing world – greatly exacerbates elite-mass divisions because the majority of the population can't understand the system and certainly doesn't have the resources to hire a lawyer.

In such a system development lags. The Philippines went from being the region's most developed to one of the least developed. People love elections but hate the social outcomes. In response, a small minority joins communist or separatist or Islamist insurgencies. The majority increasingly support leaders who promise drastic change at the expense of democratic norms – Ferdinand Marcos who promised to emulate South Korea, his assassinated opponent Benigno Aquino who idolized Park Chung Hee, corrupt womanizer and movie actor Joseph Estrada, thug Rodrigo Duterte, and Bongbong Marcos. Duterte, who slaughtered thousands of people and suppressed opposition media, was the most popular president in Philippine history by far, and after his murderous pattern was well established, his followers swept the next legislative election in a landslide. India follows a version of this pattern. Initial development parity with China led to a drastic decline in relative GDP. Horrible health, education, and poverty outcomes have eventually led to majority support of a ruthless, undemocratic figure, Modi, who suppresses freedom of the press, oppresses opposition groups, tolerates or encourages violence against Muslims, represses Kashmir much as China represses Tibet, and has managed to expel his principal political opponent from the legislature, but above all promises to impose change and ignite growth.

In contrast, China has emulated the so-called East Asian development model (based on the "little dragons," South Korea, Taiwan, and Singapore)[6] that initially shared key characteristics, including:

6 Nearby countries such as Thailand, Indonesia, and Malaysia share some diluted characteristics of the Asian Miracle economies and have achieved proportionate success with proportionate problems. They are effectively hybrids between the Asian miracle model and the peasant democracy model. India, Sri Lanka, Brazil, and a good many others fit the peasant democracy model. Until the late

- An order of priorities: agriculture, light industry, heavy industry, domestic politics, and international politics, the exact opposite of Soviet priorities, as I emphasized in *The Rise of China* and earlier articles.
- Intense fear of national catastrophe – South Korea after the Korean War, Taiwan after China's civil war, Singapore after brutal separation from Malaysia, and China after the Great Leap Forward and the Cultural Revolution – leading to national mobilization, characterized by:
- An overwhelming priority for economic growth.
- Highly centralized economic management.
- Authoritarian political control, used to implement policies that would otherwise have been politically unfeasible or unacceptably delayed (e.g., Taiwan and South Korea land reform, Park Chung Hee's diplomatic rapprochement with Japan, China's 1994 tax reform, Zhu Rongji's forcing GITIC to accept bankruptcy, the Jiang Zemin/Zhu Rongji post-1998 military enterprise reform that would have been impossible in Indonesia or Thailand).
- Marxist-Leninist ideology, in various forms and varied degrees of explicitness.
- Technocratic, meritocratic institutions (*gaokao*, merit promotion, think tanks that bypass the inertia of the bureaucracy and train an elite of future top officials).[7]
- A high degree of initial egalitarianism – for example, land reform, rural development programs, and mass education – and intense efforts to reduce absolute poverty.
- A gradual opening of the economy to domestic market forces and to international trade and investment.
- Intense competition.

1990s, Thailand was a hybrid that developed very rapidly from a base as one of Asia's poorest countries. Later it became a caricature of an electoral oligarchy alternating with a self-serving military government.

[7] There has been regrettably wide acceptance of an argument that China's promotion system is not (relatively and with some flaws) meritocratic. This is largely based on a regression analysis that applies an inappropriate method to an invalid dataset and then amplifies the findings with a fallacy of division. See Shih et al. (2012); Victor Shih's work in the special issue on China of the *Journal of East Asian Studies*, Volume 16, Special Issue 01, March 2016; and my critical analysis in *China's Crisis of Success*, pp. 176–188. Of course, Xi Jinping has subsequently weakened meritocracy. For evidence that meritocracy increases growth, see Li and Zhou (2005).

- An emphasis on building infrastructure beyond what Western development institutions consider prudent (see the Seoul-Pusan highway, rejected by AID and the World Bank, subsequently the backbone of Korean development; periodic Taiwan railroad building plans....)

The construct itself does not provide a forecast. It provides a context for exploration of the extent to which China is likely to follow or deviate from the pattern.

These systems typically experience a generation of extremely rapid growth, typically near 10 percent annually, and then come to a crisis of success that occurs because easy wins are exhausted, bubbles develop, and rapid growth transforms a relatively simple economy and society into a very complex economy and society. The latter, which I call a complexity revolution, renders centralized, hierarchical economic and political control more difficult. Taiwan had its 1979 Kaohsiung riots and much later the financial crisis of the forty Guomindang-owned infrastructure conglomerates. South Korea in 1979 experienced an explosion of national inflation and foreign debt, a financial crisis of the chaebol, and the assassination of Park Chung Hee. It took a decade or more for those countries to accommodate a newly complex economy and society by moving to more market-oriented economic and political management.

China is now in the midst of a parallel crisis of success but is attempting to manage it by suppressing complexity and centralizing further. Once the developmental construct is explicit, then all the specialist skills of the economist, the political scientist, the historian, and the country specialist become not just useful but essential. To what extent are economic, social, and political trends consistent with the template? In what ways are these trends different? What modifications of a prediction do those differences entail? This is where the detailed work occurs. To establish that China fit the growth template of the little dragons was the subject of my book, *The Rise of China: How Economic Reform is Creating a New Superpower*, along with numerous articles.[8] To establish that it fit the template of their crisis

[8] Among many, see "The China Model," *Fudan Journal of Humanities and Social Sciences*, June 2011, pp. 1–18, originally a paper presented at the World Forum of China Studies, Shanghai, November 6–7, 2010, sponsored by the Shanghai Academy of Social Sciences and Fudan University. It became clear at that Forum that, surprisingly, most Chinese scholars initially thought the

of success was the subject of *China's Crisis of Success*. Those forecasts have worked. What of the future?

The Growth Pattern of the Asian Miracle Economies

The little dragons typically grow at about 10 percent per year for a generation, then slow to 7 percent for a few years, then settle down to about 3 percent. (South Korea from 2001 to 2015 was 2.85 percent.) Will China follow this pattern? It has so far generally tracked the overall pattern in terms of economic growth rates and is now experiencing the first deceleration. However, instead of accommodating the complexity revolution, China is fighting it. It is trying to push back the tide rather than channeling it. We know from watching South Korea, Taiwan, and Singapore that political and economic accommodation (elections, market pricing, competition, acceptance of most market outcomes, and openness) are conducive to subsequent high incomes, high technology, and social stability. China's fundamental divergence from the accommodation model is obviously crucial. Exploring the details of this decisive break from the earlier pattern, the basic shape of China's economic growth curve will remain similar, but most aspects of the "fighting complexity" strategy will further depress growth.

China's economic aspirations and policies have evolved rapidly. What has remained constant for centuries is a determination to return to the domestic wealth and international power that most Chinese view as the only acceptable norm for a civilization that long led the global economy. Comprehending the continuity of this deep aspiration is essential when later we consider the long-term prospects of the Xi Jinping approach to management.

Under Deng Xiaoping and Jiang Zemin (1978–2002), the leadership's model of how to achieve that evolved rapidly in the direction of market-oriented reform and international opening to trade and investment, along with political and administrative institutionalization, meritocracy, and increasing differentiation among Party, government, and markets. Under Hu Jintao (2003–2012), economic reform and opening as previously understood largely stagnated; that administration's

China model was unique and didn't realize the extent to which Deng Xiaoping had emulated the earlier Asian successes. Deng asked the question, why are our neighbors doing so well while we are doing so poorly? Then he followed through very decisively on the answer.

achievements focused on eliminating some unfair treatment of farmers, spreading the economic miracle to China's interior, and surviving the 2008 Global Financial Crisis. However, Hu's administration also included significant efforts to institutionalize governance, including collective leadership, enhanced meritocracy, increased intra-Party democracy, and experiments with local democracy. Hu's legacy included these achievements but also worsened problems of coordinating parts of the central government, dissonance between the central and local governments, and a spectacular increase in the visible scale of corruption. Many of Hu's colleagues saw all these, including the governance changes that appeared to Western observers to be important steps forward, as threats to Party rule. Hence they chose a successor, Xi Jinping, who was determined to consolidate Party rule, impose stability, and reduce corruption.

China's Changing View of the Western Model

Until the mid-2000s, China looked up to western economies and western polities much as South Korea, Taiwan, and Singapore did. That absolutely did not mean that they intended detailed copying of them, but they saw them as models of how both mature economies and mature polities work. They took most World Bank advice. They imported Hong Kong officials wholesale in the belief that Hong Kong's market-friendly structure provided a primary economic model for China. At the turn of the century, the Central Party School under Hu Jintao was working on three models for democratization, including one modeled on Japan (elections mainly influencing the balance among factions within a dominant party) and one on Taiwan. At a RAND Corp. conference in November 2001, during a debate about Taiwan, the political leader of a Central Party School delegation surprised the Americans by declaring, "We hate everything Lee Teng-hui is doing in cross-Straits relations, but we admire the way he has taken Taiwan politics to a new level." The Carter Center and the International Republican Institute were advising on village elections. There was even high-level discussion of whether Taiwan's Guomindang Party might one day be allowed to compete and win an election in China's Fujian Province.

Three things changed that reverence for supposedly more mature Western models. The Global Financial Crisis of 2008 shocked and damaged China and convinced officials there that the Western model of economic management was fatally flawed. The emergence of Donald Trump and Boris Johnson, along with regional examples like the Philippines and Thailand, reduced to absurdity, in their view, any argument that Western democracy would ensure governance in the interest of the people or the power of the state. And China's own positive experience of mobilizing state-controlled institutions to overcome the 2008 financial crisis convinced a working consensus of China's leadership that state control of the financial system and the pinnacles of the industrial economy was essential. (In crisis such controls are indeed valuable, and even the most capitalist Western economies rebalance in favor of central controls in times of war or other crisis. The problem with the conclusions many Chinese leaders drew about the superiority of centralized, state-led economic management is that, of course, most of the time economies are not in crisis.)

The combination of domestic insecurity and disillusionment with the Western model led to the selection of Xi Jinping and like-minded colleagues with a mandate to suppress internal dissent, overcome fractiousness within the central government, consolidate the center's control of the periphery, and crush corruption.

China's New Economic Model

Under Xi Jinping, China seeks to create a new system with extremely centralized executive leadership of the government and state enterprise leadership of the economy while retaining the full benefits of market competition. It wants to strengthen the state enterprises while retaining the benefits of a private sector that provides 90 percent of urban employment, 100 percent of net job creation, over 50 percent of exports, and, according to former Vice Premier Liu He, more than 70 percent of all innovation. Likewise, it wants to retain the advantages of foreign direct investment while preventing foreign companies from attaining a leadership role in any Chinese sector and achieving Chinese global dominance in every aspect of modern manufacturing.

In this new system,[9] state enterprises will control the commanding heights of the economy. The government will support the private

[9] For a description of the recent evolution of China's state investments and political controls on the economy, see Chen and Rithmire (2020) and Pearson et al. (2022).

sector, but every company will have a Party Secretary with ultimate decision power over strategic business decisions and every company will eventually have at least a small but controlling "golden share" of government ownership in a form that ensures the state's ability to monitor and correct socially inappropriate decisions. Chinese companies will attain dominance of advanced manufacturing in foreign countries, but foreign companies will never be allowed to dominate any important sector in China. The education system will be remodeled and shortened to rigorously support industrial needs.

Along with stability, the overarching theme of Xi Jinping's new model is "Common Prosperity," and the core promise of Common Prosperity is a fairer system without the divisive income and wealth inequality that currently plagues both China and the United States. This is an inspiring wish list – as socialist critiques of capitalism and promises a century ago were inspiring. Actual policies are accomplishing much that Western-style democracies currently seem incapable of implementing, such as rapidly eliminating extreme poverty and making exceptionally rapid progress on green energy. But it is also a wish to have one's cake and eat it too. Foreign companies and countries will reject a system where they are lured in for their technology but excluded from the kind of market access that China demands from the West. Xi Jinping's support for the private sector is sincere, but no matter how many times he tells the big Beijing banks to lend more to private companies, they still will never get their money back if they obey. (If the bank doesn't have deep roots in the local village, wily locals walk away with the bank's money. Then bank executives are punished, sometimes severely, when the money doesn't come back.) Subsidized state enterprises eat up the private ones. Private sector investment and growth have plunged.

The extensive political controls on business will either be costly or ineffective. Of course, we do not yet know, for instance, how the relationship between the Party Secretary and the CEO will evolve. China's diversity means that evolution will almost certainly be diverse. We do know anecdotally that among the big companies in Beijing, the Party Secretary and the CEO often have quite different agendas; that outcome will impede growth. It is reasonable to hypothesize that in Guangdong the CEOs will often co-opt the Party Secretaries, lucratively. More broadly, the role of the Party Secretary could become like a super-CEO or Board Chair in some cases and elsewhere more like an analogue of a Western bank compliance officer. Such roles will probably be beneficial in some cases (a U.S. government compliance officer on the board of Silicon Valley Bank might have averted a crisis), but on average it will likely be a net cost.

The intended insertion of political commissars, who will have veto power over strategic business decisions, into all enterprises is a microcosm of two broader trends: a shift in the balance between red and expert (political loyalty vs. technical skills) from an emphasis on expert to a priority for red; and a blurring of the differentiation, carefully cultivated by preceding reformist leaders, among Party, government, and business. That blurring reduces the cultivation of specialized expertise and clear focus in each function.

Barry Naughton, in Chapter 10 of this volume, has emphasized a related shift under Xi Jinping, away from a sharp focus on economic growth to a more diffuse set of goals that include security, growth, distribution, and a broad set of structural goals. Much of this shift would happen anywhere as development continues. When a family has enough to eat, its goals broaden. When a society has successfully provided adequate food and shelter, its goals broaden in synch with its families. But in Xi's China, the inevitable blurring of focus occurs in the context of Xi's broader blurring of boundaries and dilution of specialization. Moreover, as Naughton highlights, Xi's centralization diminishes the provinces' and cities' ability to make decisions based on their refined understanding of local conditions; this reverses Deng Xiaoping's deliberate and fruitful decentralization (Oi, 1999).[10]

Moreover, the centralization and blurring of boundaries naturally inflate corruption. While Xi Jinping has waged a valiant and politically costly war against corruption, highly centralized and hierarchical economic systems breed corruption the way a wet log breeds mushrooms. The blurring and politicization of responsibilities magnify that effect. In the days of Mao and of early reform, an official was often simultaneously the author of steel industry regulation, the implementer of that regulation, and the owner of a steel factory. Today, Party/

[10] On the flowering of local initiative that occurred, see Zhou (1996). Zhou and others rightly highlight the importance of local initiative but disregard the crucial leadership decision to accommodate and then encourage that initiative – unlike Xi Jinping.

government ownership of land, while simultaneously being beneficiaries of land sale revenues, regulators of land uses, and deciders of who gets use of a particular parcel, invites corruption. When reformers created clear divisions of labor among Party, government, and business, such incentives to corruption declined. Now they are being reintroduced. No anti-corruption campaign is as powerful as the structural incentives the Xi administration is enhancing.

As it centralizes and emphasizes the leading role of the state enterprises, Xi's administration seems to have forgotten one of the central lessons of socialism's history: political leaders believe state ownership will give them control of the economy, but the big companies inexorably end up owning the politicians (Dahrendorf, 1959). This is already happening, for instance, in healthcare. Government policy is that resources should increasingly flow downward, to the local primary care level. However, huge, powerful state-owned hospitals drive the flows increasingly upward to themselves.[11] Something similar may be happening in banking. Alibaba's brilliant use of data to analyze credit instantly and make immediate decisions was disintermediating the banking system, making finance much more efficient at the cost of weakening the big state-owned banks. These giant institutions resisted the onslaught of Alibaba and others and that seems to have contributed to the decapitation and dismemberment of Alibaba and the nationalization of its database, which was then provided to the big banks.

The German education and apprenticeship model, which Xi seems to be emulating, deemphasizes broad education in favor of a higher priority for vocational training. This provides immediate advantages for current industry, but it decreases long-run flexibility. It has largely confined the German economy to refining early twentieth-century technologies like the automobile, while the U.S., which emphasizes providing a broad education, dominates the modern service economy. The Beijing administration is imposing this new system, or important parts of it, in the context of the weakening of the core drivers that have driven China's exceptional growth, along with emerging drags on growth. More on this later.

[11] On this point I am indebted to a presentation by Winnie Yip of the Harvard School of Public Health to Harvard Fairbank Center's series on Critical Issues for Contemporary China, March 29, 2023.

The Social Program

From the era of the Chinese civil war through the early times of Mao's leadership, the Chinese Communist Party has branded itself as egalitarian. China's constitution specified an economically egalitarian political process based on struggle by peasants and workers against their erstwhile social betters. The early years after 1949 were noteworthy for a violent egalitarianism: land reform and the Three- and Five-Anti campaigns that dispossessed business leaders. Deng Xiaoping, however, proclaimed that in the interests of growth, some people must get rich first. Jiang Zemin dispensed with the constitution's emphasis on class struggle and instead promoted the ideal of a vanguard cultural and economic elite. Hu Jintao sought to moderate the ensuing explosion of inequality by emphasizing rural improvement, but his era was nonetheless marked by the congealing of a wealthy, powerful, corrupt Party-government-business privileged class.

In this context, Xi Jinping seeks to revive the Party's egalitarian credentials. He famously completed the drive to eliminate "absolute poverty," but absolute poverty was defined as such a low hurdle that it left hundreds of millions in poverty that was quite severe even if not quite absolute. Rural education remained below standard for China's level of development, albeit far above once-equal India (Rozelle and Hell, 2020). Rural health institutions remain absolutely poor. The hukou system deprives many of vital social services when they have moved to the cities in search of a better life. Pensions, health insurance, and care for the aged remain quite backward. Resources have gone to the cities, the elite, national grandeur, and the vast and vastly expensive domestic security and political control service.

Most importantly, Xi Jinping has sought to revive the Party's egalitarian brand by assembling egalitarian policies and programs under the brand of "Common Prosperity." Many policies are variations on earlier programs: helping poorer areas with transfers of income and industry, adjusting tax rates, improving social services, boosting certain kinds of education, adjusting minimum wages including for gig workers, and making special efforts to improve rural life. The novel policies include campaign-style tools: decapitation of the high-flying tech companies, breaking up Alibaba, forcing the wealthy to make large charitable donations, and the like. And they include policies that greatly enhance the power of the state, most notably nationalizing the databases that made Alibaba and Didi so efficient. These policies have been vastly destructive of wealth and have crimped China's extraordinarily successful tech sector. These consequences have led MIT's Yasheng Huang to speculate that the real purpose of the novel policies is to crimp the economic and political power of private capital in Chapter 9 of this volume. Certainly that is at least one motivation, as seen by the treatment of Alibaba's leader Jack Ma, who went from being the country's economic superhero to a couple of years of exile in Tokyo after having the temerity to criticize banking regulators.

While decisions in the name of Common Prosperity programs have imposed trillions of dollars of losses on market values and crimp the most dynamic parts of the economy, they do not include the politically difficult measures that would actually shift the economy sharply toward the fairness promised by the "Common Prosperity" slogan. That would ultimately require a substantial property tax, a highly progressive income tax, termination of the controls on rural migration to the cities, greatly liberalized rural land rights, and a shift in the balance of taxing power between the center and the localities. At least some crucial fairness policies seem politically beyond Xi Jinping's reach. Eleven years of high-level conversation about the needed property tax have failed to implement even an experimental version. Most of the Party-government-business elite's wealth consists of property holdings and that elite has a strong interest in resisting taxation of it. In many cases, there is an even stronger interest in refusing disclosure of holdings.

Ultimately, Xi Jinping and Joe Biden appear equally impotent to alter their countries' egregious maldistribution of wealth. Ultimately, both have chosen security and geopolitical glory over amelioration of serious domestic social problems. In China's case this is particularly egregious because the combined costs of the military and the vast domestic security apparatus are exceptionally high while hundreds of millions of people remain desperately poor.

China's Long-Term Economic Prospects

All these developments tend to reduce growth. Ironically, just as triumphalism is fading in China, a version of China triumphalism continues in the United States. Many commentators, particularly those associated with the U.S. Defense establishment, project superior Chinese economic growth indefinitely into the future[12] and infer that China will overwhelm the U.S. This assumption is the foundation of status panic over China in Washington, DC. Such commentators assume that superior past Chinese growth implies superior future Chinese growth – an assumption scholars can seemingly get away with even if stockbrokers are required to disclaim such inferences. In fact, the drivers of fast growth are fading. A surprising amount of higher-level "Chinese" manufacturing is actually foreign companies' production based in China. The technological progress of many Chinese industries has relied on collaboration with foreign companies that are becoming disillusioned with unfair Chinese practices.[13]

Historically, the U.S. overestimates its competitors and underestimates itself. Throughout the Cold War, Americans (intelligence agencies, economists, media opinion makers, and informed public opinion) egregiously overestimated the Soviet economy. In the 1970s and 1980s, they grossly exaggerated Japan's prospects. Most recently we have grossly overestimated Russian military capabilities. Discussions of China do not seem to have digested the lesson of these failures.

One way the prowess of Japan, the Soviet Union, and China has been exaggerated is to focus on manufacturing prowess and ignore the service economy, which is larger and more important than manufacturing even in China. (In 2015 the services sector grew to 50.5 percent of China's economy and subsequently has continued to expand.) While the opening of China's manufacturing sectors to foreign investment, together with Chinese companies' competition for overseas markets, has toughened China's manufacturing through competition, the services sector has remained relatively closed and uncompetitive. Hence, U.S. dominance of services will likely persist in an era where both economies are dominated by service industries. Moreover, it is important to remember that, in addition to being the biggest part of both economies, services are crucial to long-run innovation and vitality in manufacturing.

Within services, education and scholarship are particularly important. The government has banned for-profit private education. Official incentives to learn English have declined. In Silicon Valley, and implicitly in Western university research, the ultimate goal is

[12] See, for instance, Allison et al. (2022).
[13] On the crucial role of foreign direct investment, see Enright (2016).

a *disruptive* breakthrough, but in China, university research funds are channeled through Party Secretaries, who are selected for devotion to stability rather than for enthusiasm about disruptive ideas. Professors' and students' travel abroad, communication with foreigners, and access to information have been restricted. Political controls on curriculum and teachers have increased at all levels. Foreign scholars' access to information and to discourse with Chinese colleagues has been even more restricted. The use of Chinese students abroad as spies – on their colleagues, on foreign professors – and the willingness of a few to threaten people who disagree with them are raising questions in foreign universities about the cost of welcoming large numbers of Chinese students. The impact on future economic progress of this deteriorating environment is impossible to quantify, but it is not positive, and it is not zero.

The core drivers of China's "miracle" growth have been heavy infrastructure, property development, and urbanization. By the end of this decade, those drivers will be largely exhausted. Property already shows signs of plateauing or tipping over. Throughout China, one encounters infrastructure projects that will never pay their way; drive across impoverished Anhui Province and the wide, first-class highways will surprise anyone from potholed Massachusetts where I live. Urbanization still provides some growth, but by the end of this decade, it too will be largely exhausted. Moreover, the easy phase of technological catch up is over. The slowing effect of a more difficult phase of technological catch up is magnified by western governments' and companies' pushback against intellectual property theft and foreign investors' reaction against unfair regulation and limitations on their market shares. If China were to follow the pattern of the East Asian model construct, its potential growth should decline by decade's end to about the 3 percent that has been typical of South Korea, Taiwan, and Singapore. But all the additional drags imposed by the Xi Jinping administration's political controls, its fighting against the complexity revolution, should detract substantially from that 3 percent, perhaps comparable to the current U.S. level of 2 percent or below.

Property and infrastructure have gone beyond drivers to become bubbles. The property bubble has at least partially burst. While that bursting appears more manageable than its counterparts in Japan and the U.S., because China's banks are proportionately far less exposed, it leaves behind large debts that must be serviced over an extended period of time. Moreover, it creates a financial squeeze for local governments throughout China that are more dependent on property development income than their Western counterparts. Less obviously, the same is true of infrastructure. Amortizing China's wondrous railroads was always going to be a serious burden; as the economy slows, as local governments increasingly lack the wherewithal to fund construction of their segments and to service the railroad construction debts, growth will slow proportionately. Maintenance of all that wonderful infrastructure will be like an additional debt burden; when it is still new, maintenance costs are low but later they rise. If anecdotal evidence of inferior construction and use of substandard materials proves indicative of widespread problems, those maintenance costs could be very high.

The heavy political controls that Xi is imposing will, if they persist and are strongly implemented, slow growth. Officials' innovative entrepreneurship at all levels has been a crucial source of growth. That has been a crucial engine of China's growth. Recall that when the central government restricted local government revenues but gave them the right to create companies, almost overnight town and village enterprises were employing 110 million people. Under Xi's tight controls, that entrepreneurship has largely died. Successful local entrepreneurship used to include bending or bypassing the myriad rules; if a local official met his or her goals, few questions were asked about how that was achieved. There were so many rules that movement required infringing some of them. Now, however, everyone is terrified to act; breaking any of the gridlocking makes one vulnerable to accusations of corruption. The result is that China's sprawling Party and government bureaucracies often resemble a New York City subway work to rule – a form of strike.

A banking system that has become much more centralized and hierarchical cannot adequately service the private sector economy that provides most economic growth, all net new jobs, and most innovation. Liu He has argued that innovation will replace the old drivers and anyone who visits Shenzhen or Zhonguancun will be dazzled by the innovation energy. But on balance across China, the political controls, emphasis on state enterprise control of the commanding heights of the economy, and the collapse of private sector funding and investment will hinder innovation.

China's economy has for decades displayed a remarkable imbalance. Household incomes are proportionately very low. Investment is very high, in fact so high that its egregious scale makes consumption look much more inadequate than it is (Ma et al., 2018). More broadly, Chinese economic policy has had a one-sided emphasis on improving the supply side of the economy rather than the demand side. In 2013 Premier Li Keqiang supported a plan to emphasize boosting the demand side of the economy, a balanced approach that came to be called Liconomics. But Xi Jinping overruled him, eventually subordinating the prime minister's normal authority over the economy to Xi's expanding reach, and ensured continued emphasis on upgrading the supply side, especially infrastructure and advanced manufacturing. This imbalance continues to be a drag on the economy.

Moreover, just as Xi's policies are fighting the complexity revolution, they fight other inexorable economic tides. Xi (here sounding like Biden) wants to prevent the decline of the share of manufacturing in China's economy.[14] He and other officials laud the private sector but impose a centralized banking system that cannot support it. Xi thinks hardware is much more important than software. He wants innovation, intended to be the main engine of future growth, to be driven by top-down directives and subsidies, but historically China's great innovations have come from the bottom up. The genius of China's leadership has been, not to impose innovations from above, but to incentivize innovation from below and to wisely endorse spontaneous innovation from below, even when that innovation contradicted official policy. Most notably, when farmers started taking their land back and reverting to family farming, the leadership recognized an economic and political opportunity rather than suppressing the infringement of socialist collective production.

This collection of depressive trends and developments lies behind the collapse of total factor productivity that has already occurred. Brandt et al. (2020) calculated a two-thirds decline in China's total factor productivity growth. Zhu, in Chapter 2 of this volume, has calculated that from 1978 to 2007, China's total factor productivity grew at 4 percent, driven by domestic market reform, international opening, market-based technological diffusion and innovation, and reduced barriers to internal trade and migration. Crucial to this rapid

[14] Naughton makes this point in Chapter 10 of this volume.

growth of productivity was innovation that bubbled up from society [and leadership willingness to endorse that innovation]. He finds that capital reallocation and export expansion have contributed little to that amazing growth. Recently the most productive kinds of reform have lagged and Xi Jinping has emphasized tight controls and top-down innovation, so total factor productivity growth has collapsed to 1 percent. Thomas Rawski notes that China's productivity growth has dropped earlier in the cycle than it did in the little dragons.

In China's graying society, the number of working-age people started declining in 2015, while the welfare burden of caring for the aged is increasing. The Japanese experience shows what an extraordinary burden a graying society can be. China's graying problem is worse.

China Will Have Some Wins

China has some important positive trends and opportunities. It looks set to dominate green energy technology and the production of electric vehicles. Contract manufacturing of gene and cell therapies may become a very large and profitable sector, and China could be the world's leader. Rural reform, including education and removal of the hukou system, could yield large gains. Some room remains for technological catch up. If China can find a way to satisfy tech regulatory needs and release once again the energy of its tech companies, Alibaba, Tencent, and Didi, which were far in advance of Western competitors, could resume their success. There could be many more like that. It is more difficult to identify areas of potential breakthrough than to see looming problems, so failure to imagine areas of upside potential is a source of risk in projecting the future.

Budget Sobriety and Sand in the Gears

China is also adjusting to the end of a bull market, and a bull market mentality, in government budgets and their management. For decades of the reform era, GDP grew fast and central government revenue grew twice that rate. Double growth of revenues occurred because the economy was increasingly monetized and tax collection was improving. This created the illusion in Beijing and abroad that the Chinese government had unlimited resources. Now GDP grows more slowly and government revenue growth must converge with GDP. The slowdown of property development severely crimps local government budgets. The severe belt-tightening of the Belt and Road Initiative, and the debt problems resulting from its early extravagance, are among the many indicators of incipient sobriety.

During Xi's third term, the controversies over Zero-Covid, Russia, decapitation of the big platform companies, political controls on the economy, private sector malaise, severe political repression, and extreme decoupling of Chinese elites from global society will be sand in the gears of the economy for his five-year term, possibly followed by a historic succession struggle.

Alternative Scenarios

To summarize, China's trajectory roughly follows the template of the smaller dragons, for similar reasons. Given its loss of powerful drivers and its demographic problems, China's potential growth after 2030 is probably similar to the little dragons (3 percent) or to the U.S. (2 percent). Xi Jinping's overcentralization, Japan-style industrial policy, kneecapping of the private sector, and political controls will probably reduce growth substantially below its potential.

As we look out to the future, even if the current structures and policies of the Xi Jinping era remain relatively constant, there are many sources of uncertainty. We don't yet know the rough magnitude of China's debt or the rough magnitude of infrastructure maintenance costs. Judgments about China's ability to innovate can be informed, but ultimately they are guesses. We don't know whether there will be a pandemic or a catastrophic banking crash or a disabling succession struggle. We don't know whether there will be a great technological breakthrough or a resource discovery in China's favor. A move away from overcentralized finance, toward a system that could more effectively finance local private enterprises, could make a large positive difference. The general shape is important, worth debating, and should be about right, but it is still just a general shape.

The greatest uncertainty is the evolution of the U.S.–China relationship. It could become more constructive if both sides react against the looming dangers of confrontation. It could descend into economic warfare. At worst, there could be a real war – a limited war over Taiwan, which would itself be economically devastating, or warfare not geographically confined.

Japanification?

In *China's Crisis of Success*, I highlighted the risk of Japanification which is a slowing of development caused by a coalition of traditional industrial conglomerates and politicians that inhibits reform, competition, innovation, and internationalization. This would imply a GDP growth rate of 1.5 percent or less. Xi Jinping has heightened the risks through: wanting the core of the Chinese economy to be dominated by a group of big state firms; expecting innovation to come heavily through subsidies to those firms; giving a Party Committee veto over strategic business decisions in every firm; consolidating bank finance in giant firms that cannot fund local private firms in a creditworthy fashion; immobilizing a previously innovative state/Party bureaucracy through omnipresent fear of politically tinged accusations of corruption; seeking industrial self-sufficiency; giving control over allocation of research funds to Party secretaries whose interest is the opposite of disruption; inhibiting scholarly exchanges with the foreign world; reducing the educational and career value of learning English; and more broadly fighting against some of the most powerful tides of economic and social development.

China retains key advantages. China has facilitated the emergence of innovative SMEs, whereas Japan has inhibited them. China has facilitated the social transformation from a manufacturing economy into a services economy, whereas Japan's giant industrial conglomerates have the political clout to slow that transformation. Chinese society has remained far more outward-looking than Japan's. Frustrated, ambitious Chinese students go abroad; Japan's stay home. Chinese scientific scholarship is competitive and internationally collaborative in a way that Japan's isn't. Chinese elites speak English (and other languages) and thus have access to foreign ideas to an extent that Japanese counterparts don't. China's economy is open to GM and thousands of other foreign firms on both the supply and demand sides to a degree that Japan's isn't. Despite Xi's changes, these advantages remain strong.

But Xi has put crucial Chinese advantages at risk. One of China's greatest advantages has been its adaptability. Each leadership team (Mao/Deng/Jiang/Hu/Xi) has changed the country's politics and economics drastically to correct the failings of its predecessor. Xi has interrupted that process of change and correction, but we do not yet know whether he has curtailed adaptability or just interrupted it temporarily. Another Chinese advantage has been the sense of mobility, of everything getting better for everybody. Japan had that through the 1980s, but then decades of near-stagnation imbued Japanese youth with hopelessness; why venture abroad or aspire to disruptive innovation when one's whole life experience is deadening? China is now where Japan was in the 1970s. As China's growth becomes slow, as the Party elite congeals, and as fear quiets the intense debates about everything that have characterized Chinese society, the risks of Japanification will grow.

The Chinese response to economic and scholarly deadening is the opposite of Japan's. The Japanese stay home and don't sally abroad in search of greater opportunities. In contrast, most Chinese middle-class and elite families want their money, their children, and often themselves out of China. Beijing risks losing its most creative minds and business ideas through repression in a way that Japan doesn't, but the Chinese exodus also feeds a vast global feedback loop that historically has facilitated revitalization. We are still in a long cycle whose early phase was driven by expatriate Sun Yat-sen. China's great economic takeoff of the past four decades is part of a shorter cycle driven by Deng Xiaoping's awareness of the four little dragons' successes together with the capital, business acumen, and money of Hong Kong, Taiwan, and the overseas Chinese networks.

If we extrapolate the trends of Xi Jinping's era indefinitely into the future, Japanification is coming. But, despite its size, China changes more readily than Japan does. China's diversity and its overseas networks fuel other scenarios. Every Chinese grad student I encounter speaks of the risk of Japanification that self-awareness is itself powerful.

Structural Change?

Prediction about China's future economic path carries far more structural uncertainty today than in the 1980s and 1990s. There was a great facilitator for predictions about China's growth to superpower scale back in the 1980s and 1990s: In a society desperate for the basics of life, food, shelter, education, the reform and opening policies led to income growth for every social group. This naturally generated broad support for those policies. A political-economic virtuous circle developed. This was obvious in China at the time, and it had been clear in the experience of the smaller dragons.

On the contrary, policies that, in the name of security, worsen a decline of growth do not create such a virtuous circle. They are politically self-undermining. Moreover, a declining growth rate is not China's only political problem. As I documented in *China's Crisis of Success*, across all the important Chinese elites, many forms of suppressed discontent fester. There is an incentive to change. That does not make positive change inevitable. It means repression and the economy will either get much worse or much better, not remain the same. This itself is an important point, because there is a tendency in the U.S. to assume that China tomorrow will be basically the same as China today. Indeed, there is a strong tendency to argue that, really, China since 1949 has always been structurally the same, that Xi Jinping's China was always immanent in Deng's China and Jiang's China.

That image could hardly be further from the truth. For such a large country, China's many changes are extraordinary. As noted earlier, each leadership team has sought with considerable success to decisively correct the weaknesses of its predecessor. Deng shed Mao's autarky, collectivization, and suppression of the market. Jiang repudiated peasant-worker struggle against the elite as the core political strategy and substituted an emphasis on inclusiveness, shared interests, and vanguard (elite) modernity. Hu Jintao's "harmonious society" abandoned the rapid market reforms that had overstressed Chinese society and instead sought fairness, responsiveness, and institutionalization. Xi Jinping warred against the Hu era's disintegrative forces that seemed to threaten social stability and Party control. Each of these was a major course change. This ability to articulate the key (perceived) problem and reshape theory and practice is a distinctive feature of post-Mao China as it was of South Korea and Taiwan – a sharp contrast with Japan's stodgy stability.

Structural change could come through self-correction in the context of continued leadership by Xi Jinping and possibly a successor chosen in an orderly process. In the extreme, elite discontents and mass disillusionment over declining growth and a failure of egalitarian promises could lead to a disorderly succession and attendant economic disruption.

This discussion highlights that the main economic risks are on the downside. In a broader perspective, China's drive for wealth, power, and respect has been a centuries-long constant that has entailed rejection of many political and economic structures and many successive leaders. If the current structure turns out to mean that China will lag in incomes and technology for the indefinite future, that economic gains will be largely captured by a relatively narrow Party-government-business elite, that its dream of paramount global leadership will evaporate, and that giving up freedoms no longer pays off in rapid growth, then domestic demands for change may become very powerful. As with the crisis of success, that does not inevitably mean that leaders will do what the West sees as the right thing, moving decisively toward more freedom and more market efficiency. It could also move decisively in a darker direction. Unfortunately, the template of the East Asian model then goes blank.

The Ultimate Difference from the Little Dragons

When South Korea and Taiwan faced their crises of success, their historic choices paralleled that of China. Their economies were centrally controlled. The pinnacles were dominated in Taiwan by forty Guomindang-owned infrastructure conglomerates and in Korea by a dozen chaebol that, although privately owned, received annual production quotas, export quotas, credit allocations, and interest rate determinations from Park Chung Hee's Economic Secretary. Taiwan's leader Jiang Jingguo was a committed Marxist-Leninist, educated in Moscow, a member of the Soviet Communist Party, and a ruthless security chief who sent dissidents to Green Island to be executed. Park Chung Hee's background was a combination of early Marxist-Leninist affiliations and Japanese-style military training. From those backgrounds they confronted a new era of social and economic complexity.

Jiang Jingguo, for all his ruthless Leninist history, proved to be exceptionally sensitive to the social changes in Taiwan society. Initially resistant to change, after the Kaohsiung riots of 1979, he relented gradually. Restrictions on the innumerable local Taiwanese firms gradually relaxed and eventually the local private firms towered over the obsolescent Guomindang conglomerates. Politically, first he allowed the democratic opposition to organize while keeping it illegal. He found it useful to have them organized so he could negotiate with them.

Gradually he allowed elections. The trend continued until, under later Guomindang leader Lee Teng-hui, fully democratic elections occurred. Eventually the opposition won. In the interest of society, Jiang Jingguo had put the party at risk, in both economic and political control.

Korea's system was more brittle. Unlike Jiang Jingguo, Park Chung Hee was isolated in the Blue House. He did not understand the need for fundamental change and over time became more rigid rather than more flexible. But people around him understood that a new era had made the Park system obsolete. So one evening, the second most powerful man in South Korea, the intelligence chief, one of Park's closest friends, invited Park to dinner with two pretty girls and shot the President in the head. There followed a bumpy road through premature democratization, return to dictatorship, but gradual economic and political liberalization until Korea achieved complete democracy and a market economy (albeit an economy still dominated by a few gigantic firms, most notably Samsung).

Thus the fundamental choice of the smaller dragons was a priority for society over party. For a time China seemed to be making gradual, hesitant steps in the same direction. Social and intellectual life became remarkably free as long as one didn't challenge political stability. The gradual differentiation of Party from government from business, the gradual acceptance of rules like mandatory retirement of officials and a professional legal system, the gradual acceptance of key standards of business and government accountability and transparency, the emergence of local elections, and Hu Jintao's steps toward institutionalization and intra-Party democracy all could have become steps in the Jiang Jingguo direction. But the choice of Xi Jinping reflected a definitive choice by China's political leadership. The Party was at risk. That was intolerable. That must be prevented at any cost. As this analysis has documented, the cost has been and will be very high. China's leaders have chosen Party over society. That is the decisive difference from the smaller dragons.

A leadership that has chosen party over society will continue to experience the great paradox: While economic success has brought stability and confident internal security to other societies, including the smaller dragons, the U.S., Europe, Australia, New Zealand, and others, China's economic success brings enhanced domestic security fears and, cascading from those fears, security-related impositions on the economy that degrade future growth prospects.

Geopolitical Implications

A slower-growing China will remain a huge market and a superpower, but it will not remain today's dominant driver of growth in developing economies and dominant magnet for developed countries' corporations. Presently China's trade and investment stimulus dwarfs those of all others combined for China's neighbors and for Africa. After 2030, China will be one great economic power among several. The U.S. and EU will have similar magnetism and Japan will be large.

If the argument of this paper is correct, soon we will be in an era when China's maritime neighbors are growing twice as fast as China. Their relative ability to resist China's incursions will grow, their morale and unity might grow disproportionately, and China may struggle with imperial overreach. If the U.S. keeps growing at recent rates, the curve of Chinese GDP might rise to bounce off America's and then be left behind. That outcome would depend on efficient U.S. economic management, at best an uncertain prospect. The reality of Sino-American economic competition is that we are currently in a historic race between Xi Jinping and Trump-Biden to see which country can degrade its economic management faster through protectionism, failure to deal effectively with great social changes, and dominance of politics over economics. Presently China is winning that downward race, but the race is tight and no outcome is inevitable.

While China's GDP may still become as large as America's in nominal terms, and is already larger in purchasing power parity terms, that may not imply overwhelming geopolitical clout. Its per capita income will still be a fraction of America's, and, despite some impressive successes like its space program, its technological level may seriously lag. Harvard Professor Lawrence Summers vividly captured the comparison problem when he recently pointed out that, if the U.S. absorbed Mexico, its GDP would increase, but its international clout would not necessarily increase. Inside China are many Mexicos. Likewise, University of California Professor Bradford DeLong has characterized China as 60 million people living at Spanish levels, 300 million living at Polish levels, and 1 billion living at Peruvian levels.

These are great historical tides. On the historical record, governing elites are very slow to recognize alterations in historical tides. Changed understandings and changed policies tend to occur only when the inertia of ingrained ideas and institutionalized doctrines hits a brick wall

(Overholt and Chou, 1974). In the U.S., the assumptions that China's rise is inexorable, that Xi's policies are forever, and that the Sino-American relationship is a zero-sum game are already so ingrained in U.S. officialdom and some of U.S. academia, and they are so beneficial for national security budgets, that they are not likely to change soon in line with altered reality. The brick wall is not currently visible.

References

Allison, Graham, Nathalie Kiersznowski, and Charlotte Fitzek. 2022. "The Great Economic Rivalry: China vs the U.S." Harvard Kennedy School BelferCenter, www.belfercenter.org/sites/default/files/pantheon_files/files/publication/GreatEconomicRivalry_Final_2.pdf

Brandt, Loren, John Litwack, Elitza Mileva, Luhang Wang, Yifan Zhang, and Luan Zhao. 2020. "China's Productivity Slowdown and Future Growth Potential." Policy Research Working Paper 9298, Washington DC: World Bank. https://documents1.worldbank.org/curated/en/839401593007627879/pdf/Chinas-Productivity-Slowdown-and-Future-Growth-Potential.pdf

Chen, Hao and Meg Rithmire. 2020. "The Rise of the Investor State: State Capital in the Chinese Economy." *Studies in Comparative International Development* 55, 257–277. https://doi.org/10.1007/s12116-020-09308-3

Dahrendorf, Ralf. 1959. *Class and Class Conflict in Industrial Society*. Stanford University Press.

Enright, Michael. 2016. *Developing China: The Remarkable Impact of Foreign Direct Investment*. Routledge.

Eulau, Heinz. 1986. *Politics, Self, and Society: A Theme and Variations*. Harvard University Press.

Li, Hongbin and Li-An Zhou. 2005. "Political Turnover and Economic Performance: The Incentive Role of Personnel Control in China." *Journal of Public Economics*, 89 (9–10): 1743–1762. www.sciencedirect.com/science/article/pii/S0047272704001355

Ma, Guonan, Ivan Roberts and Gerard Kelly. 2018. "A Rebalancing Chinese Economy: Challenges and International Implications." in *China's 40 Years of Reform and Development: 1978–2018*, edited by Ross Garnaut, Ligang Song and Cai Fang, 187–214. ANU Press.www.jstor.org/stable/j.ctv5cgbnk.19

Oi, Jean. 1999. *Rural China Takes Off: Institutional Foundations of Economic Reform*. University of California Press.

Overholt, William H. 1982. *Political Risk*. Euromoney Publications.

Overholt, William H. 1993. *The Rise of China: How Economic Reform is Creating a New Superpower*. W.W. Norton.
Overholt, William H. 2017. "Duterte, Democracy, Defense." Brookings Institution, www.brookings.edu/research/duterte-democracy-and-defense/
Overholt, William H. 2018. *China's Crisis of Success*. Cambridge University Press.
Overholt, William H. and Marylin Chou. 1974. "Foreign Policy Doctrines." *Policy Studies Journal*, 3 (2): 185–188.
Pearson, Margaret M, Meg Rithmire and Kellee S. Tsai. 2022. "China's Party-State Capitalism and International Backlash: From Interdependence to Insecurity." *International Security*, 47 (2): 135–176, https://muse-jhu-edu.ezp-prod1.hul.harvard.edu/article/880543
Rozelle, Scott and Natalie Hell. 2020. *Invisible China: How the Urban-Rural Divide Threatens China's Rise*. University of Chicago Press.
Shih, Victor, Christopher Adolph and Mingxing Liu. 2012. "Getting Ahead in the Communist Party: Explaining the Advancement of Central Committee Members in China." *American Political Science Review*, 106 (1): 166–187. https://doi.org/10.1017/S0003055411000566
Zhou, Kate. 1996. *How the Farmers Changed China: Power of the People*. Westview Press.

Index

14th Five-Year Plan, 48, 87, 266
2008 Labor Law, 248

absolute poverty, 301
advanced manufacturing, 306
age dependence ratio. *See* dependency ratio
age of abundance, 99, 120
age-specific profiles of labor income and consumption. *See* demographic dividend
aggregate social financing, 9
aggregate state assets, 188
agricultural reform, 15
Alibaba, 246, 258, 270, 289, 300
Allison, Graham, 303
Annual Industrial Survey (AIS), 157, 163, 167
Ant Financial, 10, 27, 259
Anti-trust Law, 163
Asia Development Bank, 40

bailout, 147
Bank for International Settlements (BIS), 220
bank run, 147
banker, 27, 290
banking and fiscal reforms in 1994, 53
banking system, 305
Belt and Road Initiative, 68, 82, 223, 308
Belt and Road S&T Innovation Action Plan. *See* Belt and Road Initiative
bilateral currency swap agreements, 214
Bond Connect, 217
Bond Direct, 227
bottom-up institutional change, 16, 48, 55
Brandt, Loren, 53
broadly defined economic openness, 195

campaign-style governance, 266
capital investment, 13, 48–51, 61–63. *See also* fixed capital investment rates
capital misallocation, 53
capital reallocation, 47, 53, 307
central bank digital currency (CBDC), 229
centralization, 38, 53, 158, 168, 299. *See also* resurgence of the state
China Banking Regulatory Commission (CBRC), 9
China Family Panel Studies (CFPS), 107
China Household Finance Survey (CHFS), 241
China Household Income Project (CHIP), 107
China International Payment System (CIPS), 217
China triumphalism, 302
China's capital account, 228
China's exchange rate policy, 227
China's household consumption share of GDP, 37
China's trade surplus, 194
China's new economic model, 297
China's patent system, 71
  design, 71
  invention patent, 71
  utility model, 71
Chinese Dream, 242
Chinese stock market, 32
collectively owned enterprises. *See* state-owned enterprises (SOEs)
college enrollments, 109–110
common prosperity, 26, 31, 150, 239, 256, 262, 298
Communist party, 10–11, 23, 162, 195, 239, 256, 262–264, 282, 301
competitive savings motive, 194
complexity revolution, 29–30, 288–306

compulsory charity, 277
Congressional Budget Office (CBO), 14
consumer confidence, 31
consumption increases, 112
consumption share of labor income, 110
consumption stimulus. *See* domestic consumption
consumption-driven economy, 150
controlling shareholder type, 163
corporatization of SOEs, 161
corruption, 296–300
counter-cyclical adjustments, 37
counter-cyclical policy measures, 135
COVID-19 pandemic, 2, 86–87, 99–101, 136–140
crisis of success, 288, 312
cross-border payments, 234
cross-border RMB settlement, 214, 218
cross-border trade settlement in RMB. *See* cross-border RMB settlement
currency swap agreements, 217, 221
current account surplus, 24, 200
Cybersecurity Administration of China (CAC), 27, 246

Dahrendorf, Ralf, 300
debt service ratios, 291
decentralization, 30, 48, 64, 159, 168, 268, 276
decline of the share of manufacturing, 306
decoupling, 3, 68, 84, 90, 193
DeepSeek, 38
de-globalization, 68
degree of economic openness, 206
democracy
  intra-party, 296, 313
  peasant, 291–292
  western, 297
democratization, 296
demographic dividend, 17, 100–101, 103–104
demography, 17
Deng, Xiaoping, 67, 192, 196, 295
dependency ratio, 17, 50
de-risking, 3
developmental construct, 29, 290, 294
Diamond, Douglas, 147
Digital Currency Electronic Payment (DCEP), 215, 229
digital industries, 11
digital RMB, 26
digital technologies, 69, 90
disorderly expansion of capital, 258, 269
distributed ledger technology (DLT), 234
dollar overvaluation, 39
domestic consumption, 36–37, 150
down payment requirement, 146, 148
dual circulation, 24, 33, 192, 195
dual-sector growth model, 248
Dybvig, Philip. *See* Diamond, Douglas

East Asian development model, 29, 292, 312
e-CNY. *See* Digital Currency Electronic Payment (DCEP)
economic openness, 192–211
  FDI openness, 193
  Trade openness, 193–210
economic phase transitions, 7
economic slowdown, 290
economic stimulus, 8, 36, 133, 159
effective support ratio, 104
egalitarianism, 293, 301
Eichengreen, Barry, 228
electric vehicle (EV), 19, 69, 88, 307
  battery, 88
employment growth, 50–51, 61, 123–124
engines of growth, 38
entertainment industry, 245
EquiNet, 157
equity ownership network, 168, 171, 189
European Patent Office (EPO), 80
Evergrande, 123, 127, 136, 258
excess capacity. *See* overcapacity
exchange rate, 193, 200, 210, 227, 236
exchange rate manipulation, 200
exorbitant privilege, 237
expanding domestic demand, 284
expected openness, 24
export sophistication, 193, 201–202
export technological complexity, 203

factor reallocation, 47
factory manager responsibility system, 272
family planning, 17

Fang, Hanming, 32, 134, 144
FDI openness, 193
fertility, 17, 101–103, 118–119
fertility decline, 102
Firm Registration and Ownership Database, 166
firm registration types, 158
firm-to-firm equity investments, 157
fiscal stimulus, 51
fixed capital investment rates, 49
fixed-asset investment, 9–10, 14, 30, 39–40
foreign direct investment (FDI), 13
foreign reserve adequacy, 291
former Soviet Union (FSU), 9
for-profit private education, 303. *See also* private education

Gan, Li, 247
GDP targets, 28, 35
gene and cell therapies, 307
German education and apprenticeship model, 300
Gini index, 239–253
Global Financial Crisis (GFC), 3–4, 8, 14, 16, 20, 24, 39, 48, 57, 64, 127, 133, 160, 162, 217, 223, 296
Global Innovation Index, 93
government guidance funds, 265
grasp the large, let go of the small, 16, 57
green energy technology, 307
gross domestic product (GDP), 1–17, 20, 24–25, 27–32, 34–35, 37, 39, 47–52, 54, 61–64, 100–101, 119, 123, 195–197, 199, 202–209, 248–250, 252, 262, 264, 268, 283, 292, 307, 309, 314
  China, 6
  definition, 3
  drivers, 10, 16, 288, 300–304
  digital and green sectors, 11
  expenditure approach, 3
  forecasting accuracy, 6–7
  growth, 6
  Germany, 6
  high-quality, 31
  income approach, 3
  Japan, 4–6, 14, 29, 31
  Korea, 4–6, 14, 29, 31
  potential growth, 6, 13, 32, 284, 288, 304, 308
  targets, 152
  U.S., 4–6

harmonious society, 311
hierarchical distance, 159–160
higher educational expansion. *See* college enrollments
high-quality growth, 31
high-speed rail, 16
household consumption, 10, 17, 28, 30–31, 37, 39–40
household incomes, 306
household registration system (Hukou), 16, 55
household responsibility system (HRS), 16, 55
housing cost, 113
housing price index, 144
housing price-to-income ratio, 150
Hsieh, Chang-Tai, 164
Hu, Jintao, 295
Huang, Yasheng, 26
Huawei, 57–58
human capital, 6, 61, 264
hybrid economy, 123–126
hybrid model, 20, 125, 132

implicit guarantees, 126, 134
income distribution, 37
income inequality, 40, 239, 242
incorporated companies, 167
indigenous innovation, 19, 60
indirect control. *See* hierarchical distance
industrial policy, 11, 48, 59, 192, 265, 279, 308
  targeted industries, 265
industrial robots, 32
Inflation Reduction Act, 204
information flows, 278
infrastructure development, 133
infrastructure investments, 128, 134–152
initial public offering (IPO), 246, 252, 259, 261, 279
innovation, 67–95
intellectual property theft, 304
internal migration, 55

International Monetary Fund (IMF), 2–3, 10, 214
international monetary system, 215
international reserve currency, 224
invention patents, 19
investment rate
  nominal, 49
  real, 49
investment-driven growth model, 49
inward foreign direct investment, 78, 204

Japan Patent Office (JPO), 80
Japanification, 31–33, 309–310
Jiang, Zemin, 268, 295
joint ventures, 57

Korean Intellectual Property Office (KIPO), 80

labor productivity, 119, 120
labor reallocation, 15
labor share of GDP. *See* labor share of income
labor share of income, 27, 40, 247
land sales, 131–132, 137–141
  average prices, 139
  commercial, 137
  as proportion of local revenue, 128
  quantity, 137
  residential, 137–141
  tiers of cities, 140
land sales-based funding model, 132
land-collateralized leverage, 134
Lasswell, Harold, 290
laying flat, 33
learning by doing, 59
less developed country (LDC), 7
Lewis turning point, 248
Lewis, W. Arthur, 248
Li, Daokui, 247
Li, Keqiang, 240, 306
lifecycle deficit, 114, 117. *See also* lifecycle surplus
lifecycle surplus, 18, 105, 115
limited liability companies, 167
Lin, Justin Yifu, 5–6
literacy, 102
little dragons, 288, 292, 294–295, 307–312
local democracy, 296
local government
  fiscal autonomy, 21
  indebtedness, 9, 23
  competition of, 134, 275. *See also* promotion tournament
local government financing vehicle (LGFV), 9, 20, 23, 126, 133
long-term growth, 3
lower-middle-income country, 1
Lowy Institute, 7
luxury goods consumption, 113

Ma, Jack, 27, 252, 258, 302
Made in China 2025, 240
Mandarin system, 132
Medium- and Long-Term Plan for the Development of S&T (2006–2020), 70, 81
Meitong Dong. *See* Zhou, Kevin
menu of policy objectives, 257
migration, 16, 47–48, 52, 108, 148, 302, 306. *See also* internal migration
Ministry of Finance, 157
Miran, Stephen, 39
mixed ownership reform, 22
money laundering, 233
mortality, 103
mortgage rates, 148
Most Favored Nation (MFN), 54
multi-CBDC Bridge project, 234
multi-objective policy framework, 262

National Bureau of Statistics of China, 8, 17, 21, 36, 241
national champions, 156
national security, 34, 262, 265, 315
National Transfer Accounts (NTA), 18, 106
Naughton, Barry, 11, 27, 299
new development paradigm, 192, 265
new growth engines, 150
Nine Prohibitions, 259, 271
normal trade openness, 198
notional (registered) ownership, 164

offshore RMB centers, 224
one child policy, 263
overcapacity, 14, 30, 37
Overholt, William, 29
overtime work policy, 245

ownership hierarchy, 159
ownership networks, 157
ownership threshold, 22, 158, 183–186, 189

paid-in capital, 165, 167
partial SOEs, 179
Party-government-business elite, 312
patent law, 18
patentee
  by industry sector, 19, 68, 73, 76
  by ownership type, 75
  by region, 78
patentee sector, 68, 73
patents, 69, 67–95
  commercialization, 93
  international, 79
  quality, 85
  semiconductor, 89
  total number, 70
peak age of earnings, 108
peak China, 2
peasant democracy, 291–292
Penn World Table (PWT), 6
People's Bank of China (PBOC), 9, 36, 148, 215
Pettis, Michael, 40
pharmaceutical industry, 87
policy credibility, 284
policy instruments, 28, 35, 257, 277
policy objectives, 257, 262, 264–267, 272
political power of private capital, 302
population
  age structure, 100, 102–103, 105–108, 114–117
  working age, 17–18, 50, 117–119, 248, 307
population aging, 117, 119
poverty alleviation, 26
Pritchett, Lant, 6
private capital, 243
private capital share of the GDP, 249
private education, 27, 243–244, 261, 267, 303
private tutoring, 267
privately owned enterprises (POE), 53, 156. *See also* state-owned enterprises (SOEs)
production possibility frontier, 7
productivity. *See* total factor productivity (TFP)
progressive income tax, 302
promotion tournament, 134, 275
property bubble, 304
property prices, 136
property taxation, 30, 129–130, 151, 302
purchasing power parity (PPP), 1, 156, 314

Qualified Foreign Institutional Investor (QFII), 226–227
quality of trade, 197

ratchet model. *See* Weitzman, Martin
ratio of housing inventory to annual sales, 143
Ravallion, Martin, 241
Rawski, Thomas, 6–7
real estate, 31, 123–153
  debt, 123–129
  derisking, 123–153
  hybrid model, 20, 125, 132
  as proportion of GDP, 123
real estate crash, 148
real estate-collateralized debt, 135
real investment, 15
reciprocal tariffs, 39
regional decentralized authoritarian (RDA), 10
regionally administered totalitarianism (RADT), 9–10
registered capital, 167
registration type, 163
regulatory crackdown, 27, 243, 256
regulatory reforms, 269
regulatory storm. *See* summer of 2021
relative state control, 22
reserve requirement ratio (RRR), 36
resurgence of the state, 38, 158
retirement age, 13, 17–18, 32, 120
returns to capital, 8
Rhodium Group, 2, 6, 36
Renminbi (RMB)
  convertibility, 26, 215, 227
  DCEP, 215, 229
  digitalization, 215, 228
  internationalization, 25–26, 214, 216, 235

Renminbi (RMB) (cont.)
outward direct investment (ODI), 219
trade settlement, 215, 219–221, 224, 227, 235
Rogoff, Kenneth, 20, 130
Rosen, Daniel, 6, 10, 36
Rozelle, Scott, 301
Rudd, Kevin, 23
rural education, 301
rural land reform, 243
rural reform, 307
rural revitalization campaign, 243

safe-haven currency, 228
safety nets, 38
science and technology (S&T) innovation, 67
semiconductor industry, 69, 89–90
service consumption, 40
service-oriented economy, 150, 303
Shanghai International Energy Exchange, 227
share of working-age adults, 101
Shih, Victor, 293
social financing. *See* aggregate social financing
social safety net, 150
SOE reform, 56
SOEs. *See* state-owned enterprises (SOEs)
soft-budget constraints, 10, 130, 133
soft-budget problem. *See* soft-budget constraints
Solow's residual, 4
Song, Michael Zheng, 6, 8, 164
sophistication of exports, 24
Southern Tour Speech in 1992. *See* Deng, Xiaoping
Soviet Union, 28
Special Drawing Rights (SDR), 217, 224
stagnation, 10, 248
State Administration of Industry and Commerce (SAIC), 22, 157, 166
State Administration of Market Regulation (SAMR), 259
state capital, 156–189, 249
state capitalism, 156, 160
state capture, 289
State Intellectual Property Office (SIPO), 19, 68–83
state sector advances and private sector retreats. *See* resurgence of the state
state shareholding companies, 23
State-owned Assets Supervision and Administration Commissions (SASACs), 157
state-owned enterprises (SOEs), 21–22, 53–54, 56–57, 59–60, 68, 73–75, 80–81, 83, 86, 124, 127, 149, 156–189, 260, 272–282
central, 158, 161, 173, 179–184
definition, 184
ownership network, 157, 169–170
provincial, 158, 173, 179–184
shareholding companies, 23
Stock Connect, 217
Stolper–Samuelson theorem, 194, 201
structural reforms, 37
structural slowdown, 1
structural uncertainty, 310
summer of 2021, 27, 256–284
Summers, Lawrence, 314
support ratio, 17–18, 102–104, 117–118. *See also* dependency ratio
SWIFT payments system, 235
System of National Accounts (SNA), 106

tariff rate, 200
tariffs, 34, 37–39, 54, 84, 200–201
tax revenue as a share of GDP, 250
taxation, 129, 250, 302
tax-sharing reform in 1994, 131, 293
technological complexity of product, 202
technology adoption, 57
technology diffusion, 47–48, 55–60
three red lines, 21, 27, 152, 258
Three Represents, 268
three-child policy, 263
Thucydides Trap, 34
TikTok, 91
Tinbergen principle, 277
too important to fail, 126
topdown innovation, 307
total factor productivity (TFP), 4, 7, 15, 35, 47, 283, 306

agricultural, 15, 52–53, 55–56, 243
deceleration, 15
growth, 29, 39, 47–61
total registered capital, 183
township and village enterprises, 15, 53, 56, 305
trade balance, 193, 199
trade barriers, 16
trade liberalization, 16, 47
domestic, 16
internal, 54
international, 16, 54, 60
trade openness, 193–210
"normal" level, 193
trade ratio, 24
trade sanctions, 34. *See also* U.S.–China trade war
trade surplus. *See* trade balance
two-pillar policy for the RMB, 236

U.S.–China relationship, 30, 308
U.S.–China trade tension. *See* U.S.–China trade war
U.S.–China trade war, 33, 84
Ukraine–Russia war, 235
undesirable entity list, 246
university research funds, 304
upper-middle-income country, 1
urbanization, 130, 148, 304
USPTO, 19, 80–82
utility patents, 19

value added accounting, 194, 205
venture capital state, 265
video game industry, 244
violent egalitarianism, 301

Wang, Feng, 16
wealth distribution, 40
Wei, Shang-Jin, 24
Weitzman, Martin, 28, 34
welfare state, 240
wholly state-owned enterprises (wholly SOEs). *See* state-owned enterprises (SOEs)
World Bank, 1–2, 4–5, 17, 23, 26, 37, 50
World Trade Organization (WTO), 16, 54, 192, 214
Wright, Logan, 36

Xiong, Wei, 20, 123
Xu, Chenggang, 6, 9

Young Thousand Talents (YTT) program, 85
Yue, Vivian, 25

Zhao, Linda, 21
Zhou, Kevin, 18
Zhou, Li-An, 134
Zhu, Rongji, 20, 56, 131
Zhu, Xiaodong, 14, 53

www.ingramcontent.com/pod-product-compliance
Lightning Source LLC
LaVergne TN
LVHW011704200926
848484LV00004B/1067
* 9 7 8 1 0 0 9 6 4 9 3 1 5 *